In the Hill District of the 1940s, Herron Avenue marked the boundary between the upper class "Sugartop" neighborhood and the working class "Middle Hill."

SMOKETOWN

THE UNTOLD STORY OF THE OTHER
GREAT BLACK RENAISSANCE

Mark Whitaker

SIMON & SCHUSTER

NEW YORK   LONDON   TORONTO   SYDNEY   NEW DELHI

Simon & Schuster
1230 Avenue of the Americas
New York, NY 10020

First Simon & Schuster hardcover edition January 2018

SIMON & SCHUSTER and colophon are registered trademarks of Simon & Schuster, Inc.

For information about special discounts for bulk purchases, please contact
Simon & Schuster Special Sales at 1-866-506-1949 or business@simonandschuster.com.

The Simon & Schuster Speakers Bureau can bring authors to your live event.
For more information or to book an event contact the
Simon & Schuster Speakers Bureau at 1-866-248-3049 or
visit our website at www.simonspeakers.com.

Interior design by Ruth Lee-Mui
Map by Paul J. Pugliese

Manufactured in the United States of America

1   3   5   7   9   10   8   6   4   2

Library of Congress Cataloging-in-Publication Data
Names: Whitaker, Mark, author.
Title: Smoketown : the untold story of the other great
Black Renaissance / by Mark Whitaker.
Other titles: Untold story of the other great Black Renaissance
Description: New York : Simon & Schuster, [2018] | Includes
bibliographical references and index.
Identifiers: LCCN 2017019428 (print) | LCCN 2017020491
(ebook) | ISBN 9781501122439 (ebook) | ISBN 9781501122392
(hardcover : alk. paper) | ISBN 9781501122422 (trade pbk. : alk. paper)
Subjects: LCSH: African Americans—Pennsylvania—Pittsburgh—History. | African
Americans—Pennsylvania—Pittsburgh—Intellectual life. | African Americans—
Pennsylvania—Pittsburgh—Social conditions—20th century. | African American
athletes—Pennsylvania—Pittsburgh. | Jazz musicians—Pennsylvania—
Pittsburgh. | Pittsburgh (Pa.)—Intellectual life—20th century. | Pittsburgh
(Pa.)—Civilization. | African Americans—Intellectual life—20th century.
Classification: LCC F159.P69 (ebook) | LCC F159.P69 N487
2018 (print) | DDC 305.896/073074886—dc23
LC record available at https://lccn.loc.gov/2017019428

ISBN 978-1-5011-2239-2
ISBN 978-1-5011-2243-9 (ebook)

For my grandparents, Edith McColes Whitaker and
Cleophaus Sylvester "C.S." Whitaker Sr.

Left: Grandmother Edith McColes Whitaker (center in large hat and pearls) attending
a ladies luncheon in Pittsburgh, 1941. *Right:* Granddad C.S. Whitaker Sr. (right,
in suit) presiding over the burial of a black Pittsburgh war veteran in the 1950s.

Grandmother Edith was the only child of two "Old Pittsburghers," as black folks who arrived before the Great Migration were called. A striking beauty in her youth, she was among the first black graduates of Schenley High, the city's most illustrious public school, and a gifted pianist who once performed at Pittsburgh's Carnegie Hall.

Granddad was born on a tenant farm in Texas, the eleventh child of two former slaves. He came to Pittsburgh during World War I, and worked as a chauffeur for a white undertaker who helped set him up in the funeral home business. Although he never finished high school, he prided himself on appearing a man of education and means, with his wire-rimmed glasses, suspendered suits, and patent leather shoes.

Growing up, I knew none of this history. My father—C.S. "Syl" Whitaker Jr.—left Pittsburgh to go to college and never moved back. By the time I was old enough to remember family visits, Granddad had suffered a severe stroke. Grandmother had taken over the funeral home and moved it to a neighborhood called Beltzhoover after the city tore down the heart of the Hill District, long the center of black business and social life.

Then I wrote a family memoir, and while doing research I came across two photos of my grandparents in the online archive of *Pittsburgh Courier* photographer Teenie Harris. Clicking through the archive, I discovered what a remarkable world my grandparents had inhabited. I was eager to learn more, and the result is this book. I hope that they would say I had done that world justice—and them proud.

You have to be taught to be second class; you're not born that way.
—LENA HORNE

Ever up and onward.
—BILLY STRAYHORN

You can only close if you opened.
—AUGUST WILSON

CONTENTS

Preface xiii

Cast of Characters xvii

The Neighborhoods of Pittsburgh xxiii

1

THE BROWN BOMBER'S CORNERMEN 1

2

THE NEGRO CARNEGIES 25

3

THE CALCULATING CRUSADER 53

4

THE RISE AND FALL OF "BIG RED" 89

5

BILLY AND LENA 123

6

THE DOUBLE V WARRIORS   153

7

THE COMPLEX MR. B   193

8

"JACKIE'S BOSWELL"   231

9

THE WOMEN OF "UP SOUTH"   271

10

THE BARD OF A BROKEN WORLD   303

Acknowledgments   341

Notes   345

Index   385

SMOKETOWN

PREFACE

TOWARD THE NORTHERN REACHES of the Appalachian Mountains, at the point where the East Coast ends and the great American Midwest begins, three rivers meet. The Allegheny flows from the north, gathering the tributaries of western New York State. The Monongahela cascades from the south, through the hills and hollers of West Virginia. Together, they form the headwaters of the Ohio, which meanders west all the way to Illinois, where it connects to the mighty Mississippi and its tentacles reach from Canada to the Gulf of Mexico. Because of its strategic value, the intersection of these three rivers had generals named Braddock and Forbes and Washington fighting to control the surrounding patch of Western Pennsylvania two decades before the War for Independence. Because it allowed steamboats to reach the coal deposits in the nearby hills, the watery nexus made the city that grew up around it the nation's largest producer of steel and created the vast wealth of businessmen and financiers named Carnegie, Frick, Westinghouse, and Mellon whose legacies live on in the renowned libraries, foundations, and art collections funded by their fortunes.

That story of Pittsburgh is well documented. Far less chronicled, but just as extraordinary, is the confluence of forces that made the black population of the city, for a brief but glorious stretch of the twentieth century, one of the most vibrant and consequential communities of color in U.S. history. Like millions of other blacks, they came north before and during the Great Migration, many of them from the upper parts of the Old South, from states such as Maryland, Delaware, Virginia, and North Carolina. As likely as not to have been descendants of house slaves or "free men of color," these migrants arrived with high degrees of literacy, musical fluency, and religious discipline (as well as a tendency toward light skin that betrayed their history of mixing with white masters, and with one another). Once they settled in Pittsburgh, they had educational opportunities that were rare for blacks of the era, thanks to abolitionist-sponsored university scholarships and integrated public high schools with lavish Gilded Age funding. Whether or not they succeeded in finding jobs in Pittsburgh's steel mills (and often they did not), they inhaled a spirit of commerce that hung, quite literally, in the dark, sulfurous air.

The result was a black version of the story of fifteenth-century Florence and early-twentieth-century Vienna: a miraculous flowering of social and cultural achievement all at once, in one small city. In its heyday, from the 1920s until the late 1950s, Pittsburgh's black population was less than a quarter the size of New York City's, and a third the size of Chicago's—those two much larger metropolises that have been associated with the phenomenon of a black Renaissance. Yet during those decades, it was Pittsburgh that produced the best-written, widest-selling and most influential black newspaper in America: *The Pittsburgh Courier*. From a four-page pamphlet of poetry and local oddities, its leader, Robert L. Vann, built the *Courier* into a publication with fourteen regional editions, a circulation of almost half a million at its zenith, and an avid following in black homes, barbershops, and beauty salons across the country.

In the 1930s, Vann used the *Courier* as a soapbox to urge black voters to abandon the Republican Party of Lincoln and embrace the Democratic Party of FDR, beginning a great political migration that transformed the electoral landscape and that reverberates to this day. In the 1940s, the *Courier* led crusades to rally blacks to support World War II, to win combat roles for Negro soldiers, and to demand greater equality at home in exchange for that patriotism and sacrifice. In the 1950s, its reporters—led by several intrepid female journalists—exposed the betrayal of the promise of a "Double Victory" and chronicled the first great battles of the civil rights movement.

In the world of sports, two *Courier* reporters, Chester Washington and Bill Nunn, helped make Joe Louis a hero to black America and a sympathetic heavyweight champion to white boxing fans. Two ruthless businessmen, racketeer Gus Greenlee and Cum Posey, the son of a Gilded Age shipping tycoon, turned the city's black baseball teams, the Pittsburgh Crawfords and the Homestead Grays, into the most fearsome squads in the annals of the Negro Leagues, uniting such future Hall of Famers as Satchel Paige, Josh Gibson, slugger Buck Leonard, and base-stealing demon "Cool Papa" Bell. Another *Courier* sportswriter, Wendell Smith, led a campaign to integrate the big leagues, and was the first person to call the attention of Brooklyn Dodgers owner Branch Rickey to a young Negro League shortstop named Jackie Robinson. While covering Robinson's first seasons in the white minor and major leagues, Smith served as Jackie's roommate, chauffeur, counselor, and mouthpiece, helping to soothe the historic rookie's private temper and fashion the public image of dignity that was as crucial to his success as power at the plate and speed around the bases.

In the realm of the arts, Pittsburgh produced three of the most electrifying and influential jazz pianists of the era: Earl "Fatha" Hines, Mary Lou Williams, and the dazzling Erroll Garner. It was in Pittsburgh that Billy Strayhorn grew up and met Duke Ellington, beginning a partnership that would yield the finest orchestral jazz of all time. Another Pittsburgh native, Billy Eckstine, became the most popular black singer of the 1940s and early 1950s, and played a less remembered but equally groundbreaking role in uniting Charlie Parker, Dizzy Gillespie, and Sarah Vaughan on the swing era bandstands that helped give rise to bebop. Then, in the mid-1940s, in Pittsburgh's Hill District, a black maid born in North Carolina who had taken up with a white German baker gave birth to a boy who grew up to become America's greatest black playwright.

Today, black Pittsburgh is best known as the setting of August Wilson's sweeping Century Cycle: *Fences*, *The Piano Lesson*, and seven more of the ten plays he wrote depicting black life in each decade of the twentieth century. Wilson conjured it as a world full of tormented, struggling strivers held back by white racism and their own personal demons. It was a portrait that reflected the playwright's affection for the black working class, as well as the harsh reality of what became of the Hill District and the city's other black enclaves after the 1950s, when they were hit by a perfect storm of industrial decline, disastrous urban renewal policies, and black middle-class brain drain. So powerful was Wilson's imaginary universe, and so thorough the destruction of those neighborhoods, that few in the thousands of audiences that have seen his plays or flocked to the movies that are now being made from them would know that there was once more to the actual place that the *Courier* writers liked to call Smoketown.

But there was more. A great deal more. Under the dusky skies of Smoketown, there was a glittering saga.

CAST OF CHARACTERS

PEOPLE WHO WERE BORN or lived in black Pittsburgh are in boldface. Others are those with whom they interacted.

THE PAPER

ROBERT L. VANN, publisher of *The Pittsburgh Courier*

JESSE VANN, his wife and successor

IRA LEWIS, president and business manager

BILL NUNN, managing editor

P.L. PRATTIS, executive editor

JULIA BUMRY JONES, women's editor and columnist

DAISY LAMPKIN, vice president and local NAACP leader

CHARLES "TEENIE" HARRIS, photographer

EDGAR ROUZEAU, war correspondent

COLLINS GEORGE, war correspondent

THEODORE STANFORD, war correspondent
FRANK BOLDEN, war correspondent
BILLY ROWE, war correspondent, columnist, and photographer
CHESTER WASHINGTON, sportswriter
WENDELL SMITH, sportswriter
EDNA CHAPPELL, reporter
JOHN C. CLARKE, reporter and columnist
EVELYN CUNNINGHAM, reporter and columnist
A. PHILIP RANDOLPH, head of the Brotherhood of Sleeping Car Porters
JAMES WELDON JOHNSON, author and president of the NAACP
W. E. B. DU BOIS, author and editor of the NAACP journal *The Messenger*
ROBERT ABBOTT, founder of *The Chicago Defender*
JOHN SENGSTACKE, publisher of *The Chicago Defender*
MICHAEL BENEDUM, oil tycoon and Democratic donor
JOSEPH GUFFEY, Pennsylvania senator and FDR supporter
FRANKLIN DELANO ROOSEVELT, U.S. president
CLAUDE BARNETT, founder of the Associated Negro Press
BENJAMIN O. DAVIS, first black U.S. Army general
BENJAMIN O. DAVIS JR., commander of the Tuskegee Airmen
GEN. EDWARD "NED" ALMOND, commander of the 92nd Infantry
   Division
COL. HOWARD QUEEN, commander of the 366th Infantry Regiment
GEN. JOSEPH STILWELL, commander of the Ledo Road mission
JAWAHARLAL NEHRU, Indian independence leader
MUHAMMAD ALI JINNAH, Indian independence leader
MAHATMA GANDHI, Indian independence leader
HARRY S. TRUMAN, U.S. president
SALLIE NIXON, widow of voting rights martyr Isaiah Nixon
WALTER LEE IRVIN, "Groveland Four" defendant
THURGOOD MARSHALL, head of the NAACP Legal Defense Fund
MARTIN LUTHER KING JR., minister and civil rights leader
CORETTA SCOTT KING, his wife

SPORTS

GUS GREENLEE, racketeer and owner of the Pittsburgh Crawfords

CUMBERLAND "CUM" POSEY JR., manager and part owner of the Homestead Grays

RUFUS "SONNYMAN" JACKSON, racketeer and part owner of the Homestead Grays

JOSH GIBSON, Negro League catcher and slugger

SATCHEL PAIGE, Negro League pitcher

JANET "TOADALO" HOWARD, Paige's wife, a Pittsburgh native

JOE LOUIS, heavyweight boxer

MARVA LOUIS, his wife

JOHN ROXBOROUGH, Louis's manager

JACK "CHAPPIE" BLACKBURN, Louis's trainer

JULIAN BLACK, Louis's promoter

MIKE JACOBS, Louis's promoter

J. L. WILKINSON, owner of the Kansas City Monarchs

KENESAW MOUNTAIN LANDIS, commissioner of baseball

ALBERT BENJAMIN "HAPPY" CHANDLER, commissioner of baseball

JACKIE ROBINSON, player for the Montreal Royals and Brooklyn Dodgers

RACHEL ROBINSON, his wife

JOHNNY WRIGHT, Royals prospect

BRANCH RICKEY, Dodgers president

EDDIE STANKY, Dodgers second baseman

BEN CHAPMAN, Philadelphia Phillies manager

JOE GARAGIOLA, St. Louis Cardinals catcher

MUSIC

EARL "FATHA" HINES, pianist and bandleader

LOIS DEPPE, singer and bandleader

MARY LOU WILLIAMS, pianist and composer

BILLY STRAYHORN, composer and arranger

LENA HORNE, singer

EDWIN "TEDDY" HORNE, Lena's father, a Pittsburgh racketeer

LOUIS JONES, Lena's husband

GAIL HORNE JONES, their daughter

EDWIN "LITTLE TEDDY" JONES, their son

CHARLOTTE ENTY CATLIN, pianist and teacher

MARY CARDWELL DAWSON, jubilee singer and opera director

BILLY ECKSTINE, singer and bandleader

ROY "LITTLE JAZZ" ELDRIDGE, trumpeter

KENNY "KLOOK" CLARKE, drummer

ERROLL GARNER, pianist

RAY BROWN, bass player and Ella Fitzgerald's husband

FATE MARABLE, riverboat bandleader

NOBLE SISSLE, bandleader

DUKE ELLINGTON, bandleader and composer

DIZZY GILLESPIE, trumpet player and bandleader

CHARLIE PARKER, saxophone player

SARAH VAUGHAN, singer

MORRIS LEVY, founder of Roulette Records

ELLA FITZGERALD, singer and Ray Brown's wife

MARTHA GLASER, Erroll Garner's manager

GEORGE AVAKIAN, Columbia Records producer

THE CITY

CUMBERLAND POSEY SR., steamboat engineer and coal tycoon

ANGELINE "ANNA" STEVENS POSEY, his wife

LEWIS WOODSON, minister and abolitionist

MARTIN DELANY, doctor, journalist, and abolitionist

VIRGINIA PROCTOR, wig store chain owner

HOMER S. BROWN, attorney and Pennsylvania assemblyman

BYRD BROWN, his son, and local NAACP leader

AUGUST WILSON (BORN FREDERICK A. "FREDDY" KITTEL JR.), playwright

DAISY WILSON, Wilson's mother

FREDERICK A. "FRITZ" KITTEL, Wilson's father

SALA UDIN (BORN SAM HOWZE), Wilson's childhood friend

ROB PENNY, Wilson's friend and fellow poet

ROMARE BEARDEN, artist and Wilson inspiration

ANDREW CARNEGIE, steel tycoon and philanthropist

HENRY CLAY FRICK, coal tycoon and art collector

GEORGE WESTINGHOUSE, inventor and electricity tycoon

HENRY J. HEINZ, foodstuffs tycoon

THOMAS MELLON, banker

ANDREW MELLON, banker and U.S. treasury secretary

RICHARD "R.K." MELLON, banker and urban renewal advocate

DAVID LAWRENCE, Pittsburgh mayor

EDGAR KAUFMANN, department store owner

ABRAHAM WOLK, city councilman and light opera buff

LLOYD RICHARDS, stage director and drama teacher

CHARLES DUTTON, actor

PHYLICIA RASHAD, actress

WYNTON MARSALIS, trumpeter and bandleader

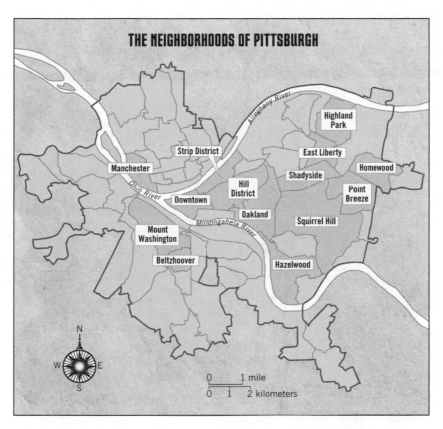

THE NEIGHBORHOODS OF PITTSBURGH

Allegheny River

Highland Park

Strip District

East Liberty

Manchester

Shadyside

Homewood

Ohio River

Hill District

Point Breeze

Downtown

Oakland

Monongahela River

Squirrel Hill

Mount Washington

Beltzhoover

Hazelwood

N
W E
S

0   1 mile
0   1   2 kilometers

Never large, Pittsburgh's black population grew from some 25,000 in 1910 to just over 100,000 by 1960. Roughly half of the population lived in the Hill District (center), which was the center of black business and culture. Blacks also resided in mixed neighborhoods to the east in Shadyside, Homewood, East Liberty, and Highland Park; across the river to the north in Manchester; and across the river to the west in Mount Washington and Beltzhoover. After the lower third of the Hill District was torn down in the late 1950s, its displaced residents moved to those other neighborhoods, causing white residents to flee and resulting in a sharp decline in the health of the economy, schools, and public services in all those previously middle-class enclaves.

On one of his many Pittsburgh visits, Joe Louis (*left*) and boyhood friend Freddie
Guinyard met at the *Courier* with Joe's favorite sportswriter, "Ches" Washington (*center*).

1

THE BROWN BOMBER'S CORNERMEN

SEVENTY THOUSAND SPECTATORS THRONGED Yankee Stadium, and the summer air was thick with cigar smoke, cologne, and the smell of history in the making. A boxing ring floated above second base, flanked by rows of seats reserved for the celebrated and the powerful. Clark Gable grinned for the cameras. Gary Cooper scribbled autographs. J. Edgar Hoover surveyed the raucous scene. It was the night of June 22, 1938, and Joe Louis was about to fight Max Schmeling for the second time. Months of breathless anticipation in the press had built it into more than a boxing bout, more than a rematch between the American champ and the German challenger who had dealt him his lone defeat in a charmed march to the heavyweight title. Set against the backdrop of Hitler's rise in Europe, the fight had taken on a metaphorical dimension, as a symbol of the struggle between Fascism and Freedom. "The Brown Bomber" versus "the Hun," the newspapers called it.

For weeks, Schmeling had issued racist taunts. "The black dynasty of pugilism must come to an end," he declared. As if to underscore the swaggering talk, Schmeling had set up training camp in a town called Speculator, in the Adirondack Mountains of New York. Two days earlier, a telegraph message had arrived there from the Führer himself. "To the coming World's Champion, Max Schmeling," the cable read. "Wishing you every success, Adolf Hitler." That spring, Louis had received his own blessing from on high while attending a Negro Elks Club convention in Washington, D.C. President Franklin Roosevelt invited him to the White House and squeezed his powerful biceps. "Joe, we're depending on those muscles for America," FDR said.

The irony of a grandson of Alabama slaves serving as the poster boy for Liberty wasn't lost on three of the men at ringside. They were out-of-towners, from Pittsburgh, the industrial city they called "Smoketown," on the western edge of Pennsylvania. Few of the East Coast or Hollywood swells would have recognized them, or perhaps even guessed that all three men were black. Robert L. Vann looked like a man of South Asian lineage, with his lanky frame, light reddish skin, and angular features. Chester Washington had straight, slicked-back hair and a round, handsome face that was so fair he could have passed for white. Of the three, only Bill Nunn fit the movie stereotype of a black male in the 1930s: a stocky, jovial man with dark skin, a wide-jawed smile, and a booming, basso profundo voice.

Yet of all the expectant boxing fans present that night, the three men had special reason to feel a mixture of excitement and anxiety. As the publisher, sports editor, and city editor for *The Pittsburgh Courier*, the nation's most widely read Negro newspaper, they had done as much as any journalists in America to make Joe Louis a hero to his own people and a sympathetic champion to the rest of the country.

Bill Nunn was the first of the three to meet Joe Louis. In the summer of 1934, Nunn traveled to Chicago to cover the black baseball all-star game known as the East-West Classic. He put himself up at the Grand Hotel, a Negro-owned establishment on the South Side, and one day Louis walked out of the lobby. The *Courier's* Chicago stringer, P.L. Prattis, recognized Louis and introduced him to Nunn. Prattis had been following Joe's first pro fights since the boxer had moved to Chicago from Detroit a few months earlier, and he was impressed. "He's going to be the next champion," Prattis predicted.

No one had a better nose for a good sports story than Bill Nunn. Although he had been promoted to city editor, sports were his first love. "Nunny," as he was known around the *Courier*, had grown up in Pittsburgh, the son of a plasterer who migrated from North Carolina to make a better life for his family. They lived in a neighborhood called Homewood, and just as Bill was entering his teens the city of Pittsburgh erected a huge new high school there to educate talented students from across the city. Nunn became one of the first black students at Westinghouse High School, and the first to earn three varsity letters, in football, basketball, and baseball. A bit too short and slow to play sports for a living, he channeled his passion into writing about the subject. He submitted his first story to the *Courier* while he was still in high school, and at twenty he quit a job as a storeroom clerk in a toy factory to work at the paper full-time.

Along with his love for athletics, Nunn was known for thinking big. As sports editor in the 1920s, he pushed to add more pages to the *Courier*'s coverage, and to create a separate entertainment section. He started sending reporters to black colleges across the country to compile an annual "Courier All-American Team" list of their best football players. He had also played a role in the creation of the first Negro League all-star game—the event that brought him to Chicago that summer. Those popular features had helped the *Courier* grow from a small local paper in the 1920s, when Nunn first joined, to a national publication that by the early 1930s was nipping at the heels of the country's largest black paper, *The Chicago Defender*.

Now Nunn was in Chicago, meeting a new rising star in the *Defender*'s backyard. Had he looked into it (which he likely did), he would have seen that the *Defender* had already published several short stories on Louis. So Nunn knew that if the *Courier* was going to win the competition to cover him, it would have to move fast.

When Nunn returned to Pittsburgh, to the *Courier*'s tiny, cramped newsroom in the neighborhood called the Hill District, he mentioned his encounter with Louis to publisher Robert L. Vann. Although Vann was consumed with the paper's business affairs—and with exercising his own political influence in Washington—he, too, was an avid sports enthusiast. As it happened, Vann also knew one of the men managing Louis, a Chicago businessman and part-time numbers racket operator named Julian Black.

Three years earlier, a Detroit numbers king named John Roxborough had discovered Louis boxing at a local youth center. Roxborough bought Joe his first pair of proper boxing gloves, and oversaw his rise through the amateur ranks, where he compiled a record of 50–4, with 43 knockouts. When Joe turned twenty, he told Roxborough he wanted to box professionally. Roxborough responded that if Joe hoped to survive in the white-run boxing world, he would need to rely on black men who wouldn't sell him cheap. To train Louis, Roxborough hired Jack Blackburn, a crafty former lightweight. To arrange for professional fights in Chicago, he brought in Julian Black.

Before the *Courier* invested in covering Louis, however, one more man needed to be convinced: sports editor Chester Washington. Like Nunn, "Ches," as everyone called him, was a hometown boy, from Pittsburgh's North Side, who had started working at the paper as a stenographer at the age of seventeen. His father was a postman with only an eighth-grade education, but Washington saved up to attend college, at Virginia Union University. When he returned to Pittsburgh, he moved into a rooming house at the YMCA across the street from the *Courier* and began working his way up from reporting on church sermons to earning a weekly sports column, called "Ches Sez."

When Washington started looking into Louis's record, he wasn't much impressed. In his first pro fight in Chicago that summer—on the 4th of July—Joe had knocked out a Norwegian-born journeyman who went by the name of Jack Kraken. By October, he had won seven more fights. But in Washington's opinion, Joe's opponents were all "paloozas," as he called them, or "damaged produce" from "Cauliflower Lane" picked by Roxborough and Black to make their man look good. His next bout, however, was against a fighter named Jack O'Dowd whom Washington respected. In his prime, O'Dowd had gone four rounds with Jack Dempsey. So in late October, Washington hopped a train to Chicago to have a look at Louis for himself.

The fight took place on the night before Halloween, 1934, and no one on the streets of Chicago seemed to know or care much about the boxing match taking place at the Arcadia Gardens. As Washington watched the boxers climb through the ropes, he thought Louis, who weighed 190 pounds, looked like a kid compared to the 210-pound O'Dowd. Then the bell rang, and Washington's "eyes popped," as he put it later. Louis weaved like a graceful cat, while O'Dowd pawed like an oversized mutt. Suddenly Joe threw a right that knocked the veteran to the mat for a nine count. O'Dowd staggered to his feet and began backpedaling as fast as he could. He survived the first round, but in the middle of the second Louis faked a right to his midsection, O'Dowd lowered his fists to block it, and Joe jolted him in the jaw with a punch with his left that put him on the mat for good.

Jack O'Dowd was finished—and Ches Washington was sold. Louis may have looked like a kid, but in only a round and a half he had exhibited the qualities that Washington looked for in a potential champion. He had quick feet, power on the right and the left, and punches that were deceptively short and fast. Under the tutelage of Jack Blackburn, the wily trainer Joe called "Chappie," Louis had also started to think like a contender. He worked O'Dowd's body until he had a shot at his head, and jabbed from one side while waiting for a chance to land a knockout blow from the other.

Washington became even more of a believer the next month when Louis finished off one of Pittsburgh's finest fighters, a body puncher named Charlie Massera, in the third round. Two weeks later, he knocked out one of the West Coast's top contenders, Lee Ramage, in the eighth. Then in January of 1935, Joe came to Pittsburgh for the first time, to take on a bruiser named Hans Birkie.

Chappie Blackburn had done a lot of fighting in Pittsburgh in his days in the ring, and he had fond memories. So he brought Louis to town a week early to train at the YMCA on Centre Avenue, across the street from the *Courier* offices. As Hill residents gathered to watch Joe work out, they couldn't believe the power in his fists. Within days, he had shredded two punching bags. But Blackburn had a new strategy for this fight: he wanted to test Louis's skills as a boxer. Don't try for an early knockout, Chappie told Joe; let Birkie wear himself out before going in for the kill.

Sure enough, Birkie didn't go down easily on the night of the fight at Pittsburgh's Duquesne Gardens. For nine rounds, he shielded his body so that Louis couldn't land hard punches. Finally, in the tenth, he lowered his guard and gave Joe an opening. Louis pounded Birkie to the canvas with three swift left jabs and a hard blow from the right. The referee took one look at the downed man's battered face and declared a TKO.

During this time in Pittsburgh, his managers paraded Louis through the Hill District to meet their friends in the city. Julian Black introduced him to Robert Vann and his wife, Jesse. Roxborough's pal Gus Greenlee, the king of Pittsburgh's numbers game, threw a dinner at his nightclub, the Crawford Grill, where everyone raised toasts of champagne and whiskey while Joe sipped a glass of milk. Bill Nunn and Ches Washington escorted him through the *Courier* newsroom, where he met Ira Lewis, the managing editor, and Julia Bumry Jones, the author of a society column called "Talk O' Town" that was read by black women across America. In his autobiography, Louis would say that he had never shaken so many hands before, and that the week in Pittsburgh was his "first test of being a public hero." It made him think: "Joe, you got to make good. You got to keep punching and winning. People all over the country are watching you and pulling for you."

Everyone on the Hill was struck by Joe's baby-faced looks and soft-spoken manner, so different from the ruthless figure he cut in the ring. They also noticed how much his managers talked about Joe's humble personality and clean-living ways. No one had to ask why. They could tell that Roxborough and Black were already preparing to see white people compare their man to Jack Johnson, the last great Negro heavy-weight. Johnson had dominated the sport and won the title a quarter century earlier; but his swagger and unapologetic pursuit of white women scandalized the public and cast a shadow of suspicion over the next generation of black fighters. If Louis was going to get a shot at the title one day, his managers knew, it would involve more than besting a string of white contenders. It would require showing the public and the white moneymen who controlled the boxing game that Joe Louis wasn't another Jack Johnson.

At the *Courier*, the editors and reporters loved nothing more than a good crusade on behalf of their people. They had fought for unionizing Pullman car porters, for taking *Amos 'n' Andy* off the radio airwaves, and for the acquittal of the Scottsboro Boys in their rape trial in Alabama. Now they saw the chance to become the public champions—and defenders— of the best and most likable Negro fighter to come down the pike in a long time. Robert L. Vann was also a shrewd businessman, and he could already sense that Joe Louis had the goods to make a lot of money, for boxing and for newspapers. Having seen the kid's potential up close, Vann wanted to get in on the action early.

LESS THAN A MONTH later, the *Courier* began publishing "The Life Story of Joe Louis," an exhaustive profile that would run in weekly installments for the next five months. Coauthored by Ches Washington and Bill Nunn, it described the upbringing of the child born Joe Louis Barrow and his seven brothers and sisters on a farm outside Montgomery, Alabama. As a boy, Joe helped his mother, Lillie, with chores and accompanied her to church every Sunday. (The story didn't mention that his father, Munroe Barrow, suffered a breakdown when Joe was two years old and was con-fined to a mental institution.) The profile followed Joe to Detroit, where his mother moved the family when he was twelve years old, and described how he fell in love with boxing and was taken under John Roxborough's wing. Then the story took Louis to Chicago, describing every detail of his first pro fights, including how much he made for knocking out Jack Kraken—$51.37.

In April 1935, Washington and Nunn traveled to Detroit to see Louis take on his toughest opponent yet. He was a scrappy Jewish boxer named Natie Brown who hadn't lost in eighteen months and had never been knocked down. The bout took place in Olympia Stadium, the city's largest indoor arena, and nearly fourteen thousand fans showed up to cheer on the hometown boy. In the crowd were dozens of East Coast sportswriters who had gotten wind of Joe Louis and had come to take his measure. Many of them arrived on a Pullman car chartered by Mike Jacobs, a New York boxing promoter who was in negotiations with Roxborough and Black to promote Joe's bouts. Although Brown managed to go the distance, he did little more than hang on after Joe floored him with a savage left in the first round. By the time he lost a unanimous eight-round decision, Natie's face was a bloody pulp.

To strengthen its claim to be "the Joe Louis paper," the *Courier* held its presses to splash the fight on the front page. The paper was printed over the weekend, on a massive Hoe & Co. press attached to the newsroom on the Hill. The bout took place on Friday night, with an opening bell at 8:15 p.m., and as soon as it was over Bill Nunn drove the three hundred miles back to Pittsburgh with photos purchased from the *Detroit News* and Ches Washington's blow-by-blow account.

Outside the *Courier* offices, Hill residents waited through the night to get their hands on the edition. "JOE LOUIS BATTERS NATIE BROWN," crowed the banner headline, while a panel of pictures depicted key moments in the fight. Although Brown had "blood streaming down his face," Louis was still "a good kid," Washington assured his readers. Already drumming up anticipation for a title bout, the paper promised an autographed photo of Louis to the *Courier* reader who predicted how soon he would get to take on the reigning champ. "When Will Joe Louis Be Ready for Max Baer?" it asked.

Back in Detroit, as Natie Brown was taken to the hospital to get his face stitched up, Louis and his handlers went to a black nightspot to celebrate.

Mike Jacobs went along, and before the evening was over the parties ducked into the men's room and signed a contract that gave the white promoter rights to Joe's fights for the next three years. Jacobs, who was trying to break Madison Square Garden's monopoly on prizefights, would stage the bouts at Yankee Stadium, and the first one would be against Primo Carnera, the mountainous, six-foot-six former champ from Italy.

Word of the Carnera bout quickly shot through the gaggle of East Coast sportswriters who had come to Detroit. Suddenly they all wanted to interview Louis and his managers. But as the white reporters lined up outside John Roxborough's office, Ches Washington was already inside, recording the scene for *Courier* readers and telling them what Joe Louis was like in private. "He's quiet and reserved," Washington reported. "He doesn't say much, but he's got an infectious, friendly grin that endears him to people. He's cocksure without being cocky; confident without being condescending. He's the type which everyone likes. Nothing Uncle-Tom about him. And the whites don't try to make him appear funny and ludicrous. Because Joe has the knack of knowing how to say the right thing at the right time. It isn't much, but it sorta gets under your skin."

The rest of the Negro press was playing catch-up, too. *The Chicago Defender* and the *Baltimore Afro-American*, the other two leading black papers, had increased their coverage of Louis, but neither could match the *Courier*. At the National Association for the Advancement of Colored People, officials demanded to know what its publication, *The Crisis*, had in store. Roy Wilkins, the editor, responded with a contrite letter to an NAACP board member named William Pickens. "There is nothing left for The Crisis to say," Wilkens confessed. "*The Pittsburgh Courier* . . . has been running for the past five weeks a serial story of the life of Joe Louis. . . . As far as I can see, the ground has been covered thoroughly."

As the Carnera bout approached, Washington installed himself at the Louis training camp in Pompton Lakes, New Jersey, and filed weekly updates. "Joe Louis Flattens 245-Pound Chicago Giant," read one headline—about a knockout of one of the huge sparring partners that Chappie Blackburn had found to get his fighter ready to take on the towering Italian. At the request of Julian Black, Ches agreed to answer Joe's mail, which was flooding in at a clip of three hundred letters per fight. Fans from as far away as Berlin and Norway pleaded for tickets. A Georgia farmer begged Joe to send him a mule. An Irish mother from Brooklyn whose boy was dying of cancer asked for an autographed copy of Joe's picture, which Washington sent Special Delivery.

The Carnera fight took place on a Tuesday, and this time Vann chartered a plane to bring Bill Nunn back to Pittsburgh with the story and pictures. When Louis knocked out Primera, Washington wrote a minute-by-minute account. "JOE LOUIS WINS!" read the headline on his story. "'Ches' Tells How Joe Won; Paints Vivid Picture." For five rounds, Louis kept up a "cool and panther-like attack" Washington reported, then in the sixth he unleashed a "volley of TNT-laden punches which floored Primo three times." When the referee stopped the fight, Yankee Stadium erupted. In the bleachers, where most of the black fans were seated, there were screams and tears of joy. Across the East River, the people of Harlem poured out of bars and brownstones and car horns honked up and down Seventh Avenue. The mood, as one observer put it, was "Everything is hotsy-totsy and the goose is hanging high."

Aboard the chartered plane to Pittsburgh, Nunn scrawled emotionally on a notepad, trying to capture the larger meaning for black America. "Bill Nunn Writes His Story 10,000 Feet in the Air," boasted the headline on Nunn's story. "Special Plane Wings Through Night and Thus Makes Glorious History for Negro Journalism." Reminding readers of the *Courier*'s special relationship with Louis, Nunn described what he had come to represent to so many of them. "To those of us know him well," Nunn wrote, "we know that Joe is the answer to our prayers . . . the prayers of a race of people who are struggling to break through a dense cloud of prejudice and studied misunderstanding . . . a race of people who ask nothing more than a CHANCE . . . a race of people, who though bowed by oppression, will never be broken in spirit."

(The victory meant something else to black fans as well: a gambling windfall. "Hundreds of thousands of dollars changed hands on the fight," another

Courier story reported, as the "smart money" on the "Gay White Way" that had made Carnera an 11-to-10 favorite came crashing down with him.)

With the Carnera win under his belt and Mike Jacobs's promotional muscle behind him, Louis was on the way to the big time—and the big money. Over the next year, he fought four more contenders, requiring a total of ten rounds to knock them all out and take home tens of thousands of dollars in prize money. One victim was the once seemingly unstoppable Max Baer, who shook his head in befuddled surrender in the fourth round after Joe knocked him to the deck for the third time. White bigots, particularly in the South, still couldn't stomach seeing a Negro boxer go so far, so fast. Before the Baer fight, *Washington Post* sportswriter Shirley Povich described them as clinging to the chance that Baer "will surpass himself in the knowledge that he is the lone White Hope for the defense of Nordic superiority in the prize ring." But when the Associated Press named Louis "Athlete of the Year" for 1935, it was a sign that the rest of America had started to embrace "the Brown Bomber" as their hero, too, particularly as he prepared to defend the country's honor in a fight against the German Max Schmeling.

In the pages of the *Courier*, meanwhile, Ches Washington saw the Joe Louis story as a vindication of the Great Migration, the exodus that had brought so many Negroes to Pittsburgh and other cities across the Northeast and Midwest. "Today Joe Louis stands as America's Public Hero No. 1," he wrote in his weekly "Ches Sez" column. "He has scaled the ladder of success by ability and diligent application in his chosen field in this land of Opportunity in the North. But what might have happened if Joe Louis had stayed down in that little community near Lafayette in prejudiced Alabama? He wouldn't have had a chance. His opportunities would have been curtailed. His ambitions would have been smothered. He probably would have been 'kept down' in some menial job and even browbeaten into an inferiority complex by his Nordic neighbors. That vicious Jim Crow complex of the state of Alabama would have 'licked' Joe Louis in his struggle for survival. It might have 'knocked him out.' He never would have arrived at the threshold of the world's championship, where he now stands."

That spring, the bonds between Louis and Pittsburgh grew even closer as the city experienced the worst flood in its history. It had been a cold and snowy winter, followed by an unusually warm March thaw. The Allegheny and Monongahela Rivers had already swelled to the official flood line when a torrential rainstorm added another twenty feet of water. On St. Patrick's Day, the rivers jumped their banks and submerged the city. Thousands of homes were inundated. Steel mills shut down. Roads were washed out. Trains and trolleys were stranded. Electricity went out for a week, casting the city into darkness, freezing the pumps at its water plants and leaving firemen helpless to fight blazes that raged for days above the sodden horizon. As the rivers receded and the fires subsided, Pennsylvania's athletic commissioner, D. W. McClelland, called Chester Washington at the *Courier*. Might he be able to persuade Joe Louis to appear at a benefit for the flood victims? McClelland asked. Washington immediately got Joe on the phone. "I'd like to come over, Ches," Louis responded, "and I'll try to make it."

But on the morning of the planned benefit, McClelland received a worrisome telegram. The private train compartment that had been reserved to bring Louis, Roxborough, and Julian Black to Pittsburgh was empty. "What'll we do now?" he asked Washington. "I'll call Detroit," Ches replied. It turned out that their guests had had an accident on the way to the station and missed the train. Instead they were making the trip to Pittsburgh by car. Around 6:30 in the evening, they pulled into town in a green Packard. After dinner at the home of Julia Bumry Jones, the society columnist, they proceeded to the Syria Mosque, where hundreds of fans engulfed Louis like the rivers that had swamped the city just weeks before. He signed everything in sight—photos, gloves, even pants pockets—until his hand cramped up.

When McClelland tried to offer Roxborough reimbursement, the manager waved him off, telling him to consider the visit a gift to the people of Pittsburgh. Before leaving town, the Louis party paid their respects to Gus Greenlee at the Crawford Grill, confirming the status of the red-headed racketeer as the King of the Hill and of the Grill as one of the top black nightspots west of Harlem. "Veni, vidi vici!" Washington declared in a gushing column describing the visit.

By now, Washington had grown so close to Louis, and so influenced by his special access, that he refused to believe the talk that Joe wasn't training hard enough for the Schmeling fight. Ed Sullivan, the columnist and future TV variety show host, had given the fighter a book on golf, and other sportswriters noticed that Louis was suddenly sneaking off for long rounds at a course near his training facility in New Jersey. With his new bride—Marva Trotter, a stenographer he had married before the Max Baer fight—home at their new apartment in Chicago, there were also rumors that Louis was consorting with comely showgirls who were part of the curious crowd buzzing around the training camp. Washington returned there to try to reassure *Courier* readers. "JOE IN TIP TOP CONDITION—CHES," read one headline. Week after week, he filed accounts of impressive sparring sessions, confident assurances from Chappie Blackburn, and predictions of why it would be "Louis Before the Fifth" for the 10-to-1 favorite.

Washington liked to compare Joe to a panther, and in one column he explained why cats are better fighters than dogs, because of their ability to attack from all angles. "Just like a cat beats a dog, the panther-like Louis will lick Max Schmeling!" he wrote on the eve of the fight, as thousands of Negroes arrived in New York City aboard trains and buses from across America, filling the hotels of Harlem. "Joe's left is as disturbing as a taxicab meter to a college boy," Washington wrote. "It clicks on and on, like an electronic clock that will never stop. . . . When the right lands solidly, the foe usually has a right to sing the blues. Because the right plays such a tune on the face and body that the opponent feels like singing, 'I Just Couldn't Take It, Baby.'"

Yet by the end of Joe's first encounter with Max Schmeling, at Yankee Stadium on June 19, 1936, it was legions of Louis fans who were singing the blues. The thirty-year-old German had trained hard for his younger opponent, and it showed. He got to Joe with a right cross in the second round, and knocked him down with another in the fourth, the first time Louis had gone to the mat as a pro. From then on, Louis seemed disorientated, unable to elude Schmeling's jabs or land solid blows of his own. By the twelfth round, Louis could barely see out of one eye. Schmeling pounded him with two rights to the body and the jaw that put him down for the count. From Harlem to the Hill, from the Deep South to the Far West, black America went into mourning. "I walked down Seventh Avenue and saw grown men weeping like children, and women sitting in the curbs with their head in their hands," poet Langston Hughes recalled. "All across the country that night when the news came that Joe was knocked out, people cried."

After the fight, Washington went to the Yankee Stadium dressing room and found Louis with his blood-streaked head in his hands. He accompanied the fighter and his entourage back to their hotel and helped apply an ice pack to Joe's swollen jaw. Ches tried to console him, to tell him that he would "come back smarter and better than ever before," but Joe was like a brokenhearted kid. "I'm not worried about myself," he said somberly, "but I'm sorry that I let down all those folks who were for me."

Washington was aching, too, but he was also embarrassed. In their own way, he and the *Courier* had also let down their readers, with their overconfident predictions. Less starstruck coverage of their hero in the pages of the rival *Chicago Defender* was making them look like shills. To prove that the *Courier* was truly "the Joe Louis paper," they would have to be honest about their man's poor performance. In his next column, Washington faulted Louis for not heeding Chappie Blackburn, who had warned him about Schmeling's right and told him to circle away from it.

Bill Nunn was even tougher in a piece that he stayed up to write on the night of the fight. "I confess that I'm still groggy, Joe, but I do want so hard to try and be fair," Nunn wrote. "I know that my people—and a lot 'em can't take it—are going to be searching both Heaven and Hades for an alibi. I know what they're going to say. They're going to talk about dope—and a fix—about 'wise money'—about this and about that. But you know, Joe—and so do I—that you were beaten by a man who was your mental superior within that hempen arena tonight. Tonight, Joe . . . you were beaten by a Better Man."

AT THAT MOMENT, EVERYONE assumed that Louis had also lost his shot at the title, and that Schmeling would get the next chance to fight Jim Braddock, the reigning champ. Yet what followed was a six-month standoff that ended with the announcement that it was Louis, not Schmeling, who would take on Braddock first. In "Ches Sez," Washington attributed the turn of events to "Economics, Liberality and Popularity." In a sign that attitudes toward Negroes were improving, he wrote, calls for a Louis challenge had come from Americans of all races. Washington praised more than a half dozen white newspapers for speaking up in favor of a Louis-Braddock bout. Most of all, he credited the power of cold hard cash. "While it is true that Schmeling deserves a shot at the title," he wrote, "it is also true that all parties concerned are likely to make more money under the new setup for the heavyweight championship merry-go-round."

That was an understatement. The reality was that Louis had been the beneficiary of one of the most cynical deals in the shady annals of boxing. By all rights, Schmeling did deserve a shot at the title, and Madison Square Garden, which had a contract to promote the next championship bout, had supported him. But almost everyone in the fight game thought that Schmeling could take Braddock, the "Cinderella Man" whom they considered lucky to have beaten Max Baer. If that happened, there was loud talk that Hitler would refuse to let Louis take on Schmeling again.

At the same time, Braddock knew that he could expect a much fatter gate if he fought Louis. And his manager, Joe Gould, figured that he had Mike Jacobs, Joe's promoter, in a corner. So Gould offered to let Louis cut in line in front of Schmeling in exchange for 10 percent of Jacobs's profits for the next ten years—including whatever he might make from future Louis fights if Joe won the title. Once in cahoots, Jacobs and Gould conspired to fend off a legal challenge from Madison Square Garden and to drum up threats of anti-Nazi protests if a Braddock-Schmeling fight went forward.

Whatever scheming was involved, Louis didn't want to blow his chance this time. As the Braddock fight approached, he went to train in the woods of Kenosha, Wisconsin, far from the temptations that lurked around his New Jersey camp. Ches Washington tagged along and recorded his every move. No detail of Joe's grueling workout routine or evening relaxation ritual was too small to share. (At night, Joe liked to play badminton and organize sing-alongs of "Dedicated to You," his favorite ballad.) And no omen of victory was too distant to invoke. (In 1758, Ches reminded *Courier* readers, another Braddock—General Edward Braddock, the British commander of the American colonies before the Revolutionary War—had met his doom at the hands of soldiers fighting for France's "King Louis" at the Battle of Fort Duquesne, the site where the city of Pittsburgh was founded shortly afterward.)

On Tuesday, June 22, 1937, Ches Washington, Bill Nunn, and Robert L. Vann were at ringside for the title bout at Comiskey Park in Chicago. After suffering an early knockdown, Louis patiently peppered Braddock for seven rounds, then knocked him cold with a brutal left-right combination in the eighth round. As the announcer lifted Joe's arm in victory, the crowd went wild. The *Courier* men joined the deafening roar, then rushed home to assemble the special edition they had dreamed of for three years, since their hero's first trip to Pittsburgh. Rather than wait until Saturday, the usual printing day, the *Courier* editors went to press the next day, on Wednesday, so they could have the paper in the hands of readers across the country by the weekend. "The King is dead, long live the King!" proclaimed Washingon's front-page story. In a celebratory ode entitled "Our Champ," the editors captured the emotion felt by millions of Negroes who danced in the streets of Chicago, New York, Pittsburgh, and so many other cities and towns that night, overjoyed to see one of their own, a black man, so decisively disprove notions of black shiftlessness and corruptibility:

In days of old,
When men were bold,
They had no foe
Like Bomber Joe
He clouted up
The Fistic path—
And dealt his cup
Of Fistic wrath.
His eyes were set
Upon his goal—
He never bet
Away his soul.
He courted fame
And power, too;
But stayed the same
To me and you.
And now he's won
He's broken camp.
His task is done—
He's now OUR CHAMP!

The next day, the new champ dodged hundreds of reporters who were begging to talk to him by spending the day looking after John Roxborough, who was ill, at the fighter's apartment on Chicago's Michigan Avenue. But in the afternoon, he invited Ches Washington over and offered him an exclusive account of the title bout. Louis admitted that the early Braddock barrage that put him on the mat in the first round—and threw a scare into his fans—was a "clean knockdown." But he shook it off and listened to Chappie Blackburn's advice to take his time. "Jes be careful, Joe," the trainer told him. "Just wait for your chance. You got fifteen rounds if you need 'em."

By the fourth, Louis told Washington, he could feel Braddock weakening. In the fifth, he hit him with a left to the midsection that "knocked all the wind out of him." Finally in the eighth, another left to the body made Braddock lower his guard and "left the jaw wide open," Joe recalled. Seizing the chance for a "payoff punch," Louis reared back and threw the hardest right he could. Braddock fell to the canvas and Joe walked away, knowing that the fight was over.

Louis had finally earned the name that Blackburn and Roxborough called him in private—"Champ." But he told Washington that he wasn't satisfied. As far as he was concerned, he wouldn't deserve the title until he avenged his loss to Max Schmeling. Praising the valiant Irishman he had just beaten, he offered a few choice words about his German nemesis. "There was never a gamer fighter than Braddock," Louis said. "He's a tougher fellow than Schmeling." How did it feel to be champion? Washington asked. "I don't feel any different," Joe replied. "But I do want to beat Schmeling."

The following New Year's Day, after defending his new title several times, Louis invited Washington to Detroit and declared his resolution for 1938. "I'm going to beat Schmeling if I fight him this year," Joe vowed as the two dined at the Brown Bomber Chicken Shack, a restaurant opened with the champ's winnings. But this time, Louis had another motive for giving his favorite reporter a private audience. The week before Christmas, Joe had been spotted enjoying the company of several beauties at a nightclub in Harlem while his wife, Marva, was home in Chicago. Walter Winchell, the syndicated gossip columnist, had described the champ as "contributing to the hilarity of the Uptown House on West 134th Street." Winchell went on to report that "insiders of the sports world will wager anything that the Louises are definitely apart." So it was no accident that when he arrived in Detroit, Ches found Joe and Marva reunited, sharing the holidays with Joe's mother, Lillie. "There's nothing to it!" the fighter told Washington about the latest reports of his wandering eye, a response that the watchful guardian of Louis's wholesome image was only too happy to repeat on the front page of the *Courier*.

Soon a date for the second Louis-Schmeling fight was set—June 22—and as it approached the political symbolism surrounding it continued to build. When the rivals had met two years earlier, Adolf Hitler had only begun to make good on his expansionist bluster by remilitarizing the Rhineland. Since then, Hitler had formed alliances with the Fascist regimes in Spain, Italy, and Japan and declared Germany's right to *Lebensraum*. By March 1938, Nazi troops had occupied Austria and incited demands for the surrender of Czechoslovakia's Sudetenland. Across America, Negroes burned with memories of the disrespectful treatment of Jesse Owens at the Berlin Olympics, and Jews rallied to Louis as Hitler's anti-Semitic designs grew more ominous. As Joe would put it in his memoir: "The whole world was looking to this fight. . . . Germany was tearing up Europe, and we were hearing about the concentration camps for Jews. A lot of Americans had family in Europe and they were afraid for their people's lives. Schmeling represented everything that Americans disliked and they wanted him beat and beat good."

Louis had his own reasons to want to beat Schmeling soundly. He hadn't forgotten the "tech" the German had thrown in round five of the first fight—boxer talk for a dirty punch landed after the bell. While reading the comics and sports pages one day, Joe had also come across a story from Germany in which Schmeling bragged about why he would win. He was in the best shape of his life, Schmeling boasted, and Louis feared him because he had discovered his weakness. What Max didn't know was that Joe and Chappie had figured out the weakness, too. In the first bout, Louis had dropped his left too often, opening himself up to Schmeling's right. Since then, Chappie had drilled Joe on keeping his left glove high at all times—all jabs, no hooks. They were sure that if the German came looking for that chink in his armor again, he wouldn't find it.

On the day of the fight, Louis was as antsy as a caged cat. In the morning, he drove into New York from Pompton Plains for the weigh-in, but he barely spoke and remained poker-faced throughout the staged ritual. In his dressing room, where he usually waited to warm up until several minutes before fight time, he shadowboxed for forty minutes. "Okay, Chappie, I'm ready as a radio," he said to his trainer as he made his way to the ring. Once inside the ropes, Joe bounced and shuffled to keep loose. The first time he had fought at Yankee Stadium, against Primo Carnera, the boisterous crowd had startled him, but this time he barely noticed what was happening outside the ring.

It was pandemonium. Seventy thousand people rippled out from the VIP seats to the corners of the outfield, jostling to get a better look. "Attaboy, Max!" Schmeling's backers shouted. "Kill that Nazi, Joe!" answered the Louis crowd. More than a quarter of the spectators were black: Hollywood stars such as Bill "Bojangles" Robinson; smartly dressed Negro businessmen who had come from Chicago, Washington, Pittsburgh, and Detroit; working men and women who had paid to sit in the cheap seats and cheer on "our Joe." Looking around, the *Courier* reporters at ringside counted no fewer than forty other members of the Negro press among hundreds of newsmen from around the world. In Harlem, the streets were choked with vehicles from forty states, including a convoy of two hundred cars from Pittsburgh. Across America, seventy million listeners huddled around radios for the live NBC broadcast.

At last the referee summoned the fighters to the center of the ring. The opening bell clanged. Louis went to work with a burst of left jabs. Schmeling threw a roundhouse right that grazed the champ's head. The two clutched at mid-ring, trying to land more punches. Then as Schmeling backed away toward the ropes, Louis saw him lower his guard. He drilled a right into the German's jaw and a second into his midsection. A yelp resembling that of a stuck pig, a sound Joe remembered from his boyhood on an Alabama farm, rose from his opponent's throat. Suddenly Schmeling was helpless to fend off a furious barrage. Louis could smell fear. The German clung to the ropes to keep from falling. When he pulled away, he shot a panicked look toward his corner. Louis moved in and pounded him to the mat with a savage combination. Schmeling staggered to his feet, but another one-two punch knocked him to one knee. As Max rose again, Joe threw a left and a right to his head and floored him for a third time. A towel appeared in the ring, thrown from Schmeling's corner. The referee tossed it back, refusing the attempt at surrender. But as the count reached eight, Schmeling was still crawling on the canvas, dazed and wounded, and the ref declared the fight over.

Revenge had taken a total of two minutes and four seconds. Louis had made such short work of Schmeling, in fact, that he needed only a brief rest before he joined the wild celebration that erupted in the streets of New York City and went on through the night. After calling Detroit to speak to his mother, who was so nervous she had gone for a car ride instead of listening to the fight, Joe showered and headed to Harlem. As his car inched through the teeming streets, thousands of revelers applauded him from the sidewalks. On one corner, a man waved a "Joe Louis for President" sign. Finally, Joe reached the apartment on St. Nicholas Avenue where Marva had listened to the bout on the radio with friends. He teased his wife about the $15 bet she had made that it would take him until the fourth round to win. The next morning, Louis went with John Roxborough and Julian Black to the office of Mike Jacobs to pick up his share of the earnings. The check was for $349,288, a third of the million-dollar gate.

"Joe was murderous," the normally reserved Robert Vann wrote in an ecstatic letter to his wife, Jesse, who was touring Europe with lady friends from Pittsburgh. "If the referee had not stepped between him and the German boy, I am sure a death would have resulted in the ring." The *Courier* edition that Vann published several days later was even more jubilant. "JOE KO'S MAX," proclaimed the paper's largest headline ever, and four large photographs on the front page and nine more inside re-created the decisive moments of the brief match. "To the poet, there is nothing so rare as a day in June," Ches Washington waxed poetically, "but for Joe, this magic June night was the night of nights for the bronzed monarch of the rope-circled kingdoms."

Another *Courier* author captured the vicarious glee that so many felt in seeing such a fine example of black manhood—strong but dignified, popular yet never servile—obliterate the personification of white supremacism. "It was as if each [black person] had been in that ring himself, as if every man, woman and child of them had dealt destruction with his fists upon the Nordic face of Schmeling and the whole Nazi system he symbolized," the author wrote. "It was more than the victory of one athlete over another, it was the triumph of a repressed people against the evil forces of racial oppression and discrimination condensed—by chance—into the shape of Max Schmeling."

For Robert L. Vann, Bill Nunn, and Chester Washington, there was more to celebrate beyond Joe Louis's victory. In less than four years, their investment in covering his rise had more than doubled the *Courier*'s circulation, from under 100,000 in 1934 to almost a quarter of a million in 1938. According to the Audit Bureau of Circulation, the scorekeeper of the publishing industry, all but 20,000 of those weekly buyers lived outside Pittsburgh. Across the country, thousands more read the paper as it was passed around homes, barbershops, and beauty salons. The *Courier* was now by far the most widely read black publication in the land, well ahead of its longtime rival, *The Chicago Defender*, whose circulation had plummeted from 200,000 in 1925 to as little as 73,000 a decade later. Having established that lead, the *Courier* would maintain it for the next two decades, through a world war, the integration of Major League Baseball, and the beginning of the civil rights movement.

From its origins as a four-page pamphlet of poetry and local oddities sold only in Pittsburgh, the *Courier* had grown into a thriving business. It had seventy-two employees in Pittsburgh, twenty-three more in Harlem and other cities across the country, an $80,000 annual payroll, and enough profit to return a dividend to its shareholders. In a letter to a Pittsburgh steel company executive, Vann proudly cited the paper's contribution to the city's economy. "We have an investment here of $170,000 and we pay a federal state and city tax, mind you, of close to $10,000 a year," Vann wrote.

By championing the champion of their people, the colored men and women of Pittsburgh had also confirmed their place at the vanguard of black America. By the late 1930s, they had helped propel a sea change in the allegiance of Negro voters, fielded the two best teams in black baseball, produced musicians who had started to rewrite the language of jazz, and built nightclubs and watering holes so vibrant that the Hill District had come to be known as "little Harlem." So many influential black cultural and political figures passed through Pittsburgh that the corner of Wylie Avenue and Fullerton Street in the Hill District would come to be known as "the Crossroads of the World." And with Hitler's forces on the march in Europe, black Pittsburgh was about to find itself at the center of a national debate over how Negroes should regard the prospect of war and what it would portend for black soldiers in uniform.

How did it happen? How had a community of fewer than a hundred thousand black people—half of them living on less than two square miles of steep, dusty streets under the soot-filled skies of northern Appalachia—produced a culture of such drive and accomplishment? It's a story that traced back almost a century, to Pittsburgh's first Negro settlers before the Civil War, and to a slave boy born in Maryland who grew up to ride the Ohio River wielding a deckhand's broom and harboring an improbable dream.

Cumberland "Cap" Posey Sr., his wife, Anna,
and their home in Homestead, circa 1900.

2

THE NEGRO CARNEGIES

THE BOY'S NAME WAS Cumberland Willis Posey, and a river called out to him from his earliest days. It was the Port Tobacco River, on the southeastern tip of Maryland, stretching out from the town of the same name to the wide Potomac four miles away. In 1858, Cumberland Posey was born seven miles from there, to two slaves who worked for a white family in Charles County. Their names were Alexander Posey and Elizabeth Willis Posey, and they were literate Negroes, Bible readers who attended gatherings of the African Methodist Episcopal (AME) Church. Although it is not known for sure, it is also likely that they were house slaves, the sort who would have been sent into the town of Port Tobacco to fetch supplies and who might have brought their young son along, to gaze out onto the river and watch the steamboats chugging into the distance.

The boy had faith and ambition in his veins. Cumberland's mother, who died when he was seven years old, barely experienced Emancipation, but as soon as he had his freedom, his father was ordained as a minister of the AME Church. Four years later, Alexander Posey took his children to Winchester, Virginia, where he became one of the first Negroes to head a congregation of the larger Methodist Episcopal Church. A half century earlier, a Philadelphia Methodist, Bishop Richard Allen, had led the AME schism in protest over the church's treatment of Negroes, who suffered such indignities as being forced to sit in separate balconies and told they were not good enough to kneel in prayer. But as the Civil War loomed, blacks who had remained in "full connection" with the white Methodists formed their own conference and sought permission to build a church in Winchester. They named it the John Mann Street Chapel, and in 1869 Alexander Posey was appointed its chaplain.

According to church records, Alexander Posey lived for only five more years, riding the circuit of black Methodist congregations up and down the western edge of Virginia. Before he died, however, he must have concluded that his children would face a better future in Ohio, a state that had been on the side of the Union and long a refuge for free Negroes. As Cumberland Posey was entering his teenage years, his father moved him and his two younger siblings to the town of Belpre, on a nook of the Ohio River that had once served as a crossing point for the Underground Railroad. It lay directly across the river from Parkersburg, West Virginia, which was connected to a town south of Winchester by the only passable toll road running across the Allegheny Mountains. There is no record of whom Cumberland lived with in Belpre after his father died, but there is of the job he had secured by the age of nineteen: working for a steamboat operator named Payton sweeping the decks of a riverboat called the *Magnolia*.

For the young Posey, the boat became a classroom as well as a workplace. When he was finished with his rounds, he would study the two men who presided over the engine room. One was the "assistant engineer," who fed cords of wood and shovelsful of coal into the furnace, carefully prodding the fuel to maintain an even burn. Occasionally, this man would also climb onto the deck to observe the color and quantity of the cloudy exhaust belching from the smokestack that thrust up from the center of the boat. The other man was the "chief engineer," who monitored a cluster of round gauges that measured the pressure of the steam in the water tanks heated by the furnace. Behind the gauges, pistons powered by that steam pushed and pulled the axle of a paddle wheel. Alongside the hull, the wheel's wide buckets gulped and spit out large quaffs of the river, propelling the boat forward.

As Posey observed and asked questions, he came to understand the function of each part of the miraculous mechanism. Like any good boatman, he also began to read the vessel with his other senses. Closing his eyes, he could listen to the symphony of crackling, hissing, thrusting, and lapping, and know what mood the boat was in at any moment, when she was demanding attention and when she was communicating that all was well and that she could be left alone.

Posey set his sights on running the engine room of a steamboat. It was something that no Negro had ever done before, and that many a white man in the trade would have said could never happen. But Posey found a believer in his employer, and with his help he began working toward the goal. First Mr. Payton helped Posey secure a position as an assistant engineer, minding the furnaces on a steamboat called the *Striker*. A year later, Posey became the first black man ever to receive a chief engineer's license. A riverboat owner named Stewart Hayes took a chance on him, and he was soon won over by Posey's fierce work ethic and taciturn, no-nonsense manner.

For the next fourteen years, Posey oversaw the operation of several of Hayes's vessels. He earned a salary of twelve hundred dollars a year and continued to study the steamboat business, learning everything he could about shipbuilding as well as engine maintenance. As word of his standing spread, he acquired a nickname of respect among Negroes up and down the Ohio River: Captain Posey, or "Cap" for short.

Sometime in his early twenties, Cap Posey had occasion to travel west along the narrow Hocking River to the town of Athens, Ohio, where he fell in love. The object of his affection was Angeline Stevens, a schoolteacher with pale skin, delicate cheekbones, and wise eyes. Her father, Aquilla Stevens, was an illiterate railroad worker and stonecutter. Her mother, Eliza Brackston Stevens, had stayed at home raising eleven children in the community of farmers and laborers where they lived outside of town. But from an early age, "Anna," as the family called her, showed an appetite for learning. There is evidence that she was the first Negro to graduate from high school in Athens, and that during the graduation ceremony she impressed an overflow crowd at City Hall with a speech entitled "The Visible and the Invisible," expounding on what she called "the invisible influences by which we are surrounded in life."

By the age of seventeen, Anna Stevens passed the tests in grammar, arithmetic, and geography required for certification as a teacher in Athens County. She went to work in the county school system, which consisted almost entirely of one-room structures where students from the first to the eighth grade were taught together. Athens didn't have a large enough Negro population for a separate school, so in many classrooms black children mixed with white students. They sat at the same desks and recitation tables, warmed themselves by the same potbellied stoves, and relieved themselves in the same outhouses. (The Negro students were required to use separate hooks, however, to hang their coats by the schoolhouse doors.) With her upswept hair and calm voice, Anna exuded maturity beyond her years, and she swiftly mastered the art of making her students sit still as she drilled them in lessons from *McGuffey's Readers*, *Harvey's Grammar*, and *Ray's New Arithmetic*.

By twenty, Anna had such a favorable reputation as a teacher that the local newspaper, the *Athens Messenger*, singled her out for praise as a model of racial achievement. "Progress in the march of events is, in one direction, chronicled in the fact that Miss Anna Stevens, of African lineage, is teaching in the public white school west of Mr. Joseph Herrold's suburban residence," the paper reported in 1880. "Miss Stevens has previously taught in York Township and at other points where she has uniformly been highly personally esteemed. As a teacher she possesses rare tact and efficiency and her services in this line have been in wide demand."

Yet a year later, an event occurred in Athens that showed the limits of that progress. In the wee hours of a November morning, thirty armed white men stormed into the town on horseback. Some moved to surround the church, so no one could sound an alarm from the bell tower. Others forced their way into the home of the sheriff. They overpowered him and seized the keys to the town jail, where a mulatto farm hand named Christopher C. Davis was imprisoned. A month earlier, Davis had been arrested for attacking Lucinda Luckey, a fifty-two-year-old white widow. She said that Davis had broken into her house, sexually assaulted her, and struck her on the head with an ax. Now he was awaiting trial, but the men had come to take justice into their own hands. Throwing a noose around the mulatto's neck, they led him to the South Bridge, where they gave him three minutes to pray before they hung him to death over the river.

After the lynching, many in the small community of Negroes in Athens chose to move elsewhere. Anna was well regarded enough that she likely had little to fear, and she was earning a respectable living, as teachers in that part of Ohio were paid an average of $22 a month and as much as $48 if they had a permanent position. But Anna must have sensed the prospect of a better future when she met the dark, broad-shouldered man who didn't talk much but had possessed the drive to become a steamboat engineer. When Cap Posey proposed, Anna accepted, and on May 9, 1883, an Athens magistrate joined them in marriage. Soon afterward, she left Athens and followed her husband to a new life in the town of Homestead, just south of Pittsburgh, in Pennsylvania.

For an ambitious young man in the boating trade, there were many sensible reasons to put down stakes in the Pittsburgh area. The first was geography. For well over a century, the city's perch at the nexus of three great rivers had made it a logistical prize. During the Seven Years War, the British governor of Virginia had dispatched men to build a fortress at the head of the Ohio River. French forces promptly seized it and renamed it Fort Duquesne. General Edward Braddock, the commander of the British colonial army, led a raid to reclaim the fortress. It ended in a humiliating defeat; Braddock and more than five hundred of his men were killed before his young aide-de-camp, George Washington, organized a hasty retreat. Later another British general, John Forbes, returned with Washington and an army of six thousand and chased away the French. "I have used the freedom of giving your name to Ft. Duquesne," Forbes wrote to William Pitt the Elder, the leader of Britain's government, to inform him that he had renamed the stronghold Fort Pitt. A native Scot who had studied in Edinburgh, Forbes took to calling the surrounding area "Pitts-burgh."

Once the colonies won independence and Americans began to push west, Pittsburgh's long maritime tentacles stretching in three directions made it a busy trading center. To the north was the Allegheny River, stretching 325 miles to the western border between Pennsylvania and New York. To the south was the Monongahela River, flowing 130 miles through the mountains of West Virginia. To the west was the Ohio River, meandering 981 miles across six states, all the way to the Mississippi River, which could carry boats as far as the lakes of Minnesota or the Gulf coast of Louisiana.

In the early 1800s, Pittsburgh was known for its longboats, which could make it to New Orleans in four weeks. (Upriver keelboats were required to make the return trip, which could take up to four months.) As steam engine technology spread, the city became headquarters to more than five hundred steamboats that ferried passengers, mail, farm goods, and other supplies in three directions. Even after railroads came along in the middle of the century, steamers remained the only or the least expensive way to reach many rural areas in Ohio and western Virginia. Every week, dozens of vessels from three major "packet lines" arrived in Pittsburgh from towns along the Ohio, the Monongahela, the Allegheny, and their tributaries. They docked for several days while their captains sold their wares and purchased new provisions, then made their way back to the farmers, miners, and storekeepers the railroads hadn't yet reached.

By the 1880s, the opportunity to profit from booming new industries beckoned. For decades, Pittsburgh's proximity to seams of coal used for smelting had made it a hub for the manufacture of glass and of iron created from ore imported from as far away as Minnesota. More recently, it had become a laboratory for the more efficient and profitable mass production of steel. Making iron products was highly labor-intensive: artisans called "puddlers" had to stand for hours by small, searing furnaces, poking molten pig iron with long rods to refine it into wrought iron. Then in the 1850s, an English engineer named Henry Bessemer invented a method of removing the impurities from pig iron with blasts of air inside a converter, a method that yielded a substance that was more malleable and more durable than iron. Because converters were mechanized, they could also run around the clock, seven days a week, producing more than three times the output of iron ovens.

Bessemer's invention coincided with the rise of the locomotive industry, and the product he called "steel" quickly became the preferred material for railway lines. The Englishman went into business as a manufacturer and built one of his first American plants in Homestead. Pictures from the period show the Pittsburgh Bessemer Steel Company occupying a stretch of waterfront on a curve of the Monongahela River, belching dark clouds as high as the surrounding hilltops from three smokestacks and spurting steam in every direction. Yet like many of the early steel producers, Bessemer went into debt to build his mill and was unprepared for the financial toll of a worker's strike and a fall-off in demand as rail expansion slowed. By 1883, the Pittsburgh Bessemer Steel Company couldn't pay its creditors and was forced to sell the Homestead mill.

The buyer was Andrew Carnegie, the bantam-sized Scottish immigrant to Pittsburgh who was fast becoming America's most successful industrialist. Carnegie had already opened his own plant using the "Bessemer process" across the Monongahela River in Braddock. With the addition of the Homestead mill, he was on his way to building an empire that would make him one of the world's richest men and make Pittsburgh the source of more than half of America's steel. So it was, in 1883, that Andrew Carnegie planted his flag in Homestead just as Cap Posey brought his new bride, Anna, there to live. And for the next decade, the Poseys were able

to study the practices of the ingenious Scot and the city's other remarkable industrial entrepreneurs as they calculated how they, too, even as
Negroes, could profit from Pittsburgh's Gilded Age.

AS A CHILD, ANDREW CARNEGIE watched the forces of technology and corporate consolidation crush his father, and he was determined never to suffer
the same fate. William Carnegie was a weaver who produced linens on
a loom in the family's tiny cottage in the Scottish village of Dunfermline. As steam-powered looms and powerful wholesalers came to dominate the textile industry, the family's modest living was reduced to bare
subsistence. In desperation, Andrew's mother, Margaret, borrowed £20
from a childhood friend to pay for the voyage to a new life in America.
Their destination was the town of Allegheny City, just north of Pittsburgh,
where several of Margaret's relatives had already emigrated. At the age of
thirteen, Andrew went to work as a bobbin boy in a Pittsburgh cotton mill,
running fresh spools of thread to the women on the looms, and then as a
messenger for a local telegraph company. He proved so able that one of his
customers, the manager of the local office of the Pennsylvania Railroad,
hired Carnegie as a personal telegraph officer and then as a full-time assistant.

Carnegie spent the next decade working for the Pennsylvania Railroad,
eventually rising to run the Pittsburgh branch himself. Yet he would build
his first fortune not from his working wages but from the investments he
made, with the help of his superior and the owner of the railroad, in companies with which they had sweetheart contracts. When Carnegie was
wealthy enough to move his family to the neighborhood of Point Breeze,
on the eastern edge of Pittsburgh, he became friends with a neighbor who
put him into a lucrative oil company stock. By his late twenties, Carnegie
had assets of almost $50,000, all but 5 percent of which came from his
crony investments.

Standing barely five feet tall and weighing less than 110 pounds, Carnegie cut a diminutive figure that belied his ferocious business instincts.

In his early thirties, he quit the railroad company so that he could be even freer to exploit his connections. He began investing in firms that made railroad bridges and tracks, and selling bonds to finance them. He became fascinated by breakthroughs in iron processing that promised to create more durable rail lines to replace the ones that had been destroyed and degraded during the Civil War. When over-borrowing in the early days of railroads and steel mills led to a cascade of bankruptcies, Carnegie pounced. He had managed his finances prudently enough that he was in position to buy out competitors, dictate terms to customers and creditors, and expand into new products. Over the next three decades, Carnegie's virtual monopoly on the steel mills of Pittsburgh would bring him vast riches that he used to build a mansion in Manhattan, to erect a castle in Scotland, and to fund a legacy as one of history's most generous philan- thropists, donating $350 million to libraries, concert halls, peace research, and other causes before he died.

While Carnegie was making Pittsburgh the steel capital of the world, four other entrepreneurs were turning it into a powerhouse in other in- dustries. In the late 1860s, George Westinghouse, a young inventor from New York, moved to Pittsburgh to test the use of steel in his railroad pat- ents. He began experimenting with electricity, and soon he was compet- ing head-to-head with Thomas Edison, the inventor of the incandescent light bulb and the first electrical power grid. Partnering with the Italian inventor Nikola Tesla, Westinghouse devised a method of alternating high and low currents that made distributing electricity more practical and less expensive than Edison's direct current method. Despite Edison's attempts to discredit AC technology—including trying to associate it in the public's mind with the electric chair—it emerged as the winner in the "war of the currents." By the 1890s, Westinghouse was employing thousands of work- ers in four separate electricity, railroad, gas, and steam-power plants in the Pittsburgh area.

In 1869, Henry J. Heinz, the son of German immigrants, began selling foodstuffs in the town of Sharpsburg, north of Pittsburgh. He founded a company to make horseradish, and when it went bankrupt he regrouped and started producing tomato ketchup. By the 1880s the H. J. Heinz Company had opened a factory in Pittsburgh and was claiming to make "57 Varieties" of food products. In fact, that number was made up: Heinz had lifted the marketing gimmick from a New York shoe store that advertised "21 styles" and came up with 57 because he thought the number had special subliminal resonance. Over time, however, Heinz would more than deliver on his famous slogan. He would sell ketchup, pickles, baked beans, mustard, chutney, and hundreds of other products, as well as introduce innovations in technology and sanitation that made working in his factories among Pittsburgh's most desirable manufacturing jobs.

Another son of immigrants transformed the city into a banking hub. Andrew Mellon was still in his teens when he dropped out of college and used a loan from his father, Thomas, a local judge and banker who came from Ireland, to begin investing in lumber and coal. By the 1880s, Andrew had taken over his father's bank, formed two others, and become the principal financier of numerous firms that came to dominate their industries. (One was the Aluminum Company of America, better known as Alcoa, which was also based in Pittsburgh.) By the 1920s, when Andrew Mellon served as secretary of the treasury under three presidents, he was America's third richest man, and Pittsburgh ranked second to New York City as a repository of U.S. financial assets.

The fifth titan in this formidable group owed his fortune to both Mellon and Carnegie. The grandson of a local Pittsburgh whiskey maker, Henry Clay Frick was a sickly child and a poor student, and he never finished school. He went to work as bookkeeper in his grandfather's distillery, and then gravitated toward the coal business, seeing opportunity in the large seam of coal deposits south of Pittsburgh. With loans from Thomas and Andrew Mellon, Frick cornered the local market in coke, a high-burning coal concentrate. He invested in hundreds of "beehive ovens" to bake raw coal at the minefields, and in a transportation network to get the coke to the Pittsburgh mills, where it was used in the blast furnaces that made pig iron hot enough to purify into steel. By his thirtieth birthday, Frick was supplying a hundred railroad carloads of coke a day to Carnegie's steel mill in Braddock, and he had already made his first million dollars.

By then, Carnegie saw that he needed Frick as much as Frick needed him. When Frick traveled to New York on his honeymoon in 1881, Carnegie invited him to dinner and toasted their partnership. After Carnegie bought the Homestead steel plant two years later, he decided to take the business relationship a step further. He offered to buy 50 percent of H. C. Frick & Company, to pay all of its debts, and to invest millions to ensure a guaranteed supply of coke for his mills. After his brother and business partner Tom Carnegie died prematurely, Andrew decided that Frick was the man to take over day-to-day management of his Pittsburgh empire while he devoted himself to travel and philanthropy. In 1887, Frick went to work for the Carnegie Brothers and Company, and by the end of the decade he was named its chairman and president.

Both Carnegie and Frick were intent on curbing the growing power of labor unions in their mills. In the late 1880s, they succeeded in breaking two brief strikes by the newly formed Amalgamated Association of Iron and Steel Workers, forcing it to accept a sliding scale of wages based on the sale price of steel. When the Homestead contract came up for renewal in the summer of 1892, the owners thought they could win more concessions. But this time the union dug in. As both sides prepared for a walkout, Frick hired Pinkerton guards to bring in strikebreakers. To protect them, he ordered the construction of a three-mile, eleven-foot-high fence that encircled the Homestead plant and ran down to the river. Three strands of barbed wire stretched across the top of the fence. Small holes were bored into its planks to allow snipers to fire out. Meanwhile, four thousand workers and sympathizers organized to prevent scabs or their protectors from reaching the plant. Lookouts took their places at Homestead's two rail stations, at the roads into town, and along both sides of the Monongahela River.

At midnight of July 6, a day after Frick set a final deadline for the union to accept his offer, a tugboat called *Little Bill* chugged out of

harbor at Bellevue, Ohio, twenty-five miles south of Pittsburgh. It pulled
two barges carrying three hundred Pinkerton guards hired to secure the
mill for the strikebreakers. Around one o'clock in the morning, a watch
party stationed on the Smithfield Street Bridge in Pittsburgh spied the
barges in the distance. An hour later, a man on horseback rode through
Homestead shouting the news. A steam whistle at the electric light factory in town sounded a coded alert. Hundreds of mill workers and their
supporters poured into the streets carrying shotguns, knives, and rocks.
Arriving at the mill, they tore through Frick's fence and took up positions. As the barges docked and the first Pinkerton guards appeared on
the gangplank, a shot rang out. Suddenly gunfire rained through the
darkness in both directions.

The battle raged into the morning and through the next day. At one
point, the workers fired a cannon from across the river. At another, they
loaded a freight car with lumber and oil, set it ablaze, and pushed it toward the river, where it toppled over before reaching the barges. More and
more townspeople arrived, brandishing everything from Roman candles to
homemade petrol bombs to hurl at the Pinkerton vessels. By nightfall, half
a dozen protesters were dead, and five guards had been killed or suffered
soon-to-be-fatal wounds. Most of the Pinkertons weren't regulars but free-
lancers, and finally one frightened recruit surrendered. Sensing victory,
the strikers stormed the barges and chased the rest of the guards onto
the waterfront. The Pinkertons were force-marched through a gauntlet of
jeering, stone-throwing townspeople, herded into town, and sent packing
on rail cars to Pittsburgh.

The union had won the battle, but it was about to lose the war. When
the town sheriff returned the next day to demand that the strikers leave
the mill, they refused. The sheriff appealed to the governor of Pennsylvania, who dispatched the commander of the state militia and four
thousand of his men to Homestead. They set up artillery and Gatling
guns on an overlook called Shanty Hill, then marched toward the mill in
battle formation, rifles and bayonets drawn. Completely outnumbered,
the strikers surrendered. The militia occupied the mill and garrisoned

the town, remaining for several weeks as nonstriking workers began returning to the mill.

A week after the siege, the strikers suffered another embarrassment when anarchist Alexander Berkman, Emma Goldman's lover, barged into Frick's office and tried to kill him. Frick was shot in the neck and back and stabbed three times before his deputy overcame Berkman and got him to spit up a capsule of mercury that could have blown them all up. Although the anarchist was making a political statement that had little to do with the strike, the attack won public sympathy for Frick and made him more determined than ever not to give an inch to the union.

As Christmas neared and the workers faced the prospect of a long winter with no work or pay, the union finally gave in. But Frick and Carnegie hadn't exactly won the battle of Homestead, either. The standoff had made headlines around the world and cast their empire in a harsh new light. Carnegie, who had posed as a friend of the union movement, was denounced as a hypocrite. Critics began to question whether his philanthropy was a form of expiation for his ruthless business practices. The crisis also put a harsh damper on his partnership with Frick. Carnegie had been on vacation in a remote area of Scotland during the crisis, but he had remained in close touch by mail and telegraph and had encouraged Frick's tough line every step of the way. Now word got back to Frick that Carnegie was second-guessing his decisions and claiming that he hadn't been fully aware of what was happening in Homestead. Although they remained in business together, their relationship would never be the same.

One man did benefit from the bloody Homestead strike, however: Cap Posey. In 1892, the year that Frick and Carnegie crushed the union, Posey made his first investment in coal boats. He went on to organize a small mining company, the Delta Coal Company, serving as its general manager and treasurer. Selling his shares in that company, he founded Posey Coal Dealers and Steam Boat Builders, a company that is said to have manufactured twenty-one steamboats. By the end of the decade, he had become a major shareholder in the Marine Coal Company and earned a yearly salary of $3,000 to manage the business. By this point, another account suggests, Posey oversaw a payroll of one thousand employees and had nine white investors. Without specifying the exact connections, numerous accounts describe Posey as a business partner of Henry Frick and a supplier to Andrew Carnegie's steel mills, which he almost certainly would have had to be to move ahead in the coal mining and steel shipping businesses at a time when those two men controlled so much of both industries.

By the 1890s, Carnegie was becoming known for his support of Negro causes, so it stands to reason that he would want to help an ambitious striver like Cap Posey. Carnegie had befriended Booker T. Washington and begun making substantial donations to Tuskegee Institute, which Washington founded, and Hampton Institute, where he had gone to school. Later Carnegie would give a speech titled "The Negro in America," which foresaw slow but steady progress toward more racial harmony.

After the Homestead strike, Carnegie and Frick had other reasons to welcome a black business partner. Once the siege was over, they refused to rehire most of the workers who had gone out on strike, the majority of whom were white European immigrants. They were in the market for new workers who hadn't taken part of the union movement, and Negroes qualified. While blacks had largely been shut out of the mills and the unions before the strike, a decade later there would be 346 Negroes working in three Carnegie steel mills in the Pittsburgh area.

Posey was in a position to help recruit those workers, and to project a positive image of the Carnegie empire within Pittsburgh's growing black community. In 1909, a writer named Helen A. Tucker visited Pittsburgh to write an article called "The Negroes of Pittsburgh" for the journal *Charities and the Commons*. She visited Cap Posey in Homestead and hailed his business success as a sign that "there is here [in Pittsburgh] a chance, such as perhaps few northern cities give, for the industrial Negro to succeed." Tucker also cited three men who disputed the charge that the only reason for the rise in Negro employment in the steel mills was that blacks had been brought in as scabs. This was not true, the sources insisted; most of the blacks had been hired after the strikes were over. Tucker identified two of her sources as "an official of the Carnegie Company" and "a Negro who went to work in the Homestead Mills in 1892." The third source was "a leading colored resident of Homestead"—very likely Cap Posey, doing a public relations favor for Carnegie and Frick in exchange for all the business they had sent his way, business that now made Posey the wealthiest black man in Pittsburgh, surpassing even the first generation of Negroes who had emerged as commercial and community leaders in the decades before the Civil War.

FOUR YEARS AFTER THE Declaration of Independence proclaimed that all men are created equal, Pennsylvania became the first state of slave owners to pledge to work toward living up to that ideal. The "Act for the Gradual Abolition of Slavery," passed by the state legislature in 1780, declared that from that point forward all children born to slaves in Pennsylvania would be free—once they turned twenty-eight. Before then, they would be classified as indentured servants, while their parents would remain slaves unless manumitted by their owners. It was a complicated and porous law that required careful tracking to ensure that Negro births were registered, that pregnant slaves weren't shipped elsewhere to deliver their offspring, and that slave owners from other states didn't hunt down blacks who tried to escape to Pennsylvania in hopes of seeing their children gain freedom. In short, it made a lot of work for dozens of white and black antislavery activists who lived and worked in Pittsburgh over the next eighty-five years.

Of the white abolitionists, the most prominent was Charles Avery, a rotund Methodist cotton mill owner whose travels through the South fired his anger over the plight of Negroes and persuaded him that education was the key to their salvation. In 1849, Avery took over a red-brick building in Allegheny City, north of Pittsburgh, and founded the Avery Trade School for Colored Youth. He filled it with seven hundred books, equipment to teach crafts and sciences, and an AME chapel on the third floor. In the basement he installed trapdoors leading to an underground tunnel. The tunnel opened onto a nearby canal, where rowboats ferried runaway slaves who hid in Avery's school to and from the Ohio River. Before his death in 1858, Avery also bequeathed $300,000, more than a third of his fortune, to support missionary work in Africa and black education in America. Among the legacies of that gift was a $25,000 endowment to support twelve scholarships a year at Pittsburgh's leading college, the Western University of Pennsylvania, for outstanding "males of the colored people in the United States of America or the British Providence of Canada."

The most influential black abolitionist in pre–Civil War Pittsburgh was Lewis Woodson, a minister and businessman whose intense gaze, high cheekbones, and broad forehead gave him a particularly distinguished look. His parents, Thomas and Jemima Woodson, had bought their way out of slavery and moved to western Virginia, where Lewis was born, and then to Ohio. At the age of seventeen, Lewis Woodson became active in the Ohio abolitionist movement, traveling across the state to preach in black churches and teach in black schools. Moving to Pittsburgh in his mid-twenties, he married a Virginia native, Caroline Robinson, and they had fourteen children, seven of each sex. While ministering at the Bethel AME Church, Woodson began opening barbershops in downtown hotels. He enrolled his children in the Avery School but also insisted that they learn trades—barbering and tailoring for the boys, dressmaking and millinery for the girls. By the time of his death, Woodson's sons and sons-in-law ran five thriving barbershops across the city, catering to as many white as black patrons.

Persuaded that learning was the key to racial liberation, Woodson founded an all-black school called the Pittsburgh African Education Society. In the summer of 1831, a nineteen-year-old boy named Martin Delany walked 150 miles on foot, all the way from the middle of Pennsylvania, to study at Woodson's school. Descended from African tribal nobility on both sides of his family, Delany had pitch-dark skin and fierce ambition. He sought out Pittsburgh doctors who taught him the art of "leeching and cupping" so that he could administer the popular bloodletting treatment to black patients. In his early thirties, Delany founded the first black-edited journal west of the Allegheny Mountains, *The Mystery.* He traveled to Rochester, New York, to help Frederick Douglass publish his *North Star* journal. Then Delany set out for Boston, where he talked his way into Harvard Medical School and became its first Negro graduate.

Returning to Pittsburgh to practice medicine, Delany continued to write articles and books and became an early proponent of the doctrine later known as "black nationalism." Decades before the rise of Booker T. Washington, he urged blacks to study trades so that they could be economically self-sufficient. Well before Marcus Garvey, Delany traveled to Africa to scout locations where American blacks might form their own colonies. Frederick Douglass himself marveled at how strongly Delany celebrated and embraced his black identity, in contrast to Douglass's own emphasis on equality between the races. "I thank God for making me a man simply," Douglass wrote, "but Delany always thanks him for making him a *black* man."

Along with Woodson and Delany, three more prominent black Pittsburgh businessmen of the day were also committed abolitionists. John Vashon, a mulatto born in Virginia, owned a bathhouse as well as a barbershop and was said to be the city's wealthiest black man. At the same time, Vashon founded the Pittsburgh Anti-Slavery Society in his home and allowed his businesses to be used as hiding places on the Underground Railroad. John Peck, who owned a clothing store, was active in the Anti-Slavery Society and served on the board of Delany's journal. Benjamin Tucker Tanner, a member of one of Pittsburgh's oldest black families, gave up his career as a barber to devote himself full-time to preaching, teaching, and editing an abolitionist AME newsletter, *The Christian Recorder.*

In the 1830s and early 1840s, most of these men lived and had their businesses in an area known as Arthursville, to the east of the meeting point of Pittsburgh's three rivers. It was named after a white wagon maker and land speculator named William Arthurs who bought one hundred parcels in 1809. Three decades later, Arthursville was still a verdant neighborhood of pleasant homes and small shops, surrounded by grassy fields and tall chestnut trees. More than a hundred black families lived there, and thirty-six of them owned property. Led by the Anti-Slavery Society, they could be counted on to harbor runaway slaves and speed their passage west to Ohio, or north to Canada.

Then in 1845, a warm, windy afternoon in April changed the future of Arthursville and the rest of Pittsburgh forever. Around noon on that day, a servant for a white colonel who lived in the downtown area left a fire she had set to heat her washing pail unattended. A spark ignited the colonel's barn. When firemen arrived, they discovered that their hoses were dry. A rainless spring had left the city's reservoirs low and its wells muddied with grime from the factories. As the winds picked up, the fire tore across the city, to the north, south, and west. A deafening roar filled the sky and an enormous cloud of black smoke blanketed the city. By the time it lifted that evening, after the winds died down and the fire burned out in the rivers, a third of the city had burned to the ground. Immigrant shacks and stately mansions alike were destroyed. Gone were some of the city's best-known landmarks, including the mayor's office and the Bank of Pittsburgh, its only remnant a charred iron vault recovered from the ashes.

The Monongahela House, the finest hotel in Pittsburgh, was one of the casualties. When it was reopened two years later, with three hundred rooms and an elegant glass-domed rotunda, it was one of the few places where visitors from out of town could stay in the devastated downtown area. With so many of the old hiding places gone, it became a new depot for the Underground Railroad. After Congress passed the Fugitive Slave Law allowing for the recapture of runaway slaves in 1850, Woodson and the other ministers established a Vigilance Committee to watch out for bounty hunters, and to kidnap back fugitives who were apprehended. The hotel's black waiters, cooks, and maids became eager accomplices in the spy network. One day, Martin Delany helped them free a slave who had been taken into police custody at the hotel. Another day, a fourteen-year-old servant girl who had arrived with a rich white family from Arkansas befriended members of the hotel staff and then suddenly vanished, carrying a trunk full of soiled clothing that was later recovered as the only proof of her escape.

After the Great Fire of 1845, businesses accounted for most of the rebuilding in the downtown area. Wealthy whites who had lost their homes began moving to enclaves to the east of the city. Before he decamped to New York, Andrew Carnegie built a stately house for himself and his mother in the neighborhood of Point Breeze. Henry Frick followed, erecting an eleven-room mansion that he christened "Clayton" and later expanded into a twenty-one-room European-style château. One after another, the tycoons who had made their fortunes in the railroad, steel, coal, banking, and food processing businesses settled in the part of town that came to be known as the East End. Next door to Frick, Henry J. Heinz built a home called "Greenlawn" that featured its own private museum and grounds planted with cuttings harvested at the Vatican. A half mile away, George Westinghouse occupied a ten-acre estate called "Solitude."

Frick became an avid art collector, and he filled his mansion in Point Breeze with European masters. Every week, he also hosted a poker game at Clayton. Regulars included Andrew Mellon, George Westinghouse, and Philander Knox, a Pittsburgh attorney who would later be elected to the U.S. Senate and serve as attorney general and secretary of state. On days when Andrew Carnegie joined in the game, one historian has estimated, as much as 60 percent of America's industrial wealth was represented around Frick's card table.

By the end of the century, the East End was home to more millionaires than any neighborhood in America. It also boasted amenities that only those men could have made possible. Thanks to Westinghouse, its mansions were powered by an AC electric grid and enjoyed air-conditioning in the summer. Thanks to Mellon, they had phone lines that connected directly with the major banks of Pittsburgh and Wall Street. Thanks to the Pennsylvania Railroad executives who made their homes there, the East End had its own train station, on a line that stretched to New York and Washington, D.C. In the late 1890s, President William McKinley pulled into that station to visit his friend George Westinghouse. Over the next three decades, five other Republican presidents would visit the neighborhood to seek out its powerful residents and their riches.

Poor factory workers and merchants who had been displaced by the Great Fire, meanwhile, searched for new housing closer to their workplaces. In the late 1840s, Thomas Mellon met that demand by buying up large tracts of the hills that had belonged to William Arthurs and to a Revolutionary War hero named Adamson Tannehill. Mellon divided the land into small plots and sold them to speculators who carved narrow streets and threw up small homes that could be sold cheap or rented out to roomers. Jewish immigrants were among the first to move in. As the iron and steel plants proliferated, newcomers arrived from England, Ireland, and Germany. An area where coal workers settled became known as "Minertown." The section at the bottom of the hills, where Negroes congregated, was called "Little Haiti." The top of the hills, where river vistas stretched in all directions, was known as "Sugartop." Like the East End, the entire neighborhood also acquired a name it would be known by from then on: the Hill District.

By the time Cap and Anna Posey arrived in the Pittsburgh area in the 1880s, the black population was nearing ten thousand. A majority of Negroes lived in the Hill District, but there were exceptions. A number of well-to-do families resided in more comfortable neighborhoods on the western fringes of the East End. The children and grandchildren of Benjamin Tucker Tanner had homes in Oakland, adjacent to the Hill. A contractor named Robert Jackson lived in a neighborhood known as Shadyside. John Writt, a caterer, made his home in Homewood. Writt was a tall, attractive man who favored waistcoats and winged collars, sported a handlebar mustache, and parted his graying hair down the middle. East End millionaires trusted Writt to bring a small army of cooks and waiters into their homes. Observing his operation, Thomas Ewell, a reporter for *The Colored American Magazine*, wrote: "Our caterer is not a man of 'soft snap.' He is a man of business, and a very delicate business at that."

Small groups of Negroes also settled among white immigrants in neighborhoods across the rivers from the Hill. On the North Side, Caroline Wiley and her husband, Thomas, lived on a plot of land first purchased by her grandfather, a fugitive mulatto slave, for the sum of $100 in 1832. On the West Side, a handful of families had homes on the steep streets of Beltzhoover and Mount Washington, otherwise known as "Coal Hill." One resident of Mount Washington, Samuel Rosamond, taught himself stenography and became proficient enough to be hired as the private secretary to George Westinghouse's chief electrician, O. B. Shallenberger, the inventor of the meters essential to the monitoring of AC power systems. Eventually Rosamond's prowess as a clerk led him to high-ranking jobs at the Post Office and the Civil Service, where he once took dictation for Theodore Roosevelt when the future president was the service's commissioner.

When the Poseys first moved to Homestead, they lived in an area called Munhall that was populated largely by factory workers. But once Cap Posey became an industrial mogul, he decided that he, too, like the East End barons, required a residence that reflected his stature. He moved his family into a home in Homestead that was the most ornate ever owned by a Pittsburgh Negro. Towering above all the houses around it, the Posey mansion had two floors with fifteen-foot ceilings and seven enormous windows looking out on the street. Six columns flanked a wide porch, and a two-tiered staircase led down to the curb. The first tier went from the front door to the bottom of the house; the second continued down another ten feet through a manicured hedge rimmed with stone. In the library, the Poseys filled the bookshelves with literary classics and covered a center table with periodicals. In the dining room, they displayed china that Anna Posey decorated by hand. A talented artist, Anna painted oils and watercolors that hung throughout the mansion as well as in the homes of other members of the Negro elite.

Along with families of new wealth like the Poseys, the Writts, and the Rosamonds, their circle included heirs of the Arthursville abolitionists who continued to number among Pittsburgh's leading black businessmen. Lewis Woodson's daughter Virginia married a barber named Jacob Proctor who counted members of the Carnegie and Westinghouse families among his clients. One afternoon, an East End matron whose husband was getting a shave decided to pay Virginia Proctor a visit. The woman was wearing a wig, and Virginia asked if she could inspect it to see how it was made. Shortly afterward, she opened a wig store on the second floor above the barbershop, and "Mrs. Virginia Proctor's Hair Shop" became one of the most successful Negro enterprises in the city, with branches downtown as well as on the Hill.

For the men of the black elite, social life revolved around a handful of fraternal orders—the Knights of Pythias, the Knights Templar, the Reformers, the Odd Fellows—and the city's most prestigious black social establishment, the Loendi Club. Located off Wylie Avenue in the bottom part of the Hill District, it was modeled after the Duquesne Club, the Romanesque refuge of the city's white lords of rail, steel, electricity, and finance. Like its counterpart, the Loendi Club was known for its elegant dining room, where members discussed business over lunch; for its card and billiard rooms, where they relaxed after work; and for its library, where wide leather chairs were suitable for reading and napping. The floors were draped with expensive carpets, and the walls adorned with the paintings of Henry Ossawa Tanner, the son of the Arthursville barber, who had moved to Paris and become a notable figure in the Impressionist movement.

Wives and daughters had their own societies. In the summer of 1897, a group of Negro women met in the home of Rachel Lovett Jones, the spouse of a businessman, to form what would become the longest surviving book club in black America. They called it the Aurora Reading Club, and they adopted as their motto "Lifting as We Climb," a slogan borrowed from the Washington, D.C., matrons who had formed the National

Association of Colored Women the year before. Every week, the reading club's twenty-five members met to discuss books and to organize support for local charities. One was the Aged Women's Home, a refuge for indigent widows. Another was the Working Girls Home, a boardinghouse on the Hill that welcomed penniless young migrants from the South who might otherwise have become working girls of another sort.

In 1890, Andrew Carnegie gave Pittsburgh a gift of $1 million to build one of the first of the more than sixteen thousand libraries that he would finance during his lifetime. A decade later, it opened a branch on the Hill, a stately red-brick building with a huge Beaux Arts arched entrance. The librarian, a Mrs. Wilson, founded another book club there, for colored girls of high school and college age. On the second night of every week, the thirteen members of the "Tuesday Evening Study Club" met at the Carnegie library on Wylie Avenue to hear lectures from guest speakers and to study the history and literature of foreign countries that they dreamed of visiting one day.

For the Poseys and the other elite Negro families, no cause was greater than the education of their children. Most of them attended the city's white public schools, thanks to a law passed by the Pennsylvania legislature outlawing segregated education in 1883. The members of the Tuesday Evening Study Club went to Pittsburgh High. The Posey children were enrolled in the Homestead schools. When Thomas Ewell, the writer for *The Colored American Magazine*, visited the Poseys in 1901, he described the eldest, Beatrix, as "a charming little belle of seventeen summers," who had achieved "a bright record in the Homestead high school."

Later Beatrix would graduate from California State Normal School and become a teacher like her mother. Her thirteen-year-old brother was just starting high school. His name was Stewart Hayes Posey, after the steamboat owner who had first hired Cap Posey as a chief engineer, but everyone called him "See." They also had a ten-year-old brother named Cumberland, after his father, who was nicknamed "Cum." But his academic record was a different story.

A small, skinny boy with his mother's light skin and long face, Cum

Posey preferred sports to books. His first love was basketball. He played guard, and what he lacked in height—he would grow to only five-foot-nine and 140 pounds as an adult—he made up in quickness and court sense. At Homestead High, he was a mediocre student but the star of the basketball team. Admitted to Penn State, he led the freshman squad and made the starting varsity as a sophomore. But Cum's grades were so poor that he was dropped from the team, and rather than go without basketball he quit college. (A *Courier* sportswriter who later profiled Cum Posey wryly described him in his college years as an "adventurous and turbulent spirit [who] brooked no faculty interference with his desires.")

Returning to Pittsburgh, Cum teamed up with brother See to form a semipro basketball team called the Monticello-Delany Rifles, named in honor of the abolitionist physician Martin Delany. Semipro ball was a difficult life, but Cum brought to it a crafty business sense that matched his athletic ability. He recruited a player who worked as a janitor for the city Recreation Department so the team could practice at a field house on the Hill during hours when blacks weren't officially allowed. He arranged for an exhibition match with Howard University, considered the best team in the black college leagues, which put the Rifles on the map when they won in an upset. Capitalizing on their sudden fame, Posey cut a sponsorship deal with his father's social club and renamed the team the Loendi Big Five in exchange for funds for uniforms and travel.

During the summers, Cum Posey threw himself into sandlot baseball. At the age of nineteen, he joined a team of Negro steelworkers who played at Homestead Park on the weekends and called themselves the Murdock Grays. Two years later, the team renamed themselves the Homestead Grays, and Posey persuaded the manager to let him schedule their games. For most of his twenties, he tried to juggle three sports at once. Briefly returning to college, at Holy Ghost, the future Duquesne University, Cum became captain of the golf squad as well as starring for the basketball team under the name Charles Cumbert. (It would later be said that Posey used the pseudonym to pass as white, but it is just as likely that he did it to protect his amateur status, which would have been jeopardized by knowledge of his semipro career.) Then Cum dropped out again and went to work for a railway mail service. Only then, when it looked like he had no other future, did he agree to take the job of manager of the Homestead Grays. Although it seemed like a dead end at the time, it was a path that would eventually lead Cumberland Posey Jr. to outshine even his remarkable father as a historic figure in the annals of black business.

As his son was embarking on his career as a sports entrepreneur, Cap Posey was eyeing a new area of investment. To that date, there had been only sporadic attempts to create publications for the Negroes of Pittsburgh. The first were white-run pro-abolitionist journals with names like *The Christian Witness*, *The Temperance Banner*, and *The Saturday Evening Visitor*. The first black-edited journal, Martin Delany's *The Mystery*, had briefly gained national attention with its coverage of the Great Pittsburgh Fire of 1845. But Delany's coverage of slave hunters and blacks whom he accused of abetting them had attracted a series of libel suits that drove him to the verge of bankruptcy and forced him to close down *The Mystery* after five years.

Yet as Cap Posey could tell from the periodicals stocked in his library, publishing had become a thriving business by the 1900s. William Randolph Hearst, Joseph Pulitzer, and other press barons were growing as rich as the industrial giants of the East End. And Pittsburgh's white-run dailies and weeklies were flourishing, particularly once a murder trial involving the son of an East End coal tycoon became the most sensational crime story of the decade.

In the winter of 1910, Cap Posey was presented with an opportunity to invest in a fledgling publishing venture. It was the brainchild of Edward Nathaniel Harleston, a stocky, smooth-faced South Carolina native with a pompadour of loose curls who worked as a security guard and messenger at the H. J. Heinz Co. pickle factory. After working as a census gatherer in Charleston, Harleston had moved to Atlantic City and taken a job as the custodian of Heinz Pier, the boardwalk attraction where free pickles were given away. But his first love was writing poetry. While in Atlantic City, Harleston had used his savings to publish a collection of verse he called

The Toiler's Life. He dedicated the volume to his mother, and an ode to her was typical of its sentimental contents:

> *In the dawning of the morning*
> *When rays on dewdrops shine,*
> *I'll think of thee, O Mother,*
> *For thy love, thy boy doth pine.*

Shortly afterward, Harleston moved to Pittsburgh to work at the main Heinz factory. Still eager to share his poetry, he began printing pamphlets of new verse and selling them for 5 cents apiece on the Hill. When that proved to be a less than roaring business success, Harleston decided to turn the pamphlet into a newspaper. He recruited friends from the pickle factory to help, and they laid out the first issue in the room that Harleston rented in the home of the Tanner family. He called the paper the *Courier,* after a Charleston publication he had read as a boy, and mailed it to a printing company. When the first copies came back, one of the Tanner daughters borrowed $3.49 from her mother to pay the postal bill, and the first edition appeared in January 1910. Harleston quickly ran out of savings, however, at which point one of his factory friends suggested that he seek financial support from the well-to-do denizens of the Loendi Club.

When Cap Posey met Harleston and read his little publication, he saw potential. Also intrigued were his fellow clubmen Samuel Rosamond, the Post Office official; William Nelson Page, a secretary at Carnegie Steel; and William Hance, a real estate man. But none of them had any intention of serving as a piggy bank for the enterprising but romantic pickle worker. If they were going to invest in the *Courier,* they wanted to own stock in a proper company. And they all agreed about who should handle the legal work: Robert L. Vann, an able and sober-minded young Negro attorney who had just passed the bar examination and set up shop in downtown Pittsburgh.

On a cold day in March of that year, the editor and the four businessmen trudged through a thin layer of snow to Vann's office on Fourth

Avenue, in the downtown business district. By the time the meeting was over, they had signed papers declaring *The Pittsburgh Courier* an official corporation. The four investors had taken shares in the new venture, and Cap Posey had accepted the title of president. But it wouldn't take long for him to conclude that the wrong man was running the newspaper. Cap Posey wanted his money on the practical lawyer, not the dreamy poet.

Robert L. Vann at the estate he purchased in Oakmont, in the Pittsburgh suburbs, after the *Courier* became the bestselling black newspaper in America.

3

THE CALCULATING CRUSADER

ROBERT LEE VANN HATED kitchen odors. As a boy, trying to get to sleep on sticky North Carolina nights, he smelled the grease and charcoal smoke that hung in the air from the day's meals at John Askew's plantation, where his mother worked. It filled his nostrils and reminded him of where he was, and of who he was. During the day, Vann was allowed to play with the three Askew children, to share their toys and race through the family mansion with its wide pillars. Sometimes John Askew himself would take Vann on his horse as the farmer inspected the groves of oaks and gardens of pink magnolias on the property. Mrs. Askew quizzed Vann on his ABC's and offered him friendly lectures about Christian virtues. But at night, he was the son of the family cook, sleeping on a tiny bed alongside hers next to a hot stove in the kitchen cabin. Vann hated its odors so much that later, as an adult, he refused to eat in kitchens, and he would open a window whenever he smelled anything that reminded him of those nights.

Vann's mother, Lucy Peoples, was the daughter of ex-slaves who ran a general store in the town of Ahoskie, North Carolina. As a teen, Lucy went to work as a cook for wealthy white families in the region. Her first employer was Albert Vann, and it was his name that she gave her son, along with the given name Robert Lee, after her grandfather. Some thought Albert Vann might have been the boy's father, but there is evidence that it was more likely a field hand named Joseph Hall who lived with Lucy at her second place of employment, Old Dr. Mitchell's Farm in Ahoskie. Whatever the truth, no man followed Lucy when she went to work for the Askew family, bringing "Vann," as she called her six-year-old son, along with her.

Apart from the kitchen smells, Vann would remember the years on the Askew plantation as the happiest of his youth. He even had warm memories of the Springfield Colored School, the overcrowded one-room schoolhouse he attended with sixty other Negro children between the ages of six and fourteen. Although the walls were unpainted and the books were hand-me-downs, Vann mastered his three R's well enough to be able to teach his unlettered mother how to read and write. By middle school, Vann was writing poetry. At his graduation ceremony, he used verse to announce the profession he had chosen for himself, one that would allow him to escape the fate of all the black men in the fields of Ahoskie County:

All can marry whom they like
I know an easier life
A lawyer need not soil his hands
But live by others' strife.

By then, Vann had a more urgent reason to seek an easier life. Lonely for a man, Lucy Peoples had married a dirt farmer named John Simon and taken her son to live with him on a property he called Red Hill. By Vann's early teens, his stepfather had him setting traps for raccoons and rabbits and driving an ox plow under the blazing summer sun. "I learned to split rails, dig ditches, hoe cotton and corn, cure tobacco in the barns, and everything else that a plow boy of a poor Negro farmer would have to know," he recalled. When work ran out on Red Hill, Simon loaned Vann out as a tobacco picker and once, to his humiliation, as a cook at a Virginia lumber camp. The comedown from the life on the Askew farm haunted Vann for the rest of his teens, and made him more determined than ever to escape the control of "the world's most worthless man," as he called Simon. "My stepfather thought I was big enough to work," he recalled, "but he never knew how the first ten years of my life constantly rebelled against the six years of torment I encountered under his juris-diction."

At sixteen, Vann began to see a way out. He managed to get a summer job working at the post office in Harrellsville, as a janitor and a clerk. The postmaster was a Negro—A. C. Boothe—the first black man Vann had ever seen in a position of high authority. Boothe took a liking to Vann, and after a while began allowing the boy to close the post office in the evening and open up in the morning.

One day before leaving, Vann accidentally locked the stamps in the safe. He didn't want to admit his blunder to Mr. Boothe, so he borrowed a bicycle, rode eight miles to a nearby town, and procured stamps from the post office there. By the time he returned to Harrellsville, he was bathed in sweat, but he had enough stamps to open the post office in the morning without Mr. Boothe being the wiser.

The $16 Vann earned that summer allowed him to enroll in the best school available to Negroes in that part of North Carolina. It was the Waters Training School, a private academy founded by a Baptist preacher named Calvin Brown and run out of three small buildings in the town of Winton. Brown charged $5 a month for tuition and room and board. Vann was able to afford four months of study, saving a dollar a month by living at home during the weekends. When his money ran out, he worked another summer at the post office to earn enough to return to the Waters Training School in the fall. Winter came early that year, however, and one weekend after walking eleven miles from Red Hill in the wet snow Vann collapsed of exhaustion. Impressed by the boy's determination, Pastor Brown arranged for him to live at the school from then on, and to earn his keep by chopping wood and doing other chores.

When Vann was nineteen, a friend at the Waters School announced that he was going to Boston to find work for the summer. Did Vann want to come along? the friend asked. His mother opposed the idea, but Vann insisted, and a white fellow who worked on the Askew farm loaned him money for a train ticket. Vann had never experienced rail travel before, and he was too captivated to chafe at riding in a segregated car. A distant aunt who lived in Boston put him up, and he found employment bussing tables at the Copley Square Hotel, where President McKinley stayed when he was in town. Emulating the hotel waiters, Vann began to part his hair in the middle. After putting aside money to repay the train ticket, he bought a pinstripe suit, a pair of tan shoes, a raglan overcoat, and a derby hat. At the end of the summer, he brought his dandyish new sense of style back to North Carolina, and it would stay with him for the rest of his life.

When Vann was selected valedictorian of his graduating class from Waters Training School, he hailed Abe Lincoln as his hero. "Never would Abraham Lincoln have risen from his humble cot to the presidency had he not first chosen the position and, after choosing this lofty height, he strove with earnest and persistent efforts, ever keeping in view that executive mansion which marked his course from boyhood to the day of his greatest attainment," Vann proclaimed in an impassioned graduation speech. "Once having found what he is best suited for, the individual should pursue aggressively his goal. Opportunity would then almost inevitably come his way. To every individual there comes as much as once in a life an opportunity which, seized at its flow, leads on to fortune; omitted, all his life is a spectacle of failure and disgrace, and he together with his once glittering talent soon sinks into oblivion and despair."

That impatience to make the most of his talent was evident the next fall when, at the recommendation of Pastor Brown, Vann enrolled at Virginia

Union University, a Baptist school in Richmond. He studied Greek, wrote for the college journal, and spent long evenings debating the wisdom of Booker T. Washington's appeals to Negroes to see to their own advancement. A classmate whose parents taught at the university invited Vann to dinners and dances at their home, where he mixed with the sons and daughters of Richmond's black elite.

Yet in his time in Richmond, Vann also came to see that opportunity for Negroes in the South was shrinking fast. In state after state, legislatures were rebelling against the legal rights granted Negroes under Reconstruction and passing Jim Crow laws segregating public facilities. The town's newspaper, *The Richmond Planet*, ran editorials calling for repeal of the Fifteenth Amendment granting blacks the right to vote. When Vann returned home to North Carolina, he found Democrats shoving aside a Fusionist alliance of Republicans, Populists, and blacks with angry appeals for a return to "a white man's state, and a white man's government." In Wilmington, a riot broke out after gun-toting white thugs chased blacks away from the polls. Afterward, local Negroes began packing up their possessions and heading north.

It was the precursor to what would become known as the Great Migration, and Vann decided he had no choice but to join the exodus. He set his sights on the Western University of Pennsylvania, in Pittsburgh, and the scholarships for twelve promising Negro students a year that had been established by the abolitionist cotton mill owner, Charles Avery. Vann applied for one of those places, and when he was accepted he returned to Ahoskie County to deliver the news.

While at the Waters School, Vann had proposed to a girl named Mattie Davis and bought her a small diamond ring. Now he told Mattie that she could keep the ring but that the engagement was off. "I'm going North," Vann said curtly. "There will be no wedding plans." Then, on a hot August day, Vann went to Red Hill to bid goodbye to his mother and good riddance to his stepfather before heading to the nearest rail station and boarding a train for his new home in Pennsylvania.

Even after Boston and Richmond, nothing could have prepared Vann for Pittsburgh, for how different it was from the farmlands of his youth. The first thing he must have noticed was the smell. Miles before his train pulled into Union Station, a stench akin to rotten eggs would have reached him, stronger than any of the kitchen odors he detested as a child. It came from the sulfur that was emitted by iron ore and coke in the 4,000 degree heat of the city's steel furnaces and excreted in piles of gray slag that littered the landscape. As Vann emerged from the train station, his eyes would have felt the sting of air suffused with smoke from the mills along the banks of the three rivers. By day, viewed from the top of its many hills, Pittsburgh could be every bit as ugly as Birmingham and the other British industrial cities to which Charles Dickens himself, after a visit to America, had once compared it. Miles of smokestacks striped the horizon, blackening the sky over the grim factories. Yet by night, the city could also be a thing of eerie beauty, as the still burning lights from the factories haloed the city's bridges and caused their reflections to shimmer in the dark mirror of the rivers below.

By 1903, when Vann arrived, Pittsburgh was very different from the place Cap Posey had first encountered only two decades earlier. It was a year after Andrew Carnegie sold his mills to J. P. Morgan's U.S. Steel Company, making U.S. Steel the world's largest producer of the globe's most desired industrial product. With steel, coal, gas, aluminum, glass, and pickles all in record demand, as many as fifteen thousand new immigrants a year were arriving in Pittsburgh to look for work. Poles, Lithuanians, Croatians, Slovaks, and Hungarians joined the Jews, Italians, and Irish of previous waves.

By 1907, the black population surpassed twenty thousand when Pittsburgh merged with Allegheny City, the town to the north where Andrew Carnegie lived as a child. Only a small fraction of the city's Negroes now inhabited the elite world of the Poseys and the rest of the city's eighty-five black business owners and roughly 150 professionals. Blacks who found work in the steel mills and the coal mines still numbered in the hundreds. Of the new arrivals, more than half of the men and almost all of the women had to settle for more menial jobs—as maids, laundresses, and janitors, or, if they were lucky, as shop clerks, railway porters, and brick-toting hod carriers.

A majority of the new Negro migrants settled on the Hill, boarding with white immigrants or crowding one family to a room in rickety, unpainted frame houses. Erased were all traces of the old Arthursville farms. Coal dust covered the streets. Sewage ran through the back alleys. Greenery had disappeared. Typhoid fever and respiratory disease were spreading. So were crime, prostitution, and cocaine use. During her visit in 1909, Helen Tucker, the writer who heralded the opportunities for the "industrial Negro" in Pittsburgh, winced at conditions on the Hill. "The poorer Negroes live in a network of alleys on either side of Wylie Avenue," she reported. "In some alleys there were stables next to the houses and while the odor was bad at any time, after a rain the stench from these and from the dirt in the streets was almost unendurable."

Yet if Vann had been born just as poor as the new migrants, no one would have guessed that now. When he presented himself at Western University, the registrar took one look at his elegant suit and copper complexion and asked if he wished to enroll as an Indian. No, Vann replied with a mixture of pride and practicality, he was a Negro who was there to claim his Avery scholarship. That stipend and a part-time job waiting tables at a white boardinghouse allowed Vann to rent a spacious second-floor room in a home in Allegheny City. The owners, the Moore family, were members of the tribe of "Old Pittsburghers," or "OP's," as the families who had settled in the city before the Great Migration were known, and they introduced Vann to their world.

Soon Vann was worshipping with the Moores at the Brown Chapel AME Church, the second oldest west of the Allegheny Mountains, at the brand-new gold-brick chapel the congregation had erected on the North Side. He was also invited to lunch at the Loendi Club, where his elegant looks and erudite demeanor drew admiring attention. He grew friendly with William Nelson Page, the private secretary to the assistant manager of sales at the Carnegie Steel Company, and became a frequent guest at the Page home. Vann also made the acquaintance of Cap Posey, then the club president, and learned of his remarkable rise from steamboat engineer to one of the richest Negroes in America, a story that can only have confirmed Vann's belief that Pittsburgh was a place where a man bent on emulating Abe Lincoln could seize opportunity at its flow.

At Western University, Vann studied literature, excelled at debate, and wrote for the school journal, *The Courant*. In his senior year he was elected editor-in-chief, the first Negro to hold the post. As graduation neared in 1906, he briefly considered heading east to study at a new school for journalists that Joseph Pulitzer had endowed at New York's Columbia University. But worries about the cost held him back. Instead Vann stayed true to his boyhood plan and moved on to Western University's School of Law, where he was the only black face in his class. To pay his tuition—and his tailor bills—he worked as a sleeping car porter. On many days, he would race to Union Station as soon as he was done at the law school, don a porter's uniform, board an overnight train to Ohio, and then return to Pittsburgh the following day in time for his next class.

It was a satisfying time for Vann, marred only by the sorrow of losing his mother. The spring after he arrived in Pittsburgh, he received word that Lucy Peoples was ill. After traveling back to Red Hill to see her, he returned to Pittsburgh with a bout of pneumonia that kept him in bed for months. Before he could visit his mother again, he received a letter from one of her neighbors informing him that she had passed away. With no siblings, a father who had abandoned him, and a stepfather he detested, Vann now had only a souvenir to connect him to his North Carolina past: a gold watch that his mother had given him to celebrate his graduation from the Waters Training School.

Then, in the fall of his senior year of law school, Vann found someone to fill the void left by his mother. He went to a dance and met a nineteen-year-old girl named Jesse Matthews. Like many of the women of the "OP" elite, she had light skin and a dignified manner. She had come to Pittsburgh to live with her aunt after being orphaned as a young child and passed around among relatives in her hometown of Gettysburg. Touched by her story and taken with her bearing, Vann suggested that Jesse move in with the Page family. Soon she and Vann were courting, meeting for tea, and taking long walks during which they shared their common bonds of hardship, loss, and aspiration.

After just a few months, Vann proposed—in his no-nonsense fashion. "My intentions are serious," he told Jesse. "If yours are not let me know. I don't want to waste your time and I have no time to waste." Though startled at his bluntness, Jesse accepted. They agreed to marry—once Vann passed his bar examination. After graduating, Vann sent Jesse back to Gettysburg, telling her "courting and studying do not mix." Six months later, he sent a telegram with the good news—"Passed O.K."—and soon afterward she returned to Pittsburgh where they were wed in the home of William Page.

As only one of five Negro lawyers in all of Pittsburgh, Vann wanted to make a good impression. He decided to set up shop in the white business district downtown. He found a building on Fourth Avenue that would rent to a Negro tenant and filled an office with secondhand furniture. But business was slow. Vann's dream was to argue criminal cases, but no whites and few blacks believed that they stood a chance before the white judges and juries of Pittsburgh with a Negro advocate. Instead, Vann spent most of his days processing wills and property claims.

In his free time, Vann began submitting items to *The Pittsburgh Courier*, the little pamphlet of verse and community news that had begun to appear around town. He befriended the poet who had founded the publication, Edward Nathaniel Harleston. One day, Harleston confided that he had run out of money and told Vann that he was seeking new backers. Vann suggested his Loendi Club acquaintances, and when they agreed to invest he was offered five shares of stock in lieu of a legal fee to draft incorporation papers. All at once, Vann was no longer just a protégé of William Page and Cap Posey; he was their business partner.

At the same meeting in Vann's office, Harleston argued that he should also get stock in payment for his work as editor. But the four businessmen refused. It was a recipe for friction—and tension soon ensued. The new shareholders pressed Harleston for changes, and he balked. By the fall, they insisted that Vann join the paper as treasurer. Within a year, Harleston quit in a fit of anger. Weary of his moodiness, the investors did nothing to keep him. Instead, they offered the job of editor to Robert L. Vann.

The job paid only $100 a year, which Vann also agreed to take in the form of *Courier* stock. But the money wasn't important to him, at least for now. Here, finally, was the opportunity he had foreseen since his high school days would "inevitably come his way": to pursue his passion for journalism as well as law, and to join the club of Negro businessmen and community leaders that he had circled and admired since first arriving in Pittsburgh. And while he didn't yet have a plan for making *The Pittsburgh Courier* a financial success, Vann could see from reading the city's white newspapers what kinds of stories attracted readers.

"CORPSE AND PISTOL FOUND IN BASEMENT OF PALATIAL HOME" shouted a front-page headline in *The Pittsburgh Press* on the 13th of March, 1910, the same month that Robert L. Vann, Cap Posey, and the others met to incorporate *The Pittsburgh Courier*. The *Press* reported that Thomas Laughlin, the heir to one of Pittsburgh's largest steel fortunes, a man said to be worth $20 million, had committed suicide in the basement of his East End mansion after a long bout with "melancholia." He had put a bullet through his brain while his wife was in Washington, D.C., visiting her sister, the wife of President William Howard Taft. The story, accompanied by a photo of the mansion and a family portrait with Laughlin's rotund brother-in-law, was the sort of tabloid fare that made the *Press* the most popular newspaper in Pittsburgh at the time, ahead of its more dignified morning rival, the *Gazette*. Returning home from long days in the factories, mines, and shops, the city's new immigrants (and more of its old guard than would have admitted it publicly) turned to the afternoon tabloid to revel in the particulars of murder trials, divorce proceedings, natural disasters, and financial scandals.

In the five years before Robert Vann became the *Courier*'s editor, one story more than any other had obsessed papers like the *Press*. Two Pitts-burgh natives happened to be at its center. Harry Kendall Thaw was an-other East End heir, to a coal and railroad fortune, and a psychotic spoiled brat. As a child, he hurled china at the servants. As a Harvard undergradu-ate, he waved a shotgun at a cab driver and was expelled. Thaw abused drink and drugs and sexual partners of both sexes, while his doting, wid-owed mother kept him in allowance and paid off anyone who threatened to expose him.

Evelyn Nesbit was a working-class girl from outside Pittsburgh with doe-eyed beauty and limited talent. Along with her meddlesome mother, she moved to New York City in her teens and became a showgirl and artist's model. Stanford White, the famous architect and notorious roué, became her lover and relieved her of her virginity. But it was Harry Thaw, after seeing Nesbit in a chorus line, who determined to marry her. Thaw wined and dined Nesbit and took her on trips to Europe until she agreed to be his bride. Then he set out to destroy his romantic rival.

On a June night in 1906, Thaw and Nesbit were in New York en route to another European vacation. They decided to attend a revue called *Mam'zelle Champagne* at Madison Square Garden, then still at its origi-nal location on Madison Square. The production had been moved to the rooftop, because the night was so warm. When Stanford White appeared shortly before midnight, Thaw became agitated and began circling White's table. As the cast sang the finale, "I Could Love a Million Girls," Thaw pulled a pistol from his overcoat and fired three shots. A cloud of black gunpowder exploded in White's face, incinerating the architect's handle-bar mustache and covering him in blood. "He had it coming!" Thaw cried as he stood over the dead man's body, before police arrested him and took him to The Tombs prison.

But that was only the beginning of the story. A three-month murder trial gave newspapers sordid new details of the love triangle to report, em-bellished by tipsters hired by both sides. White had kept a suite of rooms above his apartment full of mirrors and erotic furniture that he used to seduce Nesbit and other conquests. A red velvet swing was among the contraptions. On a trip to Europe, Thaw had imprisoned Nesbit in an Austrian castle for two weeks and repeatedly whipped and abused her. With his fortune, Thaw was also buying royal treatment on "Murderers Row." He was allowed to sleep in a brass bed, eat steaks from Delmonico's, and drink wine and champagne with his meals. Promised a payoff and a divorce from Thaw by his mother, Nesbit testified on her husband's behalf, and a split jury failed to reach a verdict. But the saga didn't end there. A second trial, a guilty-by-reason-of-insanity verdict, an escape, a manhunt, and a recapture all followed before a third jury acquitted Thaw eight years later and set him free.

When Robert Vann took the helm of the *Courier*, he claimed that he didn't want to go "yellow" like the tabloids. He was critical of *The Pittsburgh Press* for its demeaning caricatures of black people. He also looked down on the luridness in *The Chicago Defender*, the leading Negro newspaper at the time, with its screaming headlines in bright red type. Nor did the *Courier* have anything like the resources that the white press devoted to the "crime of the century" saga of Harry Thaw and Evelyn Nesbit. Only eight pages, it did little more than record the comings and goings of Negroes in the Pittsburgh area. The paper was produced out of a storeroom above a Wylie Avenue funeral parlor, with a staff of only four employees: a reporter, a sports editor, a secretary, and a proofreader who also served as a mailing clerk and messenger. Yet as soon as Vann took over the *Courier*, the first noticeable change was an increase in coverage of crime stories of interest to Negro readers.

In August 1911, in another steel town in eastern Pennsylvania called Coatesville, a black migrant named Zachariah Walker was returning home from a tavern one afternoon when he got into a drunken brawl with white workers from a local mill. A security guard for the mill tried to break up the dispute. In the ensuing tussle, Walker shot the guard dead. Later Walker was found hiding in a tree; he tried to shoot himself, but he survived and was taken to a hospital. That night, a group of men broke into the hospital, unchained Walker from his bed, and took him into the woods, where they lit a bonfire and burned him to death. Hundreds gathered to watch the spectacle, pushing Walker back into the flames as he tried to escape. The next morning, dozens of men and boys picked through the ashes, and later parts of Walker's body were sold in town as souvenirs.

For the next six months, the *Courier* gave front-page coverage to each new twist in the savage Coatesville lynching case. It ran stories on the arrest of fifteen men and boys for the brutal act, and on debates among Negro leaders in Pittsburgh about how to press for justice. The *Courier's* owners started a fund to send a delegation to Harrisburg to lobby the governor. When all fifteen defendants were acquitted and the state did nothing to retry them, Vann wrote a mournful editorial. "There is no escaping the shame," he lamented. "The whole state should shoulder the curse."

Vann also awarded banner treatment to crime stories in which blacks were acquitted, particularly if a Negro lawyer handled the case. In one front-page story, New York attorney John Frank Wheaton was celebrated for convincing a jury that a black man named William Simms had killed a white Schenectady resident in self-defense. In another, Scipio Africanus Jones, Esq. of Arkansas was hailed for doing the seemingly impossible— clearing a black man charged of rape by a white woman in the Deep South—by proving that the suspect was at his lumber factory job a hundred miles away. Presenting "possibly the most complete, the most sweeping and the most irresistible alibi that has been produced in the court in recent years," the *Courier* cheered, "[Jones] utterly annihilated the state's testimony, forcing the state to an unconditional surrender, with the result of 'Not Guilty' by the jury."

Vann's coverage of criminal justice stories also allowed him to advertise his own legal services. A front-page story in 1912 chronicled the case of Thomas Cash, a suspect for whom Vann had been appointed court's attorney. Cash was charged with a murder that had taken place fourteen years earlier. Two railroad construction workers in Unity, Pennsylvania, had gotten into a fight over a crap game. One pulled a gun and shot the other. While serving time for another crime in New York, Cash was said to have confessed to a fellow inmate. Yet despite testimony from that prisoner, Vann persuaded a white jury that Cash was innocent. According to the *Courier*'s melodramatic account, it took the jury just eight minutes to reach its verdict. When it was announced, a crowd of Negro spectators shouted in triumph and carried Cash out of the courtroom on their shoulders. Vann bought Cash a new overcoat to replace his soiled blue jumper coat, put him up in hotel for the night, and accompanied him to the train station the next morning. Not surprisingly, after the story appeared, demand for Vann's legal help grew.

By 1913, the *Courier*'s readership was inching upward, but the paper was still in dire financial straits. Printing costs exhausted a third of its tiny budget. Advertising—from a handful of black-owned businesses and mail-order products with names like "St. Joseph's Liver Regulator" and "The Original Poro Hair Grower"—brought in as little as $15 a week. Gimmicks to build circulation had gone awry. One promised a car to the reader who sold the most new subscriptions. When a well-known local clubwoman named Daisy Lampkin won the contest, the *Courier*'s board was forced to confess that they couldn't afford an automobile. Instead, they gave Lampkin a check, which promptly bounced. Finally, they had to pay up in stock (beginning what would eventually blossom into a valuable partnership when Lampkin became a vice president of the *Courier* as well as the local chapter head of the NAACP).

The *Courier*'s financial prospects began to look up, however, after Vann made a fortuitous hire a year later. He brought on Ira Lewis, a small but inexhaustible young clerk from his law office. Explaining how tight his budget was, Vann offered to pay Lewis $3 a week plus a 25 percent commission on any ads he sold. Lewis pulled out a sheet of paper. "I've already started to work," he said. "There's my first ad and I've got the payment in my pocket." Hired as a sportswriter, Lewis quickly became the paper's business manager as well. In one year, he doubled the paper's circulation and began expanding its base of advertisers beyond mail-order charlatans. Around the office, *Courier* staff started referring to Vann as "the Big Chief" and Lewis as "the Little Chief."

By the second half of the decade, Vann had concluded that the *Courier* needed more than just better business management to succeed. It had to develop a more powerful voice. As the United States entered World War I, the Great Migration began. A new wave of Negroes—not just from border states like Maryland, Virginia, and North Carolina, but increasingly from the Deep South—were heading north in hopes of taking the place of white factory workers who had gone to war. In Pittsburgh, the black population would increase by half before the end of the decade, to 36,000, and its labor force would double to more than eighteen thousand. To attract the new migrants as readers, brief stories on crime, sports, and local church and society news wouldn't be sufficient. The *Courier* needed to crusade on their behalf.

In his weekly editorials, Vann began naming the friends and enemies of the Pittsburgh Negro. He praised U.S. Steel and other businesses that hired the new migrants, and denounced those that didn't. Meanwhile, he admonished blacks to make the most of new opportunities. When the Westinghouse factory hired four hundred black workers and some of them proved to be unreliable, Vann delivered a stern lecture to the community. "If our boys ever expect to take part in the onward march of the country and to be respected for their skills and usefulness," he wrote, "they must learn that the steady man, the constant man, has a better chance to become efficient, and thus gain promotion, than the man who works until payday and loafs until his wages are spent."

As the new migrants crowded into the Hill District and other black enclaves, the *Courier* railed against the obstacles and indignities they encountered. It editorialized about squalid living conditions, usurious rents, mistreatment in white hospitals, and the absence of Negroes among Pittsburgh's doctors, policemen, and schoolteachers. The newspaper launched quixotic campaigns to raise money for a Negro hospital, and to persuade blacks to found their own real estate and mortgage agencies.

The resistance that blacks faced when they tried to move into white neighborhoods was another subject of outrage—and one that Vann experienced firsthand. The year after he became editor of the *Courier*, he and Jesse managed to find a white man who would sell them his house in

Homewood, the neighborhood east of the Hill where some of the Negro elite lived. But six years later, when Vann purchased the house next door and began renting it to another black family, his white neighbors revolted. In what became known as the "Battle of Monticello Street," they printed handbills and held meetings to protest the influx of "undesirables." When months of grumbling failed to dislodge Vann or his tenants, the whites began to move away, and within a decade most of the residents on the block were black.

Of all the battles Vann waged, his most passionate was to "abolish every vestige of Jim Crowism in Pittsburgh," as he put it. Although Pennsylvania had passed a law officially prohibiting it in 1887, blacks still confronted routine discrimination in public places. Downtown theaters refused to sell them tickets or made them sit in separate balconies. Nickelodeons charged them double price. Restaurants wouldn't serve them, or, when they did, waiters put salt into their coffee, pepper in their milk, and extra charges on their bills. Department store clerks ignored Negroes and served white customers first. When W. E. B. Du Bois, A. Philip Randolph, and other black dignitaries visited Pittsburgh, they could stay in white hotels only if they entered through the back door and used the service elevator. Instead, they frequented black-run hotels or stayed at the homes of prominent Negroes like the Vanns or Daisy Lampkin.

For a time, Vann held out hope for a new civil rights law that would spell out harsh fines and punishments for discriminatory practices. After a state legislator from Pittsburgh named A. C. Stein proposed such a measure in 1915, Vann threw the full weight of the *Courier* behind it. When the Stein law passed the state House and Senate, Vann wrote triumphant editorials, only to see the governor veto the legislation on the grounds that the existing 1887 statute made it unnecessary. Vann was crushed. Drained from his lobbying efforts, he fell ill and didn't recover for several months. When he did, he wrote a bitter editorial on the fecklessness of the white political system. "The Negro need not heed the promises this year," he concluded glumly.

Slowly but surely, Vann was becoming convinced that his editorial crusades didn't go far enough. If their battles were ever to be taken seriously, Negroes needed to become a more organized—and more feared—political force. And if Vann was going to play a role in making that happen, he first needed to turn the *Courier* into a newspaper with national reach, and a national reputation.

MEETING WITH THE *COURIER'S* board of directors in 1919, the Little Chief argued that something bold needed to be done. The paper was selling sixteen thousand copies per issue, Ira Lewis pointed out, but it was barely scraping by. It had only $102 in the bank and had never paid more than $100 in dividends. The only hope for profitability, Lewis argued, was to double the sale price, to 10 cents. To persuade readers that the extra cost was worth it, he proposed expanding the newspaper to ten pages, adding more feature stories, and running more photographs. He suggested sponsoring a beauty contest and printing pinups of the winners. Robert Vann, Cap Posey, and the other board members approved of the ideas, but they worried that the *Courier* was still too small to go it alone. Its much larger rival, *The Chicago Defender*, also cost a nickel, and the *Courier* had little hope of competing with it at twice the price.

So Vann set out to persuade the *Defender* to lift its price to a dime as well. After the board meeting, he began writing persistent letters to the *Defender's* publisher, Robert Abbott. The son of former Georgia slaves and stepson of a mulatto missionary raised in Germany, Abbott had founded the *Defender* in 1905, five years before the *Courier*. Almost overnight, it became the top Negro newspaper in the country by focusing coverage on the Great Migration. It specialized in graphic horror stories about Jim Crow, glowing tales of success in the North, and pictures and classified ads touting the jobs and housing that awaited blacks in Chicago. Fourteen years later, the *Defender* was on its way to a readership of 200,000. But it barely turned a profit, either, due to the high cost of printing and labor. Finally, after Ira Lewis made a special trip to Chicago, Abbott agreed to the price-fixing scheme—a decision that he would later come to regret as the *Defender* slowly began to lose ground to the *Courier*.

The price hike didn't pay off immediately. At first, the *Courier*'s circulation plummeted. Two years later, it still had less than $300 in its account with the Potter Title and Trust Company. (When the bank refused to issue a loan, Lewis indignantly withdrew the tiny sum.) By the mid-1920s, however, things began to turn around. Vann hired the Ziff Corporation to sell advertising space to national brand names such as Pillsbury, Colgate-Palmolive, Lever Brothers, and Vaseline. He had to pay an onerous commission—a third to a half of the cost of the ads—but the accounts increased revenue by a quarter and gave the paper a new air of sophistication. Circulation rebounded, too, as readers responded to the pinup girls and other changes that Lewis had suggested. For the first time, Vann officially agreed to emulate *The Chicago Defender* and add more "yellow" to the paper's mix. Addressing the board in 1922, he conceded that while he was still "opposed in principle to sensationalism," he had come to see that "the weekly sales of the *Courier* could be greatly increased by the publication of more sensational and morbid stories."

Yet what attracted new readers more than anything else was the *Courier*'s growing roster of memorable writers. Vann was proving to have an eye for distinctive talents, and a flair for showcasing them. By the early 1920s, a writer named John L. Clark was filling a column called "Wylie Avenue" with Runyonesque accounts of the nightlife and lowlife on the Hill's main thoroughfare. A trio of talented sports writers—Bill Nunn, Chester Washington, and W. Rollo Wilson—was turning out four pages of lively coverage and commentary every week, and creating wildly popular traditions such as the *Courier*'s All-America football team and its coverage of the annual game between Howard University in Washington, D.C., and Lincoln University outside Philadelphia, otherwise known as "the Negro Harvard-Yale."

A decade earlier, shortly after assuming the reins of the newspaper, Vann had hired a young woman to take dictation. But he quickly realized that Julia Bumry was destined to be more than a stenographer. A native of Parkersburg, West Virginia, Bumry had attended Wilberforce University, where with her round, expressive face and lively personality she became a star actress and leader in the Delta Sigma Theta sorority. When Bumry quit to take a teaching job down south, Vann lured her back by offering to make her a writer. She settled down in Pittsburgh and married a local waiter, Henry Jones. In 1920, Vann promoted Julia Bumry Jones to a new position—women's editor—in charge of covering black Pittsburgh's social calendar of teas, dances, and weddings. Under the breezy byline of "Jules," Jones began writing a column entitled "Talk O' Town," mixing chatty gossip with sly political observations and appeals to the *Courier*'s female readers to exercise their economic and voting power.

Vann added other columns aimed at attracting a national readership. "Sylvester Russell's Review" covered the theaters and dance halls of black Chicago. In New York, Floyd J. Calvin opened a bureau in Harlem and hosted *The Courier Hour*, a short-lived talk radio program that was the first of its kind for a Negro audience. Walter White, the young writer and NAACP official, wrote a column on the latest news from the Harlem Renaissance crowd. In 1925, at Ira Lewis's suggestion, Vann made his most important addition to the paper since the Little Chief himself. He hired George Schuyler, an acerbic Harlem-based columnist whose arch reports on "Aframerica" helped increase the *Courier*'s circulation by 10 percent in six months.

The same year, Vann and the *Courier* lost Cap Posey. He died in midsummer after a brief illness, following his beloved Anna to the grave by seven years. Posey was eulogized at the Loendi Club, buried with elaborate Masonic honors at the Homestead Cemetery, and remembered as a "pioneer of industry" in a front-page tribute in the *Courier*. Yet rather than slow Vann down, Posey's passing ignited even more ambition, as though he was determined not only to succeed his mentor as the most influential Negro in Pittsburgh, but to surpass him.

The following year, Vann took the daring step of issuing $25,000 worth of new *Courier* stock, at a time when the paper was only beginning to become profitable. His stated purpose was to fund a new printing plant. But Vann may have sensed that there would be limited demand for the offering, because when that proved to be the case, he dug deep into his own savings to buy up most of the new shares. Now Vann was not only the paper's editor but also its majority owner.

To celebrate, Vann treated himself to a coveted status symbol among successful Negroes. Although he had never been a good driver—he had crashed his first car, a Lincoln, soon after buying it—he decided to splurge on a Cadillac. But the first dealer Vann visited in Pittsburgh refused to sell him the roadster he wanted, worried that his white customers would start to view the Caddy as "a nigger car." Vann had to go all the way to Altoona to find a willing seller—and even then the dealer insisted that he pay the list price, $3,570, entirely in cash.

In 1926, Vann also waded into two very public fights that drew more national attention to the *Courier* and elevated his own national reputation. The first battle was with James Weldon Johnson, the renowned author and executive secretary of the NAACP, and W. E. B. Du Bois, the legendary editor of that association's journal, *The Crisis*. Until then, the *Courier* had shown deference to the venerable civil rights group and its leaders. But in October 1926, it printed a bombshell headline on the front page. "NAACP 'SLUSH FUND' AIRED," it read.

The story below was just as dramatic. It charged that James Weldon Johnson had abused his position as the sole black board member of the Garland Fund, an endowment for the support of liberal causes that had been established by the rebellious son of a Wall Street millionaire. Of the $35,000 that the fund had donated to Negro causes, the story alleged, "the lion's share" had gone into the coffers of the NAACP, paying for executive salaries and "expensive and palatial offices on Fifth Avenue." Most of the money had been meant for the defense of Ossian Sweet, a black physician from Detroit who had been charged with murder when a white mob tried to prevent him from moving into a white neighborhood. Yet only $5,000 had made its way to Clarence Darrow and Sweet's other attorneys, the *Courier* alleged. Meanwhile, another $5,000 had gone to W. E. B. Du

Bois "for study of Negro education in South Carolina"—an outrageous sum, the paper suggested, for such a narrow project.

Johnson wasted no time in firing back. Less than a week later, he issued an angry press release insisting that the donations to the Sweet case had been fully audited, and that the stipend to Du Bois was for study of black education across the entire South. Then Johnson unleashed a vicious personal attack on Vann. "He has written a more poisonous attack than has emanated from any white Southerner in the entire history of the NAACP," Johnson seethed. "I think the colored people of American have a little account to settle with Mr. Robert L. Vann, Editor of the Pittsburgh Courier." Arriving in Pittsburgh several days later, Johnson gave a hot-tempered address denouncing Vann as a "liar" and "scoundrel." The paper responded with a mocking account of the speech. "He came, he 'cussed,' and he went," the paper reported, under the headline: "JAMES WELDON JOHNSON AIRLY SLUSHES OVER SLUSH FUND."

The feud grew even nastier as Du Bois joined the attack on the *Courier*. In the year-end issue of *The Crisis*, the editor published a list of "Assets and Liabilities" for Negroes in 1926. The liabilities included "31 Lynchings" and "Vann." The *Courier* lashed back at "The Pope of Fifth Avenue," as it described Du Bois. "The army of readers of the Pittsburgh Courier will merely smile when they hear the characterization of Mr. Vann as a Race 'Liability,'" the paper jeered. "About 20 times more of them read the Pittsburgh Courier than read Dr. Du Bois. . . . If Du Bois is a sample of the Highly Educated Negro, there is little wonder that his following of twenty years ago can now be numbered on the fingers of the one hand. The old boy is dead on his feet and doesn't know it."

Before long, virtually every black newspaper in the country had weighed in on the slush fund dispute. *The Chicago Whip, The Cleveland Gazette, The Detroit Owl,* and the *Tucson Times* echoed the *Courier*'s calls for an investigation. *The Baltimore Afro-American, The Philadelphia Tribune, The Chicago Bee,* and *The Richmond Planet* backed the NAACP. Others argued that blacks couldn't afford such intramural squabbles and called on both sides to back off. Finally, after three years, they did. In a carefully orchestrated reconciliation, the *Courier* and *The Crisis* published public letters in which Vann expressed regret for his attack, and Johnson and Du Bois accepted the apology. "NAACP-Courier 'BURY THE HATCHET,'" read the headline in the *Courier*.

Yet even then, the hard feelings lingered. Vann was particularly incensed that Johnson had tried unsuccessfully to get him booted from the prestigious black fraternity Sigma Pi Phi, otherwise known as "the Boulé." When Johnson died a decade later, Vann informed Walter White, the new NAACP chief, that he would not attend the service. "I say about his funeral," Vann wrote, "the same thing I said about Huey Long's funeral—'I shall not be present, but I am glad it happened.'"

The second battle allied Vann with black America's most prominent labor leader and against the *Courier*'s rival, *The Chicago Defender*. In the summer of 1925, A. Philip Randolph, the editor of the radical New York–based journal *The Messenger*, took up the cause of black railway porters. In a series of articles, he lamented their outrageously low pay, grueling hours, and humiliating need to beg for tips and to pay for their own uniforms. At a meeting in Harlem, Randolph called for organizing the workers and agreed to lead a new union, which he named the Brotherhood of Sleeping Car Porters. But most of the Negro press was cool to the effort, particularly the newspapers in Chicago, where many of the porters lived and where their chief employer, the Pullman Company, was based.

Vann sided with Randolph. He began publishing weekly stories tallying the union's recruits and touting Randolph's speeches. When Randolph came to Pittsburgh, Vann met him at the train station, put him put up on Monticello Street, and gave banner coverage to his address at the Loendi Club. At the same time, Vann made no bones about what he expected in return. "There are 10,000 Pullman porters and I am perfectly willing to fight their battle . . . but I think they ought to be willing to give me a little financial support," Vann wrote to an associate. "I want the Courier to go into the home of every porter." In addition to new subscribers, Vann gained access to *The Messenger*'s national sales agents, and to hundreds of porters whom he recruited to hand-carry the *Courier* to remote parts of the country where he couldn't ship the newspaper.

For two years, the Brotherhood's membership grew, and so did the *Courier*'s circulation. Then in 1928, Vann abruptly turned on Randolph. The Pullman Company had refused to come to the bargaining table, and Randolph was threatening a strike. In series of editorials, the *Courier* argued that the union was still too weak to stage a successful walkout, and that Pullman executives would never deal with Randolph because of his socialist past. In an open letter to Pullman porters and maids, Vann called for Randolph's resignation. "The Pullman Porters ought not to suffer because Mr. Randolph years ago decided to be a socialist," he wrote. "He is now at the place where he can go not farther and it is time the porters realized it and worked out some other way to get some of the things they want."

Randolph was irate. In an impassioned reply in *The Messenger*, he disputed the notion that he could no longer lead the union and implied that Vann was conspiring with the Pullman Company to get rid of him. "There is a certain colored gentleman in the woodpile somewhere and the Brotherhood will smoke him out before this fight is over," Randolph wrote darkly. In fact, Vann may have well believed he had the interests of the porters at heart, but he had commercial motives as well. The *Defender* had finally come around to supporting the Brotherhood, so the *Courier* now had a competitive incentive to take a different position. *The Messenger* had also lost circulation, so access to its sales network was no longer of great value. According to one Randolph biographer, many in the Brotherhood also suspected that it was no coincidence that just as Vann began to show sympathy for the Pullman Company's point of view, the *Courier* suddenly had enough money to start building a new printing plant.

Whether or not he took a payoff from the Pullman Company, owning a printing press had become Vann's top priority by the end of the 1920s. At long last, he was determined to free himself from the $25,000 a year he paid to a white-run printing company that counted a Ku Klux Klan newsletter among its accounts. Yet even after the 1926 stock offering, the paper was still short of its goal. Then, out of the blue, an East End tycoon came to the rescue. His name was Michael Late Benedum, and he had made a fortune drilling wildcat oil wells in West Virginia. After moving his headquarters to Pittsburgh, Benedum began donating to Negro causes, and in 1928 he loaned Vann enough money to buy a residential plot on Centre Avenue on the Hill to build a new headquarters for the *Courier*, combining a newsroom and a printing plant.

A year later, on December 14, 1929, Vann and his staff gathered to watch the first issue of the *Courier* come to life in their new home. In the printing annex, dozens of linotype operators clacked away on the towering machines that cast lines of hot type. In the center of the room stood an enormous multilevel press built by R. Hoe and Company, the inventor of rotary printing technology, and designed to print up to twenty-four pages at once. As the press roared into action, cylinders covered with hot type spun at dizzying speed. Wide swaths of paper swooshed through their teeth, emerging covered with densely packed stories and advertisements on both sides. Other parts of the contraption sliced, folded, and stacked the paper into bundles, all at a rate of 250 copies per minute. It was a wonder to behold, and it hadn't come cheap. The *Courier*'s new facility had cost $104,000, far more than Vann had first anticipated, and more than he would have dared spend if the project hadn't already been under way six weeks earlier, when panic seized Wall Street and caused American business to lose a quarter of its value in two days.

To reinforce the message of investing in the future, Vann turned the job of writing about the new press over to a student intern. Ramon Clarke was a graduate student at the University of Pittsburgh, the name that Western University had taken shortly after Vann's graduation. In a star-struck story, Clarke praised the printing plant as "the greatest inspiration the youth of this community have ever been afforded." He compared Vann to such Negro pioneers as George Washington Carver,

Paul Robeson, and mathematician Benjamin Banneker. Echoing Vann's lecturing editorials, Clarke held up the printing press purchase as "an economic challenge to every potential Negro enterprise to become more productive, for in productivity rests the economic salvation of the Negro as a group. The Pittsburgh Courier steps out into a new field of activity—can others be far behind?"

Yet as a new decade dawned, Vann's mind wasn't only on economic advancement. After a decade of hard work, the *Courier* was selling sixty thousand copies a week across America, just as the post–World War I phase of the Great Migration pushed the size of Pittsburgh's black population past that same number. Its talented writers and colorful crusades had no less than H. L. Mencken praising the *Courier* as "the best colored newspaper published." With a powerful new press, Vann had the ability to meet new demand for the paper as far into the future as he could imagine.

Now Vann could afford to turn his attention back to the one territory that he had yet to conquer: politics. And in Michael Benedum, he had a new benefactor—"the Great White Father," as the oilman was jokingly referred to around the *Courier* offices—to whom he owed a huge debt.

MIKE BENEDUM HAD ALWAYS had a nose for untapped resources. Growing up poor in Bridgeport, West Virginia, he quit high school to work in a gristmill. In his early twenties, he became intrigued by talk of prospectors looking for oil in the river basin around Parkersburg. He saved up enough to buy a train ticket, and on the way there he met an oilman who offered him a job negotiating leases with farmers. Benedum showed a knack for shrewd bargaining and "creekology," as the locals called it, or the art of reading creek beds to determine if there might be oil in the area. He went into business with a geologist named Joe Trees, and several years later they hit their first gusher. Soon they were drilling wildcat wells across West Virginia and as far away as Louisiana and Texas, and Benedum was on his way to amassing a fortune in the hundreds of millions. He was also fighting a battle with the Internal Revenue Service over unpaid taxes that would drag on through three Republican presidencies and turn Benedum into an ardent supporter of the Democratic Party.

As the 1932 presidential race approached, Benedum was working to drum up support for Franklin Delano Roosevelt, and he sensed a political wildcatting opportunity in the Negro vote. One day Benedum asked his black valet, Joseph Howard Gould, what he thought it would take to win support for the Democratic candidate among Pennsylvania's registered Negro voters, who after three decades of northern migration now numbered more than 180,000. Gould, who belonged to a professional association of Pittsburgh butlers and maids that had been formed with the help of Robert Vann, suggested that his boss talk to the *Courier*'s Big Chief.

After the loan for the printing plant, Vann was only too happy to meet with Benedum. And when the oilman made his pitch for FDR, Vann was ready to listen. "What has the Negro ever gotten by voting the Republican ticket?" Benedum asked, to which Vann had a glum one-word reply. "Nothing."

It was a bitter conclusion that had taken Vann several decades to reach. Like most blacks of his generation, his devotion to Abraham Lincoln, the hero of his high school graduation speech, had long made Vann a loyal Republican. Since moving to Pittsburgh, he had taken pride in the city's place in Republican history: the first party convention had been held there in 1856, and Lincoln had passed through Pittsburgh and spent a night at the Monongahela House on the way to his first inauguration. At the *Courier*, Vann had reliably thrown the paper's support behind Republicans at the city, state, and national level. But he had grown progressively disillusioned by what he saw as a lack of quid pro quo, for his people or for himself.

In 1920, Vann attended his first presidential convention in Chicago, as an alternate delegate, and watched Warren Harding get nominated on the fifth ballot. He gave Harding the *Courier*'s enthusiastic endorsement only to see the new president offer up no political spoils and refuse to sign an anti-lynching law for fear of offending Southern "lily-whites" in the party. After Harding's sudden death, Vann had such high hopes for his successor that the *Courier* endorsed Calvin Coolidge for election in 1924 in his first days in office. Yet despite serving as vice chairman of a committee to get out the Negro vote, Vann was again denied any kind of appointment after Coolidge's victory. Instead, he watched a plum patronage job go to the editor of a rival black paper in Philadelphia.

In 1928, Vann was impressed enough by Al Smith's anti-lynching stand that he flirted with endorsing a Democrat for the first time. But when he put out a feeler to Jim Farley, the Democratic boss, Farley snubbed him, believing that Pittsburgh didn't have enough black votes to justify Vann's request for "appreciation" should Smith win. In the end, the *Courier* backed Herbert Hoover and denounced the Democratic Party convention in Houston as proof of the sway of its racist Southern wing.

In November 1928, Pittsburgh's black vote went overwhelmingly for Hoover and helped him sweep Pennsylvania on the way to a huge Electoral College victory. But yet again, the only thanks Vann received was a token appointment to a World War I memorial committee, which he turned down in a sarcastic editorial. Judging by another item in the *Courier*, he placed part of the blame for the patronage slights on Andrew Mellon, the Pittsburgh banking giant who served as treasury secretary under both Coolidge and Hoover. "The Mellons just won't give employment to a Negro," sniped a *Courier* gossip column.

By 1932, Vann had seen enough. Two years earlier, he had helped turn out enough black votes to help Gifford Pinchot, a reform Republican, win a tight Pennsylvania governor's race, and still he had received no reward. Meanwhile, he had watched the deepening Depression under Hoover ravage the city of Pittsburgh and its Negro residents. Shares in the U.S. Steel Corporation crashed. Mills all but ground to a halt. The jobless now numbered more than 75,000. More than a third of the black population was in need of assistance, and the *Courier* had begun organizing a "Neediest Family Drive" with support from everyone from the mayor and the City Council to Gus Greenlee and his lieutenants in the numbers racket.

Yet if Vann was going to defect, he wanted assurances that the Democrats would make it worth his while. He decided that the man to see was Joseph Guffey, the tough Irishman who ran the FDR campaign in Pennsylvania. But Vann didn't want to make the overture directly. Better, he decided, to go through Guffey's closest adviser—his sister, Emma Guffey Miller, the most influential female Democrat in the state.

Through Vann's contacts in the butlers and maids society, he knew that Mrs. Miller had her toenails and fingernails trimmed and painted by a Hill resident named Eva DeBoe Jones. A former servant to the wife of Pittsburgh's mayor, Jones had learned the art of manicuring and was now a favorite with the matrons of the East End. Summoning Jones to a meeting, Vann asked if she could pass along a message to Guffey's sister, and at the next opportunity she did. "Mrs. Miller," Jones said as she tended to her client's cuticles, "Mr. Vann'd like to see your brother."

Mrs. Miller passed on the message, but at first Guffey wasn't interested. His cynical response was that Negroes needed to be bought, and that the Democrats couldn't afford them. (Along with playing on the legacy of Lincoln, Republicans had a long history of passing around cash to secure the black vote.) But Miller persisted and eventually Guffey relented, as he was known to do when his sister demanded her way.

When Guffey finally met with Vann, he was struck by the depth of the publisher's disaffection with the Republicans and by his vision of the impact that the *Courier* could have. There were now more than a quarter of a million Negroes of voting age in Pennsylvania, Vann argued—more than any other Northern state—as well as hundreds of thousands more in other states that were likely to be closely contested. If he could swing enough of them to the Democratic ticket, it could make the difference on Election Day.

Guffey was persuaded. With the help of his young Irish protégé, David Lawrence, he even arranged for Vann to travel to Hyde Park to meet with FDR. Roosevelt turned on the charm, and Vann returned to Pittsburgh more motivated than ever to help him win the White House. With the blessings of campaign bosses "Big Jim" Farley and Louis Howe, he formed a "Colored Advisory Committee" to the Roosevelt campaign. Vann was named to a "Big Four" leadership group along with black FDR backers from Boston, Kansas City, and Ohio. In western Pennsylvania, he recruited two hundred members to the Allied Roosevelt-for-President Clubs. To the east, he convinced the editor of a leading black paper in Philadelphia to endorse FDR, a major coup given how many Negro voters that city had and how loyal they had been to its Republican machine.

But Vann was determined to do more. He wanted to show that he could have an influence beyond his home state, by framing the choice that blacks faced in a way that would echo across the country. And as the fall campaign began, he was presented with just such an opportunity "to seize at its flow," in the form of an invitation to address the St. James Literary Forum, a prominent public speakers program in Cleveland.

For weeks beforehand, Vann labored over a speech that was as polished as any closing argument he had made before a jury. In this case, it might have been called the Negro People v. the Republican Party. Vann titled the address "The Patriot and the Partisan," and he began it by explaining why love of country trumped devotion to party. Then he launched into a historical review of Republican betrayal of black loyalty.

In a passage drawn from his childhood memories of the Askew farm, Vann argued that Northern Republicans who took control of the vanquished Confederacy did so with no regard for "the human kindness that had been woven between the aristocratic whites and the subjugated blacks of the South." Driven only by their interests, the carpetbaggers pushed through Reconstruction laws and placed Negroes in political office with a haste that was bound to antagonize Southern whites, and then offered no support once the Jim Crow backlash began. In another passage dripping with personal bitterness, Vann pointed out how quickly GOP enthusiasm for awarding patronage to Negroes had vanished with the Harding presidency, once Republicans took the black vote for granted.

Next Vann introduced examples of Herbert Hoover's treachery into evidence. There was Hoover's order to disband the 24th Infantry and the

10th Cavalry Regiments, the Negro divisions that had fought for their country from San Juan Hill to World War I. There was the case of the "Gold Star Mothers," the program that invited mothers of war dead to visit their children's graves in Europe but required that black participants travel on a separate ship. There was the slighting of Negroes in Hoover's relief and home lending bills, and the insult of his failed nomination of Judge John J. Parker, an avowed Southern foe of black enfranchisement, to the Supreme Court.

But like any good courthouse lawyer, Vann didn't just want to argue facts. He wanted to appeal to the heart. And when it came to Negroes and the Republican Party, nothing was more emotional than their devotion to Abe Lincoln, the Great Emancipator whose picture so many black families still kept in a place of honor in their homes.

September 11, 1932, was a warm Sunday in Cleveland. A capacity crowd filled the St. James AME Church in the city's Fairfax district to hear Vann's afternoon address. He began slowly and deliberately, waiting until he was halfway through the speech before making his first reference to Lincoln. "So long as the Republican party could use the photograph of Abraham Lincoln to entice Negroes to vote a Republican ticket," Vann argued, "they condescended to accord Negroes some degree of political recognition. But when the Republican Party had built itself to the point of security, it no longer invited Negro support. It no longer gave Negroes political recognition. It no longer invited the black man into its councils."

From there, Vann veered off on several long tangents before circling back, in a rousing close, to Lincoln's photograph. "As for this year of our Lord, Negroes everywhere I have seen are aroused," he proclaimed. "They are determined. They are dissatisfied. They are patriots, yes; but not monotonously partisan. . . . I see in the offing a horde of black men and women throwing off the yoke of partisanism practiced for over half a century, casting down the idols of empty promises and moving out into the sunlight of independence. I see hordes and hordes of black men and women, belonging to the army of forgotten men, turning their faces toward a new course and a new party. I see millions of Negroes turning the picture of Abraham Lincoln to the wall. This year I see Negroes voting a Democratic ticket."

Vann knew that he had conjured a memorable image, and he wanted to make it stick. In its next issue, the *Courier* printed Vann's entire speech under the banner headline "This Year I See Millions of Negroes Turning the Picture of Abraham Lincoln to the Wall." Other black newspapers across the country reprinted the address, and Vann paid to have pamphlets of it distributed in cities where the *Courier* was sold. For the next two months, Vann continued to barnstorm, expounding on the theme of Republican betrayal wherever he went. Meanwhile, the *Courier* pounded away at Hoover and mocked his eleventh-hour bid to shore up black support by inviting a group of Negro leaders called "the Committee of One Hundred" to the White House.

When Roosevelt traveled to Pittsburgh three weeks before the election, Vann was given his first reward for the support. He was invited to be part of the public welcoming committee for what would be one of FDR's most memorable speeches of the campaign. For months, Hoover had tried to scare voters with the prospect that the profligate Democrats would make the free-falling economy even worse. But before a raucous crowd of 32,000 at Forbes Field, Roosevelt turned the tables and argued that it was Hoover and Mellon who had been reckless, by refusing to cut spending and raise revenues once the crisis began. Sensing that he had an attentive audience in Pittsburgh, a city built on business, Roosevelt offered a detailed (and remarkably conservative, by modern standards) lecture on the dangers of government deficits. If elected, he vowed to cut the cost of the bloated federal bureaucracy by a quarter—while slyly leaving himself a loophole for new programs aimed at "the direct relief of unemployment."

During a fifteen-minute pre-speech rally, the normally reticent Vann threw himself into whipping up the crowd, which he had made sure was full of black faces. One of them was gossip columnist Julia Bumry Jones, who gushed about the speech in her "Talk O' Town" column later that week. "For the first time in my young life, I am voting with the Dems," Jones confided. "Franky Roosevelt impressed me heap much as he propounded under the clear, blue skies at Forbes Field the other night." Then Jones dropped a hint to her readers that a powerful Republican ally on the Hill might also be warming to the Democratic cause. "I believe it was Gus Greenlee," she wrote, "who told me a LONG time ago that 'a change of pasture is good for the cow.'"

Two weeks later, on the Friday before the election, scores of the black residents of Pittsburgh's Fifth Ward, representing the Lower Hill, filed into a cold high school auditorium to hear a last appeal from Republican leaders. Many of the Negroes were janitors, cleaning ladies, and other laborers on the payroll of the city political machine, but they were in a sullen mood. They barely responded when ward chairman Harry Feldman took a shot at Vann, who as a resident of Homewood would be voting in the Thirteenth Ward. "Why should a citizen from the Thirteenth Ward tell you what to do?" Feldman barked. "We will not let this ward go Democrat because of one man!" Then the atmosphere abruptly shifted as a W. T. Poole, a black mortician, rose to speak. "We are tired of being used and not considered!" Poole shouted at the ward bosses. "The reason for so many Negro Democrats is because they don't feel they have had a just deal!" Suddenly all the blacks in the room broke into wild cheering that lasted for two minutes and was carried by loudspeakers out on the streets of the Hill.

Five days later, a majority of blacks on the Lower Hill for the first time voted to send a Democrat to the White House. They brought Roosevelt within a hair of winning the Fifth Ward, despite a Republican registration edge of four to one. In the Third Ward, representing the Upper Hill, Negro support handed FDR a comfortable margin of victory in a district that had previously voted 80 percent Republican. Allegheny County went Democratic for the first time ever—by 37,000 votes, with 35,000 coming from Negroes. And while Vann failed to achieve his goal of tilting the entire state, the race across Pennsylvania was closer than it had ever been.

Hoover barely held on to Pennsylvania's thirty-six electoral votes, without which Roosevelt's 472–59 vote landslide would have been an even more historic rout.

A week later, the *Courier* went so far as to suggest that Negroes had tipped the race to Roosevelt. Based on the highly conjectural assumption that two thirds of registered blacks had gone to the polls, it estimated that two million Negroes had voted nationwide. More than half of them were in key states that had gone Democratic after voting Republican in 1928: New York, Ohio, Missouri, Indiana, New Jersey, California, Tennessee, Kansas, West Virginia, and Maryland. Given the scope of FDR's victory, the *Courier* argued, those black voters represented a "determining factor" in securing the Democrat's victory.

In fact, the hard evidence of black contribution to Roosevelt's win in 1932 was much less clear. When Negro ballots in the Northern cities with the largest black populations were officially tallied, they still tilted heavily toward Hoover. Roughly three out of every four Negroes had voted Republican in Chicago, Cleveland, and Cincinnati; in Detroit, it had been two out of three. Only in New York City, FDR's home state, did he win a clear majority of Negro voters.

Yet by making the case that the memory of Lincoln should not have a permanent hold on black voters, and by proving that he could shift Negro allegiances in one of the country's most Republican states, Vann had begun to change the calculus of American politics. Once Roosevelt took office, he would go out of his way to court Negroes with relief assistance under the Works Progress Administration, and in the next campaign Big Jim Farley would give top priority to courting the black vote. The resulting Great Political Migration of blacks to the Democratic Party in 1936 would reshape its identity and gradually, over the next eighty years, transform the Electoral College map. By the late 1930s, no less an authority than Joseph Alsop, the widely read political columnist, would credit Robert Lee Vann as "the real originator of the Democratic Party's celebrated capture of the Negro vote."

FDR didn't need much persuading that he owed a debt to Vann. Two days after the election, Joseph Guffey traveled to Hyde Park and urged the president-elect to reward the publisher with a high-level appointment. When Roosevelt asked what he had in mind, Guffey suggested a post as special assistant in the Justice Department. Roosevelt's only question was whether it would require Senate confirmation, since he didn't want to risk an early fight with Southern Democrats. When Guffey replied that it would not, FDR grinned and agreed to the Vann appointment. "The job's yours, Joe!" he said.

The appointment, officially announced that summer, was big enough news to make the prestigious "The Presidency" report in *Time* magazine. As Vann prepared to depart for Washington, some of the most powerful men in the new administration traveled to Pittsburgh to pay him homage. At a Democratic Party banquet at the William Penn Hotel, Vann was seated at the head table along with Mike Benedum, Joe Guffey, Jim Farley, and Harold Ickes, the powerful FDR aide who had been named secretary of the interior. The next month, Guffey, his sister Emma, and David Lawrence all turned out for a banquet that Ira Lewis threw in honor of Vann at the Pythian Temple on the Hill. Vann was presented with an Elgin wristwatch; his wife, Jesse, received a bouquet of flowers; and Julia Bumry Jones declared that the event was "the finest, most representative affair of its kind every given in Smoketown."

After the testimonials from Guffey and Lawrence, Vann, clad in black tie and winged collar, rose to speak. He was effusive in his praise for the new president and for his political advisers, but as blunt as ever in insisting that Negroes should never again blindly serve any political master. "I came to the Democratic Party because the Republican Party no longer serves the interest of the people," Vann said to murmurs of agreement and laughter, "and when this party gets to where they no longer offer my people any service, I'll either go back to the Republican Party or to some other party."

Vann's caveat would prove prophetic, but he didn't know that yet. For one shining evening at the Knights of Pythias, the Big Chief was only too happy to bathe in the adoration of his colleagues and the five hundred other proud Negroes in the room. At long last, Vann was off to conquer Washington, just as a new King of the Hill—who had also risen from modest beginnings in North Carolina, but along a much less straight and narrow path—was reaching the height of his power.

Gus Greenlee (center) at the Crawford Grill, his nightclub in the Hill District, with *Courier* sportswriters Bill Nunn and Wendell Smith (left) and Pittsburgh Crawfords pitching ace Satchel Paige (in suit).

4

THE RISE AND FALL
OF "BIG RED"

IN THE EARLY AFTERNOON of April 29, 1932, a rare joyful date in that dark year of Depression on the Hill, thousands of locals gathered at the corner of Bedford Avenue and Junilla Street to attend Dedication Day at Greenlee Field. When the gate opened around four o'clock, they pulled out the quarters, dimes, and nickels they had saved up to be among the first to enter the stadium's brick walls. Inside, they took their places on new wooden bleachers supported by gleaming steel beams and braced by sturdy blocks of concrete. For the next hour and a half, they watched the visiting New York Black Yankees, then their hometown Pittsburgh Crawfords, take batting practice on a field as lush and manicured as any they had ever seen at a major league ballpark.

Shortly before six o'clock, the teams lined up behind a marching band and made their way to a flagpole in center field. As Old Glory was raised, the band struck up "The Star Spangled Banner." Robert L. Vann, the slender, abstemious publisher of the *Courier*, gave a short dedication speech, then he asked for a show of appreciation for the husky, high-rolling rack-eteer who had made the day possible by spending no less than $100,000. As the crowd of six thousand cheered and rose to their feet, a red Packard convertible made its way around the infield, with the man they called "Big Red" waving from the backseat, dressed in a white silk suit and smoking a Cuban cigar.

The first game in the house that Gus Greenlee built turned out to be a classic pitching duel. Satchel Paige, the mercurial ace whom Greenlee had lured to Pittsburgh, was on the mound for the Crawfords. At the top of his form at age twenty-six, Paige hurled one fastball after another—no spitballs, grease balls, or brush-back pitches. He had no need to resort to "smoke at the yoke," he liked to boast; he could get you all day with "peas at the knees." Going into the ninth inning, Paige had struck out ten, and allowed only three hits and no runs. But he had been matched inning for inning by the portly ace for the Black Yankees, Jesse Hubbard, who had given up only three hits and kept the Crawfords scoreless.

Stadium lights had yet to be installed and darkness was falling as the game entered the ninth inning. With one out and one on, Ted Page, the Yankees right fielder, hit a grounder and raced to first to beat a double play. Page promptly stole second, raced to third when the pickoff throw sailed past the second baseman, and scored when teammate Hawk Thomas hit a Texas Leaguer to right. With two out in the bottom of the ninth, Josh Gibson, the fearsome Crawford slugger, had a chance to even the game. All six thousand fans rose to their feet in hope that the man known as "the black Babe Ruth" might smack one of his mighty homers.

Gibson hit a drive to deep center, and for a second it looked like the ball might go out. But Hawk Thomas snagged it out of midair, and the game was over. The Black Yankees had won, 1–0. As the drained Crawford fans filed out into the night, they had to settle for the satisfaction of witnessing a game in their own ballpark, the first ever erected by a black man. Behind the dugouts, meanwhile, the players experienced another first. At Forbes Field, Yankee Stadium, and every other major league stadium where Ne-groes played, they weren't allowed to use the locker facilities. But tonight the men of the Crawfords and the Black Yankees didn't have to change at a boardinghouse or on a bus. Tonight, thanks to Gus Greenlee, they slipped out of their sweaty uniforms and muddy cleats in the dignity of their own locker room.

Like Robert Lee Vann, William Augustus Greenlee was born in North Carolina, in a mill town at the base of the Blue Ridge Mountains called Marion. Unlike Vann, his parents had some means. Greenlee's father was a masonry contractor who made a tidy sum helping to rebuild Marion's courthouse, hotels, and other buildings after a horrendous fire destroyed most of the town. His mother, the mulatto daughter of a black slave and her white owner, put great store in education: two of her sons grew up to become doctors, and a third, a lawyer. But Gus was a restless and rebellious child who disliked school and made it through only one year of college before dropping out.

"On the dogs with father," as one of his brothers put it, Gus hoboed his way north at the age of nineteen with nothing but some patched-up clothes and a pair of canvas shoes, making for a nasty surprise when he stepped off the freight train into the snow and cold of Pittsburgh's winter. At six-foot-two, with a shock of red hair framing his wide, freckled face, Greenlee immediately cut a striking figure on the Hill, and he displayed drive to match. He shined shoes, worked in a steel mill, and chauffeured for a white undertaker until he had saved up enough money to buy his own taxicab.

When America entered World War I, Greenlee enlisted. He was assigned to the 367th Infantry at Fort Dix, New Jersey, one of the Negro regiments that were assembled to form the 92nd Division and given the title of Buffalo Soldiers, after the all-black units of the Union Army and the Spanish-American War. In June 1918, the Buffalos set sail from Hoboken, New Jersey, for a training facility in the French town of Bourbonnes-les-Bains, known for its hot spring spas. From there, they were dispatched to an area in the eastern Vosges Mountains, which hadn't seen much action and where the French generals under whose command they had been put thought it would be safe to park Negro servicemen for the rest of the war.

But as soon as they arrived, the sector named for the town of Saint-Dié came under intense German ground and air attack.

One morning in early September, the men of the 367th looked up from their positions, where Greenlee manned a machine gun, and saw German planes buzzing overhead. Round objects began to fall from the sky. At first the soldiers took them for gas shells. Instead, they were scrolls of paper with a message addressed "TO THE COLORED SOLDIERS OF THE AMERICAN ARMY." "Hello boys, what are you doing over here?" the pamphlets read. "Fighting the Germans? Why? Have they ever done you any harm? . . . Do you enjoy the same rights as the white people do in America, the land of Freedom and Democracy, or are you rather not treated over there as second-class citizens? . . . Now, this is all different in Germany, where they do like colored people, where they treat them as gentlemen. . . . Come over and see for yourself. . . . Don't allow them to use you as cannon fodder. To carry a gun in this war is not an honor, but a shame. Throw it away and come over into the German lines."

Far from answering the call to desertion, the Buffalos fought bravely, repelling several German advances and suffering dozens of casualties and scores of injuries. Their white American officers pleaded with the French commanders to let them go on the attack, but instead the French replaced them with white soldiers. General John Pershing, who had commanded the Buffalos in previous wars and knew what they were capable of, arranged to have them assigned to him, to help in the Grand Offensive to push the crumbling German army out of France. Although the official order of battle in Pershing's advance through the Argonne forest region indicated that the men of the 367th were assigned to supply and field hospital duties, some must have found their way to the front as well, for machine gunner Gus Greenlee returned to America in the spring of 1919 with a shrapnel wound suffered in the Battle of Saint-Mihiel.

Greenlee's taxicab was waiting for him when he got back to Pittsburgh—and so was a new opportunity to use it. After "June thirsty-first," as they called the July 1, 1919 implementation of the Wartime Prohibition Act, the first step toward banning all liquor sales in America—Greenlee became a bootlegger. Four Italian brothers named Tito used him to make deliveries of the illegal beer and whiskey they manufactured in a brewery in the town of Latrobe, southeast of Pittsburgh. Soon Greenlee's cab was logging so many miles on his liquor runs that he acquired a new nickname: "Gasoline Gus."

Later there would be stories that Greenlee hijacked liquor trucks operated by the likes of Al Capone and Lucky Luciano. But there is more evidence that the gangster wars of the Prohibition Era had the opposite effect, of encouraging the shrewd, entrepreneurial redhead to pursue less perilous enterprises than rum-running. By 1922, Greenlee had opened his own speakeasy in the Hill District, the Paramount Inn on Wylie Avenue. Police promptly raided it and closed it down, charging, according to white newspaper accounts, that the club was the site of "drunken orgies" where "blacks and whites mingled freely and danced together frequently." Rather than give up, Greenlee took steps to make the Paramount more respectable, reopening the club with a full-time orchestra and forming a talent-booking agency that he ran out of an office upstairs.

Legend also had it that Gus Greenlee brought the numbers racket to Pittsburgh. Some even said that he was the man responsible for introducing numbers to the United States, after traveling to Cuba and watching the locals play "la bolita," a game where small balls inscribed with numbers were placed in a bag and gamblers bet on which ones would be pulled out. But more credible accounts suggest that the numbers first arrived in Pittsburgh from New York City, via railroad porters who took bets for Madame Stephanie St. Clair, the "Policy Queen of Harlem," and other Eastern numbers bankers who were already in operation by the early 1920s.

By the time Greenlee got into the game, a doctor on Centre Avenue who tried to start his own numbers racket had gone bust. So Gus took the time to study the details of the enterprise, soaking up the wisdom of a visiting numbers king from Philadelphia. In 1926, he began to organize his own racket, working with a partner named William Harris. Known as "Woogie," Harris owned an ideal front for numbers running: the Crystal Barber Shop on Wylie Avenue, where scores of men came in each day to get a haircut and a shave and to swap tall tales under the French-paneled mirrors.

It was slow going at first. One of the first "numbers runners" that Greenlee and Harris deployed was Woogie's younger brother Charles, whom everyone called "Teenie." (Teenie was indeed short of stature, but he acquired the nickname because of his good looks; when he was a child, a visiting relative took to calling him "Teenie Little Lover.") Teenie was sent to collect bets in McKees Rocks, a mill town north of Pittsburgh, and some days he would return with less than $2 worth of betting slips. But gradually the business grew, and by the early 1930s Gus Greenlee and Woogie Harris were taking in as much as $25,000 a day in bets and employing five hundred runners across the city. Working as "cut buddies," sharing financial gains and losses, they amassed enough money to buy side-by-side Tudor houses in the elegant Penn Hills neighborhood on the eastern outskirts of Pittsburgh.

Greenlee and Harris usually derived their numbers from the stock market, coming up with a three-digit figure every day based on the quantity of stocks that rose, fell, and stayed even. (Occasionally the number was also drawn from newspaper reports of commodity sales, or horse track results.) Between eight and ten o'clock each morning, their runners filled the streets of black Pittsburgh, in cars and on foot, collecting wagers that were recorded on slips of paper. While lookout men armed with guns under their topcoats stood guard outside, the runners delivered the slips to the Paramount Inn and the Crystal Barber Shop, where women in back rooms tallied the day's take on adding machines. The next day, a winning number was calculated from the morning stock market tables, and payouts were made to anyone who "hit the number."

For the gamblers, the bets bought a long shot at a dream, and a day's worth of hope during a deepening Depression. Greenlee and Harris set their odds in advance, usually at 600-to-1. A hod carrier could bet a penny for a chance to win $6; a steelworker, a dime to make sixty; a Loendi Club man, a dollar to score $600. It was a game rigged in favor of the house, given the number of people who played every day, and the fact that most wagers were under a dollar. But it also meant that a banker had to be good to his word when lucky winners hit the number, an occurrence that Greenlee and Harris turned to their advantage one Thursday in the summer of 1930.

Pittsburgh was in the middle of a brutal August heat wave. Weeks of 90 degree heat with no rain had baked the city streets and ravaged farmland for miles around. Water was being rationed, and the price of milk had shot up due to the drought. Too exhausted to come up with anything more creative, hundreds of Pittsburgh gamblers wrote the simplest number they could think of on their betting slips: the date, "805." Usually it was a sucker's wager, because betting the date was so obvious, but on that day the number hit. Suddenly racketeers across the city were faced with a huge payout. Most couldn't cover it. Some paid only a fraction of what they owed. Others skipped town, fleeing to hideouts in Philadelphia, Cleveland, and Chicago. One banker became the object of a bitter ditty: "805 was a burner. Where the hell is Jakie Lerner?"

As it happened, Woogie Harris was on vacation in Europe, and he had left his little brother Teenie in charge of the numbers operation. Woogie had warned Teenie to watch out for overplayed numbers and to lay them off on other racketeers. But Teenie didn't act quickly enough. When he reached his brother with the bad news, Woogie sent Teenie to a secret address downtown to collect $25,000 in cash to pay off the first wave of winners. In the following weeks, Woogie and Greenlee pawned many of their own possessions and took out new mortgages on their Penn Hills homes in order to pay off all of the "805" hits in full. Then, like Andrew Carnegie before them, they moved in and took over the territory of competitors who had gone under.

Having weathered the "805" crisis, Gus Greenlee had the means to make his most ambitious investment yet. He bought a block-long hotel called the Leader House on the corner of Wylie Avenue and Crawford Street and transformed it into a nightclub he called the Crawford Grill. On the first floor, be built a huge bar and a small, elevated stage with a mirrored piano. One floor up, there was a theater that stretched the length of the floor and had a revolving stage. On the third floor, Greenlee created a private "Crawford Club" where he entertained personal guests with his finest liquor and counted his gambling spoils. Overnight, the Grill became the hottest nightspot on the Hill, a place where black and white hipsters came to mingle over the club's famous daiquiris, and where all the top Negro entertainers who performed at the dance halls of the Hill or the Stanley Theatre downtown headed after their concerts were over.

To keep the authorities at bay, Greenlee plied police with free bets and fat envelopes of cash. On most days, a visitor to the Hill could see dozens of runners milling around the corner of Wylie Avenue and Crawford Street as patrolmen walked the beat, paying them no mind. But once in a while a raid would be staged, usually during election years. In the spring of 1934, a vice squad barged into the Crawford Grill and demanded that a locked storage room in the basement be opened. Inside were a half dozen slot machines gathering dust, a discovery that allowed authorities to charge Greenlee with operating a "gaming house" and Gus to beat the rap by insisting that the machines hadn't been used in years. Several months later, police used axes and crowbars to bust through a partition at the Belmont Hotel, pulled a false bottom out of the bar, and found hundreds of numbers slips and accounting books. They arrested Teddy Horne, a Greenlee associate who ran the hotel, along with Gus's brother George, but both men were later released without serving any jail time.

If Greenlee and his lieutenants always seemed to beat the rap, it was no accident. Along with greasing palms, Greenlee courted the Republican politicians who ran Pittsburgh and surrounding Allegheny County by delivering Negro votes. He became the treasurer and enforcer of the Third Ward Voters League, the most powerful black political organization on the Upper Hill. At Christmastime, he invited the distressed citizens of the ward to the league's headquarters for hot meals and free turkeys. On Election Days, he used his network of numbers runners to remind them of his generosity and get them to the polls. Although the league had an official policy that a vote of the entire board of officers was required to ratify all decisions, Greenlee quietly passed the word to Pittsburgh's major, Charles

Kline, and its powerful state senator, Jimmy Coyne, that to get whatever they wanted, they need only come see Gus.

(The deal kept everyone happy—until the 1932 election approached and it became clear that voters on the Hill were listening to Robert Vann's calls to turn Lincoln's picture to the wall. For years, Greenlee had used his political connections to arrange for tax relief for Hill residents who voted Republican. But in the summer of 1932, he was informed that he was under investigation for defrauding the state of tax revenue. After months of embarrassing headlines, he was cleared, but it left a sour taste. When *Courier* gossip columnist Julia Bumry Jones quoted Greenlee as saying that "a change of pasture is good for the cow" just weeks before Election Day, it wasn't an accident; between the lines was a signal that Gus wouldn't hold it against the voters of the Third Ward if they voted for Roosevelt.)

Throughout black America, the Depression gave racketeers a chance to play community hero, and nowhere was that more true than in Pittsburgh. As white-run banks stopped doing anything for Negroes except take their money, Greenlee became the top lender on the Hill, doling out loans to cover rents, prevent foreclosures, and pay doctor and funeral bills. Breadwinners laid off from factory jobs could count on temporary work in his numbers operation. Families in distress found bags of groceries and buckets of coal at their doorsteps. At the same time, Gus made sure everyone could see just how much cash he had to spread around. On any given day, he could be seen driving around the Hill in one of six different automobiles—a Lincoln, a Cadillac, a Chevy, a Buick, a Ford, and his flashy red Packard convertible. Gus held court at the Crawford Grill in silk double-breasted suits and sported an expensive bowler hat in a picture that appeared regularly in the *Courier*. In his back pocket, he carried a money clip stuffed with hundred-dollar bills that he flashed at every opportunity.

To help burnish his reputation as a modern-day Robin Hood (who in this case took from the poor to give to the poor), Greenlee hired a part-time publicist. Conveniently, John L. Clark also happened to be the author of "Wylie Avenue," the *Courier*'s widely read column on the business and politics of the Hill. Clark had begun work on an exposé of racketeering in Pittsburgh when one day Greenlee summoned him to the Crawford Grill. Gus offered the columnist a syndication deal with the "West Penn News Service," an apparently fictitious front with offices in a building owned by Greenlee. The racketeering exposé never appeared, and from then on Clark's "Wylie Avenue" column became a regular source of attacks on Greenlee's enemies and tributes to his financial generosity and political clout.

Big Red became so well known for his largesse, in fact, that sometimes he had to go out of his way to demonstrate its limits. One of his closest white friends, and a regular at the Crawford Grill, was an Irish sandlot athlete who dabbled in ward politics on the North Side and was saving up to buy a semipro football team. Decades later, when that team became the Super Bowl champion Pittsburgh Steelers, Art Rooney would tell his biographer a story about a scene he witnessed at the Grill while huddling in a back booth with Gus Greenlee and Jimmy Coyne, the Republican Party boss.

A woman came over and whispered to Greenlee that she needed some money. He told her to get lost. "That's not how you talked last night," the woman purred. "That was last night," Gus growled. "When I'm hard, I'm soft. When I'm soft, I'm hard. Now beat it!" The three men went back to their political plotting until, moments later, an ashtray came flying through the air and barely missed connecting with Coyne's head. Greenlee laughed it off but Coyne was not amused, and from then on the state senator insisted that the three meet at a location that he controlled in the Oakland district.

Greenlee was kinder to a group of struggling sandlot baseball players who approached him for support around the same time. They called themselves the Pittsburgh Crawfords, and they had gotten their start thanks to Teenie Harris, the little brother of Greenlee's partner Woogie Harris. A talented athlete, Teenie had been the captain of the baseball team at Watts High on the Hill. After playing a hard-fought championship game against McKelvey High one year, Teenie and the McKelvey captain had decided to join forces and form a semipro sandlot team with the best black players from the two squads. They named the team the Crawfords after a bathhouse on the Hill that sponsored them for a few hundred dollars, and Teenie dropped out of school to play for them while continuing to moonlight as a bag man for Woogie.

By the early 1930s, the Crawfords had assembled a raw but imposing roster, including a teenage slugger named Josh Gibson. (They had become so good, in fact, that Teenie had quit to devote himself to his other athletic love, semipro basketball.) Yet for all their success on the field, the "Craws," as locals called them, were always on the brink of financial collapse, since the city wouldn't let them charge for attendance at the public park where they played. To stay afloat, the Crawfords passed a hat. Even then, they often saw little of the meager contributions they collected. During one Memorial Day weekend game in 1930, they raised $8 but had to pay out $6 to the umpire and the visiting team. Afterward, sportswriter Ches Washington wrote an impassioned column chastising the "cheapsports" of the Hill who wouldn't even pay a nickel to watch a "young team with all the earmarks of future greatness." Washington called on local businessmen to save the Crawfords, and the white owner of a local sporting goods store responded by offering to buy the team for $1,000.

The players decided to approach Greenlee instead. At first Gus told them he wasn't interested. He would donate money for uniforms and travel, he said, not no more. Then a week later, he summoned the youngsters to the Crawford Grill to announce that he had changed his mind. He was ready to buy the team and put all the players on salary.

Greenlee didn't say what caused the reversal, but the question became a source of fascination on the Hill. Some said he was thinking about the upcoming election, when his ally Jimmy Coyne would be on the ballot. (Sure enough, the Crawfords were soon taking the field with "Coyne for Commissioner" stitched on their uniforms.) Others thought Greenlee was taking a page from his friend Alex Pompez, a New York numbers banker who owned a baseball team called the Cubans and used it to launder money. Still others assumed Gus was just doing a favor for the Crawfords because of their connection to Teenie Harris, his cut buddy's brother.

Yet given what happened next, it's likely that Gus Greenlee had a more competitive motive as well. He was already a big man in black Pittsburgh, but buying the Crawfords gave him a chance to go head-to-head with the heir to the biggest Negro dynasty in town: Cap Posey's son, Cumberland Posey Jr.

IN THE SUMMER OF 1930, just as Gus Greenlee was about to purchase the Pittsburgh Crawfords, Cum Posey introduced night baseball to the East Coast. That spring, the Kansas City Monarchs had become the first Negro League team to illuminate their home stadium so games could be played past dark, five years before white major league teams embraced what at the time they still viewed as a gimmick. But it was Posey's bright idea to approach J. L. Wilkinson, the white president of the Monarchs, and propose that he send his team and lighting gear on a monthlong barnstorming tour with the Homestead Grays. Once Wilkinson agreed, Posey cut deals to take the road show to a dozen cities across Ohio and Pennsylvania, including Cleveland, Akron, Youngstown, Greensburg, Altoona, and Beaver Falls as well as Pittsburgh.

Cum Posey may have been a late bloomer, but since becoming manager and owner of the Homestead Grays he had shown just how much drive he inherited from his father. Posey had benched most of the original players from the Homestead steel mills and set out to lure top talent from the sandlot ranks and the disorganized world of professional Negro ball. He offered salaries to players whose teams only paid by the game. He negotiated with the Pittsburgh Pirates to use Forbes Field while the white major leaguers were out of town. (The locker room, however, was kept off-limits.) Posey even rewarded his players by bringing their favorite sandwiches to games.

In 1925, the year Cap Posey died, his namesake made his most ambitious move yet. Cum hired Joe Williams, the six-foot-six, half-black, half-Comanche Texan who was considered the most fearsome black pitcher in the game. In New York, where he had played in his younger days, Williams was known as "Cyclone" because of the way his fastballs flew by hapless batters. Once he arrived in Pittsburgh, he acquired a new nickname: "Smokey Joe," for all the smoke he threw in Smoketown.

Over the next five years, Posey added a half dozen other future legends to the Grays roster. They included slugger John Beckwith, triple-threat outfielder Oscar Charleston, and Martin Dihigo, the hard-hitting Cuban second baseman who was the first black Latin player to become a star in America. Judy Johnson, the clutch-hitting third baseman, joined the team as a player-coach. Watching the way Posey went after players he wanted—and after women on the road—Johnson marveled at the owner's relentlessness. "Posey played the saint, but he was anything but a saint," Johnson recalled. "He was a terrible womanizer and ruthless in raiding other teams. He just wasn't a man you could trust with your wife or anything else."

Under Posey, the Grays projected an image that combined professionalism with extreme toughness. He demanded that his men dress in suits and ties off the field and prohibited card playing during games. But he also courted players with hair-trigger tempers and did little to keep them in check. Oscar Charleston, the scowling first baseman, had once been charged with assault for attacking an umpire, and had been fired from his previous team for throwing a punch at the owner. During one team fight, third baseman Jud "Boojum" Wilson dangled shortstop Jake Stephens out of a hotel window by his heels. During another, Ted Page, the veteran outfielder who would later be traded to the Black Yankees, had a knife pulled on him by one of his teammates.

In the night game series against the Kansas City Monarchs, the teams stood even in their series as they arrived in Pittsburgh on a Friday in mid-July. The morning of the game, twelve trucks loaded with lighting gear pulled up to Forbes Field. Crewmen positioned towers around the inside of the park. A generator powered by a 250 horsepower engine was set up. At half past eight, just as the sun was setting, the Grays and the Monarchs took the field in front of seven thousand spectators, one of the largest crowds ever to attend a Negro League game in Pittsburgh.

But as soon as full darkness fell, a problem became apparent. The lighting system had been designed for the much smaller parks where the Monarchs usually played, not a stadium as large as Forbes Field, with its three tiers of steel bleachers and center field stretching to almost 450 feet. The towers were too small. The bulbs kept flickering on and off. For the fans, the action on the field was a dim blur. Even the players couldn't even see one another clearly.

When Smokey Joe Williams took the mound for the Grays, he couldn't make out the fingers that catcher Buck Ewing used to call pitches. They settled on two signals: glove up for a fastball; glove down for a curve. Ewing still had trouble tracking Smokey's bullets, and midway through the game he caught one at the top of his mitt and broke a finger. Ewing had to leave the game, and his backup, who was playing center field, informed the coach that he had no intention of trying to catch Smokey Joe's smoke in the dark. With no other options, coach Judy Johnson turned to the stands and spotted Josh Gibson, the young sandlot catcher for the Crawfords who had begun hanging around Grays practices. Johnson yelled out at Gibson to suit up, and the teenager caught the rest of a wild game that didn't end until close to midnight, in near total darkness, when the Grays finally won, 5–4, in the twelfth inning.

Or at least that was Judy Johnson's account of how Josh Gibson came to play for the Homestead Grays. According to another version, Cum Posey deliberately poached Gibson. The day before, he sent his brother See Posey to an out-of-town Crawfords game. See met Gibson behind the stands, gave him a contract to sign, and drove back to Pittsburgh. Yet however it happened, Gibson remained in a Grays uniform from them on. He helped the Grays win the series against the Monarchs, and by the end of the season he was the team's full-time catcher and Buck Ewing had hung up his mitt.

Still only eighteen, Gibson had the face of a choirboy and the build of a lumberjack. Josh and his family had arrived in Pittsburgh from Georgia three years earlier, and his growing frame had been hardened by work in the iron mills alongside his father. His play behind the plate was still erratic, but there was no question that he could hit. Gibson's power came not just from his thick muscles but also from his economical hitting technique. He held his 40 ounce bat cocked and tucked into his right side and stood in a wide stance, giving him until the last second to read pitches before he swung at them with a short step forward and a lighting flick of his mighty arms and wrists.

Several weeks later, in a game against the Baltimore Black Sox, Gibson blasted a home run that everyone present proclaimed the longest drive they had ever seen at Forbes Field. By September, he had helped position the Grays for a showdown with the New York Lincoln Giants for the "Colored Championship of the East." After taking a 4–3 game lead, the Grays arrived at Yankee Stadium for a doubleheader that included another Gibson homer in the first game, one that became the stuff of baseball legend.

Judy Johnson later claimed that he saw the ball clear the roof, fueling the myth that Josh Gibson had "hit one out of Yankee Stadium." According to numerous other accounts, the ball actually sailed into the third-tier bleachers and dropped into the bullpen. In either event, Gibson's hot bat helped the Grays win the series against the Lincoln Giants, 6–4, and the bragging rights to the Eastern championship. In the *Courier*, Chester Washington praised the 1930 Grays as "without a doubt the greatest aggregation of players in the history of the Homesteaders, and one of the most brilliant Negro teams ever to cavort around a diamond-shaped arena."

The next year, the Grays got even better. They played 153 games against teams of all stripes and won all but 17 of them. They crushed semipro teams across the South in a spring training tour. In a doubleheader exhibition against Connie Mack's All Stars, a white team that included Lefty Grove and several other Hall of Famers, the Grays swept both games, the second by 18–0. There were no established Negro leagues that year, but the Grays won every series they played against other top black teams.

Although reliable statistics are hard to come by, Josh Gibson was said to have hit seventy-two home runs, and he and at least four other teammates batted over .300. When the Grays won a season-ending series with the Kansas City Monarchs, Posey proclaimed it as good as a world championship. "For the first time since Hillsdale defeated Kansas City in the Colored World Series of 1925," he crowed in the *Courier*, "there is an undisputed National Championship Team of the United States. And there is occasion for a little vanity when I say the Homestead Grays were the champions of 1931."

Having succeeded in assembling the best team in the Negro game, Posey set his sights on becoming its new czar. There hadn't been one single unified black league since the original one founded a decade earlier by Rube Foster, the Chicago legend who had gone into an early decline and passed away in a mental hospital. In the *Courier*, Posey called for the formation of a new "East-West League" and cast himself as champion for all the other black owners. The Grays were enough of a draw that they could make money remaining independent, Posey claimed; but teams from smaller cities like Baltimore, Detroit, and Newark couldn't survive without a league that could guarantee quality opponents and weekend games. Posey also argued that the new league would free black teams from their heavy reliance on white booking agents who arranged games with white semipro and exhibition teams—but also took a 10 percent cut of revenues that made it almost impossible for most of the teams to see any profit.

What Posey failed to mention was the new challenge he faced in Pittsburgh. For while the Grays were reaching the pinnacle of the Negro game in 1931, Gus Greenlee was turning the upstart Crawfords into a team that could compete for top dollar in the world of semipro and exhibition games—and increasingly posed a threat to the top-tier black teams as well. Greenlee had replaced the sandlot manager, Hooks Tinker, with a wily, no-nonsense veteran of the Negro leagues, Bobby Williams. He had hired seasoned players such as second baseman "Pistol Johnny" Russell from the St. Louis Stars, shortstop Chester Williams from the Memphis Red

Sox, and spitballer Sam "Lefty" Streeter from the Cleveland Buckeyes. By June 1931, the Crawfords had won ten games in a row, and Streeter had pitched an impressive no-hit shutout against the Book Shoe, one of the best teams in the independent Pittsburgh City League.

Then, in the middle of the season, Greenlee seized an opportunity created by the deepening Depression. After Smokey Joe Williams, the most feared black pitcher of the day was Leroy "Satchel" Paige, the lanky six-foot-four right-hander famous for his leggy windup and blazing fastball. Paige was also notorious for living up to his nickname—which he had acquired carrying suitcases as a seven-year-old railway porter in his hometown of Mobile, Alabama—by always being ready to pack his bags and jump from team to team depending on who was willing to pay him the most. Satchel had begun the season playing for the Nashville Elite Giants and its owner Tom Wilson, another racketeer who had signed Paige despite Satchel's open flirtation with Wilson's live-in girlfriend. But in mid-season, Wilson had moved the team to Cleveland, where it promptly went bankrupt because it couldn't fill enough seats. As soon as Greenlee heard the news, he wired Paige an offer of $250 a month to finish the season in Pittsburgh.

The day Paige arrived on the Hill, he headed straight to the Crawford Grill. As he entered the door, Greenlee rushed over to greet him. "'We're going to open against the Homestead Grays," Gus said. "They're the best there is, Satch. You beat them and you're number one right from the start." In early August, the Crawfords were scheduled to play their rivals for the third time, and Greenlee saw an opportunity to show off his new acquisition and embarrass Cum Posey at the same time.

When the day came, the Crawfords jumped out to an early lead before the Grays evened the score at seven-all in the fourth inning. Then Bobby Williams called in Satchel Paige, who made his signature lazy walk from the bullpen to the mound as the crowd in Forbes Field went wild. Over the next five innings, Paige struck out six batters and kept the Grays from scoring another run while the Crawfords pulled ahead for a 10–7 victory. Hooks Tinker, the former manager who was playing his last game in a

Grays uniform, marveled at Paige's mixture of speed and control. "He was mowing those guys down like mad," Tinker recalled. "He was throwing nothing but aspirin tablets."

After the game, Greenlee invited the team to the Crawford Grill and locked the door for a private celebration. The men all wanted to shake Paige's hand, and the waitresses buzzed around to flirt with him. "They mobbed me like money'd rub off on me," Paige recalled. But one girl kept her distance, a light-skinned beauty with a wide mouth and such large eyes that her friends teasingly called her "Toad," or "Toadalo." Naturally, she was the one who caught Paige's eye. "Lo, I'm Satch," he said, extending his long dark hand. "I know you all right, Mr. Paige," she replied. "Everyone knows who you are. I'm Janet Howard."

Until then, Paige would write in his autobiography, he had always thought of marriage as "like walking in front of a firing squad without anyone making you do it." But in Janet Howard, he would discover that he had met his match. "Right then and there, she was starting to write the end of my bachelor days," he wrote. "I didn't even know it."

Smitten, Paige offered to walk Howard home and asked if he could take her out again. When he got back to the Crawford Grill, he told Greenlee he needed extra cash for the date. "I'll do better than that," Gus responded. "Tomorrow you go down and buy yourself a couple of suits and hats on me." Greenlee was so thrilled with Paige's first win that he even offered to pay him $700 that month, a bonus over his $250 salary. "That ought to keep you happy enough to stay with me," Gus joked. The next day, Paige charged two suits to Gus and bought three more with his own money, as well as an assortment of bright red, blue, green, and yellow ties. "You look like a walking barber pole," Howard said when he showed up for their date. Then she grabbed Paige's arm tight, as though he already belonged to her. "You look fine!" she said.

With Paige and Streeter on the mound, the Crawfords had a strong finish to the 1931 season and would have seemed like a natural addition to Cum Posey's new East-West League. But Posey made no effort to include them, instead huddling secretively with the owners of clubs from

Cleveland, Detroit, Philadelphia, Baltimore, and Newark. When Gus Greenlee approached him about joining the new league, Posey presented him with a list of high-handed conditions. The Crawfords would only be considered "associate members." The league would have veto power over any games they played in the same territory as the Grays. It would impose a salary cap on the Crawfords' spending and have the right to transfer its players to other teams. The Grays owner even told Greenlee that he should install his brother See Posey as manager of the Crawfords.

Greenlee scoffed at the conditions, and for good reason. By then, he had launched his ambitious plan to build a professional-quality stadium "closer to where Negroes live," as he put it. He had identified a property on the Hill occupied by a bankrupt brick factory and secured the blessing of the cemetery and the hospital on either side. He had formed a corporation called the Bedford Land Company and taken 20 percent of the stock, doling out the rest to the brick factory owner and his old bootleg suppliers, the Tito brothers, who were given the concession business and the job of keeping away Pittsburgh's Italian mobsters. With an investment of cash, land, and construction of more than $100,000, the last thing Gus Greenlee planned to do was let Cum Posey dictate who could and could not play in Greenlee Field.

So instead of playing ball, Greenlee went to war. Dangling the lure of a brand-new stadium and hard cash from his numbers business, he began to raid Posey's best players. By January 1932, he had convinced Oscar Charleston, the hot-tempered first baseman, to leave the Grays and join the Crawfords as a player-manager. He wooed away shortstop Jake Stephens and Ted Radcliffe, the pitcher known as "Double Duty" because he had once hurled the first game of a doubleheader and caught the second. Then Greenlee went after his biggest prey: Josh Gibson.

On a Wednesday in February, Gibson had signed a new contract with Posey for $150 a month. But the very next day, Greenlee summoned Gibson to the Crawford Grill and offered him $250 a month to join the Crawfords. Without saying anything about the Grays deal, Gibson signed the second contract. When Posey found out what had happened, he was furious and tried to shame Gibson into honoring the first deal with several stern columns in the *Courier*. But Greenlee had the more binding contract, witnessed by a notary public, and soon Gibson was back in a Crawfords uniform.

Later that month, as Posey traveled to icy Philadelphia for another tense league meeting, Greenlee took his team on a tour of the sunny South. He bought a bus with six cylinders and a shiny grille, painted "Pittsburgh Crawfords Baseball Team from Greenlee Field" on the side, and amused his players by getting behind the wheel. First Greenlee treated the team to ten days of spring training in Hot Springs, Arkansas. Then he accompanied them on a six-week barnstorming tour of exhibition games against local sandlot and semipro teams. In Louisiana and Texas, he arranged for wealthy black families to invite the team to their homes and serve them fresh-cooked meals. And to build anticipation in Pittsburgh—and no doubt to annoy Cum Posey—Gus made sure that the trip got ample coverage in the *Courier*. He invited John L. Clark, his part-time publicist, to cover the trip and sent back a photo of his team in Hot Springs. "CRAWFORDS BASKING IN SPA'S SUNLIGHT," read the headline.

When the Craws returned to Pittsburgh in early April, more hoopla greeted them as they prepared to open their season at Greenlee Field. Greenlee hosted a black-tie welcome-home dance. Stepping up his courtship of the *Courier*, he invited Robert L. Vann to throw out the first pitch. By May, Posey finally realized that the Crawfords had gotten too big to ignore. Word leaked that he was in talks with Greenlee to bring the Craws into the East-West League, and the feuding owners agreed to an exhibition series. It took place over the long weekend of Memorial Day, and in a whirlwind of five games played in three different stadiums in two days, the Crawfords won the series, 3–2.

Finally, Cum Posey threw in the towel in his fight with Gus Greenlee. In June 1932, it was announced that the Crawfords would join the East-West League for the second half of the season. The Grays agreed to merge with the Detroit Wolves, to lessen the competition for crowds in Pittsburgh. But by then, it was too late to save Posey's brash venture. He had chosen the worst year of the Great Depression to launch a new league, and several of its teams were sinking fast. In July, the Philadelphia franchise known as Hilldale, the winner of the first Negro World Series in the 1920s, folded after selling only 295 tickets over two weekends. Suddenly, even the survival of the Grays was in question. Several players became so worried about getting paid that they demanded cash in advance, and they walked out in the middle of a Saturday doubleheader when Posey rebuffed them. By the end of the summer, the new East-West League had folded, and Cum Posey's dream of becoming the next Rube Foster was dead.

THAT FALL, GUS GREENLEE opened his weekly copy of the *Courier* to discover that Cum Posey was still finding ways to snub him. When the paper asked Posey to name the best black baseball players of 1932, he included only one Crawford in his "All-America Ball Club"—Chester Williams, as a benchwarming "utility" man. Missing from his starting lineup was not only Satchel Paige at pitcher but three former Grays players who would have been on virtually anyone else's list: Josh Gibson at catcher, Oscar Charleston at first base, and Judy Johnson at third. Meanwhile, in describing his picks, Posey praised one in particular: "Cool Papa" Bell, the longtime outfielder for the St. Louis Stars. Bell "could play centerfield and bat on anyone's club," Posey wrote.

So in typical fashion, Greenlee targeted Cool Papa Bell as his next conquest. Bell was playing in the Mexican winter league in early 1933 when he got a call from Greenlee inviting him to Pittsburgh. Although the clean-living teetotaler was wary of his host's gangster reputation, he was won over by Gus's generosity. Greenlee treated Bell to dinner at the Crawford Grill and showed him around Greenlee Field, wowing the Mississippi native who had grown up playing on dirt sandlots in the South. Laying on the flattery, Greenlee "told me that I had a chance to be part of the best team in the history of black baseball and that I was the key," Bell recalled. The Crawfords already had the best pitcher and the best hitter in black baseball, and when Greenlee signed Bell they gained the fastest base runner, too. (Among the many stories of Cool Papa's speed: Satchel Paige swore he once saw Bell turn off a hotel room light switch and get in bed before it went dark.)

Over the winter of 1933, Greenlee also moved to fill the vacuum created by the collapse of Posey's league. He called a meeting of owners from around the country in Indianapolis and proposed a resurrection of Rube Foster's Negro National League. To serve as chairman, Greenlee nominated himself. Unlike Posey, he offered no grandiose mission statements or racially charged talk about curbing the power of white booking agents. Instead, he appealed to the financial interest of the most strapped clubs, by stressing how much money they could make when Satchel Paige and Josh Gibson came to town or they got a cut of the gate at Greenlee Field.

At first, Posey appeared to go along with the new effort and joined the other club meeting in Indianapolis. But it was only a matter of months before he pulled the Homestead Grays out of the new league. In a sign of how rancorous relations had become between the two owners, Posey also waded into a bitter tit-for-tat over the circumstances of the withdrawal with Greenlee's publicist, John L. Clark, in the *Courier*.

In an open letter to the sports department, Posey insisted that he had quit the Negro National League because he owed it to his players. He complained that Greenlee was forcing teams to kick back revenues to the league and that the Grays could earn more by remaining independent. Clark fired back that Posey had been booted from the league for poaching rival players. He went on to mock the Grays owner for being afraid to compete with the Crawfords and for not having any "business enterprise other than baseball" to support his players. The war of words continued more than a month, titillating *Courier* readers with details of the nasty, closed-door league disputes.

Yet if Gus Greenlee was able to succeed as a baseball czar where Cum Posey had failed, it wasn't just because of his ownership of marquee players and his own ballpark. It was also due to another stroke of competitive one-upmanship and clever marketing. Just as Greenlee's new Negro National League was getting off the ground, white pro baseball announced its first All-Star Game. It was held at Chicago's Comiskey Park in early July 1933 and saw Babe Ruth swat a two-run homer to lead the American League to a 4–2 victory against the National League.

As it happened, Roy Sparrow, a black stringer for the evening *Pittsburgh Star-Telegraph*, had been floating the idea of a black all-star game for some time. Once the white contest was announced, Sparrow arranged to meet with Cum Posey and Bill Nunn of the *Courier* at the Loendi Club to brainstorm how to make a black version happen. The three men mused about holding the game at Yankee Stadium, and Posey agreed to reach out to "Bojangles" Robinson, the well-connected movie star, to see if he could make introductions.

But later that night, Nunn and Sparrow went to the Crawford Grill and mentioned the all-star game proposal to Gus Greenlee. Once Greenlee heard that Posey was involved, he countered with the idea of holding the game in Chicago and said he would enlist the help of "King" Cole, the owner of the Chicago American Giants of the Negro League. Together, the two owners booked Comiskey Park for later that summer, decided to call the game the "East-West Classic"—and cut out Cum Posey. To gin up fan interest, Nunn suggested that the *Courier* and the *Chicago Defender* poll readers to select the players—an innovation that it would take the white major leagues decades to copy. Greenlee also brought in Abe Saperstein, the owner of the Harlem Globetrotters, to handle publicity, offering him 5 percent of the gate.

Played on a raw, rainy September day in the Windy City, the first East-West Classic didn't exactly live up to that description. Twenty thousand fans showed up, but many were disappointed to find that the Crawfords' main attraction, Satchel Paige, wasn't there, having opted for a bigger payday elsewhere. Though Greenlee's other top players—Josh Gibson, Cool Papa Bell, Oscar Charleston, and Judy Johnson—were all in the Eastern lineup, they turned in a lackluster performance, managing only seven hits compared with fifteen for the Western squad, which won, 11–7. Still, the maiden "Classic" of 1933 made headlines in Negro papers across the country and marked the beginning of what would quickly turn into the biggest and most anticipated annual sporting event in black America. Over the next few years, it would grow to draw fifty thousand or more spectators every year and, under a profit-sharing agreement, throw off enough cash to keep dozens of black teams that lost money the rest of the time in business.

Looking back, virtually everyone who witnessed the Pittsburgh Crawfords of the mid-1930s agreed that Gus Greenlee had made good on his vow to Cool Papa Bell to assemble "the best team in the history of black baseball." The Crawfords boasted five of the Negro League players later to be named to the Hall of Fame—Paige, Gibson, Bell, Charleston, and Judy Johnson. Those future legends were surrounded by more than a half dozen other standouts, including pitchers Nate Hunter and Leroy Matlock and outfielders Jimmie Crutchfield and Ted Page, the former Black Yankee whom Greenlee lured to the Crawfords with a side job as a lookout man for his numbers operation.

At their best, Greenlee's Crawfords were unforgettably electric. At one point or another, they trounced every other Negro League team. They routinely made short work of white exhibition teams as well, dominating not only with pitching and power but with a blur of bunts, fakes, and steals. In one game against a white squad with pitcher Dizzy Dean on the mound, the Crawfords pounded the St. Louis Cardinals ace for eight runs on the way to an 11–1 victory. In another exhibition against a U.S. Marine Corps team, they ran up a 12–0 lead before taking pity on the Leathernecks. "This is really unpatriotic," Gibson said to Paige during a trip at the mound. "I agree," Paige nodded. "The Marines have to score at least one run." On the next play, Paige threw a lob over the plate and the batter hit a dribbler down the first base line. Gibson scooped up the ball and fired it past the first baseman into right field, where Ted Page made a wild throw to home, allowing the player to score. When the game was over, Gibson sidled up to the lucky Marine. "I had a feeling you were going to be a hero," he said.

Just as in 1932, however, the record books for 1933 failed to reflect the Crawfords' dominance due to disarray in the black baseball ranks. Paige recalled going 31–4 in games against other Negro League teams that year, with 16 shutouts. Greenlee claimed that Josh Gibson finished the season with 55 homers and 239 hits, for an astonishing .467 average. According to various accounts, Oscar Charleston and Cool Papa Bell also hit well over .300. But while Greenlee's new Negro National League started the season with seven teams, it ended with only three: Chicago, Nashville, and Pittsburgh, which was declared champion by default. After Posey's Grays pulled out, Baltimore followed, and teams from Columbus and Detroit went under.

In a defiant piece in the *Courier*, Greenlee spokesman John L. Clark charged that other teams had left his boss "holding the bag." Greenlee had been forced to make up a $1,100 deficit, and would thenceforth require that all teams wishing to join the league put down a cash deposit. Looking for more financial stability, Greenlee issued invitations during the off-season to other black racketeers who owned baseball teams on the side: his pal Alex Pompez, the owner of the New York Cubans, and Abe and Effie Manley, the husband-and-wife team behind the Newark Eagles.

Yet while his new league may not have been initially profitable, Greenlee was making plenty of money from his two most valuable assets: Satchel Paige and Josh Gibson. Once Paige arrived in 1931, Gus started booking as many extra exhibition games as possible, often forcing his players to sleep on the bus as they traveled from city to city. As Paige put it: "That fast ball of mine was popping against town druggists who were playing only on Sundays, and against major leaguers who were earning a few more bucks after the regular season was over." Wherever they played, Greenlee supplied posters guaranteeing that fans would see Gibson hit at least two home runs and Paige strike out the first nine men he faced—and the two routinely made good on the promise.

The duo were in such demand that Greenlee could pay them hundreds of dollars a month in addition to their regular salaries. He also stroked Paige's ego by giving him top billing on the posters. At first, Paige basked in the attention, and the extra income. "If it hadn't been for Gus, I never could have kept those offers to pitch straight," he recalled. "He was my agent, booking around when I didn't have to pitch for the Crawfords. He was a sharp—a real one. . . . He was so sharp that they must have a school for what he could do and he learned real good at that school."

Greenlee also tried to school Paige on how to manage his windfall—to no avail. "You can keep this up for ten years and save some dough and you'll be in great shape," Gus told him. But Satchel was having too much fun living high: eating and drinking at the finest establishments, buying fancy clothes and a collection of as many as fifteen shotguns. As usual, he would sum up his spendthrift ways in a colorful turn of phrase decades later: "You can't tell the guy who's got good gravy all over his front shirt that the gravy bowl is going to be empty some day."

Paige was also enjoying life as the prince of Pittsburgh. Whenever the Crawfords were at home, he had the run of the city, holding court at the Crawford Grill and drawing big crowds at the Centre Avenue YMCA, where he sparred with John Henry Lewis, a boxer whom Greenlee had signed and who was on his way to becoming the light heavy-weight champion. "The whole town was glad to see me," Satch recalled. "I'd walk down the streets in Pittsburgh and everybody tried to talk to me."

In 1934, Paige rewarded Greenlee and the fans of black Pittsburgh with the best season of his career. Against other Negro National League teams, he was 14–2 in regular games and 2–0 in exhibitions, with 144 strikeouts and an earned run average of 2.16. Outside the league, he won another 21 games without a single loss—raising his overall total to 35–2, with an ERA of 1.38. To Greenlee's delight, Paige saved his best performance of the season for a July 4th game against the Homestead Grays, after Cum Posey grudgingly agreed to start playing exhibition matches with the Crawfords again.

More than ten thousand fans crowded into Greenlee Field for the showdown—so many that hundreds had to stand in the bleacher aisles and along the infield perimeter. After walking Homestead's star slugger, Buck Leonard, in the first, Paige began striking out one Gray after another. He fanned the first batter in every inning and seventeen overall, matching his previous high. By the end of the game, the Grays had reached base only one more time, on an error, and gone hitless for the first time ever. Bewildered by the way Paige's fastball rose just as it crossed the plate, Leonard kept asking the umpire to inspect the ball for evidence of tampering. When the ump finally threw out one ball that appeared to be scuffed, Paige sneered. "You might as well throw 'em all out because they're all gonna jump like that," he shouted from the mound.

In the stands, Gus Greenlee gloated while Cum Posey fumed. Posey was smoking his favorite cigars—Toby stogies from Marsh & Co.—and the *Courier* reported that he "ate two boxes" of them by the time Paige's no-hitter was over. Meanwhile, one of Greenlee's assistants brought along a first-aid kit to use on his boss in case the Crawfords lost. But there was no need for it: the Crawfords beat the Grays, 4–0, and afterward Greenlee grinned from ear to ear as he posed for a picture with his pitching ace.

Greenlee was all smiles again two months later, when Paige helped make the second East-West Classic worthy of its name. This time, the early September sky over Chicago's Comiskey Park was clear, and some 25,000 fans showed up. The game was still scoreless in the sixth inning when the leadoff batter for the West hit a double. The East's manager motioned for Paige. Taking his usual slow walk from the bullpen, he stopped to throw his warm-up jacket into the dugout. "It's Paige," he heard a fan cry out. "Goodbye, ballgame." Climbing the mound, Paige glanced toward third base, brought his elbows to his chest, and waited several more seconds before unleashing a blazing fastball for strike one. Ten pitches later, he had retired the side with a strikeout and two forced outs. After that, he pitched three more flawless innings, striking out five more batters and giving the East the time it needed to finally score a run in the eighth. Another Crawford, Cool Papa Bell, produced the winning run by walking, stealing second, and dashing home on a blooper over second base.

By 1934, the crowd for "the Classic" included several thousand white fans and dozens of white reporters. Their reaction showed that Greenlee's all-star game was becoming more than a treasured rite for black Americans. By exposing whites to the best Negro players, and showcasing their thrilling defense and base running as well as pitching and hitting, it was advancing the case for integrating the major leagues. In the *Chicago Daily Times*, columnist Marvin McCarthy reflected the newfound respect in a piece headlined "Black Matty" that compared Satchel Paige to pitching legend Christy Mathewson. "To try to enumerate all the endless diamond miracles the East and West colored boys wrought would be a wasted effort, like wiping sweat off an old fish's brow," McCarthy wrote. "Trying to stretch hits on the outfielders was as crazy and self-destructive as a rooster crowing next door to a colored camp meeting. . . . But, of course, there were none to stretch off Black Matty (or Black Magic if you prefer)."

Back in Pittsburgh, Big Red showed his gratitude to his "Black Matty" with two very public displays of appreciation. As soon as Paige returned from the all-star game, Janet Howard told him that she wanted to set a wedding date, and he agreed to late October. Greenlee offered to hold the ceremony at the Crawford Grill, and Paige asked Bojangles Robinson, his longtime bachelor running buddy, to be best man. When the day came, so many people thronged the streets of the Hill District that Greenlee had to lock the doors. Then after the preacher pronounced Paige and Howard man and wife, Greenlee announced that he had another surprise for the groom. "Satchel won't be leaving us, don't worry about that," Gus told the crowd. "I have a new contract here for him." In front of everyone, Greenlee presented Satch with a new two-year deal, which he signed as Janet and Bojangles stood over his shoulder. "'Satch' Says 'I Will' Twice," cheered a *Courier* headline.

But as 1935 began, Paige was back at the Grill with his hand out for more cash. The cost of keeping his new wife in style had created "a powerful lightness in his pocket," he recalled, so he asked Greenlee to sweeten the new deal. This time, Greenlee refused. "Don't forget those games we got coming up," was all Gus said, in a cold voice. Furious, Paige went home, packed his suitcases and told Janet they were getting out of town. It wasn't long before an opportunity presented itself: an auto salesman from Bismarck, North Dakota, offered Satchel $400 a month and a new car to jump to his local semipro team for the rest of the 1934 season.

When Paige ignored an order to report to spring training in early 1935,

Greenlee began hurling hardballs of his own. He dealt Paige's new contract to a Jewish semipro team called the House of David and announced that Satch had been banned from the Negro National League for the year. Greenlee also spun the story to the black press, where interest in Paige was starting to take a backseat to the rise of Joe Louis. "Heroes come and go," Chester Washington sniffed in the *Courier*. "The champ of today can be the chump of tomorrow. . . . Satchel apparently made the mistake of regarding the contract as a 'scrap of paper' and now he must pay the price."

Fortunately for Greenlee, the Crawfords were so good by 1935 that they didn't need Satchel Paige. With Leroy Matlock stepping in as their ace and five starters batting over .300, the Craws won the first half of the season and ended up in a playoff with the second-half winners, the New York Cubans. After losing three of the first four games, Pittsburgh clawed back to even the series at three-all. The Cubans were leading the final game 7–5 when their ace, Louis Tiant Sr., gave up solo home runs to Josh Gibson and Oscar Charleston. With the game tied, Cool Papa Bell worked his base-running magic. He singled, stole second, and then raced home on an infield error, giving the Craws the game and the title. At the party thrown at the Crawford Grill, the normally unflappable Greenlee couldn't disguise his glee. "Gus was really happy," recalled Judy Johnson. "I think it gave him even more satisfaction to win the championship without Satchel."

By the next spring, Greenlee and Paige had patched up their differences again. Although lucrative, Paige had found his year in Bismarck stressful: one of his mostly white teammates had responded to his brashness with a muttered taunt of "dirty nigger," and in another game his outfielders refused to take the field behind him after he criticized their play. (Satch pitched nonetheless and struck out the side.) As the 1936 season began, the *Courier* reported in a breathless "Flash" headline that Paige was returning to Pittsburgh for a salary that was rumored to be the highest in the Negro National League. He helped the Crawfords finish in first place for the second half of the season, and to dominate a Denver tournament that took the place of a league playoff in 1937. But then the fraught relationship between Greenlee and Paige took its strangest turn yet when Satch joined the Crawfords for their Southern spring training tour in 1938.

When the Crawfords reached New Orleans, several mysterious, dark-skinned men dressed in ivory suits and Panama hats started showing up at their games. Greenlee suspected that they were from the Caribbean baseball leagues, where black players had been spending more and more time to supplement their meager earnings in America. "Haitian pirates, that's what they are," Greenlee fumed. At one point, he even tried to have a local court throw the scouts in jail for "conspiracy." But after several weeks, one of the men approached Paige and introduced himself as Dr. José Enrique Aybar, from the Dominican Republic. He explained that he was an envoy from a team called Cuidad Trujillo. He offered Paige $30,000 to spend the season in the Dominican Republic and bring eight players with him, with the money to be divided as Satchel saw fit. When Paige expressed skepticism, Aybar came back the next day with a statement showing that $30,000 had been deposited in a bank in the name of Satchel Paige.

It appeared that Rafael Trujillo, the Dominican Republic's military strongman, was looking to shore up his sagging popularity. Knowing how passionate his countrymen were about baseball, he had taken over the two best teams in Santo Domingo and created a new squad named in his honor: Los Dragones de Cuidad Trujillo. But the Dragons had started losing to provincial teams, and Trujillo had grown worried that their disappointing play might cost him the next election. So he dispatched Dr. Aybar—who was also the dean of the University of Santo Domingo and a member of the National Assembly—to America with a promotional flyer bearing Paige's picture so that he could hunt down the fabled pitcher and bring him back to rescue the Dragons.

When Greenlee learned that Paige had taken the money and run yet again—and was using Trujillo's cash to lure away other Crawfords—he was furious. But this time, he was in no position to fight back. Since his last showdown with Satch, Greenlee's financial fortunes had taken a precipitous turn for the worse. He had invested thousands of dollars in his boxing prospect, John Henry Lewis, who had won the light heavy-weight crown but was having trouble breaking into the heavyweight ranks. A newly elected Democratic mayor was putting the squeeze on gambling in Pittsburgh, and word was that Greenlee had lost a small fortune when one widely played number hit.

Adding to Gus's woes, Greenlee Field had become a perennial money-loser. Greenlee's partners had refused to pay for a roof for the stadium, leaving it vulnerable to rainouts and heat waves that kept fans away. His bootlegging friends, the Tito brothers, insisted on hiring white cronies to man the turnstiles and sell popcorn in the stands, offending blacks from the surrounding neighborhood. Attendance at Crawford games had dropped to less than 1,700 a game, hardly enough to cover Greenlee's $4,000 a month payroll and the other costs of operating a ballpark and taking the team on the road.

Paige soon pulled out of the Dominican Republic deal, after Trujillo's goons started following him around day and night and warning of dire consequences if he didn't keep winning. But when Paige approached Greenlee about returning to the Crawfords, Gus offered him only $450 a month, with a $15 fine for any game he missed. "I wouldn't throw ice cubes for that kind of money," Paige responded arrogantly, so Gus sold the rest of Satchel's two-year contract to Abe and Effie Manley of the Newark Eagles for $5,000. (The Manleys didn't have any better luck changing Paige's mercenary ways: he refused to move to Newark and spent the next few seasons playing in the Mexican League and jumping from exhibition to exhibition until he eventually settled down again—at least for a few years—with the Kansas City Monarchs.)

Meanwhile, Cum Posey sensed Greenlee's weakness, and he was fi-nally in a position to capitalize on it. After years of trying to bankroll the Homestead Grays on his own, Posey had brought in his own racketeer to help finance the club. His name was Rufus "Sonnyman" Jackson, a smooth-faced, ebony-dark numbers man who also owned the top night-club in Homestead. Posey named Jackson president of the Grays and cut a new deal to play their games in Forbes Field, throwing Greenlee Field further into the red. Then, in March 1937, Posey and Jackson traveled to New York City for an owners meeting that would shift the power balance of Pittsburgh baseball yet again.

"GRAYS GET GIBSON," exclaimed the headline in the *Courier* the following week. After three days of secret negotiations, Greenlee had agreed to trade Josh Gibson, his top slugger, and Judy Johnson, his all-star third baseman, to Cum Posey in exchange for two players and $2,500 in cash. In a further sign of Greenlee's financial predicament, he had dealt pitcher Harry "Tin Can" Kincannon to the New York Black Yankees "for an unannounced sum." The owners reelected Greenlee as president of the league, but now that looked like no more than a consolation prize. The real news was "the biggest player deal in the history of Negro baseball," as the *Courier* put it, one that would "make the Homestead ninery one of the most formidable members of the league."

That turned out to be an understatement. In Gibson and first baseman Buck Leonard, the Grays now had the most formidable slugging duo in the Negro game. With Gibson's arrival, Vic Harris, the Grays' manager and center fielder, and Ray Brown, a curveballer who was married to Posey's daughter Ethel, also came into their own. Starting in 1937, the Grays won eight of the next nine Negro National League pennants, as well as three of the first black "World Series" contests against a rival league that sprang up in 1942. In another shrewd move to ensure the team's financial survival, Posey and Jackson cut a deal to start playing half of their games in Washington, D.C., where they came to be known as the Washington Homestead Grays.

Back on top of the Negro baseball world, Cum Posey began to take a public stand on integrating the big leagues. In February 1938, he and Chester Washington interviewed the president of the Pittsburgh Pirates and got him to endorse the idea. "If the question of admitting colored players into organized ball ever becomes an issue, I would be heartily in favor of it!" said William Benswanger, singling out Josh Gibson and Satchel Paige as two players of "big league caliber." On the *Courier* sports page, meanwhile, Wendell Smith, the paper's newest sports columnist,

THE RISE AND FALL OF "BIG RED"   121

took up the integration cause. "If Pittsburgh Pirate officials weren't afraid, they'd sign Ray Brown, Buck Leonard and Josh Gibson and stop worrying about whether their team is going to cop the N.L. pennant or not," Smith wrote in October 1938.

The next month, bulldozers rolled onto the corner of Bedford Avenue and Junilla Street and began tearing down the house that Gus Greenlee built. In its latest New Deal experiment, the FDR administration was awarding millions of dollars to cities across America to erect housing developments for the poor, and Pittsburgh had decided to locate its first one in the area surrounding Greenlee Field. The city's Housing Authority offered Greenlee $38,000 for the land and threatened to seize it if he didn't take the deal. Greenlee never commented on the matter, but his spokesman John L. Clark didn't hide his bitterness in a story called "The Rise and Fall of Greenlee Field." Greenlee had tried everything to save the park, Clark wrote—issuing stock, selling season tickets—but nothing worked. "Greenlee Field joins the list of banks, industries and other enterprises which should not be again attempted in this city for 100 years," Clark concluded glumly. "It is safe to say that Pittsburgh is no place to attempt big things for Negroes."

A year later, Gus Greenlee sold the Crawfords to a new owner in Toledo and resigned from the Negro National League. He suffered another blow when his prize boxer, John Henry Lewis, finally got a shot at Joe Louis and went down in the first round, ending his career. But his mouthpiece's moroseness notwithstanding, Gus Greenlee had achieved much by attempting big things in Pittsburgh. He had made heroes of Satchel Paige and Josh Gibson. He had reorganized black baseball, revolutionized its marketing, and created the wildly popular "East-West Classic." And he had gotten the worst but also the best out of Cum Posey, a debt that Posey acknowledged once Greenlee left the league. Over the next decade, Greenlee's health would steadily decline, but his ambition never would, and before long he would be back, joining Wendell Smith as a key player in the events that changed baseball forever in another ballpark—Ebbets Field, in Brooklyn.

When they finally met and became instant soul mates,
one of the first things Billy Strayhorn and Lena Horne talked
about was their mutual ties to Pittsburgh.

5

BILLY AND LENA

IN THE FALL OF 1935, a young *Courier* reporter named Ralph Koger walked into the newsroom carrying an armful of posters. A wiry go-getter whose nickname was "Projoe," Koger had started working for the paper as a student at Westinghouse High School. In addition to running track, debating, and editing the yearbook, he filed stories to the *Courier* on events such as the meetings of the local NAACP youth group. Now, just two years after graduating, Koger had taken a second job as publicist for a new theatrical production called *Fantastic Rhythm*. According to the posters, which Koger posted around the *Courier* and in stores up and down the Hill, it would be a "Musical Comedy Revue" in the style of *Shuffle Along*, Broadway's first all-black extravaganza. The show would feature "50 Beautiful Shapely Girls," an "All-Star Cast" with the city's fleetest tap dancer and one of its loveliest cabaret singers, and the popular Moonlight Harbor Band. For the show's two-night run at Westinghouse High, Koger arranged to sell tickets at the *Courier*, Ramsey's Barber Shop, and Lincoln Drug

Store—at prices of 26 cents for adults, 16 cents for children, and 47 cents for reserved seats.

More remarkable yet, the composer and lyricist of *Fantastic Rhythm* was even younger than Koger. Still months away from his twentieth birthday, Billy Strayhorn had only graduated from Westinghouse High School himself the year before, in the class of 1934. As reserved as Koger was outgoing, Strayhorn stood only a few inches over five feet, wore owlish wire-rimmed glasses, and talked in a soft voice that sometimes barely rose above a whisper. But in his four years at Westinghouse, Strayhorn had emerged as the star of the school's renowned Music Department, a whiz not only at playing the piano but composing original music and arranging scores as well.

For an annual senior class talent contest called "Stunt Week," Strayhorn had written a collection of songs called "Musical Divorces." It was so successful that the next year's class invited him back to compose more numbers. This time Strayhorn outdid himself, creating a twenty-minute skit featuring twenty students and a live band that he called *Fantastic Rhythm*. The conductor of the Moonlight Harbor Orchestra, a debonair operator known as "Boggy" Fowler, saw the revue and was so impressed that he offered to help turn it into a full-scale production, with professional singers, dancers, and costumes. Once the cast of fifty was chosen, Strayhorn spent four months rehearsing them in his family's cramped four-room wooden house in a back alley of Homewood, bringing the performers into the house in shifts because the space was so tight.

On the second day of November, a sellout crowd filled Westinghouse High's 1,200-seat auditorium for the premiere. Although the plot wasn't much to speak of—a flimsy story about a group of newspaper reporters that served mostly to link song-and-dance numbers—the tunes sparkled with musical sophistication and the lyrics with humorous winks at life in Smoketown. The opening number, "We Are the Reporters," was a jaunty send-up of office politics at the *Courier*. A blues number called "Let Nature Take Its Course" spoofed the loose sexual morality of Wiley Avenue. Two love songs, "Something to Live For" and "My Little Brown Book," were as polished as the ballads heard on the dance floors of the Savoy Ballroom and the Pythian Temple on the Hill. In the finale, the entire cast tap-danced to the show's title song, a homage to George Gershwin that also suggested the influence of Fletcher Henderson.

Despite a torrential rainstorm, another sellout crowd showed up the following night. The show received a rave review in the *Courier* and generated such enthusiastic word of mouth that *Fantastic Rhythm* continued to be staged periodically in schools and theaters across western Pennsylvania over the next two years. As the curtain fell on the first two performances, Strayhorn stepped out shyly from the orchestra, where he accompanied Fowler's band on the piano, to acknowledge the raucous applause for the biggest homegrown theatrical sensation black Pittsburgh had seen in years.

In his youth, his mother called Billy Strayhorn her "miracle baby" because he came so close to death as a newborn. Lillian Young was a dignified, studious only child who grew up in the small town of Mars Hill, North Carolina, and attended a Baptist school for women in Raleigh. At eighteen she met James Strayhorn, the twenty-year-old son of a well-to-do couple in nearby Hillsborough. As moody and restless as Lillian was poised, James had dropped out of school after the eighth grade and begun working for a living. Once they were married, he took Lillian away to Dayton, Ohio, the home of the Wright brothers, where James hoped to get a job in the electricity business.

Over the next three years, Lillian gave birth to a son named James Jr. but lost two other children. So when a fourth child was born with rickets, she superstitiously identified him only as "Baby Boy Strayhorn" on his birth certificate. For months afterward, Lillian massaged the child every night with greasy dishwater to strengthen his crooked limbs. When he was a year old, the family moved again. James had lost his job as a wirepuller and was working as a janitor, and in frustration he took Lillian and their two sons to live with his sister in New Jersey. Four years later, they came west again to the Pittsburgh area, moving from town to town along the Monongahela River as James struggled to hold a steady job. Finally, in

1926, the Strayhorns settled in Homewood, the mixed neighborhood east of the Hill District, in a flimsy wooden house in the alley known as Tiago Street Rear. By now, Baby Boy Strayhorn had a name: his mother called him Bill and to everyone else he was known as Billy.

Having failed at other work, James Strayhorn was laboring as a hod carrier, hauling heavy metal plates covered with plaster to bricklayers on construction sites. He became a nasty drunk, and he was particularly cruel toward his small, introspective second son. When Billy started wearing glasses, his father mocked him, stepping on the spectacles when Billy put them down from reading. Lillian tried to shield her son from his father's tirades and beatings, but there was only so much she could do. So when Billy was eight, she started sending him over the summer months and during school holidays to stay with her husband's parents in North Carolina.

A descendant of whiskey distillers who had flourished after the Civil War, Jobe Strayhorn lived with his wife, Lilly, in a large Victorian house in the black section of Hillsborough. They were wealthy enough to own a Victrola, and Lilly delighted in playing recordings for her grandson when he visited. Her most prized possession was a polished upright piano that sat in the parlor. A devout Baptist who played the piano at her church, Lilly passed the evenings filling the parlor with religious music as Billy listened and watched. Eventually he was able to sit down at the keyboard and imitate Lilly's fingerings to play entire songs by himself. The first song he mastered was "When the Roll Is Called Up Yonder," one of his mother's favorites.

At age eleven, Billy returned from North Carolina to Pittsburgh with a grand plan: he intended to buy his own piano. To save up for it, he took a job delivering newspapers. One of his routes took him to Shadyside, the predominantly Jewish neighborhood west of Homewood, where he dropped off papers at a pharmacy called the Pennfield Drug Store. Seeing how familiar Billy was with addresses in the neighborhood, the druggist began tipping him to make deliveries. Billy proved so adept at that task that the owner gave him clerical chores and let him fill in behind the soda fountain. Before long, Billy had squirreled away enough money to purchase an old player piano that no one else wanted because its roll was broken. He installed the bulky upright in a corner of the Strayhorn shanty on Tioga Street Rear and thrilled his mother by hammering out the spirited chords of "Brighten the Corner Where You Are."

With the cash Billy earned on his paper route and working at Pennfield Drug Store, he went to Volkwein's Music Store, Pittsburgh's largest, to buy sheet music and to take piano lessons. In his authoritative biography of Strayhorn, cultural critic David Hajdu would identify his first piano instructor briefly as "Charlotte Catlin, a black teacher associated with Volkwein's." But Charlotte Enty Catlin was no ordinary music store teacher. Of the many fine black pianists in Pittsburgh, she was among the most accomplished and most active. Known for the distinctive way she wore her hair—parted in the middle, with large circular braids covering her ears—Catlin was also descended from two of the oldest and most distinguished Negro families in the region.

Charlotte's father, a contractor, had the given name of "Clever"—perhaps for the energy and intelligence he exuded at birth—and later became known as "Frank." His American lineage traced back to Tobias Enty, a native of the Bahamas who arrived by boat to Philadelphia in 1783. Tobias Enty I married twice, the second time to a woman identified by family historians as "dark-skinned," indicating that she was either black or mulatto. He fought in the War of 1812 and was rewarded with a plot of land in Schuyler County, north of Philadelphia. One of his sons, Peter Enty, set off to make his fortune as an engineer and miner in the coal and ore-rich hills of Western Pennsylvania and had sixteen children of his own, one of whom was Charlotte's grandfather, Tobias Enty II.

Charlotte's mother's family story also dated back the 1780s. Born Mary Jane Little, she was said to be descended from a white slave owner from Virginia named William Little who had inherited land from George Washington's brother. One of William's slave offspring, James Edward Little, either escaped or was freed and made his way to the Georgetown area of Washington, D.C., by the mid-1850s. James Edward fought in a colored unit of the Union Army during the Civil War and moved to Pittsburgh after his discharge. A hard-drinking brawler of a stevedore in the postwar years, he eventually became a minister, married a widow from Virginia, and had four children with her, one of whom was Mary Jane. The family moved onto Tioga Street in Homewood—just steps from the back alley where Billy Strayhorn's family settled—and Reverend Little helped found the Homewood AME Zion Church and arrange for the construction of its sanctuary on the corner of Tioga and Dunfermline Streets.

Along with industry and faith, the Little family was known for its musical prowess. Charlotte's uncle, George Little, served as organist for the Homewood AME Zion Church, and later gave the first live musical performance on KDKA, America's oldest broadcast radio station, born out of George Westinghouse's patents for transmitters and receivers. By the age of twelve, Charlotte's mother was playing the organ at the Bethel AME Church, the oldest in the Hill District. By her early twenties, Charlotte herself was beginning a career as a soloist and accompanist in black churches across the city, at the Carnegie Recital Hall and other prestigious concert venues, and in the homes of white aristocrats from Pointe Breeze to Allegheny City on the North Side.

The man Charlotte married, Charles Catlin, had never finished high school but had a secure and well-paying job for a black man of his time, as a custodian for the city post office. Charlotte herself earned a BS in Music from Carnegie Tech, and went on to take postgraduate instruction on the pipe organ. In her early twenties, she met with seven other local graduates at the Centre Avenue YMCA on the Hill and founded the Pittsburgh chapter of the black sorority, Alpha Kappa Alpha. Catlin became a regular at the Loendi Club and a close friend and bridge partner of the grande dames of the *Courier*—Jesse Vann, Daisy Lampkin, and Julia Bumry Jones. By the time Billy Strayhorn was taking lessons from her, she had moved with her husband and parents to a home on Monticello Street, a block away from the Vanns. Billy would continue to study with Charlotte until he was nineteen. During that time, she was in a position to expose him not only to an ever-widening musical repertoire but also to the lifestyle of Pittsburgh's "blue vein society," as the well-to-do and mostly light-skinned residents of enclaves such as the Upper Hill and Homewood were sometimes called.

By studying with Charlotte Catlin, Strayhorn also became connected to a musical tradition that stretched back for a century in black Pittsburgh and was unique for its blend of classical, religious, and jazz influences. Like the Catlin and Little families, many of the city's earliest Negro settlers had been freed or former house slaves who came from northern and eastern regions of the Old South where there was a long tradition of blacks learning to read sheet music and play classical instruments. By the turn of the century, Pittsburgh boasted two Negro classical orchestras. At the city's many black churches, choir members banded together in groups of "jubilee singers" that performed for black and white audiences alike. One of the most successful of those groups was formed by a talented young migrant from North Carolina, Mary Cardwell Dawson, who later went on to found America's first Negro opera company in Homewood.

Of all the classic instruments, none was more revered by the early migrants than the piano. Every year, the social calendar of the "Old Pittsburgher" elite was full of piano recitals at the Loendi Club and the many Baptist and AME churches around town. Then, shortly after World War I, a man arrived on a steamboat from New Orleans and began to teach Pittsburgh musicians how to blend classical music with ragtime jazz. A slender, balding gentleman who drank his gin from a water glass, Fate Marable would install himself for the winter at the nightclubs of the Hill and tutor anyone willing to accept his methods. Those included learning to read music and practicing Bach and Beethoven as well as Jelly Roll Morton. (Among Marable's disciples was Louis Armstrong, who played in his riverboat band as a teenager. However, it was said that Marable initially turned Armstrong away until he learned to read sheet music.)

As the Great Migration gathered force, pianos became status symbols for new arrivals as well. In Duquesne, a steel town south of Pittsburgh, a coal dock foreman named James Hines bought a parlor organ for his wife. She taught their three-year-old son, Earl, to play a few notes, and he caught on so quickly that they traded in the organ for a piano so that he could take lessons. When Earl mastered everything a kindly Negro lady from the town of McKeesport had to teach him, his father arranged for him to take lessons from a German immigrant named Von Holz, a task-master who demanded that Earl learn to read music and practice Czerny exercises and Chopin etudes.

When Earl reached high school age, his father was determined to give him the best musical education available, so he set his sights on a new school that was the talk of Pittsburgh. Opened in 1916, Schenley High School had cost a million and a half dollars to build, more than any public secondary school in America up to that point. It was located in Oakland, east of the Hill, on a large plot of land donated by Mary Schenley, the heir to a Pittsburgh real estate fortune. Designed in the shape of a triangle by one of the city's top architects, Edward Stotz, the school's Indiana lime-stone facade stood four stories tall and spanned over 150 yards. It had 180 rooms, including 40 classrooms, 11 science labs, 2 gyms, a 1,600-seat auditorium, and 2 music rooms.

Schenley High admitted a small number of black students every year, roughly a tenth of every grade. James Hines had a sister-in-law who lived in East Liberty, so he sent Earl to live with her so that he could attend Schenley. For the next two years Earl studied classical music in school, while his Aunt Sadie's friends introduced him to jazz. One of her admir-ers was Lois Deppe, Pittsburgh's best-known crooner. Hearing that Earl could play the piano, Deppe handed him the sheet music to a new Irving Berlin tune, "I'll See You in C-U-B-A." When Earl played the song flaw-lessly by sight, an astonished Deppe asked Sadie's permission to let the youngster spend the summer playing with his band at the Leader House, Gus Greenlee's speakeasy on the Hill.

For Earl, the summer at the Leader House was an education in more ways than one. He learned to hustle pool, to smoke cigars, and to keep company with Wylie Avenue streetwalkers. But he also continued to seek knowledge from older musicians, spending much of his $12-a-week sal-ary on gin, beer, and Camel cigarettes that he traded for lessons. One pianist taught Earl the slide piano trick of stretching the left hand to play "tenths," or chords spanning two octaves, with a thumb and pinkie finger. Another showed him how to play melodies in between, using his middle fingers. Soon Earl was playing tenths, tremolos, and melodies all at once, creating a thunderous sound on his upright piano that carried over Deppe's megaphone and the other instruments in the band. He called it his "trumpet style."

When Earl returned to Schenley High the next fall, he could outplay any pianist in the school. Concluding that he was "a kind of genius" who had little more to learn from them, Earl recalled, his instructors blessed his decision to leave school to play full-time with Deppe. Over the next few years, the Deppe band toured across Pennsylvania and Ohio and performed for Pittsburgh's KDKA radio station, marking another of the first occasions that Negro musicians were heard live over the airwaves.

Eventually Hines and Deppe parted ways, and another friend of Aunt Sadie's, pianist Eubie Blake, encouraged Earl to leave Pittsburgh. "If I catch you here again I'm going to take this cane and wrap it around your head," Blake said. So when Harry Collins, a club owner on the Hill, announced that he was opening a new nightspot in Chicago, Sadie encouraged Earl to follow him. "If you run into trouble," she said, "you can always wire home, and I'll see you get money to come on back."

A decade later, Earl Hines did come back—as a national star. In 1932, he was booked for an entire week at the Stanley Theatre, the largest concert hall in Pittsburgh. By then Hines had spent four years as the headliner at the Grand Terrace Café, the top "black and tan club" in Chicago, owned by Al Capone and his brother Ralph. He had also forged a musical partnership with Louis Armstrong, who had traveled north from New Orleans to become the toast of Chicago. They had met playing pool at a musicians' union hall, and Armstrong had invited Hines to record with his Hot Five band. The result was a string of sides for the Okeh label— "Weather Bird," "West End Blues," "Tight Like This," "Two Deuces," "Beau Koo Jack," and "Muggles"—that were instantly hailed as among the best jazz performances yet to be captured on records.

In the years after Earl Hines left Pittsburgh, two other exceptional prodigies emerged from its competitive world of young black pianists. At the age of six, a bubbly, dark-skinned girl named Mary Elfrieda Scruggs arrived from Georgia with her older sister Mamie and their mother, Virginia Riser, who had left the girls' father, a drifter named Joseph Scruggs. Mary Lou, as she was called, had learned her way around a keyboard by the age of four, sitting on the lap of her mother, known as Ginny, as she played a reed organ in their shotgun shack. When the family moved to Pittsburgh, they settled in the East Liberty neighborhood and Ginny married a professional hustler named Fletcher Burley. Burley started taking Mary Lou to gambling dens and pool halls, where she would play the upright in the corner for tips that the two split between them. She became known as "the piano girl of East Liberty" and was in such demand that she could charge a dollar an hour to perform at Saturday hops and at the rent parties, or "chitlin' struts," that neighbors threw to collect bill-paying money.

In the early 1920s, another Pittsburgh high school—Westinghouse—became the first in the city, and perhaps in the country, to cost more than $2 million. After issuing a $3 million bond offering to upgrade Pittsburgh's school system, city officials opted to spend two thirds of it turning the Homewood school into an early version of a magnet academy that could accommodate talented students from across the city. The expansion included erecting a new limestone edifice that spanned a full city block, constructing a 1,200-seat auditorium and flanking the school with an athletic field big enough to host track meets and football games. Like Schenley, Westinghouse also admitted Negro students from its earliest days, and by the end of the decade they included honors students, star athletes, and participants in dozens of after-school clubs.

In ninth grade, Mary Lou Scruggs transferred from her school in East Liberty to Westinghouse. She caught the attention of teachers who took her to hear opera and concert orchestras, to play for University of Pittsburgh faculty, and to perform at the homes of the Mellon family, for whom two of her aunts worked as maids. Mary Lou left Westinghouse in her sophomore year, however, to help support her family. She spent a summer touring with a vaudeville act sponsored by the Theatre Owners Bookers

Association, known by its initials TOBA and jokingly referred to as "Tough on Black Asses." When Fletcher Burley fell ill, Mary Lou went on the road and joined a band called "John Williams and the Syncopators." At age seventeen, she married the bandleader and took the name by which she would be known from then on: Mary Lou Williams.

A decade later, another self-taught piano phenomenon began commuting from his home in East Liberty to Westinghouse High in Homewood. Erroll Garner was the baby of a middle-class, music-loving family that worshipped at the St. James AME Church on Euclid Avenue, where both his parents sang in the choir. The Garners had an upright piano and a Victrola in the parlor of their brick row house, and by age three Erroll could put both hands to the keyboard and reproduce tunes he heard on the record player. When his older sisters started studying piano with a teacher named Madge Bowman—one of the most respected in the city, along with Charlotte Catlin and Mary Cardwell Dawson—Erroll would watch them and then re-create everything he had heard as soon as Miss Bowman left. Eventually he took a few lessons from her but stopped because he could play so well by ear that he had no patience for learning how to read music.

When Erroll arrived at Westinghouse High, teachers didn't quite know what to make of him. He had no mind for academic subjects, and scored so poorly on intelligence tests that he was placed in a remedial reading, writing, and math classes. But he would happily spend hours in the music room, playing the piano from memory and mastering the tuba by ear. He liked to watch the school orchestra rehearse, and one day, as they were preparing for the annual year-end concert, the pianist couldn't get the hang of a difficult passage. The other students urged the faculty adviser, Carl McVicker, to let Garner have a try, and he improvised a new passage that was so much better than the original that the band adopted it and invited him to share the piano chair.

Of all the talented musicians who attended Westinghouse High in that era, however, Billy Strayhorn stood out. McVicker, the head of the music department, had arrived from a small high school in Erie, Pennsylvania, in 1927. A tall, imposing man with a wavy mane of hair, he began teaching jazz as well as traditional music. He organized a swing band in addition to the school orchestra, horrifying some older teachers. McVicker would recall that at first Strayhorn refused to join the swing band, envisioning himself only as a classical pianist. But under McVicker's tutelage, Billy soon became fascinated with the art of writing and arranging music and composing for jazz instruments.

The department's other stalwart was Jane Patton Alexander, a stern taskmistress who taught music theory. To drill the principles of harmony into his head, Strayhorn recalled, Miss Alexander made him learn chord progressions over all twelve keys. Billy said that he "hated" the exercise but that it proved "invaluable" once he started to write his own music. Eventually he became so expert at music theory that Miss Alexander would ask Billy to fill in for her whenever she was called away from her classroom.

By his senior year, Billy was first pianist for the Westinghouse school orchestra. For its spring recital, he led the orchestra in Edvard Grieg's demanding Piano Concerto in A Minor. He was also starting to write his own original music. For his graduation ceremony in the winter of 1934, he wrote and performed an entire "Concerto for Piano and Percussion." Outside of school, he was also getting his first taste of appearing in front of large public audiences as the pianist for the Orchestra Club, a twenty-five-piece ensemble that Mr. McVicker selected from among his best students to play at hotel banquets and other social functions around Pittsburgh.

After graduating from Westinghouse, Billy spent much of the next two years writing and producing *Fantastic Rhythm*, his impressive professional debut as a theatrical songwriter and lyricist. But his first love remained classical music. When he was nineteen, the National Association of Negro Musicians held its annual convention in Pittsburgh. The three-day gathering included a morning devoted to performances by young artists, and Strayhorn chose to play a solo piano piece he had rehearsed with Charlotte Catlin. Called "Lotus Land," it was an impressionist tone poem by a minor British composer named Cyril Scott who was sometimes referred to as "the English Debussy." Continuing to work at Pennfield Drug Store, serving soda and ice cream behind the counter and doing other odd jobs, Strayhorn saved up enough money to enroll in a small private conservatory called the Pittsburgh Music Institute so he could study with its highly regarded director, Charles N. Boyd. But when Boyd died of a heart attack in his second term, Billy dropped out.

In his early twenties now, Billy seemed resigned to the life of a soda jerk by day and a musician for hire by night. He became friendly with two white musicians, a clarinetist and a drummer, and they formed a trio called the Mad Hatters that played Benny Goodman tunes in dance halls around town. He earned extra pocket money writing arrangements for white swing orchestras. But privately, Billy hadn't given up his ambition to compose his own songs.

In his spare time, Billy began to work on a solo piano piece he called "Life Is Lonely" that combined the Debussy air of "Lotus Land" with blue note inflections. When he later wrote and recorded it under another title, "Lush Life," it would be seen as a bitter ode to heartbreak, born of Billy's despair of ever finding happiness as a gay man. What would be less noticed was the song's evocation of another longing Billy had observed growing up in Pittsburgh: the drive for worldly success that romantic urges can undermine ("Romance is mush, stifling those who strive . . .").

At the time, Billy had no intention of recording the song. He viewed it as a little something he played for his friends, or when performing in quiet moments in nightspots around the city. One of those places was a small club tucked in the corner of a big Victorian house on Apple Street, not far from the Strayhorn home in Homewood. By day, the house was taken over by Mary Cardwell Dawson, the jubilee singer who ran a music school that she would later expand into the National Negro Opera Company. But by night, it was known as "the Mystery Mansion," a club that was rented out for special occasions and also served as a quiet destination for patrons who weren't ready to go home after the bars on Wylie Avenue closed, the sort of place where a young pianist could soothe the melancholy of lonely hearts under the influence of "too many through the day twelve o'clock tales."

Like everyone who worked there, Billy knew that the owner of the

Mystery House was Woogie Harris, the top man in Gus Greenlee's gambling empire. What he didn't know yet was how Gus Greenlee would help change his life, or that he would one day become best friends with another musical prodigy who had just moved to the Hill to live with her father, also a key lieutenant in Big Red's numbers operation.

TEDDY HORNE WAS AN unlikely racketeer. He had moved to Pittsburgh from New York City, where his parents belonged to the light-skinned black upper crust. His father, Edwin Horn, was a Native American mulatto— half-British, half-Blackfoot—who had been raised in Indiana and become a successful journalist and storeowner in Tennessee. His mother, Cora Calhoun, was the eldest daughter of a former butler to the white Southern Calhoun dynasty who after the Civil War started his own businesses in Georgia and Alabama. After meeting in Birmingham, Edwin and Cora had come north to escape Jim Crow. They added an "e" to the end of their name for extra refinement, and moved to the then comfortably middle-class Bedford-Stuyvesant neighborhood of Brooklyn. Through connections with Tammany Hall, Edwin got work as a fire inspector, and Cora became a full-time volunteer for the NAACP, the Urban League, and other worthy causes.

The Hornes of Brooklyn had four sons. The eldest, Erroll, enlisted with the Buffalo Soldiers in World War I and died of influenza at the front. The third, Frank, was an eye doctor and part-time poet who got a job in FDR's second administration. The youngest, Burke, served as an Army sergeant during World War II and was briefly engaged to the first Negro woman accepted into the Navy's female volunteer WAVES program.

Of the four, the second, Edwin Jr., known as "Teddy," was the most handsome—and the most rebellious. Before the age of nine, he had talked his way into a job as a page at the Astor Hotel in Manhattan. As a teen, he gambled with Dutch Schultz's henchmen in Harlem and was rumored to have made money on the Black Sox fix. To his parents' dismay, he skipped college and instead married Edna Scrotton, another fair-skinned, middle-class Brooklynite who had her own unconventional dreams of becoming an actress. But the impetuous union lasted only a few years, just long enough for Edna to give birth to a baby girl, an event her father missed for a high-stakes card game.

The baby was named Lena, after Cora's beautiful younger sister. Like her great-aunt, she had soft ringlets, high cheekbones, and bright, wide-set eyes. But with divorced and undependable parents, she was fated to endure a lonely, itinerant childhood. First she was left in the care of her strict grandmother and kindly grandfather in Brooklyn. Then her mother snatched Lena away and took her on the road while Edna tried to make a living on the stage. When that became impossible, Lena was sent to live with her uncle Frank, at the time a dean at a Negro academy in the South.

Throughout these early years, Lena's father remained a dashing but mysterious figure. Teddy Horne had moved west, she knew, but for years she wouldn't see him. Then he would suddenly pop up out of nowhere- — to attend a prizefight in New York, or on a road trip in a gleaming Pierce-Arrow convertible. Mostly, Lena knew her father by the expensive gifts he sent her at Christmastime: a winter fur coat, or a giant "Mama" doll from the Effanbee company.

In fact, Teddy Horne had fled to Seattle, where he married a second wife named Irene. From there they moved to Chicago, then to Detroit, before eventually settling in Pittsburgh. To some, it might have seemed an oddly provincial choice given everything Teddy had going for him: his elite pedigree, his New York worldliness, his easy charm and the angular good looks of a darker-skinned Fredric March. But Teddy found he could make good money in Smoketown. He took over the Belmont Hotel in the Hill District and turned its back room into a gambling den he called "the Bucket of Blood." Just as appealing was the seamless way his two worlds intersected in Pittsburgh. In older cities such as New York, Boston, and Washington, the Negro aristocracy looked down on mobsters, as the Hornes of Brooklyn had on Teddy's Harlem friends. But in Pittsburgh, all worlds met on Wylie Avenue. The racketeers were part of the elite. Men like Teddy Horne and Woogie Harris could run numbers out of the

Belmont Hotel and the Crystal Barber Shop by day, then go around the corner and dine at the Loendi Club at night.

By the time Lena was sixteen, her grandparents had passed away and she was living in the Bronx with her mother and a new stepfather, a hot-tempered white Cuban called Mike, for Miguel. They had no money but a big dream for their daughter: to turn her into a nightclub star. Edna took Lena to audition at the Cotton Club, where she landed a job in the cho-rus line. Before long, Lena had dropped out of school so she could sleep during the day and work until four in the morning, while her mother sat vigil in the dressing room. One day, Lena was pulled out of the chorus to perform duets with a male singer. When her untrained voice became hoarse by the third show, her mother demanded that she start taking sing-ing lessons.

While Lena was performing in Harlem, Teddy Horne showed up one night and watched her from a stage side seat. It was a double surprise, since Negroes were rarely allowed in the audience at the Cotton Club. Lena would often encounter "friends" of her father's in Harlem who said they had been told to look after her, but now she saw how powerful those connections were. During his brief stay, Teddy also treated her to another surprise—without her mother's knowledge. He took her to New Jersey, to a town called Pompton Plains, where the boxer Joe Louis was training. Lena watched Joe work out and met a friend of her father's from Pitts-burgh, a sportswriter named Ches Washington who was covering Louis for *The Pittsburgh Courier*.

After Lena got a bit part on Broadway, Edna and Mike decided she was destined for bigger things. Though she was under contract to the Cotton Club, they arranged for a singing tryout with the bandleader Noble Sissle, then skipped town with Lena when she got the job. Lena hardly had the voice of the top female band singers of the day: Duke Ellington's Ivie An-derson, Chick Webb's Ella Fitzgerald, or Count Basie's Billie Holiday. But she had the elegant diction and near-Caucasian looks that Sissle craved for his slow-tempo repertoire. Soon Lena was touring the country playing as many garden parties as roadhouses. But when the Sissle band reached

Boston, an incident occurred that proved the final straw in Lena's contentious relationship with her mother and stepfather.

The Ritz-Carlton Hotel had booked the Noble Sissle Society Orchestra to perform on its roof, the first Negro band ever to be hired for that venue. But the hotel insisted the band come in through the back door. With Cuban machismo, Mike declared that this was no way to treat a young lady like Lena. He demanded that Sissle make a stink. Sissle shrugged. There was nothing he could do, he explained. It was how it was for Negroes in America. Mike flew into a rage, cursing the bandleader in Spanish. Lena was livid—and humiliated. Life on the road with Mike and Edna had come to feel like prison.

Shortly afterward, Teddy Horne surfaced again with what seemed like a way out. He came to see Lena perform with the Sissle orchestra in Cleveland, and brought along a young friend from Pittsburgh. The man's name was Louis Jones, and he was a minister's son who had a college degree and worked as a clerk in the Pittsburgh coroner's office. Lena was immediately struck by his good looks and gentlemanly manner, so unlike the coarseness she saw in the entertainment world. She grew to like Jones even more during a visit to Pittsburgh a few months later, in November 1936, and by the end of the year she had resolved to quit show business and move to Pittsburgh to be his wife.

Mike was furious and Edna took ill, but Lena had made up her mind. On the second day of 1937, she returned to Pittsburgh and moved into the Belmont Hotel. Lena was still only nineteen, and Teddy refused to let her go near the ballroom, but she could hear the Lindy-hopping from her room upstairs. Within two weeks she and Jones had applied for a wedding license, and when it came through five days later they decided to get married on the spot.

Lena wore a black dress and Jones slipped a diamond-studded wedding band on her finger as the groom's father pronounced them man and wife in the living room of his home in Sugartop. Teddy and Irene looked on along with their sportswriter friend, Ches Washington. Several days later, the *Courier* ran a story confirming that "the prettiest girl in Harlem" was giving up her singing career for her man. "It's love and a home," Lena was quoted as saying, underneath a photo of her and Jones sitting down to a bacon breakfast in their new "apartment," two rooms in his brother's house.

The picture certainly captured Jones's vision of the marriage. He expected his new bride to become a housewife, but the role didn't fit Lena easily. She actually knew nothing about cooking bacon, or cooking anything else for that matter. She had to learn to make the pork chops and biscuits her husband expected for dinner. She could tell Jones hated his job at the coroner's office, believing it was beneath him, but he refused to discuss it. He spent most of his time hanging around with Democratic ward heelers on the Hill, dreaming big about how they would be rewarded for helping FDR win reelection, and many nights she found herself alone while he went to political meetings. But the thing that bothered Lena most was her new husband's attitude toward money. Taught frugality by her grandmother Cora, Lena couldn't stand to see Jones spend money they didn't have on expensive clothes to keep up appearances with the Loendi Club crowd.

Within another month Lena was pregnant, however, and she focused on preparing for motherhood. She grew particularly fond of her doctor, a Pittsburgh obstetrician named Ira Cornelius whom everyone referred to as "Buster." On the day Lena went into labor, she was relieved to see Buster at the door of the hospital. "Take it easy and I'll look in on you tomorrow," he assured her. "Where are you going?" she asked. Lena didn't know that black doctors in Pittsburgh weren't allowed inside white hospitals. She became so panicked that it took her two days to deliver her baby, a little girl she named Gail. Decades later, Lena would remember being forced to give birth without the help of Dr. Cornelius as "the cruelest act of prejudice that was ever visited on me personally."

A year later, little Gail had just turned one when her mother received an unexpected phone call. It was from Ralph Cooper, the inventor and emcee of "Amateur Night" at the Apollo Theater in Harlem. Cooper remembered Lena from her days at the Cotton Club and wanted to make her an offer. He was starting a production company to make movies for black audiences, and he asked her to star opposite him in its first venture, a film called *The Duke Is Tops* that he planned to shoot in Hollywood. Lena was intrigued, but she was certain that her husband would veto the idea. Yet to her surprise, Jones gave her permission, dreaming of all the money she would earn.

For the people of Pittsburgh, it was the biggest news of the year. The *Courier* ran a banner headline. Teddy purchased Lena a first-class plane ticket to Los Angeles and threw a farewell party at the Loendi Club. Adding to their debts, Jones insisted on buying her a new coat and a tulip-shaped hat for the sendoff. Woogie Harris and his wife showed up at the Pittsburgh airport to help carry her bags. Woogie's little brother, Teenie, who had begun a new career as a photographer, snapped pictures for a two-page spread in *Flash*, a Negro version of the "newspicture magazines" that had become all the rage. "From Smokeland to Filmland!" a caption cheered.

Yet as soon as the plane left Pittsburgh, there was trouble. Turbulence forced a landing in Arizona and Lena had to complete the trip by train. When Ralph Cooper met her at the station, he was upset that the skinny teenager he remembered now had a young mother's figure. The name of his company—Million Dollar Productions—turned out to be fanciful. Financing had yet to be completed for the movie and there was no cash to pay the actors. When Lena called Jones with that news, he demanded that she quit and come home, and they had a huge fight over the phone. But she decided to stick it out and complete the shoot, since it only lasted ten days and she was enjoying her stay in the home of one of the most famous Negro radio stars of the day, Lillian Randolph, better known as Birdie the maid in *The Great Gildersleeve* show.

When *The Duke Is Tops* premiered in Los Angeles several months later, many of Hollywood's other black stars turned out, from "Bojangles" Robinson to Mantan Moreland and Hattie Noel. A Los Angeles critic praised it as an uplifting musical with "no 'Uncle Tom' bandana or calico sequences." But it was a very different scene at the Pittsburgh premiere, held the same night at the New Grenada Theatre on the Hill. The crowd was shocked to learn that Lena had refused to attend. Instead she sent a telegram to the Pittsburgh NAACP, which hosted the event, stating "PROFESSIONAL APPEARANCES SHOULD BE MADE ON A PRO-FESSIONAL BASIS." Lena wanted to be paid! the gossips clucked. She had gone downtown to a white movie instead! a rumor had it. Offended, the *Courier* reporter who covered the premiere praised Lena's singing but panned her acting, sniffing that "she is no Myrna Loy."

But the gossips didn't know the full story. The truth was that Lena didn't attend the premiere because her husband forbade it. Jones told her that he didn't want to see her bow and scrape for the uppity Negroes who would be in attendance. Yet it seemed to her that Jones just wanted to prove that he was the boss of the household, and that she was at his beck and call. Her husband was also still sore that she hadn't made money on the movie, and he had dictated the telegram that had made her look greedy. Now that Lena was home, the minister's son was again exuding contempt for her show business life—suggesting, she later recalled, "that he had rescued me from a life of sin."

So when Lena received another show business offer several months later, she kept it quiet. Lew Lewis, a New York theater producer, invited her to star in *Blackbirds of 1938*, a revival of the popular musical revue. Grudgingly, Jones agreed to let her go on condition that she take Gail, so Lena asked a Pittsburgh friend to come with her to babysit. The show tried out in Boston, but there wasn't enough money to pay the cast. Again, Jones demanded that Lena quit, but she stayed out of loyalty to the ensemble. Finally *Blackbirds* made it to Broadway, where it received luke-warm reviews and closed after a week. On the last night, Jones showed up from Pittsburgh and refused to let Lena attend the cast party, and it was then that she decided she wanted a divorce.

When Lena told her father, Teddy urged her to reconsider. He set up a family meeting with Jones's father and sister. Everyone urged the couple to think about what was best for Gail, and Lena warily agreed to give the marriage another try. Almost immediately, she got pregnant again. In early

1940, she delivered a baby boy who was named Edwin, after his father and grandfather, and nicknamed "Little Teddy."

After the birth, Lena made a new friend who finally helped her find work in Pittsburgh. Jones was part of a group that met at different homes to play bridge, the favorite card game of the Sugartop set. Lena didn't play, but sometimes she tagged along and sat in the corner. One day one of the regulars came over to talk to her, a slim, elegant lady with braids around her ears. It was Charlotte Enty Catlin, the Hill socialite and acclaimed pianist. They hit it off immediately, and before long Charlotte asked if Lena would like to go into business with her. Charlotte often played at the homes of rich white folks around the city, and she suggested that Lena come along to sing. When Lena warned that her husband might not permit it, Charlotte said, "I'll ask Louis." And sure enough, Jones couldn't bring himself to say no to someone of Catlin's social standing.

For Lena, it felt good to be performing again, without the grueling hours and miserable conditions of nightclubs and road trips. When she and Charlotte arrived at a host's home, they were ushered into a side room while the guests finished dinner. Then everyone gathered around the piano while the two entertained them with the kind of songs that went over well in the wealthy white world: "The Man I Love," "Copper-Colored Gal," "The Sunny Side of the Street." The hosts were always very polite and appreciative, and sometimes they offered coffee and cake. Cash never changed hands directly: instead a fee of $5 or $10 was discreetly sent to Catlin the next day.

The Cotton Club or the Ritz-Carlton they weren't, but the soirees helped Lena improve as a singer. In such intimate settings, she could hone her natural talent for working a lyric. Catlin recognized this as Lena's great strength—her ability to tell a story, rather than her sheer vocal prowess. Charlotte helped Lena develop that skill, teaching her how to vary her inflection and pace and projection.

Later, Lena would look back at the experience of singing with Charlotte Catlin as one of the many ways Pittsburgh changed her, for all the disappointments of her marriage. Pittsburgh allowed her to get away from her suffocating mother and stepfather, and to be treated like a grown-up by her father and his friends. It forced her to learn to stand up for herself, as a wife and a performer and a businesswoman. And it gave her a first experience of being treated with respect, by white folks and her own people. Compared with how she had been exploited everywhere else in her young life, she recalled, "the Pittsburgh work was at least straight-forward, honest work."

Still, it wasn't enough to save Lena's marriage. By the time Little Teddy was a year old, she had decided that it was over. She knew she couldn't escape Jones without her own money, so she asked her father's wife, Irene, for a loan to buy a train ticket to New York and a hotel room in Harlem until she earned enough to send for her children.

When Lena confronted Jones with her plan, they had one last terrible fight, during which he said two hurtful things that she would never forget. "You can take Gail, but you'll never get Teddy!" Jones seethed, and sadly that would turn out to be true. Gail would soon join Lena in New York and spend the rest of her childhood with her mother. But her son would stay with his father and never become as close to Lena as she wished during his brief lifetime, which was cut short by kidney disease at the age of thirty.

Yet Louis Jones would be wrong about the other harsh thing he told Lena Horne on the day she left him and his hometown for good. "Just because a bunch of Pittsburgh socialites think you're cute," he said, "doesn't mean you can make it somewhere big."

LENA HORNE AND BILLY STRAYHORN just missed meeting in Pittsburgh. If Lena had befriended Billy's piano teacher Charlotte Catlin earlier, or Billy had stayed longer, they surely would have encountered one another there. But in 1939, the year before Lena started performing with Catlin, Billy left for New York on an odyssey that began when he, too, started playing in the homes of white Pittsburghers.

At the end of 1938, Strayhorn was still working at the Pennfield Drug

Store in Shadyside, manning the fountain and making drop-offs. Sometimes he would stay to play piano at the homes to which he delivered, and as word of his talent spread he started getting work performing at private dinners and cocktail parties. A fellow employee at the drugstore named David Pearlman heard Billy play and was so impressed that he had an idea. Pearlman was studying for a druggist license at the University of Pittsburgh School of Pharmacy, and one of his classmates was George Greenlee Jr., the nephew of Gus Greenlee. One day, Pearlman pulled George aside to sing Billy's praises. "George, we have a delivery boy who's one of the finest musicians I've ever heard," he said. "Your uncle knows all the biggest musicians. Why don't you introduce him to someone?"

George had never met Billy but he trusted Pearlman, who was one of the few white pharmacy students who treated him as an equal. George happened to know that his uncle was throwing a big party that night at the Crawford Grill for Duke Ellington, who was in Pittsburgh playing at the Stanley Theatre. Assuming the festivities wouldn't start until the show was over, George waited until after midnight and headed straight to Gus's private club on the third floor of the Crawford Grill. Sure enough, Duke was there. As soon as his uncle introduced them, George made his pitch. "A good friend of mine has written some songs," he said, stretching the truth, "and we'd like for you to hear them." George figured that Duke wouldn't refuse in front of Gus, and he was right. "Well, why don't you come backstage tomorrow after the first show?" Ellington said.

An early December snow was falling outside the Stanley Theatre when Billy met George there the next day. They took in the one o'clock matinee, then made their way to Ellington's dressing room. They found Duke stretched out on a chair, head back and eyes closed, having his hair conked. Ellington motioned toward an upright in the corner. Show us what you can do, he said. Billy sat down to the piano.

"Mr. Ellington, this is how you played this number in the show," Billy said, producing a note-for-note imitation of Duke's rendition of "Sophisticated Lady" during the matinee. Then Billy said: "Now, this is the way I would play it." His fingers returned to the keyboard, and out came an up-tempo version in a different key that was "pretty hip-sounding," as George Greenlee remembered it.

Amazed, Duke got up and stood over Billy at the piano. "Can you do that again?" he asked. Billy played another of Ellington's best-known songs, "Solitude," first as Duke had performed it during the matinee, then with a different harmonization.

Ellington asked his valet to fetch Harry Carney, his baritone saxophonist. As Carney entered the room Duke whispered: "Listen to this kid play!" Carney went to alert two other stars in the orchestra, alto sax player Johnny Hodges and singer Ivie Anderson. When they got back, Duke had his hands on Billy's shoulders and was asking him to play his own compositions. Billy obliged with "Something to Live For," from *Fantastic Rhythm*. Then he played another tune he hadn't named yet. When Duke asked what it was called, Billy laughed. Later, Ellington described it as the moment he became truly captivated with Billy Strayhorn, when he first heard the sound of Billy's laughter.

In the few days Ellington had left in Pittsburgh, he gave Strayhorn assignments to see what more he could do. He asked Billy to write a lyric, then an original orchestration. When Billy returned with his handiwork, Duke was between shows in his dressing room, having dinner with a mocha-skinned beauty named Thelma Spangler, an aspiring musician and recent graduate of Schenley High School whom Ellington had met the night before at the Loendi Club. Billy spread his sheet music on the floor and Duke pored over it for several minutes. Then Ellington scooped up the pages and Thelma watched from backstage as he handed them out to the musicians on the bandstand, whispered a few words to Ivie Anderson, and then began conducting. An ethereal version of "Two Sleepy People" filled the Stanley Theatre. When it was over, Ellington beamed.

Backstage, Ellington told Strayhorn that he wanted him to come to New York and work in his organization. He handed Billy a twenty-dollar bill for the orchestration and a slip of paper explaining how to take the subway from Pennsylvania Station to Duke's apartment in Harlem.

Over the next few months, Billy agonized. He didn't know if Ellington was serious. Since his childhood visits to his grandparents in North Carolina, he had rarely left Pittsburgh. He worried about leaving his mother. He didn't have enough money to pay for a train ticket to New York City. But Lillian Strayhorn encouraged her Bill to pursue his dream, and one of his white bandmates from the Mad Hatters offered to travel with him and loan him money for the trip. First, though, Billy decided to write a song to offer Ellington when he got there. Sitting down to his used piano on Tioga Street Rear, he quickly banged out a bouncy tune based on the subway directions to Harlem that Ellington had given him.

When Strayhorn finally headed East, Ellington was on the road, and it took several days to track him down in Newark. Duke didn't remember Billy's name, but he said that he had been wondering how to find him. He asked Billy to return to New York with the band and offered to put him up in a $5-a-night room at the YMCA. Several days later, Strayhorn returned to Pittsburgh to collect his things and say goodbye to family and friends. One of the pals he phoned with the news was Ralph Koger, the young *Courier* reporter and fellow Westinghouse alumnus, who had listened to Strayhorn play the new song he wrote for Ellington. "Guess what," he told Koger. "I'm going to work for Duke. I played that tune 'A Train' for him, and he liked it. I'm moving to New York!"

Soon Strayhorn was living with the Ellington family in Harlem and exploring the exciting new world of Manhattan, including the freedom it gave him to begin exploring his sexuality as a gay man. He started writing arrangements for the Ellington orchestra and played piano on several of its recordings. Then a showdown in the music industry presented Billy with an unexpected opportunity to demonstrate his songwriting talent. The American Society of Composers, Authors and Publishers, the organization that collected royalties for songwriters, was demanding more payment from radio programs. Instead of submitting, the stations decided to form a rival organization and boycott ASCAP songs and writers. To stay on the airwaves, Ellington needed to come up with an entirely new repertoire not attributed to him, since his existing songs were all part of the ASCAP empire. So Duke told his son, Mercer Ellington, and Strayhorn to get to work.

Laboring night and day in a Chicago hotel room, fueled by cigarettes and whiskey and blackberry wine, the two men turned out a dozen new songs for the orchestra to record. Strayhorn's contributions ranged from several haunting ballads—"Chelsea Bridge," "Passion Flower," "A Flower Is a Lovesome Thing"—to a propulsive full-orchestra showpiece called "Rain Check." He dusted off several of the songs he had written for *Fantastic Rhythm* in Pittsburgh, including "My Little Brown Book" and "Something to Live For." And he wrote an arrangement for the song he had composed as a gift to Ellington that was so infectious that it became the orchestra's new signature. Until then, Ellington's theme song had been a languorous tune called "Sepia Panorama." From then on, it would be Strayhorn's piano-stomping, trumpets-blaring, saxes-purring orchestration of "Take the 'A' Train."

The Ellington orchestra made its first recording of "Take the 'A' Train" in Hollywood during a West Coast swing in early 1941. While Duke was there, he was invited to a party hosted by an MGM movie writer named Sid Kuller. Ellington played the piano for the crowd, which grew so exuberant he described them as "jumping for joy." Before the night was over, Kuller had convinced Duke to write a full-length stage show around that theme. That summer, the musical entitled *Jump for Joy* opened at the Mayan Theatre in Los Angeles with an all-black cast and a lineup of songs that included several more soon-to-be classics: "Rocks in My Bed," "I've Got It Bad and That Ain't Good," and an instrumental number that would later be put to lyrics with the title "Just Squeeze Me." Ellington was listed as the writer of all those tunes, with Billy Strayhorn credited in the program only for "musical arrangements." But Kuller and others would confirm that Billy collaborated with Duke on almost every song in the musical, a role that would have come naturally to him after his experience in Pittsburgh writing and rehearsing the entire production of *Fantastic Rhythm*.

It was also during the summer of 1941 in Los Angeles that the paths of Billy Strayhorn and Lena Horne finally crossed. Fleeing Pittsburgh for New York in late 1940, Lena had found her spot in Noble Sissle's orchestra taken. Instead she landed a job singing for a white swing band led by saxo-phonist Charlie Barnet that had won respect from black audiences with its jazzy recording of "Cherokee." Through Barnet, Lena was introduced to John Hammond, the talent scout for the Greenwich Village nightclub Café Society. On its small stage, Lena was able to display the intimate singing style that she had perfected in the drawing rooms of Pittsburgh, and her performances won new friends and admirers among the sophisti-cated mixed race crowd that frequented the club, from Benny Goodman and Paul Robeson to the artist Romare Bearden.

Lena moved into her grandparents' old house in Brooklyn, and for sev-eral months Little Teddy came to visit. At Easter time, Big Teddy also arrived from Pittsburgh, and while he was in New York he once again took Lena to see Joe Louis train in New Jersey. Joe was now the heavy-weight champ, and the shy chorus girl he had met five years earlier was a full-grown woman in a fox stole, silk stockings, and open-toed shoes. They began a secret affair. When light heavyweight champ Billy Conn challenged Louis for his title in May, Lena asked John Hammond to drive her around Central Park so she could listen to the fight on his car radio. Until Louis finally knocked Conn out in the thirteenth round, Lena was a nervous wreck, punching Hammond as though she was in the ring herself and leaving black-and-blue marks all over his arm.

The affair with Joe Louis didn't last long, but it wasn't the only dalli-ance Lena had during this time. Another Café Society regular was Duke Ellington, who liked to come downtown to mix with the bohemian crowd. Lena had first seen Ellington in her Cotton Club days, when he had no idea who she was, but now he laid on his regal charm and they, too, had a brief fling. It also ended quickly, but not before Duke helped convince her to pursue a new job opportunity in Los Angeles. A club owner named Felix Young was planning a big new spot called the Trocadero and wanted to hire Lena as a featured singer. She was reluctant at first, but Duke flattered her by telling that it was her duty to "let the whole world benefit from your incredible radiance." He also said he wanted to introduce her to a friend he called "Swee Pea" who was working on a new musical they planned to debut in Los Angeles. "You'll get to meet 'Pea because we're getting ready to open *Jump for Joy* there," Ellington said.

Shortly after Lena arrived in California, Duke sent her a ticket to one of the first performances of the show. The seat next to her was empty, but during intermission a small man sat down in it. "I'm Billy Strayhorn— Swee Pea," he said, clasping her hand. To Lena, he looked more like an elegant owl, with his round face, thick glasses, and smartly tailored suit. But his soft voice and warm manner immediately put her at ease. After the show was over, she invited him to her apartment, and they talked through the night. She figured out quickly that their relationship would never be romantic—and she even suspected that Duke had sent him as a chaper- one to keep other men away—but Lena knew immediately that she and Billy Strayhorn were destined to be soul mates.

One of the first things Billy and Lena talked about that night, Horne would tell Strayhorn's biographer, was Pittsburgh. She didn't go into greater detail, but it is very likely that they discovered their common bond with Charlotte Enty Catlin, Billy's piano teacher and Lena's accompanist. They may have marveled at the ties between Lena's father, Teddy, and Gus Greenlee, the man who had made it possible for Billy to meet Duke Ellington. Both would later speak of the similar sense of humor and world- view they discovered that evening, and it isn't hard to image that they found it in part by gossiping and laughing about the colorful characters and cultural quirks of black Pittsburgh.

Over the next few months, Billy and Lena became inseparable. They went to an L.A. sanatorium to visit Jimmy Blanton, Ellington's talented young bassist, who had started his career performing on riverboats with Fate Marable and was now sick with the tuberculosis that would claim his life at age twenty-three. They frequented Alabama and Brothers, two nightclubs in the black section of town that attracted a hip mixed race crowd. Billy also helped Lena prepare for her debut at the Trocadero, which was still under construction. He suggested songs that matched her voice, wrote flattering arrangements and coached her on her delivery, picking up where their mutual coach Charlotte Catlin had left off.

On December 7, 1941, Billy and Lena were rehearsing at the home of friends when they heard the awful news about Pearl Harbor. They gathered around a radio and listened speechlessly, sensing that the attack would change everything but not yet knowing how. For Lena, it would mean that her move to Los Angeles would turn out very differently than she had expected. As war rationing went into effect, Felix Young canceled his plans for a grand nightclub and instead opened a tiny venue he called the "Little Troc." Instead of show-stoppers, Strayhorn helped Lena develop tunes and arrangements to fit the smaller space, songs such as "Honeysuckle Rose," "There'll Be Some Changes Made," and Harold Arlen's "Blues in the Night." Lena's extended run at the Little Troc would make her the toast of the Los Angeles music scene, and lead to a series of wartime film roles that turned her into one of black America's leading movie stars.

Back in Pittsburgh, meanwhile, America's entry into World War II would get the steel mills and other factories humming at full capacity, as Smoketown answered FDR's call to create an "Arsenal of Democracy." And at *The Pittsburgh Courier*, it would give rise to a new crusade, to mobilize support for the war effort and for black soldiers at the front, that was the culmination of everything Robert L. Vann had fought for during his contentious time as a Negro in the bosom of the New Deal.

A Pittsburgh resident shows support for the *Courier*'s
"Double V Campaign" during World War II.

6

THE DOUBLE V WARRIORS

WHEN PERCIVAL LEROY PRATTIS left Chicago in the summer 1935, on the odyssey that would take him to a new home in Pittsburgh, he couldn't bring himself to say goodbye in person. For more than a decade, Prattis had worked for Claude Barnett, the founder of America's first black wire service, the Associated Negro Press. Although Barnett paid him a pittance, the two men had become close friends, and "P.L.," as Prattis called himself, was in Barnett's debt. Barnett had taken a chance on him even though he had come late to journalism. From a poor family in Philadelphia, Prattis was waiting tables in Grand Rapids, Michigan, to put himself through school when a customer asked if he would like to write an article for a local paper. Barnett was also willing to hire Prattis after he lost his first job in Chicago, with the *Defender*, following a personal dispute with publisher Robert Abbott. Most of all, Prattis owed Barnett for recommending him to the editors of *The Pittsburgh Courier*, who by the early 1930s were looking for someone to investigate the crooked sales agents who were pocketing most of the profits from the 150,000 copies of the *Courier* that were sold in Chicago every week.

The part-time job for the bosses in Pittsburgh had worked out well. Prattis made the sales agents pay up; he also lifted the *Courier*'s profile by encouraging the editors to send copies to Chicago VIPs. He had sharp editorial instincts, too, such as his tip to Bill Nunn about the young Joe Louis and his suggestion that Julia Bumry Jones put more Windy City gossip into the Chicago edition of the paper.

During all this time, however, Prattis's personal life was falling apart. In his twenties, he liked to joke, he had been so poor that "I couldn't afford to look at a girl." Short, balding, and bespectacled, he also resembled an accountant more than anyone's idea of matinee idol. So at age thirty-seven, Prattis had married a longtime acquaintance named Lillian Sherman, despite knowing that she was an unpredictable spirit who had broken off several previous engagements. Now, after three turbulent years of matrimony, Lillian had run away from Prattis, too—to New York—and he had decided to run after her.

On the August day when Prattis left the Chicago office of the ANP for good, he felt "alone in the world," as he later put it. He had just turned forty, and he was certain half of those years had been wasted. He told himself that he needed to do something "to become some sort of somebody." Instead of breaking the news face-to-face, Prattis left a farewell note for Claude Barnett. "This is merely to let you know I have gone," he wrote. "It's the hardest thing I have ever done in my life—to part with so much of what we have been together. To have said goodbye in words would have been too hard, for you and for me. . . . I am unhappy in my private life and my work, I shall try to find work, any kind of work. If you can help me, I know you will." Prattis ended the note with a forwarding address in New York and a wistful wish for his boss and friend. "Let us see if there are not things we can do," he wrote, "far as we may be apart."

While en route to New York, Prattis stopped off in Pittsburgh for a day to meet with Robert L. Vann and Ira Lewis. They didn't offer him a full-time job, but they did enlist him to be part of the team the *Courier* was sending to Joe Louis's next fight in New York, against Max Baer, the former champ who had lost his title to Gentleman Jim Braddock. As it turned out, Prattis got an even bigger scoop that day: about Joe's secret marriage to his nineteen-year-old girlfriend Marva Trotter just hours before the fight. Prattis was the first to report details of the rushed ceremony in a fourth-floor apartment on Edgecombe Avenue in Harlem. Impressed, Ira Lewis phoned him long-distance with an official offer to work at the *Courier*'s headquarters, at a salary of $40 a month, more than Prattis had ever made. Lillian protested, but after several weeks he talked her into moving with him and they shipped their belongings to Pittsburgh.

The arrangement didn't last long. Within a year, Lillian fled to New York again to take a beautician's course, announcing that she intended to open a hair salon. Then she abruptly returned to Pittsburgh and convinced her husband to invest the little savings he had accumulated into a new eatery on the Hill, which she called the "P & L Chicken Shack." When Lillian flew off once again, Prattis divorced her. Before long he was dating a clerk in the *Courier* sales office, Helen Sands, a quiet, churchgoing young lady who had grown up on Sugartop and left Pittsburgh only briefly to attend Cheney College outside Philadelphia, where she made the honor roll. When Prattis proposed marriage, he wrote to Claude Barnett that he had deliberately chosen a levelheaded bride with deep Pittsburgh roots as a sign to his colleagues at the *Courier*—and to himself—that he planned to stay put. He was forty-three now, and at last he had found the place and the position that would allow him to become some sort of somebody.

Although Prattis was quickly promoted to city editor, he was seen as an outsider among the tightknit group that had worked at the paper since the 1920s. He had a particularly wary relationship with Bill Nunn, the loud, backslapping newsroom general who in personality and appearance was his polar opposite. Unlike so many others, Prattis was also not charmed by the earthy tongue and bawdy humor of Julia Bumry Jones. Forced to share the same table in the *Courier*'s tiny newsroom where Jones received guests and made reporting phone calls for her gossip column, Prattis later described his discomfort with her "unrestricted and unrestrained coarseness."

But Prattis found favor with the Big Chief, Robert L. Vann. Although Vann was far too aloof to say it out loud, he probably saw something of himself in Prattis. Like Vann, Prattis had grown up extremely poor, in a black neighborhood of Philadelphia. He had also put himself through college—at Hampton University in Virginia—before moving to Michigan to study at the Ferris Institute. Like Vann, Prattis spoke in a learned manner and dressed in a fashion that belied his humble origins: in double-breasted suits, trousers braced with suspenders, and conservative rimless eyeglasses.

But what Vann admired more than anything about Prattis was that, unlike any of the other *Courier* editors, he had served in the military. Drafted at the age of twenty-two, Prattis had been assigned to the all-black 813th Pioneer Infantry Brigade and had arrived in France in August 1918 just in time for the Meuse-Argonne offensive. After less than two months, he was promoted to sergeant major and he proudly wore his olive green officer's uniform under General Pershing's command in the push across France that put an end to the war.

Of all the crusades that Vann had waged in his quarter century at the *Courier*, none was dearer to his heart than the cause of Negro soldiers. After World War I, he had run editorials calling for a monument to honor black troops who died in the trenches. Hamilton Fish, the Republican congressman from New York who had commanded a "Harlem Hellfighters" unit during the war, agreed to introduce Vann's monument bill, only to be thwarted by another Pittsburgher—David Reed, a flinty Republican on the Military Affairs Committee. When Congress voted to disband all but four black Army units in the 1920s, Vann sent reporters to expose the conditions at their segregated bases, where the soldiers were denied combat training and relegated to shoveling out horse stables and other menial tasks. Now, in the late 1930s, Vann was becoming increasingly convinced that another world war was possible, and he was determined to use the *Courier*'s growing reach and influence to make certain that black soldiers were taken seriously and treated justly this time.

For Vann, it had been a sobering time since he departed for Washington,

D.C., in the first year of the Roosevelt presidency. His reward for calling on black voters to turn "the picture of Abraham Lincoln to the wall"—an impressive-sounding post as "Special Assistant to the Attorney General"— had turned out be a frustrating sinecure. When Vann showed up at the Justice Department, no one had assigned him an office or a secretary. He was given tedious administrative chores such as writing memos to remind staffers to fill out their time sheets. He was never asked to meet with Attorney General Homer Cummings, and was kept at arm's length by the group of Negro aides and advisers known as FDR"s "Black Cabinet." To make matters worse, Vann had to spend four months of his first year in the job convalescing from a near-fatal skull fracture, after he impatiently tried to pass a truck on a drive home to Pittsburgh and his Packard sedan slammed into a car coming down a hill in the opposite direction.

With little to do in Washington, Vann decided to take a monthlong cruise with his wife, Jesse, in the fall of 1935, traveling by ship around the Gulf of Mexico all the way to California. While the Vanns were in Los Angeles visiting the Hollywood set where their friend Bill "Bojangles" Robinson was shooting a movie with Shirley Temple, they received a surprise gift from Pittsburgh. On the week that the *Courier*'s circulation passed 100,000 issues for the first time, everyone at the paper had signed the last copy off the presses for them. The gesture touched Vann—and made him realize that he could do more good running the paper than trying to fight the bureaucracy in Washington. In a mordant letter, he explained his decision to his friend H. L. Mencken. "The work got a little tedious for me," Vann wrote of the Justice Department post, "because it developed that such a job as I held was a splendid pastime for old men who are seeking a soft place in their declining years. I did not want to get into the rut of an old man because the only difference between a rut and the grave is that the grave is a little deeper."

As luck would have it, Vann returned to Pittsburgh just as the biggest foreign crisis of the time was erupting. The Fascist regime in Italy, led by Benito Mussolini, had invaded its former colony of Ethiopia, governed by the dynamic young Emperor Haile Selassie. Still in Chicago, P.L. Prattis sent Vann a letter pointing out how interested black readers would be in this David and Goliath story and suggesting that he send a reporter to the front. Prattis hoped that he would get the assignment, but instead Vann gave it to a writer who was better known to *Courier* readers: Joel Augustus Rogers. A self-taught Jamaican, Rogers had originated a popular feature called "Your History" that appeared every week on the *Courier* editorial page. Illustrated in the manner of "Ripley's Believe It or Not," the column touted the exploits of famous Negroes through history—and delighted readers by asserting that many Great Men assumed to be white, such as Beethoven and Haydn, were in fact part black.

The war correspondent idea was an expensive gamble—one that no other Negro publisher could have afforded at the time—but it paid off handsomely. For six months, Rogers filed melodramatic dispatches from "the front" that the *Courier* touted with banner headlines. In reality, like most white reporters covering the war, Rogers witnessed little combat. He relied almost entirely on Ethiopian government sources, and as a result he vastly overestimated the progress of Selassie's thinly armed forces and underestimated the advantage the Italians had, particularly once they started using mustard gas and other chemical weapons. After fleeing the capital of Addis Ababa, Salessie gave a loudly ballyhooed interview to Rogers in which the emperor claimed to be winning the war when actually he was weeks away from giving up and leaving the country. One of the British correspondents, Evelyn Waugh, would later spoof the wildly erroneous reporting on all sides in his comic novel *Scoop*. Still, the war coverage proved a huge boon for the *Courier*, lifting its weekly sales by 70 percent to 170,000 copies.

In the summer of 1936, Vann gave himself the assignment of reporting on the eighteen black athletes who competed for the United States at the Summer Olympics in Berlin. He interviewed a "grateful" Jesse Owens after he won the 100-yard dash—the second of Owens's historic four gold medal victories. Even more satisfying, Vann described the surprise victory of a hometown boy: Johnny Woodruff, a nineteen-year-old University of Pittsburgh freshman and native of the nearby mining town of Connellsville, who escaped from inside a pack of runners to win the 800-meter race.

Seated directly below Vann in Berlin's Olympic Stadium, in a box that jutted out from the stands, was Adolf Hitler. In Vann's bullish stories for the *Courier*, he reported that Hitler "saluted" the U.S. athletes (likely a reference to the Nazi salute that Hitler extended to everyone) and that the German crowd went "literally crazy" for them. But in Vann's letters home, he conveyed private bitterness at how the black Olympians had been treated. Hitler "found it convenient to leave the stadium" rather than shake their hands, he complained to one friend, while telling another that the German press had dismissed the gold medals as "points scored by the American African Auxiliary."

When her husband returned from Berlin, Jesse Vann hosted a welcome-home picnic. It was held at their stately new residence: an eleven-room Tudor house surrounded by wide lawns and tall poplar trees in the wealthy Pittsburgh suburb of Oakmont that Vann had purchased for $50,000 from a white banker. Jesse invited the entire *Courier* staff: the editors, the ad salesmen, the circulation managers, the stenographers, the proofreaders, the bookkeepers, the pressmen, the mail clerks, even the janitor and the telephone operator. As everyone feasted on Chicken Maryland, potato salad, and Heinz pickles, Vann and Ira Lewis hailed the remarkable progress they had all achieved together in just a few short years. Boosted by coverage of the Ethiopian war, the Berlin Olympics, and the rise of Joe Louis, the *Courier* was now selling more than 200,000 copies across the United States, surpassing the circulation of all its top competitors combined (including its longtime rival *The Chicago Defender*, whose fortunes had plummeted with the declining health of Robert Abbott).

For the rest of the fall, Vann threw the *Courier's* clout and his own personal influence behind Franklin Roosevelt's bid for reelection. Showing how determined they were to win Pennsylvania, one of the few states FDR had lost in 1932, the Democrats held their convention in Philadelphia, and Vann was among thirty black delegates. While the *Courier* editorialized in favor of FDR, he traveled across the state as an official representative of the campaign and adviser on the Negro press. Most white newspapers forecast a close outcome in the state, but the *Courier* presciently predicted a sweeping Democratic victory. Roosevelt trounced Republican Alf Landon by 663,000 votes in Pennsylvania on the way to the most decisive Electoral College victory in U.S. history. Of the roughly 190,000 blacks who voted statewide, three out of four chose Roosevelt, contributing in particular to his wins in Philadelphia and Pittsburgh.

Yet once again, Vann didn't receive the thanks he believed he deserved. Once the Democrats saw that they could capture black votes across the state, they turned to courting Negro leaders in Philadelphia, with its larger population. With Joe Guffey serving in the U.S. Senate, his ambitious protégé, David Lawrence, now in charge of the state party operation, began to assert his independence. The rift would break wide open in 1938, when Lawrence backed another candidate over Guffey for governor. When Lawrence's man won the Democratic primary, Vann opted to endorse the Republican in the general election. Vann viewed it as a gesture of loyalty to Guffey, but Guffey didn't see it that way. He publicly accused Vann of a "deceitful and dishonest" betrayal of the Democratic Party, and the two men rarely spoke again.

After the 1936 election, Vann grew increasingly vocal in his criticism of Roosevelt. Three issues in particular rankled him. One was FDR's foot-dragging on anti-lynching legislation, which Vann viewed as a cowardly concession to Southern Democrats on Capitol Hill. The second was the president's handling of the Supreme Court. After a reporter for the morning daily *Pittsburgh Post-Gazette* uncovered the fact that Hugo Black, FDR's latest appointee, had once belonged to the Klu Klux Klan in his native Alabama, Vann became one of the strongest national voices calling for Black to step aside. Meanwhile, Vann's high-minded opposition to FDR's bid to "pack the Court" with additional justices was so eloquent that the *Chicago Daily Tribune* named one of his *Courier* essays on the subject its nationwide "Editorial of the Day."

(For a brief period, Vann himself was touted as a potential Supreme Court candidate. A chorus that included H. L. Mencken, the Urban

League, and the head of the National Bar Association urged Roosevelt to consider Vann as a counterweight to Hugo Black. As Mencken put it, "If the white Crackers of the South, in return for their votes, deserve to have a reliable agent on the Supreme Court, then why should the colored faithful of both North and South, not to mention East and West, be denied?" In letters to friends, Vann said he found it hard to take the idea seriously—no Negro had ever served as more than a messenger at the Supreme Court—but that he hoped the speculation might set a precedent. "We will never get anything of this kind until somebody is led to believe we ought to have it," he wrote, "and I am letting my name be used solely for the purpose of creating a favorable impression toward the idea.")

Vann's third and most passionate cause was the future of blacks in the U.S. military. One day in early 1938, he summoned P.L. Prattis to give him a special assignment. Vann asked Prattis, as the only veteran among the *Courier* editors, to help him get a letter to dozens of military leaders, congressmen, newspaper editors, church leaders, and college presidents. In the letter, which he also published in the newspaper every week for two months, Vann listed all the military branches that excluded Negroes— "the air corps, the coast artillery corps, the tank corps, the engineer corps, the chemical warfare service, the field artillery, the signal or any of the other special services." Then he solicited opinions about the best way to increase opportunities for black soldiers. "Do you believe that all branches of the army and naval service should be opened to Negroes?" the letter asked. "Or do you think there should be an entire Negro division, including all arms of the service and officered, at least in the line, by educated colored men, in the army; and a squadron manned by Negroes in the Navy?"

Over the following weeks, the *Courier* published dozens of responses to Vann's survey. While views differed, a majority concluded the most realistic place to start was with a segregated Army division. (The more elitist Navy wasn't ready for a black squadron, most agreed.) Armed with the feedback, Vann enlisted his old ally, Hamilton Fish, to introduce three bills in Congress to test the waters. The first called for opening all

branches of the military to Negroes. The second proposed a full but separate Army division. A third demanded that two blacks per year be admitted
to West Point for officer training. Fish sent a cable to Roosevelt asking for
his support, and the president responded by inviting Vann to the White
House for a courtesy call.

But opposition to what became known as "the Pittsburgh Courier bills"
arose from an unlikely source. Walter White, the executive secretary of
the NAACP, thought his organization should lead the fight for ending discrimination in the military, and that nothing short of full integration was
acceptable. White's deputy, Roy Wilkins, disagreed. Wilkins applauded
the *Courier* for forcing the debate and thought that public hearings would
benefit the cause. "Although we began the agitation years ago and have an
excellent record on the question," he wrote White, "the fact remains that
the Courier at the psychological moment whipped up the enthusiasm of
the country into a campaign which has assumed such proportions that this
Association could not issue any statement which would seem to be 'cold-
watering' the Courier's crusade. I think you will realize how unpopular
that would make us." But White overruled Wilkins and lobbied quietly to
kill what he privately belittled as the *Courier's* proposal for a "Jim Crow
division."

In late October 1938, Vann sought a second audience with Roosevelt.
With his usual noncommittal bonhomie, FDR agreed that America might
soon be forced to enlarge its military, and that a Negro division might be
considered. But in the end, he did nothing to support the Fish legislation, in part because the anti–New Deal Republican had become such a
thorn in Roosevelt's side on other issues. Without backing from the White
House, the "Pittsburgh Courier bills" never made it out of the House
Military Affairs Committee, where twelve of twenty-six members were
Southerners.

Vann refused to give up on his military crusade, however. With his own
money, he funded a group called the Committee for Participation of Negroes in the National Defense to lobby for more gradual reforms. In 1940,
he finally won a victory as Congress began implementing a mandatory

draft. With Vann's encouragement, Fish proposed an amendment to the Selective Training and Service Act that stated "no Negro because of race should be excluded from the enlistment in the army for service with colored military units now organized or to be organized for such service." After the bill cleared the House by a margin 121 to 99, the *Courier* congratulated itself for the breakthrough, declaring that it took "pardonable pride" in "the fact that PARTIAL success has been won in the fight to secure participation of Negroes in national defense."

For P.L. Prattis, 1940 was shaping up as a particularly gratifying year. He and his new bride, Helen Sands, had moved into a small brick house on Junilla Street in the Hill District. After a year of marriage, they began trying to have children, a step that would result a year later in the birth of a daughter they named Patricia. At work, Prattis had been given his own weekly column, entitled "The Horizon," in addition to his editing duties. In May, he wrote his friend Claude Barnett in Chicago to share the good news that he had been promoted to managing editor. "This is the first time anybody but Mr. Vann or Mr. Lewis has served in that capacity," Prattis explained proudly.

Five months later, Prattis learned very different news that shattered his newfound sense of security. Until then, Robert Vann had told only a few of his oldest associates at the *Courier* that he had been diagnosed with abdominal cancer. Vann had quietly undergone surgery to have the growth removed. Still frail from the operation, he had willed himself to attend both of that summer's presidential conventions to lobby for the cause of black servicemen. In Philadelphia, the Republicans nominated Indiana businessman Wendell Willkie and adopted a platform declaring "discrimination in the Civil Service, Army, Navy, and all other branches of the government must cease." In Chicago, where Roosevelt was selected to run for a third term, the Democrats paid lip service to civil rights for the first time since Reconstruction, but failed to address the military question beyond commending Negro soldiers for their "achievements" in past wars.

Returning to Pittsburgh, Vann told his editors that the *Courier* would endorse Willkie. Some of his reasons were personal: Vann was opposed in principle to a third presidential term. He approved of Willkie as a fellow self-made businessman, and he hadn't forgotten the slights he had suffered in FDR's Washington. But most of all, Vann couldn't forgive Roosevelt's seeming indifference to the millions of blacks who had voted for him. A letter to Mary McLeod Bethune, a member of FDR's "Black Cabinet," about the plight of Southern farmers captured Vann's annoyance. "You cannot afford to travel around the country and talk about the blessings of the New Deal unless there are some real blessings to talk about," he wrote Bethune. "The Negro Farmers of the South are not getting the benefits intended for them. . . . The President has a fine attitude, but attitude is not bread and butter. Attitude is not corn and wheat. Attitude is not pork and potatoes."

On days that Vann came to work at the *Courier*, he had a custom of swinging by the newsroom to greet his reporters. "Hey gang!" he would call out. But on an October morning in 1940, he went straight to his office and called for Julia Bumry Jones, his old friend and one of the first employees he had hired twenty-five years earlier. "Rose," Vann said gravely, using his pet nickname for Jones, "I have to make my plans for the future. I have tried to build the Courier so it will live on without me. Now, there are some things we must face, regardless of how we feel . . ."

Vann's voice began to break, and Julia's eyes welled up as she realized what he was saying. His cancer had returned. Jones began to weep. "Now, have your cry," Vann said, "but listen to me . . ." For the next half hour, they talked about how the *Courier* would carry on. They reminisced about the days when it had been just the three of them—Robert Vann, Ira Lewis, and Julia Bumry Jones—and a handful of others. Recalling the conversation, Jones invoked the motto of the National Association of Negro Women: Vann and Lewis were always "climbing, climbing and lifting as they climbed," she wrote. "They started with the three of us and kept adding until there were more than a hundred. It was a long pull and a hard pull . . . [until] they reached the top of the hill."

It was Vann's last day at the *Courier*. Shortly afterward, he checked into Shadyside Hospital, and within days he slipped into a coma. "Don't worry about me, I'll be all right," he said in his last words to his wife, Jesse, who was at his bedside. Two days later, minutes after seven in the evening on Thursday, October 24, 1940, Robert Lee Vann passed away, less than two months past his sixty-first birthday.

The next issue of the *Courier* was a monument to Vann's legacy, in more ways than one. There was a front-page story, "NATION EULOGIZES VANN," and seven pages of obituaries, tributes, and photos. But there was also another headline that Vann had helped make possible: "DAVIS FIRST NEGRO GENERAL." In one of his last acts as editor, Vann had published a letter from a *Courier* reader protesting the Army's failure to include a black officer, Benjamin O. Davis, in a group of colonels promoted to general. The oversight had become an eleventh-hour election issue, and on the day after Vann died Roosevelt had promoted Davis to brigadier general, making him the first Negro to hold such a high rank. The *Courier's* editorial writers welcomed the news, but it didn't stop them from obeying Vann's final wish and endorsing Wendell Willkie. "This last minute desperate maneuver will not swing a single Negro vote," they declared, "if, as seems likely, it was designed to snare needed support."

As it turned out, FDR didn't need the *Courier's* backing in 1940. While a handful of other black newspapers joined it in supporting Willkie, most of the Negro press endorsed Roosevelt—including *The Chicago Defender* for the first time, now that the staunchly Republican Robert Abbott had died and left his nephew John Sengstacke in charge. Across the country, two out of three Negro votes went to Roosevelt. In Pennsylvania, FDR won every district with a sizable black population, and on the Hill he captured four out of five black ballots. In the end, the political migration that Robert L. Vann had started in 1932 had overtaken the philosophy behind it. The black vote was no longer the "liquid asset" that Vann envisioned but a fixed resource for the Democratic Party, and it would remain so for the rest of the century and well into the next.

Respectful of faith but frequently critical of the black clergy, Vann had left instructions that his funeral be held not in a church but at his beloved property in Oakmont. Hundreds of mourners attended, from leaders of the Negro press such as John Sengstacke of the *Defender* and Claude Barnett of the Associated Negro Press, to scores of influential politicians, businessmen, ministers, and scholars from across the country. Floral tributes were sent by Gus Greenlee, Joe Guffey, Joe Louis and his managers John Roxborough and Julian Black, and hundreds of other admirers. Chester Washington delivered a eulogy and Reverend C. E. Askew, a boyhood friend from North Carolina, recalled Vann's early hardships. From Oakmont, a caravan of cars followed the hearse bearing Vann's casket to Homewood Cemetery, where he had purchased a huge stone mausoleum decorated with stained-glass figures that symbolized his three passions: the Book of Knowledge, the Scales of Justice, and the Gutenberg Press.

After the Reverend Charles Foggie, an AME Zion pastor from the Hill, conducted a gravesite service, P.L. Prattis and dozens of other mourners stayed behind to walk through the mausoleum and share tears, hugs, and memories. For Prattis, it was a moment for solemn reflection but also for apprehension about the future—about how he would get along with the *Courier*'s old guard now that Vann was gone, and about what lay ahead for all of them as the country inched ever closer to war.

SEVERAL MONTHS AFTER ROBERT L. VANN'S death, P.L. Prattis embarked on a mission to carry on his mentor's legacy. In a leadership shuffle at the *Courier*, Prattis had relinquished his managing editor duties to Bill Nunn, who everyone agreed was better suited to running the newsroom from day to day. Prattis had assumed a new title of executive editor, freeing him to write and report and also take over Vann's old role as an ambassador to the powers-that-be in Washington. In that capacity, Prattis sought the War Department's permission to make another tour of segregated Army bases across the country. In a series of articles in the spring and summer of 1941, Prattis identified some disturbing new trends: the Army was randomly assigning black enlistees to combat and noncombat roles, for example, without regard to their level of education or literacy. But he also found promising developments, such as an increase in officer training and the use of Negro doctors and nurses on segregated bases for the first time.

Then, on an August night at Fort Bragg in North Carolina, home to more than six thousand black troops, all hell broke loose. It was "colored payday," when soldiers went into nearby Fayetteville to spend their monthly pay. Shortly after midnight, a group of fifty black soldiers boarded a military bus to return to base. The white driver told them that he wouldn't leave unless accompanied by military policemen. The soldiers asked for black MPs—who were deployed only on paydays—but the driver insisted on white ones. When the white MPs arrived, one of them struck a talkative black soldier with a club. Another soldier took a defiant tone and received blows as well. Suddenly the second soldier pulled a revolver and shot at several MPs, killing one. "I'm going to break up you MPs beating us," the black soldier cried out before being gunned down himself.

That was only the beginning of what became known as Fort Bragg's "Night of Terror." After the bus incident, MPs rounded up hundreds of black servicemen who were in the Fayetteville area that night. The soldiers were stripped of their weapons, herded onto trucks, and driven back to the camp, where they were thrown into a guardhouse and subjected to several days of beatings and verbal abuse.

After Prattis reported on the Fort Bragg story in the *Courier*, the NAACP called for an investigation. When the War Department agreed, Prattis was asked to deliver an official report. As a peace gesture to Bill Nunn, Prattis asked his newsroom rival to coauthor the report, and they gathered eyewitness accounts of the Fort Bragg crackdown as well as similar stories of indiscriminate racial violence at bases in Georgia and Arkansas. Several months after the "Night of Terror," the Army announced an unprecedented response to the *Courier* findings: Fort Bragg's commandant would be transferred. The chief of the military police who ordered the Fayetteville roundup would be replaced. For the first time, a unit of thirteen black military policemen would be put on full-time duty at Fort Bragg, not just on "colored paydays," and given the same authority as white MPs.

Within a month after the Fort Bragg shakeup, the news of the surprise

Japanese attack on Pearl Harbor reached Pittsburgh. The next day, President Roosevelt delivered his "date which will live in infamy" speech and declared war against Japan. By midweek, America was at war with Germany and Italy as well. At the *Courier*, Prattis and Nunn huddled with their counterparts on the business side: Ira Lewis, now president, and Jesse Vann, who had taken the post of treasurer. As they debated how to cover the war, a complicated question confronted them: how to demonstrate patriotism while continuing the *Courier's* crusading tradition?

Prattis and Nunn knew that many blacks were skeptical about supporting the war. Indeed, it was a view that some of the *Courier's* own opinion writers were already voicing. In a column entitled "We Remember 1919," Joseph D. Bibb recalled what had happened when blacks heeded the appeal of W. E. B. Du Bois to "rally around" the flag during World War I. Instead of the hero's welcome that white veterans received, Negro soldiers returned to vicious attacks during the "Red Summer" race riots that swept the country that year. In another column, Joel Augustus Rogers voiced his own support for the war but shared the views of "a friend" who questioned why Negroes should join a military that discriminated against them, fight another colored race in the Japanese, or help to rescue British imperialism.

Yet the editors also knew that Robert L. Vann would have wanted them to rally black America yet again, and in the days after Pearl Harbor P.L. Prattis saw a way. Some of the first accounts of the attack came from a wire service reporter named Ralph Burdette Jordan. In one dispatch, Jordan reported hearing the story of a black kitchen worker who had fired at a Japanese plane from the deck of a U.S. warship. The Navy confirmed the incident, but refused to identify the sailor. So Prattis set out to discover the sailor's name. Over the next two months, he spent some $10,000 on travel, hotel, and other expenses to shuttle from Pittsburgh to Washington, chasing down every possible lead.

Three months after the attack, the *Courier* announced the results of Prattis's reporting. "MESSMAN HERO IDENTIFIED!" a front-page headline cheered. He was Doris Miller, a twenty-two-year-old from Waco, Texas. "Dorie," as he was called, had enlisted just shy of his twentieth birthday and been assigned to the USS *West Virginia* at Pearl Harbor. On the morning of the attack, Miller was standing on the signal bridge with several white officers and enlisted men. A Japanese plane dove out of the sky and opened fire, striking the ship's captain in the abdomen. As the other men pulled the commander behind an antiaircraft gun for cover, Miller and a white lieutenant manned guns on deck and fired back at the plane. They kept up the brave fusillade even as flames engulfed the deck. Near death, the captain ordered the men to abandon ship, and Miller was one of the last sailors to escape by climbing down a rope suspended from a crane on the dock.

Comparing Dorie Miller to the black heroes of the Revolutionary and Civil Wars, the *Courier* demanded that he be recognized for his bravery. A bill was introduced in Congress calling for Miller to receive the Medal of Honor. But Frank Knox, the Republican businessman whom FDR had named as his navy secretary, refused to see the military's highest award go to an untrained Negro. Instead, Knox hastily arranged for Miller to receive the Navy Cross, news that still made headlines across America and gave blacks a sense that they, too, had a stake in the war.

In February 1942, a second opportunity to rally black support arrived at the *Courier* in an unexpected form: a letter from a young reader. James Gratz Thompson was a cafeteria worker in a Cessna plane factory in Wichita, Kansas. At age twenty-six, he personified the hopes and frustrations of the children of the Great Migration. Thompson's father had moved to Wichita from Greenville, Alabama, and worked his way up from a custodial job to running a grocery store. James's mother was a native of Natchitoches, Louisiana, who volunteered at the AME church and black YMCA in Wichita. The Thompsons had managed to buy their own home, a modest, five-room, one-story ranch house. After attending a segregated elementary school, their children had gone to Wichita High School North, where James became a star athlete.

Yet for all that progress, Thompson was keenly aware of how limited opportunities for blacks in Wichita remained. Apart from a few undertakers and storeowners like his father, most blacks could find jobs only as laborers and domestics. James himself was one of only 150 Negroes who worked in Wichita's four aircraft manufacturing plants. Despite his good looks, polite manner, and gift for reading and writing, Thompson was never able to advance out of the cafeteria, and he eventually quit after being denied a 5-cents-a-week raise.

As Thompson weighed the prospect of enlisting, he wrote a letter to the *Courier* expressing his mixed emotions. "Dear Editor," the letter began, "Like all true Americans my greatest desire at this time, this crucial point of our history, is a desire for a complete victory over the forces of evil, which threaten our existence today." However, Thompson continued: "Being an American of dark complexion and some 26 years, these questions flash through my mind: 'Should I sacrifice my life to live half American?' 'Will things be better for the next generation in the peace to follow?' 'Would it be too much to demand full citizenship rights in exchange for the sacrificing of my life?'"

Then Thompson shared an idea that had come to him after seeing pictures of Winston Churchill making the gesture that symbolized the fight against Fascism in Europe. "The V for victory sign is being displayed prominently in all the so-called democratic countries which are fighting for victory over aggression, slavery and tyranny," Thompson wrote. "If this V sign means that to those now engaged in this great conflict, then let we colored Americans adopt the double VV for a double victory: The first V for victory over our enemies from without, the second V for victory over our enemies from within. For surely those who perpetrate these ugly prejudices here are seeking to destroy our democratic form of government just as surely as the Axis forces."

As soon as they read Thompson's words, Prattis and the other editors were struck by the power of the "double VV" image. In the next edition of the paper, they printed Thompson's entire letter, along with a picture of the handsome young Kansan. Meanwhile, they asked Wilbert Holloway, a *Courier* cartoonist, to create a symbol to capture the concept. The following week, without any explanation, Holloway's drawing appeared at the top of the front page: a bald eagle, perched above two stacked

Vs, framed by the words "Double Victory" and "Democracy At Home-Abroad."

The response from *Courier* readers was overwhelming. Within days, hundreds of telegrams and letters poured into the Pittsburgh offices commenting on the "Double V" drawing and congratulating the newspaper on its message. A man from Los Angeles wrote that he had cut out Holloway's illustration and posted it on his car windshield. Another from Manhattan was having the design knit into a sweater. Dozens more asked how they could get replicas—so many that the editors began producing pins and posters and selling them through classified ads in the newspaper. A Baptist minister from Ohio summed up the hope behind all the excitement: that embracing the emblem and everything it stood for would change the image of Negroes in white America. "The 'Double V' will teach the Mr. Charlie of the South a new lesson and will shake the foundations of a hypocritical North!" the preacher wrote.

In the next edition, the editors officially announced a "Double Victory Campaign." "WE HAVE A STAKE IN THIS FIGHT," they proclaimed on the front page. "WE ARE AMERICANS, TOO!" Soon readers began sending photographs as well as letters to demonstrate their support. Beatrice Williams, "Miss Bronze America" for 1941, modeled a "double V pose"—arms crossed over her chest, with both hands flashing Vs. Singer Marian Anderson cradled a Double V statuette. A Philadelphia baker displayed a Double V cake. A Hollywood bathing beauty held up a Double V poster. Newlyweds at Niagara Falls flashed the Double V sign.

As Easter Sunday approached, the National Baptist Convention declared the holiday "National Negro Double Victory Day." Putting aside his past differences with the *Courier*, Walter White issued an official proclamation of support on behalf of the NAACP. The Elks, the largest black fraternal organization, devoted their annual convention to the "Double Victory" theme. The Pullman Porters and Maids Association endorsed the campaign, and the United Automobile Workers passed a unanimous resolution of support on behalf of its seventy thousand, mostly white, members.

Other influential white figures also spoke up. Thomas Dewey, the mob-busting district attorney who was eyeing a race for governor of New York, invited a *Courier* reporter to his office in lower Manhattan to praise the campaign. "All Americans must participate in the terrible struggle ahead," Dewey agreed. Addressing book publishers in New York, Pearl Buck, the Nobel Prize–winning author, echoed the paper's dual message. "Unless we can declare ourselves whole for democracy now, and do away with prejudices against colored peoples," Buck said, "we shall lose our chance to make the world what we want it to be."

From Hollywood, Gary Cooper, Ingrid Bergman, and Humphrey Bogart sent messages of encouragement. In New York, Clare Boothe Luce, the conservative socialite and author who was running for a House seat in Connecticut, sounded the Double V theme in a radio interview. "Let us, for the sake of our boys' lives as well as for the sake of our own souls, co-operate at home as well as aboard with our loyal colored citizens and aliens of different races," Luce declared. "We will not only feel better, but fight better, and the peace we will then win will have a far, far better chance to endure."

By spring, the campaign even had a theme song. Andy Razaf and James C. Johnson, the composers of some of Fats Waller's and Bessie Smith's greatest hits, collaborated on "A Yankee Doodle Tan (the Double V Song)." Three of the country's top black bandleaders joined the chorus. Jimmie Lunceford traveled to Wichita and took James Thompson up in his private plane. Lionel Hampton performed "A Yankee Doodle Tan" on national radio. Louis Jordan opened his act with the theme song during a sold-out six-week tour of the South and Midwest.

In the early days of the campaign, Julia Bumry Jones suffered a stroke, and her young secretary, Edna Chappell, took over editing the Women's Activities pages. Excited to play a part in the war coverage, Chappell filled the section every week with news of Double V dances, Double V bake sales, Double V quilting bees, and Double V gardens. There were pictures of Double V dresses, Double V hats, even a Double V hairdo, the winner of a contest at the Madam C. J. Walker College of Beauty in Chicago. The paper took to naming a "Double V Girl of the Week" and, as summer arrived, there were photos of Double V bathing suit contests.

By June, the *Courier* announced that membership in "Double V Clubs" across the country had surpassed 200,000. Along with generating tens of thousands of dollars for the war effort from the purchase of pins and posters, the clubs had sold millions of dollars' worth of war bonds and sent tons of clothes, shoes, books, magazines, candy, cigarettes, and ashtrays to black enlistees reporting for duty across the country.

Yet instead of gratitude for the *Courier's* help in mobilizing black support for "Victory Abroad," the Double V Campaign was met with a very different response in Washington. President Roosevelt and FBI director J. Edgar Hoover chose to focus instead on the demands for "Victory At Home," and what they saw as the threat to wartime morale posed by the *Courier's* continued coverage of racial injustice.

Hoover had been suspicious of the Negro press from his first days as an agent for the "Alien Enemy Bureau," the precursor to the FBI, investigating ties between black and communist newspapers during World War I. As long as the *Courier's* circulation remained modest, and Robert L. Vann was alive to trumpet his pro-American and pro-capitalist views, it had been spared Hoover's scrutiny. But now the *Courier* was squarely in the FBI director's sights. As early as the fall of 1941, Hoover had sent a request to an FBI agent in Pittsburgh to investigate whether P.L. Prattis was acting as a foreign spy when he went on his tour of segregated military bases and reported on the bloody roundup of black soldiers at Fort Bragg. The agent reported back that Prattis had done nothing to threaten "the national defense program," so Hoover backed off, temporarily.

Then, on the day after Pearl Harbor, Roosevelt put Hoover in charge of "censorship matters"—the president's euphemism for monitoring the press to identify stories that should be suppressed in the name of the war effort. Hoover began gathering and passing along evidence of seditious reporting gathered by the FBI, Army intelligence, and the ironically named Office of Facts and Figures (OFF), the wartime agency Roosevelt had created to ensure "the dissemination of factual information . . . on the progress of the defense effort." In one report analyzing the contents of five black newspapers, OFF singled out the *Courier* and the Double V

Campaign in particular, concluding that its "basic concern" was to carp about racial discrimination.

Exploiting his back channel to Roosevelt, Hoover complained that his efforts to crack down on the press were being thwarted by FDR's attorney general, Francis Biddle. Biddle, a Philadelphia patrician and disciple of Justice Oliver Wendell Holmes, believed that the press had a constitutional right to criticize the government, as long as it did not directly assist the enemy. In several tense confrontations, Roosevelt mocked Biddle's restraint and pushed him to get tougher. "When are you going to indict the seditionists?" the president demanded in several cabinet meetings. In one, he specifically brought up black newspapers and suggested that Biddle and Postmaster General Frank Walker lean on their publishers. According to Biddle's notes, FDR's instructions were "to see what could be done about preventing their subversive language."

By March 1942, FBI agents began showing up in the newsrooms of black newspapers. In Los Angeles, they barged into the *California Eagle* and interrogated its publisher, Charlotta Bass, about whether she had received money from the Japanese or the Germans to print articles critical of the U.S. military. In an editorial voicing support for Bass, the *Courier* reported that the FBI had also visited an unnamed second black paper, and there is good reason to believe that it was the *Courier* itself. Years later, Frank Bolden, then a city desk reporter, recalled being in the newsroom one day in early 1942 when a group of FBI agents appeared. They asked to speak to the editors, Bolden said, and "expressed dissatisfaction at what we were doing . . . [and] suggested that we protest in another way or wait until the war was over."

When the agents left, P.L. Prattis told his reporters not to be intimidated. He "just called them scared white people—Hoover's flunkies," Bolden recalled. "We all said that. . . . We just ignored them."

What Prattis and his colleagues couldn't ignore was the possibility that the *Courier* might not get mailed. By May, Post Office chief Frank Walker had reluctantly joined the sedition hunt after repeated goading by Roosevelt. Tipped by the FBI, a Post Office examiner concluded that one edition of the *Courier* was "unmailable." The report singled out a brief account of a speech by Harlem pastor Adam Clayton Powell Jr. in which Powell used words like "Gestapo" and "pogroms" to describe conditions for blacks in the United States. (Apparently the Post Office examiner missed the bemused tone of the story, which described the bombastic Powell as "hurling similes like a Bataan Island battery of machine guns.") The same examiner later recommended suppressing three more editions of the *Courier*, although no action was taken because the papers had already been mailed. Around the same time, Billy Rowe, the *Courier*'s well-connected Broadway critic, heard talk in New York circles that the Post Office was looking to shut down black newspapers and passed those rumors along to Pittsburgh.

Eventually Prattis became so concerned that he reached out directly to Roosevelt. Although it's not clear how he got through to the president, in May Roosevelt sent a memo to his press secretary, Stephen Early, telling him that Prattis was planning to be in Washington and had requested a meeting with Early to discuss "disconcerting reports concerning their own newspaper—coming from various sources." Early never followed up, however, and there is no record that the meeting ever took place.

Instead of Prattis, it was John Sengstacke of *The Chicago Defender* who went to Washington to plead the case for the black press. Shortly after becoming the *Defender*'s publisher, Sengstacke had persuaded his competitors to form a trade group called the Negro National Publishers Association (NNPA). In June 1942, acting as president of the NNPA, Sengstacke approached Mary McLeod Bethune, the leader of FDR's "Negro Cabinet," and asked if she could arrange a meeting with Attorney General Francis Biddle to discuss the suppression threat.

When Sengstacke arrived at the Justice Department, copies of the *Defender*, the *Courier*, and several other Negro papers were strewn across a conference table. According to Sengstacke's account, Biddle warned that he was "going to shut them all up" if the papers didn't tone down their coverage, and the publisher defiantly told Biddle to "go ahead and attempt it." By the end of the meeting, however, it became clear that both men wanted to avoid an escalation. Sengstacke agreed to urge his fellow publishers to seek more official comment on stories critical of the government. For his part, Biddle offered assurances that the Justice Department would resist formal sedition charges. After Sengstacke briefed his fellow NNPA members on the meeting, P.L. Prattis told his reporters in Pittsburgh that the threat of being shut down had passed.

In a wide-ranging history, *The African American Newspaper*, journalism scholar Patrick Washburn ranked *The Pittsburgh Courier*'s Double V Campaign as one of the three most influential crusades every undertaken by the Negro press—along with Ida B. Wells's battle against lynching and Robert Abbott's appeal for Northern migration. But Washburn also noted that virtually all of the nearly one thousand articles, letters, photos, and drawings devoted to the campaign were published in the space of six months. By the fall of 1942, mention of the campaign fell off dramatically—except for a small "vv" symbol that continued to run at the end of *Courier* stories until the end of the war.

So what happened? In *The Black Press: Soldiers Without Swords*, an award-winning documentary film, director Stanley Nelson suggested that the pullback was a response to the government's campaign of surveillance and harassment. Washburn, meanwhile, cited the *Courier*'s stake in not jeopardizing its wartime financial windfall, as a special tax on excess corporate profits encouraged cigarette and other consumer goods giants to spend money on advertising in black newspapers for the first time.

Yet if Prattis and the other Pittsburgh editors were motivated by anything in the final months of 1942, it wasn't fear or greed as much as a new sense of optimism. After years of advocating for a greater role for Negroes in the military, they were finally seeing those dreams realized. At Fort Bragg and Fort Huachuca in Arizona, all-black Army units were at last receiving combat training. Having acknowledged Dorie Miller's heroics, the Navy was starting to allow blacks to serve in other than kitchen and custodial roles. The Marines and the Coast Guard were accepting their first black enlistees. At the Tuskegee Institute in Alabama, Negroes were training to become Army pilots.

On the home front, black labor was suddenly in wide demand. By the fall of 1942, the War Production Board had decreed that government contractors hire more Negroes. From Goodyear rubber to Kaiser shipyards to Forstmann textiles, manufacturing giants were increasing employment of black workers. The Congress of Industrial Organizations, the country's largest labor union, had restated its policy of welcoming black members and was pushing the American Federation of Labor to end its discriminatory practices. By the end of the year, the *Courier* was running weekly photographs of black women working at defense plants. In one photo, smiling riveters at the Curtiss-Wright plant in Buffalo put the finishing touches on the nose and wing sections of P-40 Warhawk fighters, the planes that Tuskegee-trained black pilots would soon be flying in the skies over the Mediterranean.

When the *Courier* recapped the year, its headline was "1942 in Retrospect Shows Gains Outweigh Losses." The story didn't ignore the year's bad news: six lynchings, failure to repeal a poll tax, housing riots in Philadelphia and Detroit. But it heralded "gains on the job front" as the year's biggest story. Along with all the new opportunities in the military, the paper cited advances in pay equity for black teachers and increased government benefits for black farmers. In a blow to Jim Crow, the Supreme Court had ruled unanimously in favor of Arthur Mitchell, the lone black member of the U.S. House Representatives, in his lawsuit against a Southern railroad line that had ejected Mitchell from his first-class sleeping car while he was traveling through Arkansas.

In a column entitled "We Gain by War," Joseph D. Bibb, the skeptic about U.S. intervention after Pearl Harbor, now extolled the war's benefits for black America. "No longer will the racketeer, the gambling mogul nor the vice magnate be the criterion for our youth," Bibb wrote. "War heroes will challenge their admiration and fire their ambition. . . . Those who are keeping the home fire burning are bound to receive benefits, too. They are learning new trades, are being absorbed into new industries. They are being required to buy bonds, which is compulsory saving, and every day, they are building social security by paying for unemployment insurance.

When the war ends the colored American will be better off financially, spiritually and economically. War may be hell for some, but it bids fair to open up the portals of heaven for us."

When *Courier* reporter Frank Bolden reflected back on the Double V Campaign decades later, he compared it to a firework that fell to earth only after it had lit up the night sky. "We had knocked on the door and gotten some attention and so the editors said, 'Let's concentrate on what the people are doing,'" Bolden recalled. "For example, why would I want to read about the Double V when people are working in a war plant down the street? I wouldn't. These gains showed good faith intentions by the government and other people, and we felt we should follow suit. . . . In other words, the Double V was like a Roman candle. It flared up, it did its work and then it died down. It wasn't the sole reason things opened up, but it certainly woke people up."

By the end of 1942, P.L. Prattis had another good reason to move on from the Double V Campaign. As black troops began to ship out to the war zones of Africa, Italy, and Northern Europe, Prattis took charge of securing War Department accreditation for reporters to cover them. After the Italian-Ethiopian conflict, he and the other Pittsburgh editors knew that when it came to selling newspapers, nothing could compete with war stories from the front lines. By the end of the war, the *Courier* would dispatch a total of ten accredited war correspondents—far more than any other black newspaper—and that investment would lift its circulation to an all-time high of 466,000 copies a week by 1946. Of those reporters, the city desk's Frank Bolden would be one of the first to leave Pittsburgh, and the last to return home from the Pacific four years later.

BLAZING TRAILS WAS NOTHING new in Frank Bolden's family. Before the Great Migration, his grandfather had been the first colored man to serve on a jury in Nashville, Tennessee. After Bolden's parents moved north, his father became the first black mail carrier in the town of Washington, south of Pittsburgh. Frank was the first in his family to go to college, enrolling at the University of Pittsburgh in 1930 at the age of seventeen. A moon-faced redhead with charming freckles and a loquacious manner, he made scores of black and white friends, pledging the colored Alpha Phi Alpha fraternity but also integrating the school marching band, playing the clarinet. So it was no surprise that Bolden would major in biology and set his sights on becoming a doctor.

But when Bolden went with a Jewish friend to apply to Pitt's medical school, they were both turned away. The quota for Jewish students was filled, they were informed, and the school didn't admit Negroes. Bolden pursued a graduate degree instead, hoping to go into teaching. When he was finished, he discovered that the Pittsburgh public schools didn't hire black teachers. While in grad school, he worked part-time for *The Pittsburgh Courier*, keeping an eye on Crawfords and Grays games for Chester Washington while Ches was off covering Joe Louis. So with his other paths forward blocked, Bolden was ready to listen when Robert L. Vann offered him a full-time job.

Bolden was assigned a column on Hill District nightlife, entitled "Orchestra Swirl," and he began to display a gift for coining colorful phrases. He called the prostitutes who emerged after dark on the Lower Hill "the sisterhood of the nocturnal order." He dubbed Gus Greenlee and Woogie Harris "digitarians"—or "numbers runners with class." After covering his share of stories at the John Wesley AME Church in Sugartop and the Allegheny County Prison downtown, Bolden came up with a particularly memorable description of Wiley Avenue. It was "the only street in America that begins with a church and ends with a jail," he wrote.

In the months after Pearl Harbor, P.L. Prattis summoned Bolden to propose another first. Prattis was looking for reporters to cover black soldiers who were being deployed to the front. Under War Department rules, newspapers were required to submit candidates to be assigned to specific troop units. Once approved, "accredited war correspondents" were issued uniforms and given the honorary rank of major, while agreeing to submit their reporting to Army censors. Prattis had come to see that in reviewing Negro candidates, the War Department was impressed by one qualification above all others: a college education. Although Bolden had no military or foreign reporting experience, he did have two degrees from the University of Pittsburgh.

Thus it was that Frank Bolden became one of the first black war correspondents of World War II. In June 1942, he packed his bags for Fort Huachuca, the Army training camp in southeastern Arizona, just miles from the Mexican border. During World War I, Fort Huachuca had been home to the "Buffalo Soldiers" of the 10th Cavalry Regiment. Now it was serving as a base for the 93rd Infantry Division, the first black contingent to be designated for combat training after Pearl Harbor.

As soon as Bolden arrived at Fort Huachuca, he saw why the *Courier* had once described it as the "worst location in the U.S. for Negro soldiers." The remote location was no accident. Tucson, the nearest big city, was eighty miles away. There wasn't a town with more than a few hundred white people within twenty miles. Inside the base, white commanders enjoyed their own dining hall and social club. But for the black soldiers, there was nothing to do for recreation except buy swigs of whiskey sold out of kegs along the road outside the camp and visit tin-shack brothels crawling with venereal disease in the tiny, aptly named town of Fry nearby.

Bolden also discovered that the 93rd Infantry wasn't going anyplace soon. Although the division had fought in World War I—earning the nickname the "Blue Helmets" for the French-issued trench hats they wore— it had been disbanded afterward. Now the Army would force the Blue Helmets to undergo two years of training before giving them a chance to fight again. So for the rest of 1942 and into 1943, Bolden labored to turn the drudgery of tank maneuvers and bayonet drills into readable copy for the *Courier*. Occasionally there was an outbreak of racial violence to cover, but Bolden had to be careful. To bypass the military censors, he typed those stories on onionskin paper and gave them to black laundresses to smuggle out of the camp. After one story about a gunfight between a black private and a white MP appeared in the *Courier*, the FBI summoned Bolden to Pittsburgh for questioning.

In the middle of 1943, the Blue Helmets left Fort Huachuca for other training bases in California and Louisiana. Instead of following them, Bolden returned to Pittsburgh. The circumstances aren't known, but they may have had to do with a troubled marriage: once the war was over, Bolden's first wife, Helen, filed for divorce and ran off with another man from Chicago. So for the next year, before he finally got a chance to go overseas, Bolden watched as other *Courier* reporters beat him to the front.

The first was Edgar Rouzeau, a reporter in the Harlem bureau who was the very first black reporter to receive war correspondent accreditation. Rouzeau was placed with the first Negro unit to ship out: the 41st Engineers Regiment, known as the "Singing Engineers" because of the spirituals they chanted while training. The Engineers were sent to Liberia, to construct an airfield to serve as a transport hub for the North Africa campaign. But unhappily for Rouzeau, military censors refused to allow him to report on the mission, because Liberia's prime minister hadn't told his parliament that he had given permission for the airfield. Seven months passed before Rouzeau was able to sing the praises of the Singing Engineers in the *Courier*. He was rewarded for his patience, however, when President Roosevelt made a surprise visit to the new airfield on his way back from the Casablanca conference. For the first and last time, FDR inspected black troops in the field, and Rouzeau got the scoop.

From Africa, Rouzeau went to Italy, to cover the arrival of the 99th Pursuit Squadron, the first deployment of black pilots trained at the Tuskegee Institute. It was a rocky debut. In Rouzeau's words, the squadron was treated like an "orphan" unit and forced to complete on-site training on its own. When its single-engine P-40 Warhawk planes flew cover for Allied bombers in the invasion of Sicily, they were no match for Germany's Focke-Wulfs. In the fall of 1943, the squadron's captain, Benjamin O. Davis Jr.—the son of the black general—returned home to a hostile congressional hearing. *Time* magazine reported that Army commanders were "not entirely satisfied" with the Tuskegee "experiment" and that the only thing keeping them from confining black pilots to noncombat duty was because "the Negro press has campaigned against it."

Yet the *Courier* continued to publish Rouzeau's upbeat accounts of the 99th Squadron's occasional successes. The stories helped buy time for Davis to complete training of a full Tuskegee fighter group. When those pilots arrived in Europe with new red-tailed P-51 Mustang fighter planes, they performed heroically for the rest of the Italian campaign and later downed dozens of German planes over the skies of Northern Europe.

The white press was even more hostile to the black ground troops who fought in the Italian campaign. In 1944, the 92nd Infantry Division, the latest incarnation of the "Buffalo Soldiers," arrived in Italy, led by a white general, Edward "Ned" Almond. Also placed under Almond's command was the 366th Infantry Regiment, which had a black leader, Colonel Howard Queen. When Almond ordered men from both forces to attack Italian positions in the hills of the Serchio Valley that winter, they suffered heavy losses and had to retreat. They were pushed back again in the spring when they tried to clear out enemy positions around the Cinquale Canal on Italy's western coast.

After that setback, *Newsweek* magazine published a story entitled "A Behaviour Pattern" concluding that blacks in combat roles had been "more productive of disappointments and failure than anything else." In *The New York Times*, correspondent Milton Bracken wrote that only the "supersensitivity of some Negro papers at home" kept white commanders from telling the truth about the unpreparedness of black troops.

In Pittsburgh, P.L. Prattis had made two unlikely choices to send to the Italian front. Ollie Harrington was a cartoonist, the creator of a popular weekly strip called *Bootsie*. But Harrington was also a graduate of Yale, so Prattis submitted his name for accreditation and sent him to cover the arrival of the 92nd Division in Italy. Collins George was a former French professor who had served as a conscientious objector and only just started working in the *Courier*'s "Missing Persons Bureau," taking classified ads from people looking for runaway loved ones. But George had an even more valuable college credential: a degree from Howard University, which Howard Queen and many of the other black officers of the 366th Regiment had attended.

George arrived in Italy just in time to report a very different version of the Cinquale fiasco. According to George's sources among the officers of 366th Regiment, Ned Almond had rejected Howard Queen's request for additional training before his men were ordered into battle. Almond also told the black troops that they were only there because of pressure from "your Negro newspapers" and that he would make sure they got "their share of casualties." Then Almond sent the soldiers on the attack just as unusually muddy conditions created by a snowy winter and a wet spring had caused the rest of the Fifth Army to delay its assault on Italy's Gothic Line.

After the war, the Buffalos were widely mocked as the "hapless 92nd," and Ned Almond was hailed for exposing the failure of segregated military training. It would be decades before one of the division's regiments, the 370th, was properly recognized for its role in the final assault on the Gothic Line, after the regiment was removed from Almond's command and assigned to a mixed division with white and Japanese American troops. (One hero of the 370th was Vernon Baker, the lone surviving recipient of the Medals of Honor that were belatedly bestowed on black soldiers who fought in World War II.) But the Buffalos never forgot Collins George for sticking up for them. "He did for us what Ernie Pyle was doing for the American white soldier," a 92nd Infantry artilleryman named Hondon Hargrove wrote when George passed away in 1992. "He made us feel like we were great patriots, accomplishing great deeds for our country."

For Prattis, covering the role of black troops in D-Day and the liberation of Northern Europe proved a frustrating ordeal. Early in the war, he hired George Padmore, a black intellectual who happened to live in Europe, as London correspondent, only to discover that Padmore was better at pontificating than reporting. Then Prattis took a chance on a college graduate named Randy Dixon who until then had only reported on sports for the *Courier*. A handsome charmer with a rakish mustache, Dixon looked the part of a war correspondent, and the *Courier* spent some $18,000—a hefty investment at the time—to train him and put him up in London for fifteen months. But Dixon was more interested in reporting on the London social scene and parties thrown by British women for Negro soldiers than making his way to the front. He missed the first deployments of black troops on D-Day, and only arrived at the beaches of Normandy two weeks later.

Furious, Prattis called Dixon home and replaced him with another college man named Theodore Stanford. Stanford arrived in France in time to witness the liberation of Paris, then was assigned to the black 784th Tank Battalion as it made its way across Belgium toward Germany, supporting the infantry divisions that withstood the Nazi counterattack at the Battle of the Bulge and advanced all the way to the Rhine River. Yet because almost all the Negro troops in the European Theater of Operations worked behind the front lines—as truck drivers, bridge builders, ammunition runners, mine sweepers, and bakers of thirty thousand tons of bread a day—there was little record outside the black press that one in ten American soldiers in the ETO was black. (In Steven Spielberg's *Saving Private Ryan*, for example, the black soldiers who operated anti-aircraft decoy balloons over Omaha Beach on D-Day were nowhere to be seen.)

When the Blue Helmets did deploy in the spring of 1944, it was to the Pacific Theater. But as it turned out, Frank Bolden didn't accompany them. Instead, Prattis assigned another improbable war correspondent, Billy Rowe, previously known to *Courier* readers as the paper's New York–based theater columnist. Troops from the 93rd Infantry were assigned to a mission to liberate the Japanese-occupied island of Bougainville, and they took part in several battles. During one, inexperienced grunts panicked, adding to the charges of inadequacy that would be leveled against black troops. But in other skirmishes, they performed courageously—including one that made a minor hero of Billy Rowe himself. After a bloody day of fighting, Rowe volunteered to go back into the jungle with eight GIs to the retrieve the wounded. He shouldered rifles while the soldiers carried stretchers, and when the search party came under attack he helped the Blue Helmets circle back and kill three Japanese snipers.

Finally, in April 1944, Frank Bolden got his long-awaited letter from the

War Department. He was assigned to black troops headed for an undisclosed location in the Middle East. In his first story during the ocean passage, Bolden's excitement was palpable. Showing off his way with words, he conjured up the cast of characters on the ship. Two black GIs took over "the laundry and tonsorial concessions . . . and the trip was quite profitable for both of them," Bolden reported. A canny card sharp feigned illiteracy—an act that "would never rate an 'Oscar' . . . but was otherwise amusing." A private in charge of the KP "resembled the picture of the little man who adorns the cover page of *Esquire* and possessed a strong, booming voice somewhat like that of a rail gang boss."

Bolden's mood darkened, however, when after two months at sea he discovered his destination. It was the desert monarchy of Iran, where after seizing power from his father the young Shah had turned over large stretches of land for a "Persian Corridor" to supply Russian troops on the Eastern Front. As Bolden and the rest of the passengers disembarked in the Gulf city of Khorramshahr, it was so hot that a thermometer sitting in the sun registered 146 degrees. Black GIs who manned the port wore two layers of gloves as they unloaded metal equipment. The soldiers who had become so close during the long voyage were broken up and dispatched to new unknown locations. Meanwhile, Bolden boarded a train for the six-hundred-mile trip to Tehran across an arid landscape that he described as "making Death Valley look like the Florida Everglades."

Bolden spent several months searching for compelling stories in the Iranian desert before giving up. Instead he made his way to Burma, the British colony in Southeast Asia where black troops were at the center of the most ambitious engineering project of the war. When the Japanese army pushed the British out of the area, the Allies had lost access to most of the Burma Road stretching from India into southern China. In order to supply the anti-Japanese forces of General Chiang Kai-shek, they had to airlift men and equipment over the "Hump" of the Himalayan Mountains. So, in 1942, the Allies undertook to build a new one-thousand-mile road through the part of Burma they still controlled to serve as the main supply route into China. The project became known as the "Ledo Road," after the town in India where it originated. It was also called the "Stilwell Road," for the man who was given command of the mission, U.S. General Joseph Stilwell. To build the road, Stilwell was assigned fifteen thousand troops, almost ten thousand of whom were black—the largest deployment of Negro soldiers to a single mission during the entire war.

From the beginning, the operation was a Herculean struggle of man against nature. The first hundred miles of road traversed the mountains on the border between India and Burma, through a narrow opening known as "Hell Pass" because it was so treacherous. Bulldozers had to remove thousands of feet of dirt for every mile, along a path that twisted and turned through the dense jungle and rose more than four thousand feet from its lowest to its highest point. Over the next 350-mile stretch, until the new passage connected with an existing portion of the Burma Road, engineers had to erect bridges across a hundred rivers and 155 streams. At any time, they faced the threat of a Japanese air attack or a monsoon rain that could wash away a month's work in one day. "They don't need engineers here, they need sailors," one GI lamented to Bolden.

Bolden described the mission as "Green Hell." "Sweat, sweat, sweat . . . that's what it took, not perspiration," he wrote. "Men like these, with guts of Atlas, who helped move fourteen million cubic yards of dirt for the Ledo Road out of malaria, cobra, tiger-infested and heat-punishing, monsoon-drenched swamp land, don't perspire. They sweat!" The toll was as much psychological as physical. The nearest "Negro Rest Club," as the Army's segregated relaxation facilities were known, was hundreds of miles away, in an orphanage in Calcutta. Days seemed endless. Sleep was fitful. Fear of death was constant, yet without any prospect of glory. Disease and accidents claimed lives every day, and rescue attempts often compounded the losses. One GI drowned trying to save another who fell into a monsoon-swelled river. A black private from Birmingham, Alabama, in the heart of Jim Crow country, befriended a white soldier in his unit only to die trying to save the buddy from a burning ammunition truck.

The black GIs weren't even permitted to witness the rewards of their grueling labor. One Engineer Construction Battalion was assigned to build an airfield in a rice paddy on the Indian side of the Ledo Road. For three months, the men drained fields, hauled gravel from as far as ten miles away, and mixed and poured concrete in the 100-degree heat. They were gone, however, by the time Allied bombers began using the runway for the first land-based air attacks on the Japanese mainland. When the Ledo Road finally reached China, black truck drivers were excluded from the first convoy over the border. The decision was protested, and ten black drivers were added. When the convoy returned to Burma after only two days, there were rumors that the Chinese had turned the trucks back because they didn't want Negroes in their country.

When Bolden ran into two old friends from Pittsburgh serving with a trucking company on the Ledo Road, all they wanted to talk about was home. Sergeant Johnny Adams was the "motor dispenser" for the unit, in charge of keeping its vehicles in working order. His white officer praised Adams as "an indefatigable worker who is about the best man at his job that he had ever seen," Bolden reported. But Adams only wanted to quiz Bolden about "the girls and the 4-Fs" back in the Hill District, and about the value of the war bonds he had purchased in hopes of studying for a business degree. Sergeant Joe Walker of Homewood had logged 270,000 miles a month driving a cargo truck along the "Kidney Run," as he called it, and had come under enemy fire countless times. But Walker's mind was on "a certain Pittsburgh lovely" who was waiting for him at home and on a plan to open a haberdashery after the war was over.

When word of the victory in Europe reached Burma, it was monsoon season. The men on the Ledo Road told Bolden they were too exhausted to celebrate. "I'm actually happy but I lack the energy to show it," Sergeant James Thompkins said, adding stoically: "It'll probably be a long time before transportation will be made available to relieve us. Guess there is nothing to do but keep on working." Sergeant Herbert Boyd of Washington, D.C., who had worked on the road for twenty-two months, could only shrug. "I feel good about it but I can't indulge in hysterics," Boyd said. "There's still some monotonous work to be done here and the monsoon makes things tougher. My major interest concerns my return home to my wife." Several GIs preferred to talk about other news that had reached the jungle: that President Roosevelt had signed a new law to help returning vets finish school, buy homes, and start businesses. "I'm going straight to my wife and family, then I'm going to see about this GI Bill of Rights and try to get some loan money for my farm," said Private Eddie William Fedd of Georgia. "The next depression won't catch me this time."

With the end of the war finally in sight, Bolden left the Ledo Road temporarily in the summer of 1945 to cover the other major story in the region: India's push for independence from Britain. Lord Wavell, the British viceroy, had summoned the leaders of the movement to a meeting in the town of Simla in the northern mountains. Arriving in Simla, Bolden found the Indians curious to meet a black reporter, and eager to send messages to U.S. readers. "So you have come all the way from America as a representative of the Negro press—splendid!" Jawaharlal Nehru, the head of the Hindu-led Congress party, exclaimed as they shook hands. Questioned by Bolden about the Indian caste system, Nehru predicted that it would disappear under the "modified Socialist system" that he advocated. Nehru also waved off the idea that demands for autonomy from India's 93 million Muslims and their leader, Muhammad Ali Jinnah, could not be defused peacefully. "Even Mr. Jinnah would not welcome a civil war," Nehru insisted, calmly puffing on a cigarette. "Nationalism is our goal and not division."

Jinnah took a very different tone in his meeting with Bolden. Wasting no time on pleasantries, he launched into an attack on the Congress party for trying to dictate which Muslims could participate in an interim regime. Jinnah also charged that Mahatma Gandhi, with his saintly appeals to one-man, one-vote rule, was part of the anti-Muslim conspiracy. "Planning is Gandhi's strongest point," Jinnah scoffed. "He knew that majority rule is the essence of democracy. What good would it be to the Hindu majority if it did not have the Muslim minority under control? Yes, the Muslims must be destroyed as a separate political entity!"

When Gandhi invited Bolden for an interview, he responded with quiet fatalism to Nehru's imperviousness and Jinnah's paranoia. "If there should be chaos, God will work it out," Gandhi said, sitting cross-legged on the floor in his spare loincloth. Fixing Bolden with a soft-eyed stare, the Mahatma expounded on his theories of nonviolence—offering what for many black American readers would be their exposure to the philosophy that would one day play such an important role in their own struggle. Nonviolence did not extend to opposing all war, or even withholding support for British troops and bases, Gandhi made clear. "I do not want the Axis to win," he said. "Non-violence is the best way of fighting the enemy within the city's gates—especially when you are too weak physically and economically to exert physical force and violence."

"What about the Negroes in America?" Gandhi asked at one point. "Is their lot improving?" Bolden responded positively. He described how awful Jim Crow was in the South but how different life was for Negroes in the North. He talked about the rise in literacy and business ownership in Northern cities. He described the increase in factory jobs and the improving relations with the white labor movement. And he spoke proudly of the role his editors in Pittsburgh had played in that progress. "They will never stop, never let up," Bolden told Gandhi. "They keep probing, jabbing and screaming until they flush another reactionary victim from his smug and lucrative foxhole."

When the Japanese finally surrendered on September 2, 1945, Billy Rowe wrote the front-page story for the *Courier*. From General Douglas MacArthur's headquarters in Manila, he reported that black service troops were on ships headed for Japan and would be among the first GIs to enter Tokyo. (Due to a paperwork error, Rowe himself beat the soldiers there, becoming one of the first Americans to set foot in the ravaged capital.)

Meanwhile, Frank Bolden's story about the end of the war for the men of the Ledo Road was relegated to page nine. "Peace Means These GIs Can Leave Jungle Hell," read the headline. This time, Bolden reported, the men allowed themselves to celebrate. "We got mean drunk, because there was nothing else to do or place to go," said Corporal Willis Pickens of Long Branch, New Jersey. An Army points system gave combat troops priority in being discharged, so most of the soldiers still didn't know when they would get to leave. "I hope to be home by Christmas," said Corporal Joe Patterson of New York City, adding that he wanted to "hurry home to my sweet wife and the old Civil Service job where I hope to enjoy the ease and comfort of the best home on earth."

Bolden did his writerly best to sum up the legacy of the Ledo Road troops. "The Tan Yanks have written their names high among those who served their country well," he wrote. "The milestones along the Stilwell Road are the graves of those who made the supreme sacrifice." Yet for all of Bolden's eloquence, it was a sacrifice to little avail. More than $150 million had been spent on the Ledo Road. More than a thousand men had died, a vast number of them black. Yet the road had never become the invaluable supply route that the Allies envisioned. By the end of the war, it accounted for less than a tenth of the tonnage reaching China, the majority of which was still being airlifted over the Himalayas. Winston Churchill's prediction—that the Ledo Road would prove "an immense, laborious task, unlikely to be finished until the need for it had passed"— had proved prophetic. As soon as the war ended, the road was largely abandoned and was gradually swallowed up by nature.

In the V-J Day edition of the *Courier*, another story was tucked in the bottom corner of the front page. "600,000 Negroes Face Job Loss in Cutbacks," read the headline. The story detailed an Urban League report on the expected layoffs of wartime factory workers, and the problems it would create in cities across America for black communities whose numbers had swelled yet again with a third wave of migration from the South. Over the coming months, millions of white soldiers would return from World War II to their old jobs in the cities, or to new lives in the suburbs made possible by cheap home loans provided by the GI Bill. Postwar movies and books and the new medium of television would celebrate those veterans, including the millions of white immigrants who had proved their patriotism by serving their country. But for black GIs and their families and neighbors, and for P.L. Prattis and Frank Bolden and all the *Courier* editors who had kindled their hopes, the dream of a Double Victory that burned so bright at the start of the war would be slowly snuffed out, just like the road that ten thousand anonymous "Tan Yanks" had carved out of an implacable jungle.

In 1946, (left to right) Earl Hines, Mary Lou Williams, Erroll Garner, Billy Eckstine, and Maxine Sullivan all came home for a "Night of the Stars" gala as part of a Pittsburgh tradition known as "FROGS Week."

7

THE COMPLEX MR. B

TEENIE HARRIS JOINED THE *Courier* as its first staff photographer in 1941, just in time to capture the men of black Pittsburgh going off to war. Retiring from his former life as a numbers runner for his older brother, Woogie, Harris roamed the city with his bulky Speed Graphic camera, snapping photos with a thrifty speed that earned him the nickname "One Shot." He photographed Johnny Woodruff, the University of Pittsburgh sprinter who won a gold medal at the Berlin Olympics, in his lieutenant's uniform as Woodruff prepared to join the 369th antiaircraft regiment. Harris recorded the hero's welcome received by James Wiley, the Pitt physics major who was one of the first Tuskegee Airmen to fly missions over Italy. As black soldiers started to return home, they trooped to Teenie's private studio on Wylie Avenue for formal portraits in their dress khakis, accompanied by sweethearts in fur coats and their finest hats and jewelry.

Now it was summer of 1944, and nightlife was in full swing again as word of the successful D-Day invasion reached Pittsburgh. In the music world, the big news was that Billy Eckstine was coming home with his own big band, and a new spelling of his name. "It's Eckstine Now!" announced the *Courier* to readers who had always known Billy by his family name, Eck*stein*. On a steamy night in August, Teenie Harris went downtown in one of the luxury cars he always drove—Cadillacs and Lincoln Continentals handed down from Woogie—to photograph the Billy Eckstine Orchestra performing at the Aragon Ballroom. Climbing up onto the raised stage, he got a shot that would prove historic: of Dizzy Gillespie and Charlie Parker, the two Eckstine sidemen who would go on to revolutionize jazz, playing together while Billy eyed the camera in the background. Then Teenie climbed up to the balcony to capture a panoramic view of the entire orchestra, fronted by an as yet little known singer wearing a flowered skirt, a ruffled white blouse, and a gardenia in her hair. Her name was Sarah Vaughan.

By the time the Billy Eckstine Orchestra came back to Pittsburgh two months later, it was a national sensation. In just ten weeks, it had performed in ten different cities across the East and the Midwest and sold more than $100,000 worth of concert tickets. The band had played to sellout crowds at the country's top black theaters, the Apollo in Harlem and the Regal in Chicago. Its latest recording, a seductive ballad called "Good Jelly Blues," was on its way to selling a million copies. This time the Eckstine orchestra played at the former Pythian Temple on the Hill, now renamed the Hill City Auditorium, and Teenie Harris was there to photograph the band's newest members. Sonny Stitt and Dexter Gordon had joined the saxophone section, and the band had a new drummer, Art Blakey, who had also grown up in Pittsburgh and who played with such ferocity that his drumsticks disappeared in a blur in Teenie's photos.

As it happened, Lena Horne was in town that week in October as well, performing at the Stanley Theatre downtown. The Loendi Club threw a reception to welcome her back, and Harris covered it for the *Courier*. Yet as Teenie's photographs made clear, Billy Eckstine was as big an attraction as the guest of honor. Wherever he turned, women and men crowed around to be in his presence. When a cake was brought out, Billy helped

Lena cut it and shared the first slice. And when the guests sat down to dinner, Eckstine was placed at the head table. While Lena strained to make conversation with her ex-husband, Louis Jones, Billy sat several places away, flirting with Lena's friend and piano accompanist Charlotte Catlin as they picked at lobster tails.

Over the Thanksgiving holiday, the Eckstine band traveled to Cleveland and Youngstown, then returned to New York for Christmas. It appeared again at the Apollo and recorded a new song, "I Want to Talk About You," that became another hit. As the New Year dawned, the band made a five-city swing through Texas before heading to its first West Coast engagement, at the Club Plantation in Los Angeles. In a *Courier* column, West Coast correspondent Herman Hill drew a comparison that would follow Eckstine wherever he went for the next decade. "Bandleader Billy Eckstine, currently in our midst at the Plantation, could easily be press agented into a sepia Sinatra," Hill predicted. "He's that handsome and his voice and personality put Frankie to shame."

With his languid baritone and lounge singer looks, Billy Eckstine would come to be remembered as the black crooner who never quite made it into the same league as Frank Sinatra or Tony Bennett. In fact, the story was more complicated, and so was the man, in ways that had much to do with the culture of black Pittsburgh. Like so many of its notables, Eckstine had light features and a surface air of refinement. But he could also exhibit the grit of a Homestead steelworker and the rakishness of a Wylie Avenue racketeer. His education came in equal parts from the classroom—Pittsburgh's Peabody High School, and Howard University—and from the streets. He was a traditionalist who sang corny love songs but also a modernist who mentored musical rebels.

Most of all, Eckstine was a restless musical entrepreneur who dreamed of making it big not only in black America but in the wider world of popular culture beyond. It was a drive that took him deeper into crossover territory than any Negro entertainer had gone before, right up to the hard limits to black advancement that became more and more apparent as the heady hopes for racial progress after World War II evaporated.

His name, William Clarence Eckstein, was passed down from his pa-
ternal great-grandfather, a white German immigrant. When Wilhelm Eckstein and his wife, Anna, arrived in America in the 1850s, they settled
in Washington, D.C. Wilhelm took the Anglicized name of William and
gave it to his son, who carried on the daring family tradition by marrying a
black woman from Virginia, Nannie Cole. Their son, Clarence, moved to
Pittsburgh around the turn of the century and met a Negro girl from the
North Side, Charlotte Smith, known as Lottie. Like most migrants, the
couple worked several jobs to make ends meet. Lottie was a dressmaker,
and Clarence worked for a family of furriers, the Wolks. But it was Clarence's other job as a chauffeur for Harry Milholland, the president of *The
Pittsburgh Press*, that allowed the Ecksteins to purchase a small two-floor
house on Bryant Street in the Highland Park neighborhood and raise three
children there: two girls named Maxine and Aileen, and the baby of the
family they called "Billy."

His mother gave Billy his first taste of entertaining. When he was four,
Lottie Eckstein put him in a production staged by the Dressmakers of
Pittsburgh at a local high school. Wearing a sailor's suit, Billy was supposed to carry an American flag across the stage. Halfway, he stumbled
and fell. Rather than cry or retreat, he jumped back up and carried on as
if nothing had happened. Then Billy displayed an early sign of another
lifelong trait: instead of leaving the stage, he stood by the emcee's side and
stared wide-eyed at all the ladies in the production.

Billy made his singing debut accompanying his grandmother to church.
Mary Ann Smith was an "Old Pittsburgher," having migrated to the city
from Maryland, with her husband, Robert Smith, in the decade after the
Civil War. They settled on the North Side and joined the Avery Memorial
Church, where Mary would worship for more than fifty years until her
death at the age of eighty-two. She sang hymns in the choir, and when
Billy was six or seven she began bringing him along to perform duets.
Recognizing his gift, Lottie arranged for voice and piano lessons, which
continued through his early teen years at Peabody High School in Highland Park.

At fifteen, Billy received his first introduction to business. Aiming to teach the "art of salesmanship" to local youth, Robert L. Vann had launched a program called "the Pittsburgh Courier Newsies Club." Every Thursday, boys from across the city gathered in the *Courier* building on the Hill to collect freshly printed newspapers. They earned a commission on every copy they sold, and competed for a monthly prize for the top earner. To instill the habit of savings, Vann established a "purpose club" that encouraged the boys to put aside their commissions for use at Easter or on other special occasions. "All of the boys are of the aggressive, hustling types—anxious to do something to help themselves and their parents," the *Courier* reported in a story that listed "William Eckstein Jr." as one of thirty Newsies in the spring of 1930.

By the early 1930s, both of Billy's older sisters had graduated from the University of Pittsburgh, an indication of how much the Ecksteins valued education. Aileen went to work for the *Courier* writing a radio column called "Wave Lengths." Maxine became a schoolteacher, working in Pittsburgh and West Virginia before taking a job as a Spanish instructor at Armstrong High School in Washington, D.C. Seizing the opportunity to send their boy to Duke Ellington's alma mater, the family dispatched Billy to live with Maxine so he could finish high school at Armstrong.

By his senior year, Billy already had the look of a budding singing idol, with his gangly frame, mocha-colored complexion, and pencil mustache. He began to sing with a bandleader named Baron Lee, then won an amateur contest at the Howard Theatre, imitating Cab Calloway's version of "Stardust." When Lottie arrived from Pittsburgh to help him prepare for graduation, she discovered that Billy had snuck away to New York to compete at amateur night at the Apollo Theater. He sang the Hoagy Carmichael tune again and beat out a sixteen-year-old Virginian who had just moved in with her aunt in Harlem. A year later, that girl, Ella Fitzgerald, won another Apollo amateur night contest that led to her hiring as the lead singer in Chick Webb's orchestra.

Success didn't come as quickly for Eckstine. After graduating from Armstrong High, he enrolled in a Virginia vocational school, and then transferred to Howard University. Although he was offered a musical scholarship, he dropped out after two semesters to sing in the pit orchestra at the Howard Theatre. He was fired ten weeks later, however, and had to return to Pittsburgh. He formed a band that took on visiting "orks," as they were called, in cutting contests at the Savoy Ballroom and the Pythian Temple on the Hill. For the next three years, Billy bounced from city to city across the Northeast, working mostly as an emcee in small clubs.

In the summer of 1938, Eckstine moved to Chicago at the urging of a friend named Budd Johnson, who played saxophone in the orchestra led by pianist Earl Hines. Billy's first job there was at Club DeLisa, a black nightclub on the South Side owned by three Italian former bootleggers. A year later, in the fall of 1939, Hines finally showed up to hear Eckstine sing. The bandleader was impressed with the way Billy crooned—and how he made ladies swoon. "Goddamn," Hines said to a band member who had accompanied him. "I'm going to try to steal that boy. He will kill everybody."

Eckstine was still under contract to the DeLisas, however. Even after Hines offered him a big raise, Billy was wary about crossing the former gangsters. When they agreed to let him go, he figured that it was only because even bigger mobsters—Al Capone and his brother Ralph— were part owners of the Grand Terrace Café, where the Hines orchestra played. "When the DeLisa brothers didn't want you to go," Eckstine recalled, "they would take you downstairs and walk you into the icebox and do a number on you. Since I was spared that treatment, I knew that somebody up there with an iron fist in kidskin gloves was giving me an awful lot of help."

Eckstine lent a needed dash of youth and energy to the Hines orchestra, which had dipped in popularity since its days as the top orchestra in Chicago. Although the man they called "Fatha" was usually the one to school younger musicians, it was Billy who taught Hines how to stand up for himself. Every year the manager of the Grand Terrace Café, a greedy Capone crony named Ed Fox, booked the orchestra on a tour of the South to make extra money. Not welcome in hotels or restaurants, the band members were forced to sleep and eat on run-down buses, or in the sooty "nigger cars" behind the engine on trains. They traveled from town to town, playing in tiny dance halls where they were often the target of ugly slurs, and sometimes of hurled bottles and cherry bombs as well.

The unfailingly polite Hines put up with it all, but not Eckstine. On his first trip south with the Hines band, he insisted on carrying a gun. From the window of the bus, he fired at squirrels and cows to make sure everyone within earshot knew he was armed. When Billy saw the sorry condition of the pianos that the Southern dance halls provided, he took it as an insult to Hines and would rip out the strings and mallets before the band left town. On the train ride back north to Chicago, the black musicians were ushered into a "nigger car," where in addition to coal dust from the engine they had to endure the stench of garbage that whites in the dining car tossed into the compartment.

When the train pulled into Union Station, Eckstine jumped off the train and confronted one of the white passengers from the dining car. "Man, what were you throwing all that stuff in on us for?" he demanded. Then Billy belted the man in the face, grabbed him by the collar and hit him again. The white diner jumped on the tracks and crawled under the train to hide, but another band member came at him from the other side. "If you can stand up under there, you're gonna be a bitch," Billy shouted at the man, "because I'm gonna whip your ass across the tracks and back under again!"

Eventually Billy helped Hines get out from under the rapacious Ed Fox. Just as Eckstine was joining the band, the manager shut down the Grand Terrace Café, forcing the band to go on the road full-time. Thanks to Eckstine's popularity, they had a successful run at the Howard Theatre in Washington and at the Roseland Ballroom in New York City. The orchestra also cut several new records for RCA Victor's Bluebird label, producing Eckstine's first hit, a ballad called "Ann, Wonderful One." Buoyed by the success, Hines worked up the nerve to dispute his onerous deal with Fox, which committed him to working for the manager's children even if

Fox passed away. But when Hines appealed his contract to the musicians union, Fox canceled all of his engagements, forcing the orchestra to disband as the legal battle played out.

Worried that he would never perform again, Hines crawled into a whiskey bottle for a month. But then the musicians union ruled in his favor, and Eckstine encouraged him to fire Fox and sign with the William Morris Agency. By the end of 1940, the new agents had the Hines orchestra on the road again, on a tour that avoided the Deep South. Instead they traveled across Texas, then up and down California, ending in Los Angeles for a recording session that changed the trajectory of Eckstine's career.

The session took place at a Hollywood recording studio booked by Bluebird Records. After the band had played all the songs they had prepared, they still had an hour of studio time left. "Why don't you play some kind of blues?" a Bluebird representative suggested. While Hines and Budd Johnson worked up a melody, Eckstine stepped into another room to write the words. Twelve minutes later, he returned with a lyric inspired by a telephone conversation that he had overhead from a homesick band member. *"Hello, baby, I had to call you on the phone,"* it began, *"'Cause I feel so lonesome and Daddy wants his baby home."* Then, after a middle chorus, it ended suggestively: *"Jelly, jelly, jelly. Jelly stays on my mind. Jelly roll killed my pappy; it run my mammy stone blind."* Hines set up the vocal with a simple twelve-bar piano lead-in. Then, as soon as Eckstine finished signing, the trumpet section erupted with a series of forceful blasts and the clarinet played a screeching line above them. For any record buyers who didn't know what the word "jelly" was slang for, the orgasmic finale left no doubt.

That fall, the *Courier* broke the news that Earl Hines had signed a deal to spend the Christmas holidays performing in the Pittsburgh area. Billing it as a "triumphant homecoming" for both Hines and Eckstine, the paper reported that the band's hit single "Ann, Wonderful One" would be the "theme" of the tour. To build excitement, the promoter announced that the woman for whom the song was written was also coming to Pittsburgh. She was a former Cotton Club showgirl named Anna Jones who had caught Hines's eye. Sure enough, Jones was in the audience on New Year's Eve at the Duquesne Gardens, where seventeen thousand fans joined Eckstine in "Auld Lang Syne."

By the time the band reached New York ten days later to perform at the Apollo, however, "Ann, Wonderful One" was forgotten. Bluebird had just released "Jelly, Jelly," and it was an instant craze. As Eckstine drove through the streets of Harlem, he heard record stores playing the song to lure customers off the street. On opening night at the Apollo, so many people lined up for tickets that police had to keep order on horseback. Inside, as soon as Billy uttered the first words—"Hello, baby, I had to call you on the phone"—women in the audience shrieked. A man in the balcony grew so excited that he tipped over the banister and plummeted into the orchestra section.

For the rest of 1941, the Hines band rode the success of "Jelly, Jelly" on dates across America. In early 1942, it recorded two more Eckstine hits: "Stardust" and "Stormy Monday Blues." Yet by then, America had entered the war and Hines was faced with replacing band members, such as Budd Johnson, who had enlisted in the Army. When he asked Eckstine and his drummer, Shadow Wilson, to act as talent scouts, they went after two up-and-coming musicians who had just left other bands.

One was Dizzy Gillespie, who had split with Cab Calloway after several contentious years. Eckstine had first met Gillespie several years earlier, when he moved into a building on Seventh Avenue in Harlem. Dizzy lived a floor above, in an apartment with an upright piano. Although Eckstine enjoyed listening to Gillespie practice his trumpet, he was even more impressed with how Dizzy spent hours working out his ideas on the keyboard. "Even then, you could see that Diz had his head on straight, man, he was completely into studying," Eckstine recalled.

The other sideman was Charlie Parker, the dazzlingly inventive saxophonist known to his fellow musicians as "Yardbird." Eckstine knew Parker was available because the saxophonist had approached Earl Hines one night in Harlem and asked for a job. Parker was so desperate to leave

Jay McShann, the bandleader who had brought him to New York from Kansas City, that he offered to give up his alto saxophone and play tenor instead, as long as Hines bought him a new instrument.

Eckstine and Wilson tracked Dizzy Gillespie down at a club in Philadelphia where he was playing temporarily. As Gillespie later described it: "These greasy muthafuckas cruised me out of Philly to go with Earl Hines. They told Yardbird, 'Well, Diz is coming over here.' Then to me they said, 'Well, you know we're getting Yard.' And then Billy Eckstine and Shadow got Earl Hines to offer me $20 a night to go on the road. So I took it. They got Charlie Parker the same time—cruised him in there."

DIZZY GILLESPIE WAS FIFTEEN years old when he began trying to imitate Roy Eldridge. Dizzy had been playing the trumpet for three years in his hometown of Cheraw, South Carolina, and he liked to listen to the broadcast of the Teddy Hill Orchestra performing at the Savoy Ballroom that aired every weekend on NBC radio. At first Dizzy didn't know the name of the band's trumpet soloist, he recalled, but he knew his sound "knocked me out." Dizzy began trying to reproduce the trumpeter's scratchy timbre, his flashy runs of eighth and sixteenth notes, and his use of the high register. At night, he even dreamed that they were playing together on Teddy Hill's bandstand.

Dizzy didn't know it yet, but his infatuation with the best trumpet player to ever come out of Pittsburgh was putting him on a path to the invention of bebop.

Born on the North Side, Roy Eldridge was introduced to music by his mother, Blanche, a gifted pianist who could play almost anything by ear. By age six, Roy was banging out blues phrases on the keyboard and taking lessons on the drums so that he could play in a fife and drum corps that marched through his North Side neighborhood on holidays. Short, restless, and fiercely competitive, Eldridge burned to outdo his older brother, Joe, who played everything from the clarinet and the saxophone to the violin. It was Joe who, after hearing his younger brother play bugle in church, urged him to take up the valve trumpet. Roy began studying with P. M. Williams, a local barber and amateur musician who taught him how to breathe and hit high notes by squeezing his diaphragm. In his early teens, Roy's mother passed away and his father remarried, and Eldridge escaped the family drama by locking himself in his room and practicing the horn.

In ninth grade, Eldridge's hot temper and disdain for any study other than music got him expelled from high school. He ran away from home, joining a tent show that traveled across Ohio. At some point, he got his hands on a 78 rpm record of Fletcher Henderson's band playing a lively rag called "The Stampede." Instead of trying to copy the regal, fluid playing of the band's trumpeter, Louis Armstrong, Roy practiced reproducing the more frenetic, raspy solo of saxophonist Coleman Hawkins.

By the time Eldridge returned to Pittsburgh at age seventeen, he had developed a unique sound and a growing reputation as the king of dance hall "cutting contests." He briefly changed his stage name to Roy Elliott to organize a band called the "Palais-Royal Orchestra," then he teamed up with his brother Joe to form "The Twelve Rhythm Kings." When Eldridge moved to New York in 1935, fellow musicians astonished by how such a small man could produce such a big sound nicknamed him "Little Jazz." Soon Roy joined the bandstand of the Teddy Hill Orchestra, one of the most coveted seats in the city because of the national exposure it got through the NBC radio broadcasts.

When Dizzy Gillespie moved to Philadelphia after high school, he saw his idol perform for the first time. It was at a club called the Rendezvous, and Roy Eldridge engaged in a cutting contest with Rex Stewart, Duke Ellington's trumpet player, that made Stewart "cry," Dizzy remembered. Later Gillespie moved to New York just as Eldridge was leaving Teddy Hill's band to join Fletcher Henderson. Dizzy auditioned and got the open trumpet chair—to the annoyance of some of the older veterans in the band—because Teddy Hill was so taken with how much Dizzy sounded like Roy.

While playing with Teddy Hill, Gillespie became inspired by another

Pittsburgh musician, drummer Kenny Clarke. Kenneth Spearman Clarke had grown up in the Hill District. His mother, the former Martha Grace Scott, was also a talented pianist who taught him to play his first notes. But Martha died when Kenny was only five years old, and his father, Charles Spearman, left Pittsburgh to start another family in Washington, D.C. Kenny was placed in an orphanage in the Lower Hill, the Coleman Industrial Home for Negro Boys. The orphanage was cramped and dingy, with more than thirty boys sleeping in four rooms. But the matrons took them to church every Sunday and invited local musicians to give recitals. By nine, Kenny had foraged a set of drumsticks, and someone at the orphanage had taught him how to play the snare drum. By the time he entered junior high, Kenny was leading the marching band.

At fifteen, Clarke dropped out of school and began performing in the dance halls and clubs of Wylie Avenue. Two Irishmen who owned a local music store, Hammond and Gerlach on Penn Avenue, gave him lessons and allowed him to practice on a professional drum kit. When the drummer for a popular local dance band fell ill, Kenny got his first taste of keeping a swing tempo for a ballroom of Lindy-hoppers. But he quickly tired of thumping out a monotonous four-four beat on the bass drum.

Although not certain, it's likely that at some point Clarke heard a recording by "Papa Jo" Jones, the first big band drummer to keep time with the hi-hat, the stacked cymbals operated by a foot pedal on the side of the drum kit. By the time Clarke arrived in New York City in 1935, at the age of twenty-one, he was keeping time by "riding" the hi-hat with his left foot, freeing up his right foot to throw in bass drum accents that he called "dropping bombs." When Kenny made his first recordings with the Edgar Hayes band in 1937, he already had a sound that jazz historian Gunther Schuller later proclaimed "the beginnings of modern drumming."

Clarke joined the Teddy Hill band a year later, and he and Dizzy Gillespie clicked immediately. Dizzy loved the fast tempos that Kenny kept on the hi-hat, and the way his bombs on the fourth beat set up Gillespie's trumpet riffs. Both men dug the interplay of the horn and the cymbals, as if the two brass instruments were talking to one another. Gillespie imagined Clarke's drums as "cousins" with his horn, and listened for their encouragement to take new chances. "He infused a new conception, a new language, into the dialogue of the drum, which is now *the* dialogue," Dizzy recalled.

While everyone else marveled at Gillespie's harmonic inventions—how he improvised new music over chord changes rather than simply embellishing melodies—Clarke was fascinated by his friend's rhythmic originality. "It wasn't only his trumpet playing," Clarke said. "He had a lotta other things that people didn't see, but I saw the rhythmic aspect of it." Both men played piano, and they introduced new concepts to one another on the keyboard. "Kenny would run up to me—he played piano, too, all of them played piano—and say, 'Look here . . . bam!' Right on the piano," Dizzy recalled. "I'd say, 'Yeah, yeah,' because guys were very generous in those days with their ideas, man."

Other band members didn't dig Clarke's unconventional technique at all. They complained to Teddy Hill, who struggled himself to describe what his drummer was up to with his offbeat snare accents and bass bombs. "He does all those 'klook-mops' and shit," Teddy sputtered to Dizzy one day. So that's what Gillespie started calling Clarke: "Klook-Mop." The nickname stuck—"Klook Clarke"—but it didn't stop the grumbling from band members who could only follow tempos pounded on the bass drum. "We can't use Klook because he breaks the time too much," a trombonist who helped manage the sidemen griped to Hill. Eventually the trombonist persuaded Hill to fire Clarke.

Teddy Hill wasn't finished with Kenny Clarke, however. By the end of 1939, Hill's orchestra had disbanded and he had gone into a new line of work, managing a small nightclub in the back of the Cecil Hotel on West 118th Street in Harlem. The owner was Henry Minton, a saxophonist who was the only black delegate to the local branch of the American Federation of Musicians. Officially, the union prohibited members from performing unless they were paid. So-called walking delegates issued fines to anyone caught jamming for no money. But Minton was determined to provide cover for musicians who wanted to play after hours.

So he opened a club he called Minton's Playhouse down the street from Apollo Theater. For the house band, Minton encouraged Hill to look for confident improvisers and accompanists. To play piano, Hill brought in a self-taught prodigy whose name, Thelonious Sphere Monk, matched his eccentric clothes and otherworldly sound. To play drums, Hill hired Klook Clarke.

Over the next few years, Minton's became a nightly musical laboratory. On Mondays, the owners of the Apollo Theater treated their headliners to dinner at Minton's, and the ensuing jam sessions went until dawn. Established stars such as Lester Young, Coleman Hawkins, and Ben Webster sat in, soaking up the ideas of the younger players and testing them in cutting contests. Roy Eldridge showed up regularly to duel with Dizzy Gillespie, and before long Monk was teasing the Pittsburgh master that his disciple had surpassed him. Charlie Christian, the electric guitarist in Benny Goodman's band, crafted improvisations that stretched far beyond the four- and eight-bar solos of swing.

Charlie Parker arrived in Harlem with the Jay McShann band from Kansas City and quickly became a fixture at Minton's. While Gillespie was forever analyzing the new music, Parker came to it effortlessly, with awesome technical chops, encyclopedic command of musical quotations, and a natural ear for mixing bebop with the blues. Previously known as a stride pianist, Thelonious Monk began to experiment with unexpected pauses and dissonant leaps, sometimes becoming so pleased with himself that he would jump up and dance around his piano. Meanwhile, Kenny Clarke added rhythmic innovation, perfecting a style that supported the new music while making the drums an equal partner in improvisation for the first time.

Starting in 1942, another Pittsburgher became a nightly presence at Minton's. Mary Lou Scruggs had seen a lot of the world since her start as "the little piano girl of East Liberty." After she married Joe Williams at the age of seventeen, they moved to Memphis and Joe went on the road with Andy Kirk's "Twelve Clouds of Joy," leaving his young bride to make ends meet by working part-time for an undertaker. Eventually Mary Lou joined

Andy Kirk's band as well, and soon she emerged as a soloist, composer, and arranger. But by the early 1940s, Mary Lou had divorced Joe Williams and moved to New York City, where she befriended the new generation of bebop pioneers.

In the 1930s, Williams had become known as the queen of the swing piano, with its emphasis on keeping a steady, relaxed time. But thanks to her grounding in the sophisticated piano culture of Pittsburgh, she immediately grasped the complex new music of the 1940s, with its "millions of notes," as she put it. At Minton's, Williams acted as an unofficial den mother. She kept a wary eye out for white musicians who tried to steal material by sitting in the audience and scribbling transcriptions into notebooks and on shirt cuffs. When Mary Lou got her own gig at Café Society, the nightclub in Greenwich Village, Monk and Dizzy would show up at her apartment in the early morning, after she finished her last set, and stay for hours excitedly demonstrating their new discoveries.

After the Teddy Hill Orchestra broke up in 1939, Gillespie joined Cab Calloway's band. But it wasn't long before Dizzy became restless in the job, which kept him on the road and away from the Harlem jam scene for long stretches. The other band members were more interested in trading real estate tips than discussing music. All Cab Calloway seemed to care about, besides making money, was betting on horses at the track.

When the band reached Hartford, Connecticut, in 1941, the tension boiled over. Before the Calloway orchestra came on, a trumpeter for the warm-up band started hurling spitballs at his drummer. When Cab entered, he saw the wet debris on the stage and assumed that Dizzy was the culprit. After the curtain went down, he accused Gillespie. When Dizzy denied responsibility, Cab became enraged and climbed into the orchestra to punch him. Band members pulled them apart, and Calloway stormed off to his dressing room. When Dizzy passed by several minutes later, Cab rushed into the hallway and accused him again. This time, Dizzy pulled a knife. When Calloway got back to his dressing room, he saw blood seeping through the leg of his white tuxedo. He went to find Gillespie and fired him on the spot. "Get him outta here!" Cab shouted to his band manager, who hastily paid Dizzy in cash and hustled him onto a bus back to New York.

For the next year, Gillespie played with several other bands, but nothing lasted until Billy Eckstine persuaded him to join the Earl Hines orchestra by offering him $20 a week and the chance to play with Charlie Parker.

Although Gillespie and Parker had jammed at Minton's and other New York clubs, playing in the Hines band gave them the chance to compare notes and practice together for the first time. While the orchestra was on the road, the two men holed up during the day playing scales and etudes from the exercise books they both carried with them. (Although Gillespie denied it, Earl Hines was convinced that their early bebop improvisations were all based on those practice scales, mixed in hundreds of ways over all twelve keys.) Both men were highly competitive, but not with each other. "It was a mutual non-aggression pact, a matter of respect for one another, of respect for the other's creativity," Gillespie recalled. "We each inspired the other."

That respect extended to making sure that Parker's drug habit didn't undermine their partnership. "We were together all the time, playing in hotel rooms and jamming," Gillespie recalled about the time on the road with the Hines band. "We were together as much as we could be under the conditions that the two of us were in. His crowd, the people he hung out with, were not the people that I hung out with. And the guys who pushed dope would be around, but when he wasn't with them, he was with me. Yard was very funny about that. He never used in front of me."

One night, the Hines band found itself playing in a white dance hall in Pine Bluffs, Arkansas. During a break, Gillespie was tinkering on the piano when a customer gave him a nickel to play a special request in the next set. Dizzy tossed the coin away and went back to the piano. Later, when the concert was over and he thought everyone had left, Gillespie went to use the "whites only" men's room. As he came out, the man with the nickel cracked a bottle over his head. Gillespie tried to grab another bottle to retaliate, but five other white men grabbed him and pinned him down. Suddenly, Parker appeared. "You took advantage of my friend, you cur!"

Bird shouted, startling the assailants enough that they let Dizzy go. "That was funny," Gillespie chuckled when he told the story about the white assailant, "because I knew that peckerwood didn't know what a cur was!"

Soon after recruiting Gillespie and Parker, Eckstine came upon another raw but extraordinary young talent. Finding himself in New York City and short on money, he stopped by the Apollo to ask the manager to cash a check. He heard the sound of an intriguing female voice and poked his head into the theater. A tall, dark-skinned eighteen-year-old from Newark was standing awkwardly on stage and singing with effortless, infectious vibrato. Eckstine introduced himself to Sarah Vaughan and told her that he was going to tell Hines to hire her. But Hines balked. The band already had a female vocalist—an older and more refined singer named Madeline Green—and Hines couldn't afford *three* singers, with their high union salaries.

Fortunately, Vaughan was also an accomplished keyboard player, so Hines agreed to hire her as a second pianist, at a lower union rate. But Eckstine was so determined to make her the female vocalist that he rattled Madeline Green until she quit. With Vaughan at his side, Eckstine had a singing partner whose talent matched his own—and whose vibrato he began to emulate. Meanwhile, Parker and Gillespie gained a new friend and a musical soul mate. Soon Dizzy was writing special arrangements for Sarah, and Bird was accompanying her with bebop obbligatos. Offstage, the two men delighted in bringing out the salty tongue behind Vaughan's shy demeanor that led band member to give her the nickname "Sassy."

While playing with another orchestra before joining Earl Hines, Gillespie had composed an exotic-sounding instrumental piece that embodied many of his new rhythmic and harmonic ideas. He called it "Interlude." When he played it for Hines, the bandleader suggested another title, inspired by the headlines about black soldiers fighting in North Africa: "A Night in Tunisia." Hines also added another Gillespie number to his playlist, calling on Dizzy to shout the tune's name from the bandstand: "Salt Peanuts!"

Those stories—and the uniting of Dizzy Gillespie, Charlie Parker, and

Sarah Vaughan at such an early stage in their careers—would later lead jazz historians to label the Earl Hines orchestra "the incubator of bop." Yet sadly, there were no recordings of the band during this period. From the summer of 1942 until the early fall of 1943—the time during which the three pioneers played for Hines—the American Federation of Musicians went on strike, forbidding members to make records until the big labels agreed to share more of the new revenue that was coming in as radio stations turned from broadcasting live performances to playing recorded music.

In early August of 1943, the Hines orchestra was performing at the Howard Theatre in Washington when they read reports of a race riot in Harlem. The band was scheduled to begin a tour of the South, but Eckstine told Hines that he refused to go. A year earlier, Eckstine had married June Harris, a striking former nightclub entertainer who was urging him to settle down in New York. Billy also had no interest in seeing how he would be treated in the land of Jim Crow after the Harlem riots. When Billy informed Dizzy and Bird that he had "put his notice in" to Hines and explained the reason why, the two sideman decided that they would quit the band, too.

For a brief time, the alumni of the Hines orchestra went their separate ways. Eckstine began singing in clubs on 52nd Street. Gillespie tried to put together a bebop orchestra. But it soon became apparent that they could all make more money if Eckstine formed his own band, capitalizing on the popularity of "Jelly, Jelly" and playing in large theaters rather than small Manhattan clubs. So Billy began reassembling the old Hines bandstand, starting with Dizzy and Bird. Shadow Wilson had enlisted in the Army, so Eckstine recruited Art Blakey to play the drums. In the summer of 1944, they began the tour that brought them to the Aragon Ballroom in Pittsburgh.

On that first tour, the band also played at the Club Riviera in St. Louis. One night, a skinny dark-hued teenager showed up carrying his trumpet. The boy had just finished high school in the nearby town of Alton, Illinois, and had fallen hard for the new bebop sound. One of Eckstine's trumpeters was out with tuberculosis, so the band manager asked if the teenager had a union card. "Yeah, I have a union card," he answered. So Miles Davis was invited to sit in for the rest of the two-week engagement.

Miles struggled to keep up. Eckstine would later tease him that he "couldn't even blow your nose" at that point. Still, the experience changed his life. Davis went home to Alton determined to master the horn and make it to New York to play alongside his musical heroes again. He also came away deeply impressed with the way the bandleader everyone called "B" stood up for his musicians with the Club Riviera's white owner and white patrons. It was an unapologetic toughness that Davis would later emulate in his own career. "B didn't take no shit off nobody," Miles recalled.

For the other members in the orchestra, Eckstine was unlike any bandleader with whom they had ever played. He respected their new musical ideas and openly encouraged their rebelliousness. At their next stop in Cleveland, Sarah Vaughan joined the band, and soon she and Gillespie and Parker were up to more irreverent hijinks. When Art Blakey complained about how much the three cursed, Eckstine told him: "Art, if you're going to be in the band . . . you've got to get used to using profanity." Eckstine not only allowed his musicians to drink and gamble on the road; he mounted flashlights on wire hangers at the back of the tour bus so they could play cards through the night.

When Eckstine finally agreed to tour the South, he brought firearms. In one town, FBI agents confiscated the tour bus after receiving reports that band members were shooting crows from the windows. In another town, a hotel owner who had accepted a reservation for the orchestra claimed to have no rooms available once he saw that Billy Eckstine was not white or Jewish, as the man had assumed. While Eckstine bickered with the hotel owner, Blakey and another band member climbed up to a second-floor balcony and started urinating into the courtyard. When the owner looked up, Eckstine punched him in the face, and the musicians made a run for it.

In his first year as a bandleader, Eckstine sold out theaters wherever he went and commanded an average of $5,500 a week—not quite Cab Calloway and Duke Ellington money, but more than most other swing bands of the era, black or white. Dizzy Gillespie took over as musical director as well as lead trumpeter, creating up-tempo arrangements of old standards and adding new bebop tunes such as "A Night in Tunisia" and "Second Balcony Jump" to the band's repertoire. But Charlie Parker was another story. Within a month of joining the band, he began missing engagements due to his heroin habit, and one time he showed up without his horn because he had pawned it to buy dope. By the time the orchestra arrived at the Apollo Theater for its Christmas engagement at the end of 1944, Parker had quit to go back to performing in small clubs.

On New Year's Eve, Dizzy Gillespie gave notice as well. Eckstine quickly replaced him in the lead trumpet chair with another bebop innovator, Fats Navarro. Over the next two years, Billy continued to hire sidemen who would go on to become leading lights of the new jazz movement, including Dexter Gordon, Gene Ammons, Howard McGhee, and Kenny Dorham. All of them would later call the Eckstine band an invaluable training ground and the first authentic bebop orchestra. But eventually all of them, including Sarah Vaughan, left to join other orchestras or to devote themselves to playing the new music full-time with smaller ensembles.

By 1946, Eckstine was ready for a change as well. When he returned to the Apollo in January 1946, hundreds of white female fans packed the theater along with his usual black followers. In another sign of Billy's growing crossover appeal, he was named Outstanding New Male Vocalist for 1945 by *Esquire* magazine. White music critics who had dubbed Eckstine "the Sepia Sinatra" gave him a new nickname that made him sound less like an imitator than a competitor. By this time, Eckstine had shed the high-register, Cab Calloway sound of his early career and become known for his seductive baritone, made all the sexier by the quivering vocal technique he had learned from Sarah Vaughan. He was now known as "The Vibrato," and his female fan club called themselves "The Vibrato's Vibrators." And before the year was over, Billy Eckstine signed his biggest record deal yet, with a label that had dreams of making "The Vibrato" from Pittsburgh as big a star as "The Voice" from Hoboken, New Jersey.

"JELLY, JELLY" MAY HAVE been Billy Eckstine's bread and butter, but he privately resented singing the blues. It wasn't that he disliked the music: what bothered him was that white people thought that blacks could *only* sing the blues. In the 1930s, when Eckstine joined the Earl Hines band in Chicago, local radio stations broadcast its performances from the Grand Terrace Café. Producers always wanted ballads to be played as instrumentals, and Hines had to insist that Billy be allowed to sing romantic songs such as "Skylark" and "You Don't Know What Love Is." The broadcasters made the "bullshit" argument that the radio audience couldn't understand blacks singing slow numbers because of their Southern accents, Eckstine recalled. "Shit, man, I'm from Pittsburgh!" he would say. "What Southern accent are you talking about? The only South I know is the South Side of Pittsburgh."

Even after Eckstine formed his own band and began recording ballads, the music industry persisted in treating him like a blues singer. In 1945, Eckstine had left Deluxe Records to sign with the National label, and his first single was a romantic tune called "A Cottage for Sale." *Billboard* described it as having "a fetching blues overtone" even though, as Eckstine biographer Cary Ginell put it, "there was nothing approaching the blues about it." When sales surpassed 150,000 records, National devoted the band's next two studio sessions to love songs. But when "I'm in the Mood for Love" became another hit, *Billboard* initially insisted on listing the song on its chart of "Race" records.

By 1946, more and more white teenagers were showing up at Eckstine's concerts, and resentment over his crossover romantic appeal bubbled up for the first time. In Boston, a drunken woman became enraged at Eckstine's seductive crooning and rumors that his band had refused to enter the theater through the back door. She heckled him, and Billy answered back. The woman's companion charged the stage. Patrons fled without paying, and the rest of the engagement was canceled. Shortly afterward, Eckstine received an admiring telegram from Frank Sinatra. "Congratulations, Billy," the message said. "You have upheld the prestige and standard of the thin man's brigade."

While Eckstine's band filled concert halls, however, it didn't make money. After the cost of touring and paying sidemen, little was left. Meanwhile, white solo artists were becoming the postwar rage. For Eckstine, the point was made when Perry Como recorded a song that the Eckstine orchestra had also put out, "Prisoner of Love," and scored Billboard's top hit of 1946. So in early 1947, Eckstine announced that he was striking out on his own. Weeks later, he signed the most lucrative record deal ever awarded to an individual black artist. The MGM movie studio had launched a new record label, and it gave Eckstine a two-year contract that guaranteed the release of twenty-four singles, paid a $50,000 annual retainer, and offered the prospect of roles in MGM movies as well.

As it had been when he formed his own big band, one of Eckstine's first trips as a solo performer was to his hometown. Just after signing with MGM, Eckstine received an invitation to a second annual "Night of the Stars" uniting, as the *Courier* described them, "native sons and daughters of Pittsburgh who have risen to the glamor-laden peak of success." The occasion was "FROGS Week," a treasured annual tradition named after black socialites who in the 1910s had formed an eating club they playfully dubbed "Friendly Rivalry Often Generates Success." "Wouldn't miss this chance to come home," Eckstine cabled back. On a sweltering night in August 1947, he shared the stage of the Syria Mosque with a group that represented four generations of Pittsburgh musicians who had lifted each other as they climbed: Earl Hines, Billy's former boss; Lois Deppe, the bandleader who gave Hines his start; Mary Lou Williams, who was inspired by Hines; singer Maxine Sullivan, who had joined Williams as one of the few black female musicians headlining in small New York clubs in the mid-1940s; and Erroll Garner, the East Liberty prodigy whom the *Courier* anointed "newest sensation among the piano gentry." In tribute to the musical heavyweights assembled—and the role Pittsburgh had played in his own career—Joe Louis even showed up to close the evening with a mock sparring match.

With the support of MGM's marketing muscle, recording technology and top-notch arrangers, Eckstine was on his way to becoming one of the hottest American male vocalists of the late 1940s. His first record for the new label, "This Is the Inside Story," sold more than 100,000 copies. Three more recording sessions followed in 1947, including a marathon date that produced seven records in advance of another musicians union strike. Those songs kept Eckstine in record stores and on the radio and helped him end 1948 as *Billboard*'s top-ranked male singer, ahead of Bing Crosby, Frank Sinatra, and Frankie Laine.

Like his white rivals, Eckstine was becoming almost as famous for his look and his lifestyle as for his singing. Men snapped up shirts with collars in the shape of a "B." A young Caribbean singer just out of the Navy, Harry Belafonte, grew a pencil mustache and experimented with vibrato after seeing Billy perform at New York's Royal Roost. Tabloids oohed over Eckstine's seven-room house in Encino and aahed over his golf outings with Joe Louis. Even scandals—such as when Eckstine and his wife, June, were each caught up in marijuana busts—didn't halt Billy's rise. By the end of the decade, he was so famous that he didn't think twice about turning down the minor film roles that MGM put in front of him, believing that he was destined to play a leading man. When he was offered a part as a valet to Dan Dailey, a B-movie star, Eckstine scoffed. "I don't carry my own fucking bags," he said, "so why would I be carrying Dan Dailey's?"

In 1942, bobbysoxers had mobbed the Paramount Theatre in New York City when Frank Sinatra appeared there, launching a solo career after his time as a swing band singer. Seven years later, in April 1949, Eckstine's Paramount debut created almost as big a stir. "Billy Eckstine is doing the biggest business at the Paramount since Sinatra packed them in," Walter Winchell reported in his syndicated column. Thousands of fans on Easter break—at least 90 percent of them white, by one estimate—descended on Times Square to see Billy perform. Shrieking women threw panties and keys onto the stage. In just two weeks, the 3,654-seat theater grossed close to $200,000, and its managers rewarded Eckstine with a $3,000 bonus and an invitation to come back during the Christmas holiday season.

By the time Eckstine returned to the Paramount for a third engagement in the spring of 1950, he was an even bigger draw. The readers of *Downbeat* and *Metronome* magazines had voted him the top male vocalist of 1949. MGM had sold more than three million copies of his records. Membership in "Billy Eckstine Fan Clubs of America" had surpassed 100,000. Eckstine's former moniker—"The Vibrato"—had given way to an even loftier nickname: "The Great Mr. B."

This time, fans began lining up for tickets outside the Paramount as early at seven in the morning. At the end of his act, the theater's hydraulic stage was supposed to lower Eckstine out of sight, but when crazed admirers tried to storm the stage the theater's management had to nix the sinking exit.

In further evidence of his widening appeal, *Life* magazine commissioned a profile of Eckstine. To capture the "Billy soxers" craze, as the magazine called it, the editors assigned Martha Holmes, a twenty-six-year-old freelance photographer who had snapped one of the most memorable *Life* images of the previous year: of painter Jackson Pollock dripping paint on a canvas in his Long Island studio. Holmes followed Eckstine around for several days and captured the kind of candid moments that *Life* readers craved: Eckstine and his wife, June, dressed at their New York apartment. The singer palled around with Earl Hines and Louis Armstrong backstage. Billy arrived at the Paramount Theatre with an entourage that included Charlie Sifford, the black golf pro who moonlighted as Eckstine's chauffeur and private swing coach.

After the Paramount run, Holmes accompanied Eckstine when he went across the street to perform at a new club called Bop City. Opened the year before, the club was designed for a new generation of jazz enthusiasts who preferred to listen rather than dance. Patrons sat at tables and drank a house specialty called the "Bop-amatic." Further away from the stage, there was a gallery where fans could pay 90 cents to stand and watch.

As Eckstine was leaving Bop City one night, Holmes snapped a photo of a chance encounter with a group of white female fans. Billy was dressed in a light-colored plaid suit and a "Mr. B" collar shirt. His hair was neatly conked and his pencil mustache perfectly trimmed. The women looked young but sophisticated. They wore pearls and gold earrings and salon-fresh perms. Something amusing had just happened, because four of the women in the photo were convulsed in laughter. One of them, an attractive blonde, had fallen against Eckstine's chest. Her face was pressed into his jacket and her right hand touched his lapel. Billy seemed amused, too, as he looked down at the woman with a wide smile.

Holmes later said the photograph was her favorite of the thousands she took during her long career. Its depiction of spontaneous ease among the races "told just what the world should be like," she recalled. The *Life* editors liked the photo, too—but they realized how controversial an image of physical contact between a black man and white women would be. When a photo editor argued that it might be offensive to subscribers, the matter was put before Henry Luce. "Run it," the publisher commanded.

Even then, the *Life* editors worried about how the image might be interpreted. When the three-page feature entitled "Mr. B" appeared in the April 24, 1950, edition, the photo took up more than half a page. Beneath it, a caption tried to make the encounter sound entirely chaste. "After a show at Bop City, Bill is rushed by admirers," it read. "Most profess to have a maternal feeling for him. 'He's just like a little boy,' they say."

Life readers leapt to their own, far less innocent conclusions. For some black readers, it felt like a turning point in American culture. "When that photo hit, in this national publication, it was as if a barrier had been broken," Harry Belafonte recalled. But white readers were incensed. Furious letters from two of them appeared in the magazine's letters column three weeks later. Frank J. Roy Jr. of Columbus, Georgia, proclaimed himself "disgusted with Life for printing the picture of Billy Eckstine and his admirers." John H. Edmonson of Fairfield, Alabama, seethed that "if that was my daughter she would be lucky to be able to sit down in a while when I finished with her."

Decades later, the *Life* photograph would be widely remembered as the beginning of the end of Billy Eckstine's rise. "It changed everything," recalled Billy's friend Tony Bennett in an interview with David Hajdu. "Before that he had a tremendous following, and everybody was running after him, and he was so handsome and had great style and all that. The girls would swoon all over him, and it just offended the white community." In the view of pianist Dr. Billy Taylor, the *Life* photo gave white audiences a pretext to turn against Eckstine just as he was hitting the big time. "When he played the Paramount, that should have been his really big break," Taylor said. "Many [white] people . . . were hearing him for the first time, because he had never played in white theaters. . . .The girls loved him, everything was great. But the coverage and that picture just slammed the door for him."

In fact, the fallout from the *Life* photograph was more insidious. It only became apparent gradually, like a slow leak that Eckstine and his entourage couldn't detect at first. In the months after the *Life* issue appeared, Eckstine continued to play premier venues from L.A.'s Shrine Auditorium to New York's Carnegie Hall with a quintet featuring the white jazz pianist George Shearing. MGM signed him to a new million-dollar, ten-year contract that guaranteed sixteen singles and one album per year. In one of the first of those sessions, Billy recorded a ballad called "I Apologize" that became his most memorable hit. The next two years were the most lucrative of Eckstine's career, between record royalties and nightclub fees. By 1952, he was wealthy enough to partner in a deal to buy a nightclub on Hollywood's Sunset Strip.

Yet in retrospect, signs of a backlash were building. As Eckstine's marriage to June Harris headed toward divorce in 1951, the press began trawling for evidence of entanglements with other women—white ones, in particular. *Look* magazine published a photo of Billy on a date with French movie actress Denise Darcel. Until then, he had repeatedly been rumored to be up for romantic leads in movies. Such talk abruptly stopped, just as Frank Sinatra was about to launch his show business comeback with an Oscar-winning performance in *From Here to Eternity*. When Eckstine was cast in an MGM musical called *Skirts Ahoy!*, it was only as a nightclub singer. After that, the only major part he was considered for was the role of Joe in *Carmen Jones*, a movie version of the all-black Broadway adaptation of the Bizet opera. Eckstine later claimed that he had rejected the role as too "Uncle Tom," but others insisted he never had a chance once the producers fixed on a younger heartthrob, Harry Belafonte.

Despite Eckstine's commercial success, critics started to insinuate that he himself had become a kind of musical Uncle Tom. Instead of a balladeer treated like a blues singer, he was depicted as a crass commercial crooner who had betrayed his jazz roots. Some of the griping had to do with the undeniable fact that Eckstine's quavering baritone began to sound increasingly old-fashioned as the 1950s went on. Belafonte was popularizing the relaxed calypso sound. Sinatra was resurfacing as a swinging saloon singer. Nat King Cole had a romantic tone with more ease—and less sexual charge.

But Eckstine also couldn't win for trying. In addition to ballads, he recorded numerous up-tempo numbers for MGM, assisted by the label's talented young arranger Nelson Riddle. Yet it was only when Riddle went over to Capitol Records and began working with Frank Sinatra that he won widespread acclaim. When Eckstine did go back to his roots—touring with George Shearing and Count Basie, or breaking into scat singing to remind listeners that Sarah Vaughan had learned that particular technique from him—it went largely unnoticed.

In 1954, the bottom started to fall out. After Eckstine's divorce from June Harris was finalized, he departed on a tour of Europe. Like many black musicians of the era, he found that he was appreciated even more abroad than at a home. But that welcome only increased Eckstine's bitterness when he was forced to return to the United States to deal with financial troubles. Charging Billy with dodging taxes, the government had put a lien on his home in Encino, the beginning of decades of battles with the IRS. A nationwide tour with Peggy Lee was canceled due to lack of promoter interest. Eckstine's ten-year deal with MGM was almost half over, and he hadn't had a top ten hit since "I Apologize." In early 1955,

Jet magazine, the new weekly digest of black entertainment and social news, asked on its cover "Is Billy Eckstine Through?" The story inside criticized MGM for not giving Eckstine enough support, but also quoted industry insiders confirming his slump. "Billy needs a [hit] record very, very badly," said a *Downbeat* editor.

Soon afterward Eckstine announced that he was exercising a five-year exit option with MGM and signing with RCA Victor. But that move was eclipsed by much bigger news: RCA had snagged Elvis Presley. By April, Presley's first singles for the label—"Heartbreak Hotel" and "Blue Suede Shoes"—topped the charts. Hoping to capitalize on the rock 'n' roll craze, RCA convinced the forty-one-year-old Eckstine to record two Presley-inspired numbers: "The Tennessee Rock 'n' Roll" and the embarrassingly titled "Condemned for Life (With a Rock and Roll Wife)." Predictably, they didn't sell. Nor did anything else Eckstine produced in five studio sessions for RCA. At the last one, he recorded a tune that songwriter Jimmy Van Heusen had just written for an as yet unreleased movie starring Frank Sinatra. After RCA failed to do anything with Eckstine's version of "All the Way," it became another hit for Sinatra and Capitol Records.

In 1957, just as RCA dropped Eckstine after one year, Billy returned to Pittsburgh to bury his father, Clarence. Resigned to the end of his career as a hit-maker, Billy began to come home musically, too. He joined Count Basie, Lester Young, saxophonist Zoot Sims, and trumpeter Chet Baker for a "Birdland All-Stars" concert at Carnegie Hall. He reunited with Sarah Vaughan to record Irving Berlin tunes and a sophisticated jazz album called *Billy Eckstine's Imagination*. He signed a new deal with Roulette Records, a minor label owned by the controversial musical producer Morris Levy who would later be convicted for his ties to the Mafia. Although not widely distributed, the albums Eckstine made for Roulette showed that he could still be a musical pioneer. In one, he sang French ballads orchestrated by an up-and-coming young arranger, Quincy Jones. In another, recorded at a studio in Brazil, Billy became the first American singing star to devote an album to the Bossa Nova sound.

It was too late for Eckstine to reclaim the crossover fame and fortune that he had begun to enjoy before the *Life* magazine story in 1950. Despite the confidence that winning a global war had given the country, America still felt threatened by a black man who was as commercially successful and seductive to white women as Billy had briefly proven to be. But it wasn't too late for "Mr. B" to keep blazing new musical trails, or to offer reminders of the "don't take no shit off nobody" demeanor that had inspired his bebop protégés and to which so many black entertainers would aspire from then on.

After Eckstine had made several recordings for Roulette, he discovered that Morris Levy had a habit of falling behind on royalty payments. When Billy went to confront the hard-nosed record producer, Levy pulled a pistol from his desk. Unfazed, Eckstine hand-rolled a cigarette. Levy fired the gun. The bullet clipped the end of the cigarette and tore a hole in the office wall. Without missing a beat, Eckstine calmly rolled another cigarette and lit it. Levy couldn't help but smile with admiration at Billy's undimmed confidence and cool. "Get my checkbook!" he shouted to his secretary.

IN THE YEARS AFTER World War II, as Billy Eckstine was climbing the white record charts, Bill Nunn decided that black America deserved its own music ranking. Using his baseball all-star game survey as a model, he created an annual "Pittsburgh Courier Band Poll" to allow readers to choose their favorite jazz orchestras, singers, and soloists. To celebrate the poll's fourth anniversary in 1947, the *Courier* hosted one of the most star-studded concerts ever to be entirely conceived, booked, advertised, and sold by black promoters. On a nippy March night, a mixed race crowd of several thousand lined up outside Pittsburgh's Carnegie Music Hall to see a show that rollicked for more than two and a half hours. Ella Fitzgerald scatted "Oh, Lady Be Good!" and encored with "A-Tisket, A-Tasket." Count Basie swung. Dizzy Gillespie bopped. The Mills Brothers harmonized and the Ink Spots serenaded. Eckstine showed up to croon his rendition of "Prisoner of Love." Lionel Hampton's orchestra, the winner of that year's poll, kicked off the evening with the explosive "Air Mail Special," brought the crowd to a frenzy with "Flying Home," and sent everyone home shimmy-ing to "Hamp's Boogie-Woogie."

Yet along with touting all the famous musicians in attendance that eve-ning, the *Courier* reporter who covered the concert also took time to praise a skinny, twenty-one-year-old sideman who played the least glamorous in-strument on the stage, the upright double bass. "Dizzy Gillespie, trumpet star, and Ray Brown, his bass find, gave out with 'Hot Box,' backed by Hampton on drums," the reporter wrote. "Dizzy graciously gave Ray plenty of scope before entering into his bop exercises."

What the *Courier* didn't tell its national audience was that Ray Brown was another hometown boy. Like so many kids from black Pittsburgh, he had grown up in a family that revered the piano. His father introduced Ray to Fats Waller and Art Tatum records when he was still a toddler, took him to hear Count Basie at the William Penn Hotel, and started him on lessons by age eleven. But when Ray entered junior high, he was one of twenty-eight pianists on the school orchestra. He had to sit around all week just to get fifteen minutes of rehearsal time. Waiting his turn one day, he noticed an unused bass lying in corner of the room. "If I was play-ing that bass, I could play every day?" he asked the music teacher. "That's right," the teacher said. "We're looking for another bass player."

Like Ecsktine in his school days, Brown had a *Courier* paper route, and one of his customers was a well-known Pittsburgh bass player. Once Ray took up the instrument, the older musician invited him in to listen to recordings of the Duke Ellington orchestra showcasing Jimmy Blanton, the first bass player to play entire melodies and take improvised solos. Ray taught himself by playing along with Blanton records, and he quickly developed the remarkable versatility for which he would become known. Using his long, strong fingers, he could lay down powerful rhythmic licks he referred to as his "grits and gravy"; then he could vary his tone and pace to produce creative riffs and subtle accompaniments. By the time he was an upperclassman at Schenley High School, Ray was so good that a visiting jazz orchestra offered to hire him to replace a bass player who had been hauled off by military police for avoiding the draft. But his mother laid down the law. If Ray went on the road before getting his high school diploma, she announced, she would send the police to track *him* down.

After graduating in 1944, Brown tried his luck playing in Buffalo for a year, and then bought a one-way ticket to New York City. On his first week in town, he went to a jazz club on 52nd Street and was introduced to Dizzy Gillespie, who upon hearing that Ray played the bass offered him a job in his big band. The next night, Ray was rehearsing at Dizzy's home with Charlie Parker, pianist Bud Powell, and drummer Max Roach. Two years later he was on the road with Gillespie's band when Ella Fitzgerald joined them briefly. Despite their nine-year age difference—she was thirty, and he was still only twenty-one—Ella and Ray fell in love. On a tour stop in Youngstown in Ohio, Ray popped the question and they arranged for a hasty civil marriage before a local probate judge that same day. They began touring together before conflicting professional priorities pulled them apart and led to an amicable quickie Mexican divorce five years later. For Ray, one of those projects was recording an album with three fellow alumni from the Gillespie band—vibraphonist Milt Jackson, pianist John Lewis, and Kenny "Klook" Clarke, the Pittsburgh drummer—that marked the beginning of the phenomenon known as the Modern Jazz Quartet.

During those years, Brown was also a regular on the Jazz at the Philharmonic tours organized by promoter Norman Granz. In 1949, a young Canadian pianist named Oscar Peterson joined the tour and hit it off with Ray. It would be the start of a partnership that lasted for a decade and a half, as Brown joined Peterson in a series of acclaimed jazz trios. Finally tiring of life on the road in the late 1960s, Brown settled down in Los Angeles and became a session player and music producer. Over the following decades, he did everything from sitting in with the *Tonight Show* band and playing bass on the iconic "Mission: Impossible" theme to helping launch the careers of Quincy Jones and singer Diana Krall. When Brown passed away of a heart attack at the age of seventy-five—after playing a pre-concert round of golf in Indianapolis—Jones hailed him as "simply the best there's every been" on his instrument. The leading bass player of a new generation, Christian McBride, was even more specific. "Ray Brown was to the bass what Charlie Parker was to the saxophone," McBride said. "He took what Jimmy Blanton started to an entirely new level."

Asked about his early musical influences, Brown would credit his parents but also the "ton of music" in Pittsburgh, from the competitive school scene to the theaters where the best bands in country could be heard virtually every week of the year. He remembered one peer in particular. While still at Schenley High, Ray formed his first ensemble with several other young musicians who practiced with him at one of their homes in East Liberty. Around the corner lived Erroll Garner, the self-taught piano prodigy who had just recently graduated from Westinghouse High. The Schenley students were so in awe of Garner that they would cut short their own rehearsals to go his house to hear him play. Erroll returned the compliment by showing up at the North Side Elks Club, where the youngsters played on Sunday nights, to jam with them after midnight. "It was a lot of fun when he showed up!" Brown recalled.

There was one place Erroll Garner couldn't play in Pittsburgh, however: the musicians union hall. The local required its members to read sheet music, and because Garner played entirely by ear he couldn't get a union card. So in 1944, at the age of twenty-one, he set out for New York City. He soon found work on 52nd Street, playing in a trio fronted by bassist Slam Stewart. For a while, he relocated to Los Angeles to gig at Billy Berg's club, where he played with Charlie Parker after Parker was released from his famous dry-out stint at the Camarillo State Mental Hospital. But Garner was still viewed mostly as a supremely talented ensemble player until, in 1950, he met a white female civil rights activist turned talent manager who would help make him one of the most successful and beloved jazz headliners of the next two decades.

As it happened, Martha Glaser also hailed from the Pittsburgh area. She was born in Duquesne, the mill town south of the city where Earl Hines grew up. Her parents, Hungarian immigrants, moved the family to Detroit by the time Martha was in high school, and she stayed there to attend Wayne State University. Motivated by the 1942 Detroit race riots, she threw herself into civil rights work, taking a job in Chicago with the city's Human Rights Commission. A jazz lover, she helped Norman Granz organize the Jazz at the Philharmonic tours and moved to Manhattan to open her own management agency. When she first heard Garner play on 52nd Street, Glaser was so enthralled that she signed him to an exclusive contract and began devoting herself full-time to overseeing his professional and financial affairs.

As photos of the two illustrate, Martha lit up in Erroll's presence, charmed by his joyous smile and teasing banter. (She wasn't alone. Despite his diminutive five-foot-two stature, Garner was a discreet but busy lady's man.) Yet Glaser was also shrewd enough to see that Garner represented something unique in the jazz world by the early 1950s: a dazzling virtuoso whose music was complex enough to impress fans of the new bebop style but accessible to those who missed the simpler swing era. It required an effort to appreciate the dissonant experimentation of Thelonious Monk and Bud Powell, and even the relentless harmonic improvisation of Art Tatum. But enjoying Garner's sound, rhythmically infectious and at turns melodically playful and romantic, was no work at all. It was an appeal summed up by Ross Russell, the head of Dial Records, who signed Garner to his first record deal. While jazz was becoming "progressively cerebral and nervous," Russell wrote, "Erroll Garner's music . . . springs from the heart rather than the head."

The challenge lay in capturing Garner's genius, which was like bottling lightning. He couldn't write music, either, so there were no notations of his inventions. He also insisted on playing whatever came into his head, without warning, even to his accompanists. Shortly after signing Garner, Glaser moved him from the small Dial label to the pop music giant Columbia Records. George Avakian, the Columbia "artist and repertoire man" who oversaw recording sessions, recalled the first time he asked Garner to make a long-playing album. In Avakian's experience, it usually took three hours to produce enough music to fill two short-play 78 rpm records, with their three-minute sides. For the LP, Avakian would need a full hour of usable music. Arriving minutes after his sidemen, Garner announced that he didn't have a play list and had no need to rehearse. "Just start that tape going," he said. Erroll took a sip of coffee, loosened his tie, lit a cigarette, and proceeded to play thirteen flawless numbers back to back, with no retakes. Avakian likened it to "running the hundred yard dash in eight seconds."

In 1954, Glaser cut a separate deal for Garner to record for EmArcy, the jazz label of Mercury Records. Around that time, Erroll was flying from San Francisco to Chicago when his plane was caught in a thunderstorm. As it landed, he looked through the window to see a magnificent rainbow through a soft mist. All of a sudden he found himself fingering his knees and humming. Thinking Garner might be sick, the passenger in the next seat called a flight attendant. But he was just composing in his head, and as soon as he got off the plane he found a piano to work out the tune he would call "Misty." At his next recording date, he slipped it into another marathon of first takes that produced an EmArcy album called *Contrasts*. A few years later, after lyricist Johnny Burke put words to the melody and Johnny Mathis made it a top 20 hit, "Misty" was on its way to earning its own place in the Great American Songbook.

The following year, Glaser accompanied Garner and his sidemen to an engagement in San Francisco. To earn a little extra cash, she arranged for the group to play a one-night concert in the town of Carmel-by-the-Sea on the Monterey Peninsula. After a sixty-minute drive along the Pacific coast, the musicians and the manager arrived to find a converted high school auditorium full of local jazz enthusiasts. As the trio set up, a man carrying a reel-to-reel tape machine approached Glaser. He was Will Thornbury, a disk jockey for Armed Services Radio who wanted to record the concert for soldiers at nearby Fort Ord. Glaser agreed—on condition that Thornbury turn over the tape and rights to its contents as soon as his broadcast had aired.

Garner proceeded to deliver one of the most delightful live performances he had ever given. Invigorated by the scenic drive and buoyed by the spirited crowd, he tore through fifteen classics in his first set, including "Night and Day," "I Remember April," "The Nearness of You," "Lullaby of Birdland," and "It's Alright With Me." After a short break, he returned with seven more, including "They Can't Take That Away from Me," "Autumn Leaves," "'S Wonderful," "Laura," and ending with a seven-minute version of "Caravan." Throughout the ninety-minute concert, he teased the audience with his long, elliptical introductions, keeping them guessing about which song was coming next. Gently humming and grunting as he played, he turned to smile and wink at them, showing just how much he was enjoying himself. By the time the concert was over, Glaser knew that something special had occurred. On the plane back to New York, she kept Thornbury's tape in her lap for the entire flight.

Glaser had just signed Garner to a new exclusive deal with Columbia Records, so she took the tape to George Avakian. He recognized the genius of the piano playing, but he didn't like the sound of the room and thought the bass was slightly out of tune. (The bassist had left his instrument in San Francisco and borrowed one from Fort Ord.) Avakian turned over Thornbury's tape to Columbia's crack engineers, who used special filters and boosters to bring out the sound of the drums and the bass and to compensate for the bad acoustics. When the results were issued as an LP the next year, Columbia chose a fetching title—*Concert by the Sea*—and a cover image of an attractive young woman walking along the Monterey cliffs, waves crashing against the shore, with her arms raised as if to celebrate the liberating spirit of the music.

Within one year, *Concert by the Sea* sold 225,000 copies. Within three years, it surpassed a million in sales, making it one of the most successful albums in the history of jazz up to that point. One buyer was a gentleman who employed Erroll Garner's older sister, Ruth, as a maid. When she showed up for work one day, the employer told her that she looked a lot like the picture of a pianist on a record he had just purchased. Ruth had yet to hear of *Concert of the Sea*, but when the employer played it she recognized the sound immediately. "That's my brother," she said.

Propelled by the popularity of that album and by Martha Glaser's ambition, Garner rocketed to worldwide fame in the late 1950s and 1960s. He became the first jazz artist ever to sign a concert promotion deal with Sol

Hurok, the classical music impresario who represented Artur Rubinstein, Isaac Stern, Andrés Segovia, and the Bolshoi Ballet. He performed in the great concert halls of Europe, Asia, and South America—always sitting atop a Manhattan phone book provided for in his contract with Hurok. He became a favorite guest of TV late night and variety hosts, from Steve Allen and Andy Williams to Merv Griffin and Johnny Carson. During one *Tonight Show* appearance, Carson asked Garner what made his playing so special. When Erroll couldn't explain it, Johnny called over to the pianist in the *Tonight Show* band, Ross Tompkins, for an answer. "Happiness!" Tompkins yelled out.

By the 1970s, Garner was back to playing in jazz clubs, but he still had an avid following. In February 1975, he was in the middle of a triumphant return engagement at Mister Kelly's in Chicago when he collapsed on-stage. Taken to the hospital, he was diagnosed with emphysema, brought on by his three-packs-a-day cigarette habit. It would be his last concert, and within two years he would be dead of lung cancer at the age of fifty-three.

Because he died so young; because his looks were so unusual; and because he was so famous for not reading music, Erroll Garner would come to be remembered as an inexplicable genius, as if he had come out of nowhere. But serious students of jazz knew where the music came from—how deeply Garner had absorbed and synthesized the traditions of stride and ragtime piano, of swing and bebop, of Broadway show tunes and polyrhythmic percussion that traced all the way back to Africa. And the many talented musicians from his hometown knew where he had first en-countered those influences and developed the ambition to outshine them all—including, in the end, even great crossover heartthrob Billy Eckstine.

The year after Garner left Westinghouse High, another piano prod-igy graduated from the school. He was a skinny boy named Frederick Jones, who was known by his nickname "Fritz." As an adult, he became a member of the Nation of Islam and a leading light of bebop under the name of Ahmad Jamal. In a documentary film about Garner that came out twenty-five years after his death, Jamal had an answer for the critics who charged that Erroll was more of a gifted entertainer than a true artist. "He could make you laugh, and he could make you cry, and he could make you think," Jamal said. "That's what an artist is supposed to do."

And where did that artistry come from? "What was different about Erroll was one word: Pittsburgh," Jamal said. "Pittsburgh produced this kind of talent."

Jackie Robinson gets ready to play the Pittsburgh Pirates
at Forbes Field during his first season as
a Brooklyn Dodger, 1947.

8

"JACKIE'S BOSWELL"

ON A HOT FLORIDA afternoon in March 1946, two *Pittsburgh Courier* reporters sat in a Greyhound bus station in Daytona Beach, waiting for the two passengers they had been sent to pick up. Billy Rowe had driven from Harlem, where he was settling back into his work as the paper's entertainment columnist after two years of reporting on black troops in the Pacific. Wendell Smith, the paper's sports editor, had come all the way from Pittsburgh. With his wide face, tortoiseshell glasses, and ever-present fedora, Smith had a naturally friendly look, but today he seemed anxious. Although they were in Florida working for the paper, the two reporters had been quietly hired to keep an eye on the man who six months earlier had become the most talked about minor league baseball prospect in America. But the recruit was two days late for spring training, and no one knew what had happened to him. Looking around the bus station, Smith and Rowe were relieved to see no other reporters, but as the hours ticked by a small crowd of black citizens from Daytona

Beach began to gather. A curious white bystander asked a porter what was going on. "Don't you know?" the porter answered. "Jackie Robinson is coming in."

At last, a bus from Jacksonville pulled into the station and Robinson stepped off, accompanied by his bride of three weeks, the former Rachel Isum. Rachel appeared weary, the strain of two sleepless nights showing on her normally radiant face. Her ermine coat, a wedding present from her husband, was stained with the grime of a fieldworker who had squeezed next to her on the bench at the back of the bus. Jackie, his dark face flushed and his double-breasted suit rumpled, looked furious. "Well, I finally made it," he snapped at the two newsmen. "But I never want another trip like this one." Rowe grabbed the couple's valises and showed them to his red Pontiac sedan. "I'm your chauffeur!" he said cheerfully. Robinson was in no mood for friendly banter. "I've had better chauffeurs and I've had better cars!" he grumbled.

That night, as Rachel went to bed, Robinson stayed up and raged to Smith and Rowe about the indignities the couple had suffered since they boarded an American Airlines plane in Los Angeles two nights earlier. The following morning, the plane landed for a layover in New Orleans. When the Robinsons went to reboard, they were told that they had been bumped "for military reasons." At an airport restaurant, they were allowed to order sandwiches but not to sit down. Stuck in New Orleans for the night, they could find lodging only in a segregated black hotel with tiny, foul-smelling rooms and plastic mattresses. The next day, they boarded another plane for Daytona Beach only to have it land in Pensacola for refueling. A flight attendant informed them they would have to get off to compensate for the fuel's weight—just as three new white passengers got on.

Despairing of reaching their destination by air, the Robinsons took a train from Pensacola to Jacksonville, then boarded a bus for Daytona Beach. They stretched out in the seats in the front of the bus to finally get some rest. But as the bus filled, a white passenger told them to move to the back, calling Jackie "boy." Stifling the urge to strike the man, Robinson

Joe Louis (right) at the Loendi Club in 1938 with (left to right)
Woogie Harris, Teenie's racketeer brother; singer Cab Calloway;
and light heavyweight boxer John Henry Lewis.

From the 1920s until the 1950s, so many black luminaries passed through the
Hill District that it became known as "Little Harlem" and "the Crossroads of
the World." Visiting athletes and musicians were feted at the Loendi Club, the
black counterpart to the Duquesne Club of Pittsburgh's Gilded Age tycoons,
and gathered at the Crawford Grill, the leading nightclub on the Hill.

Teenie Harris with his light meter and Speed Graphic
camera on the streets of Pittsburgh.

Charles "Teenie" Harris was a star sandlot athlete and numbers runner who taught himself photography and worked for *The Pittsburgh Courier* for four decades. Known as "One Shot" for the speed and efficiency with which he deployed his Speed Graphic press camera, Harris left a stunning record of black Pittsburgh in its heyday—including most of the photos in this book.

Ella Fitzgerald poses in 1948 with then husband,
Pittsburgh-born bass player Ray Brown.

Louis Armstrong dines with a local singer and
journalist at the Crawford Grill in 1945.

Duke Ellington (right), Billy Strayhorn (center), and dancer
Charles "Honi" Coles at the Stanley Theatre, the show
palace where Ellington and Strayhorn first met.

In 1938, Duke Ellington was performing in Pittsburgh when he was introduced to a shy but brilliant recent high school graduate named Billy Strayhorn—beginning one of the most fabled collaborations in jazz history. Later Strayhorn became best friends with Lena Horne, who spent her early twenties in Pittsburgh reuniting with her racketeer father and struggling in a failed marriage.

*Lena Horne with her father, Pittsburgh hotel owner
and numbers runner Teddy Horne.*

*Lena sings at the Loendi Club accompanied by pianist Charlotte
Enty Catlin, who was also Billy Strayhorn's teacher.*

*Gus Greenlee holds court at the Crawford Grill, from which he
ran his racketeering empire and his baseball operations.*

In the 1930s, Pittsburgh boasted the two best baseball franchises in the Negro
Leagues—the Homestead Grays and the Pittsburgh Crawfords, They had a bitter rivalry fueled by the warring egos of Grays owner "Cum" Posey, the son of a
black shipping and mining tycoon, and Gus Greenlee, who used his racketeering fortune to purchase the Crawfords and raid Posey's best players.

Josh Gibson in a Homestead Grays uniform for the second time in the 1940s.

The fearsome Pittsburgh Crawfords of 1932, featuring Satchel Paige and Josh Gibson (back row, second and third from left) and three other future Hall of Famers.

P.L. Prattis (center, in vest) and staff gather in the
Courier *newsroom in the mid-1940s.*

After the death of pioneering publisher Robert L. Vann, his widow and protégés carried on Vann's crusade on behalf of black soldiers. Led by executive editor P.L. Prattis, the *Courier* launched the "Double V Campaign"—urging black Americans to support the cause of victory in World War II in exchange for the promise of greater racial equality at home—and sent more war correspondents to the front than any other black newspaper.

Frank Bolden in his World War II correspondent uniform.

Jesse Vann (center) and Bill Nunn (looking over her shoulder) celebrate the wartime circulation boom by signing the 300,000th issue of a 1946 edition to come off the press.

Billy Eckstine (right) and his orchestra, featuring Dizzy Gillespie (center) and Charlie Parker (to his right), perform in Pittsburgh in 1944.

Pittsburgh-born crooner Billy Eckstine was one of the most popular male singers, black or white, in America before a controversial photo of his encounter with white female fans ran in *Life* magazine in 1950 and began his slow descent from superstardom. Eckstine is less well remembered as an innovative big band leader who served as a mentor to bebop pioneers Dizzy Gillespie, Charlie Parker, and Sarah Vaughan.

The Life *photo of Billy Strayhorn with fans*
outside New York's Bop City in 1950.

Sarah Vaughan (right), who first came to Pittsburgh
with Eckstine's band, visits in 1950.

Jackie and Rachel Robinson (left) arrive in 1946 for minor league spring training in Dayton, Florida, where the Dodgers had sent two Pittsburgh chaperones to greet them.

In the late 1930s, a young sportswriter named Wendell Smith joined the *Courier* and began a crusade to integrate the major leagues. A decade later, he recommended Jackie Robinson to Brooklyn Dodgers owner Branch Rickey and served as Robinson's traveling companion and spokesman during Jackie's minor league tryout with the Montreal Royals and historic rookie year with the Dodgers.

Wendell Smith, the Courier *sportswriter who led the crusade to integrate pro baseball.*

Robinson and Branch Rickey reunite in Pittsburgh a decade after Smith connected them.

Eleanor Roosevelt and local children at a monument
to FDR in the Hill District in 1956.

In the 1930s, the Hill District became Ground Zero for the political migration of black voters to FDR's Democratic Party after Robert L. Vann proclaimed that it was time to turn "the picture of Abraham Lincoln to the wall." Twenty-five years later, the Lower Hill was destroyed in the name of urban renewal, and a decade after that, much of the Middle Hill was burned out in the riots that followed Martin Luther King Jr.'s assassination.

The Bethel AME Church, the last building to be destroyed on the Lower Hill in 1957.

Martin Luther King Jr. meets the press during his final visit to Pittsburgh in 1966.

Erroll Garner, the beloved piano virtuoso
and composer of "Misty."

Of the scores of remarkable pianists that Pittsburgh produced over the years—
from Earl "Fatha" Hines and Mary Lou Williams to Ahmad Jamal—none was
more dazzling than Erroll Garner. Although Garner was often depicted as an
inexplicable genius because he didn't read music, his peers knew better. "What
was different about Erroll was one word: Pittsburgh," Jamal said. "Pittsburgh
produced this kind of talent."

escorted his bride to the rear, where they rode upright through the night, trying not to breathe in the engine fumes that wafted through the open windows.

"Get me out of here!" Robinson pleaded to the reporters. "Just get me out of here!" He would never get a fair tryout—not here in the South, he seethed. He didn't want to put his wife, a California girl who had never experienced the worst of Jim Crow, through more humiliation. He would go back to the Negro Leagues, back to the Kansas City Monarchs.

As Robinson sulked, Smith and Rowe listened sympathetically and tried to calm him down. "You can't do that," they said, reminding him of all the people who were counting on him. They recalled what Branch Rickey, the Brooklyn Dodgers president, the man who had signed Robinson to play for the Montreal Royals farm team and hired Smith to watch over him, had said when the two men first met. Rickey had chosen Jackie not just for his skill on the field but also for his temperament, because the first Negro in the big leagues had to be man enough *not* to fight back.

Finally, after the three men had talked all night, the sun lifted and so did Jackie's mood. He would stay, he told the relieved reporters. He wouldn't let everyone down.

Wendell Smith modestly referred to himself as "Jackie's Boswell"— after the British writer known primarily for his biography of a more famous writer, Samuel Johnson—but he was far more than that. Movie and book versions of the Jackie Robinson story would dwell on Smith's role as Jackie's travel companion and mouthpiece during his challenging first years in the Dodgers organization. But long before that, Smith helped lay the groundwork for Robinson's rise with a decade-long crusade for baseball integration in the *Courier*. It was then Smith who first called Branch Rickey's attention to Robinson and who helped persuade the Dodgers president that Jackie could handle the pressure of being the first black player in the pro game. Other journalists also deserved recognition, from Sam Lacy of the *Baltimore Afro-American* and Frank Young of the *Chicago Defender* to Smith's bosses and colleagues at the *Courier*. But if Branch

Rickey was the visionary "Mahatma" of the Robinson story—the pious Methodist driven as much by moral zeal as financial opportunism—then Wendell Smith was the indispensable Sherpa, the scout who studied the terrain beforehand and who protected Jackie from danger, settled his moods, and bore witness to his historic ascent.

Unlike most blacks of his generation, Smith grew up around white people. Born John Wendell Smith, he was named for his father, who was raised on a Canadian farm and made his way to Detroit as a riverboat kitchen hand. Eventually John Sr. became the personal chef to Henry Ford. The auto tycoon started inviting the elder Smith to functions at his Dearborn mansion, and at the age of ten Wendell began to tag along. He became friends with Ford's son Edsel, and during the summers he invited Wendell over to play ball. "He's a fine looking boy," Henry Ford once remarked to John Smith as they observed the children. "What does he want to be when he grows up?" John answered that Wendell dreamed of being a major league pitcher—and didn't understand yet that that wasn't possible for a Negro boy.

At age nineteen, Smith learned that lesson the hard way. He pitched for an American Legion team, and in the playoff that year he hurled a 1–0 shutout. Wish Egan, a top scout for the Detroit Tigers, was in the stands. Afterward, Egan offered contracts to the opposing pitcher and to Wendell's catcher, Mike Tresh, who went on to have a long pro career. "I wish I could sign you too, kid," Egan told Smith. "But I can't." That night, Wendell cried harder than he ever had before. "That broke me up," he recalled to sportswriter Jerome Holtzman years later. "It was then that I made the vow that I would dedicate myself and do something on behalf of the Negro ballplayers."

The way to make good on that mission, Smith decided after graduating from West Virginia State College, was by becoming a journalist. Moving to Pittsburgh, he took a job with the *Courier* for $17 a week, writing photo captions and covering high school sports. A year later, at age twenty-four, he was promoted to sports editor and began to write a column, called "Smitty's Sport Spurts," which he turned into a soapbox on the subject of race and baseball. Seeing how the *Courier*'s crusades—from Joe Louis to the war in Ethiopia—roused readers and drove sales, Wendell proposed a new one. "I suggested a campaign for the admittance, the inclusion of Negro ballplayers in the big leagues," he recalled.

As National League teams passed through Pittsburgh to play the Pirates, Smith polled their players and managers about their views on integration. The Baseball Writers Association of America had denied Wendell's application for a press card—on the flimsy grounds that he covered other sports—so he couldn't do business inside Forbes Field. Instead he went to the Schenley Hotel, where the visiting teams stayed, and buttonholed them there. "Have you ever seen any Negro ballplayers who you think could play in the major leagues?" he asked everyone he interviewed.

Smith's investigation was a big hit with readers and his bosses, who rewarded him with a raise. Every week for more than a month, the results were splashed across the *Courier*'s sports pages. Twenty percent of the baseball men he interviewed opposed integration, Wendell estimated. Five percent ventured no opinion. But 75 percent voiced support for opening pro baseball's doors. That list included such All-Stars as Dizzy Dean, Honus Wagner, Mel Ott, Carl Hubbell, and Pepper Martin. Smith also got positive responses from managers of eight ball clubs: the Chicago Cubs, Pittsburgh Pirates, St. Louis Cardinals, Brooklyn Dodgers, New York Giants, Philadelphia Phillies, and Boston Bees. "I've seen plenty of colored boys who could make the grade in the majors—hell, I've seen a million," said Leo Durocher, the garrulous Dodgers skipper.

When America entered World War II, the *Courier* editors made the baseball crusade part of their Double V Campaign. Their scoop on Dorie Miller's heroism at Pearl Harbor had led Navy Secretary Frank Knox to end the practice of restricting blacks to mess duty. Chester Washington seized on the news to write an open letter to Kenesaw Mountain Landis, the commissioner of Major League Baseball. Washington pointed out that all the arguments marshaled against giving blacks a shot at big league baseball—tradition, training, morale—had once applied in the Navy. White sportswriters picked up on the theme. "Now that the Negro has proved himself good enough for the Navy, what must he do to demonstrate that he is fit to participate in organized baseball?" wrote Dan Parker, the veteran columnist for the *New York Daily Mirror*.

Landis, the trust-busting federal judge who had been appointed baseball's first commissioner after the 1917 Black Sox gambling scandal, prided himself on having cleaned up the game and enforced its integrity with an iron fist. But for two decades he had dodged the integration issue. Now the wartime arguments and positive statements from the likes of Leo Durocher shamed Landis into taking a position for the first time. "I have come to the conclusion that it is time for me to explain myself on this important issue," he declared in a written statement eight months after Pearl Harbor. "Negroes are not barred from organized baseball by the commissioner and never have been during the 21 years that I have served as commissioner. . . . If Durocher, or any other manager, or all of them, want to sign one, or 25 Negro players, it is all right with me."

Sensing an opening, Smith called on Landis to meet with leaders of the black press. On December 3, 1943, the commissioner finally consented, inviting a delegation from the National Negro Press Association to an annual meeting of club owners and league officials in a second-floor conference room at New York's Roosevelt Hotel. John Sengstacke of *The Chicago Defender* was scheduled to speak first, but before he could begin Landis introduced a guest: Paul Robeson, the actor and former college sports star. Landis had called Robeson away from performing *Othello* on Broadway to try to impress the newspapermen and preempt their complaints. "This man has sense," Landis said of Robeson, "and this man has not been fooled by the propaganda that there is an agreement in this crowd of men to bar Negroes from baseball."

When Robeson spoke, he didn't address the conspiracy suspicions but told the owners it was high time to allow black players into the major leagues. Sengstacke went next. But it was the third speaker—Ira Lewis, the tiny, baldheaded publisher of the *Courier*—who delivered the morning's most memorable remarks. Lewis began by appealing to the club owners as businessmen, making a dollars-and-cents argument for integration. Citing the boost that Joe Louis had given to boxing, Lewis argued that "the lifting of this ban against Negro baseball players . . . would make such a difference in your turnstiles as to make you wonder why you hadn't done this years before." Then Lewis took direct aim at the commissioner's denial of an "agreement" to bar blacks from the big leagues. "We thank Judge Landis for this statement," he said. "We believe, however, that there is a tacit understanding; there is a gentlemen's agreement, that no Negro players be hired."

Although the publishers presented a list of demands, Landis moved on to other business and then abruptly adjourned the meeting without giving any response. When Smith chased him down for comment, Landis shifted responsibility to the club owners, most of whom had fled to catch trains to their home cities. "I can't speak for the owners at all," Landis said. "Really, there is absolutely nothing I can tell you." Ford Frick, the National League president, mixed evasiveness with condescension. "I really think they were impressed by the presentation," Frick said of the owners. "But I can't say what will happen."

A follow-up letter went unanswered and another year of inaction passed until, in late November 1944, Kenesaw Mountain Landis died at the age of seventy-eight. In the *Courier*, Smith gave Landis credit for everything else he had done for baseball but did not sugarcoat his disappointment at the judge's legacy on the racial ban. "The fact remains he never used his wide and unquestionable powers to do anything about the problem," Smith wrote. "Landis played a subtle 'fence game' on this question."

Throughout the Roosevelt Hotel meeting, the journalists from Pittsburgh did notice one team representative quietly taking notes. He was Branch Rickey, the burly, bespectacled general manager of the Brooklyn Dodgers. Around the *Courier* newsroom, the question of what team might be the first to give black players a chance was a frequent topic of conversation. For a long time, the editors hoped it might be the Pittsburgh Pirates, but in 1943 owner William Benswanger had backed out of a promise to audition colored prospects.

Brooklyn was seen as another possibility. It had the kind of fans who might accept black players, and manager Leo Durocher had been unusually outspoken in his support for giving Negroes a shot. Although Rickey held his cards closely, he was known to be a man of deep religious conviction (he never attended ball games on Sunday) as well as a daring innovator (he had all but invented the farm system as an executive for the St. Louis Cardinals). So as the 1945 season approached, the Pittsburgh editors approved a scheme to test Rickey on the integration issue.

On the morning of Friday, April 6, four black men walked into the Dodger spring training camp at the U.S. Army field house in West Point, in the Bear Mountain range north of New York City. Two of them were reporters: Jimmy Smith, from the *Courier* bureau in Harlem, and Joe Bostic, the sports editor of *The People's Voice*, a smaller black paper. The other two men were veterans from the Negro Leagues: Terry McDuffie, a thirty-six-year-old pitcher for the Newark Eagles, and Dave "Showboat" Thomas, a thirty-nine-year-old outfielder for the New York Cubans. Bostic approached Robert Finch, Rickey's right-hand man, and asked if the two players could try out. Finch replied that the schedule for the day was set, but he invited the journalists to meet his boss. Over lunch at the Bear Mountain Inn, Rickey told the reporters that he didn't appreciate being put on the spot but that he would watch Thomas take batting practice and McDuffie pitch the following day.

Rickey didn't say much after the brief audition, and he didn't have to. As Smith conceded in his account for the *Courier*, McDuffie and Thomas were too old to be taken seriously as major league prospects. To be truly impressed, Smith wrote, white baseball front office executives like Rickey would have to see "young players, who have better records and greater possibilities" and would merit "a real trial, one that will last long enough for the players to adjust to the situation."

Although Smith didn't say so at the time, he had just such a player in mind. For five years, he and the other *Courier* sportswriters had been following the rise of a remarkable young athlete from Pasadena, California. The *Courier* had first written about him in 1940, while he was at UCLA, mistakenly referring to him in a headline as "Jackie Robertson." That story described the collegian as "America's top athlete" after he earned varsity letters in football, basketball, track, and baseball. Since then, Jackie Robinson had excelled in military competition during an Army stint and had made a promising start in the Negro Leagues, as a shortstop for the Kansas City Monarchs.

Now Smith was working at lining up a pro tryout for Robinson. A month earlier, Wendell had read that a city councilman from Boston named Isadore Muchnick was in a tough reelection battle in a racially mixed neighborhood. He wrote Muchnick and suggested that he appeal to black voters by coming out in support of integrating Boston's pro clubs, the Red Sox and the Braves. Smith urged Muchnick to threaten to call for a ban on Sunday baseball—a position that would win favor with Boston's Catholic Church—if the teams didn't agree to audition black players. When Muchnick agreed, the two men made a deal: Smith would select qualified players and bring them to Boston if Muchnick set up tryouts with the Red Sox and Braves.

Smith chose three players: Marvin Williams, a second baseman for the Philadelphia Stars; Sam Jethroe, a speedy outfielder and .350 hitter for the Cleveland Buckeyes; and Jackie Robinson, the rookie shortstop for the Monarchs. Of the three, Robinson was the least proven, and Wendell selected him as much for his demeanor and background as for his baseball skills. "He wasn't necessarily the best player," Smith recalled, "but he was the best player for the situation."

Like Wendell, Jackie was accustomed to being around white people, having attended UCLA and served in the Army. He knew the value of hard work, as the son of a woman who had supported five children on a domestic's wages after her husband abandoned the family. He could also stand up for himself, as he had in the Army when a driver ordered him to the back of a military bus. Jackie refused and was court-martialed for insubordination, but he managed to win an acquittal and an honorable discharge.

Just as impressive to Smith, Robinson had a winning smile and a thought-
ful, earnest manner that masked his fierce drive and prickly pride and that
would go over well with white fans and baseball executives.

Although skeptical, the players went along once Smith told them that
the *Courier* would pay for their trip. On the second week of April 1945,
they set off by train for Boston. When they arrived, they discovered that
the Braves had already departed for spring training and had canceled their
tryout. Then, as the four men were waiting for a call from the Red Sox,
they learned that President Roosevelt had died. As the nation went into
mourning, Smith and the three Negro League players waited in a Boston
hotel with nothing to do. The delay gave Wendell a chance to get to know
Jackie better, and to witness his short temper for the first time. "Listen,
Smith, it really burns me up to come fifteen hundred miles for them to
give me the runaround," Robinson fumed.

Finally the men were summoned to Fenway Park, only to find themselves in the company of high school players and prospects from the lowest
rungs of the minor leagues. Joe Cronin, the Red Sox manager, and Eddie
Collins, the general manager, sat high in the stands and observed without
saying anything. None of Boston's white baseball writers bothered to show
up. The tryout lasted only an hour, and Smith left feeling that it had been
nothing more than a cynical political sop. When a promised follow-up call
never materialized, he wrote to Collins, who claimed that the Red Sox
couldn't make any decisions because Cronin had broken his leg.

Disappointed but not wanting to waste a trip to the East Coast, Smith
decided to look into an intriguing development in the world of black baseball. The previous year, Gus Greenlee, the former owner of the Pittsburgh
Crawfords and czar of the Negro Leagues, had announced a comeback.
His coffers replenished by the wartime numbers racket, Greenlee planned
to launch a new baseball circuit called "the United States League" to compete with the two existing black leagues of the day. Now there was word
that Branch Rickey was huddling with Greenlee to discuss sponsoring a
team for the new league, one that would play in Ebbets Field while the
Dodgers were on the road.

Smith called Rickey to check out the story, and Rickey invited him to New York the next day. When they met at the Dodgers' headquarters on Montague Street in Brooklyn, Rickey asked if Wendell could recommend any players for his new team, to be called the Brooklyn Brown Dodgers. Smith mentioned the three players he had just brought to Boston. When he uttered the name "Jackie Robinson," Smith recalled, Rickey's bushy eyebrows shot up. "Jackie Robinson!" Rickey said. "I knew he was an All-American football player and an All-American basketball player. But I didn't know he played baseball." Smith told Rickey that Robinson had been the star of the Red Sox tryout, bashing homers over Fenway Park's famous left field wall and speeding around the bases. Rickey listened raptly. "You will hear from me," he said as the men parted.

A week later, Rickey phoned Smith in Pittsburgh. In a secretive tone, he said that he was sending his top scout, Clyde Sukeforth, to observe "the young man from the West." Wendell assumed Rickey was talking about Robinson, and that he had a reason for speaking in such veiled terms. "Mr. Rickey," he asked, playing along, "is there any chance of this ball player ever becoming part of the Brooklyn ball club?" Rickey dodged the question. "This may be more extensive than you visualize," was all he would say. "I don't know exactly how this is going to turn out." Still, the call was enough to confirm that the Dodgers were eyeing Robinson for *something*. A week later, Wendell saw Jackie and gave him a heads-up. "The Dodgers are trailing you," he said.

Soon afterward, Rickey called Smith again with worry in his voice. While scouting Robinson, Clyde Sukeforth had heard from a fellow scout that the Monarchs shortstop had gotten into a fight with a white umpire. Was the prospect "a belligerent individual"? Rickey asked. Wendell knew the answer was complicated, but he didn't want to discuss it at this delicate stage. "I didn't want to tell Mr. Rickey, 'Yes, he's tough to get along with,'" he recalled. "A lot of us knew that. Jackie had a sizeable temper." Smith assured Rickey that the incident was probably just a routine dust-up—but then he contacted Jackie again and warned him to be on his best behavior. "I told Jackie to watch himself, to watch his conduct," Wendell recalled. "Everything he did, on and off the field, would get back to Mr. Rickey."

Finally, in August 1945, Rickey was ready to meet "the man from the West." Robinson was playing for the Monarchs at Comiskey Park in Chicago when a pale man with a long, thin face waved at him from the stands. It was Clyde Sukeforth, come to take Robinson to Brooklyn. That night, the two men rode on a sleeper train to New York, and the next morning Jackie was in Rickey's office on Montague Street, receiving an offer to play in the Dodgers' farm system.

"Mr. Rickey told me I would have to stand a lot of gaff without losing my temper or making a scene," Robinson recalled in an autobiography written with Wendell Smith two years later. "He even acted out several situations I'd be likely to face, and then asked how I would meet each one of them. I wasn't too happy with the prospect he foresaw, but I knew, too, that I was pretty sure to run into some name-calling, some insults, some Jim Crow. I told him I felt pretty sure I would stay out of rhubarbs on the field and trouble of any sort away from it, but that I couldn't become an obsequious, cringing fellow. Among other things I couldn't play hard, aggressive ball if I were that sort of man."

The response satisfied Rickey, and by the end of the meeting he offered Robinson $600 a week and a $3,500 bonus to play for the Montreal Royals of the International League the following season. Fearing leaks, Rickey demanded that Jackie keep the deal a secret from everyone but his mother and his fiancée. Rickey also continued to play coy with Wendell Smith. Although Wendell had yet to write about Rickey's pursuit of Robinson for the *Courier*—"it would have killed it," he explained later—he couldn't be expected to sit on such a huge scoop. "I had the definite impression there was more behind [Rickey's interest] than the Brown Dodgers," he recalled, "but he never came out and said so until he signed Jackie for the Montreal Royals."

When that day arrived two months later, it caught the rest of the sports world by complete surprise. Reporters didn't know what to expect when Hector Racine, the Royals president, invited them to a hastily arranged press conference in Montreal. When Racine introduced Robinson as the team's latest recruit, sportswriters in the room rushed to find phones and telegraph machines to report the news. Once America's leading sports columnists started to weigh in, however, many didn't give Robinson much of a chance. "With every major league ball club having a backlog of young talent, proven stars, returning from the war, Robinson is a 1,000–1 shot to make the grade," wrote Jimmy Powers in the New York *Daily News*.

Shortly afterward, Smith was rewarded for his behind-the-scenes role in Robinson's scouting with two splashy exclusives for the *Courier*. One was a first-person account dictated to him by Jackie himself—the first of dozens of "diary" stories that Wendell would ghostwrite for Robinson over the next two years. The other was a two-hour interview in which Rickey explained his decision. In characteristic fashion, he portrayed it as a brave act of Christian faith rather than a calculated business bet. "When my scouts told me Robinson was good enough to play with Montreal . . . I could not turn him down because he was a Negro—my conscience wouldn't let me," Rickey insisted. "I anticipated the adverse reaction that has been expressed by certain people, but I had the shield of right and I was not afraid."

Rickey was far less charitable, however, when it came to the organization he had stepped over to sign Robinson. When Smith brought up the Kansas City Monarchs, Rickey appeared "irked" and started to rock side to side in his swivel chair. "Kansas City claims that Robinson was signed to a contract," Rickey sputtered. "Well, Robinson says he cannot remember ever having signed one. I'd like to see the contract they claimed he signed!" Then Rickey heaped contempt on the corrupt ways of black baseball. "I don't care what they say about contracts, suspensions and fines; they don't have a league," he scoffed. "They're simply a booking agent's paradise. Another thing, they have owners of ball clubs in each league serving as presidents. They are not leagues and have no right to expect organized baseball to respect them!"

In his early crusading columns, Smith had imagined that the Negro

Leagues might benefit from big league integration, by selling player contracts for top dollar and serving as an unofficial farm system. Cum Posey, the owner of the champion Homestead Grays and secretary of the Negro National League, had written that black teams would not "stand in the way" of their players getting a shot at the major leagues but would demand a fair return. "We're not here to give anything away," Posey insisted. But now Rickey was sending a very different signal to the rest of white baseball: it had no obligation to compensate black teams for giving up their best players.

For a brief time after the Royals announcement, J. L. Wilkinson and Tom Baird, the owners of the Kansas City Monarchs, cried foul. Clark Griffiths of the Washington Senators also came to the defense of the Negro Leagues, hoping to protect the hefty fees he received for renting his ballpark to the Homestead Grays. But the white owners soon backed off once they realized how bad it looked for them to stand in Robinson's way. And by the time Jackie began his season with the Montreal Royals, the one leader in black baseball tough enough to stand up for its interests was dead.

In the days after Cum Posey succumbed to lung cancer at the age of fifty-five, thousands of admirers filed by his casket as he lay in state in Homestead. David Lawrence, the ambitious FDR foot soldier who had just been elected mayor of Pittsburgh, hailed the passing as a "severe blow to the community." Gus Greenlee tipped his cap to his longtime adversary. "Although at times we opposed each other bitterly," Greenlee told the *Courier*, "I always held the greatest respect for Cum as friend, associate and rival." Ira Lewis captured the unapologetic drive that had led Posey to win more championships than any owner in the history of black baseball. "Cum Posey was a man who never forgot an enemy or a friend," Lewis said in his eulogy at Homestead's Clark Memorial Baptist Church. "He asked very few favors but was rather inclined to seek results on the merits of operation and competition. He prided himself on never being a good loser because, as he said, 'Good losers are seldom winners.'"

Now Cum Posey was gone, and with him the chance that anyone would prevent the Negro Leagues from becoming the biggest losers in the baseball revolution to come.

IT WAS THE MOST important social night of the year for major league baseball. For more than two decades, the New York chapter of the Baseball Writers Association of America had hosted an annual dinner to toast—and roast—the national pastime. The guest list included not only sports reporters and team owners but hundreds of influential politicians and businessmen. Every year, they looked forward to the dinner's main event: a burlesque show in which the writers dressed up in humorous costumes to spoof news in the baseball world. As more than a thousand attendees gathered in the ballroom of the Waldorf-Astoria on an early February night in 1946, they were eager to see how the mischievous scribes would make sport of Albert Benjamin Chandler, the gregarious Kentucky politician known as "Happy," who had just given up a seat in the United States Senate to become the new commissioner of baseball.

After cocktails and dinner, an orchestra struck up Happy Chandler's favorite song, "My Old Kentucky Home." The ballroom curtain rose to reveal a Southern mansion set. A butler in knee britches stood with his back to the audience, dusting furniture. As the butler slowly turned, the crowd could see that his face was painted black, and that he was wearing a Montreal Royals jersey. The sportswriter playing the part waited for a wave of laughter to subside before he uttered a line in "darky" dialect. "Looks like the massa will be late this evenin'!" he said before exiting the stage.

Five more sportswriters entered, all dressed as Kentucky colonels and hailing their leader: "Colonel Chandler." After singing several verses in praise of baseball, Chandler clapped his hands. "Robb-eee!" he called out. "Robb-eee!"

"Yassuh, Massa," said the butler, returning to the stage. "Here I is."

"Ah, there you are, Jackie," Chandler said. "Jackie, you old woolyheaded rascal. How long you been in the family?"

"Long time, Colonel, mighty long time," the butler said. "Ever since Massa Rickey done bought me from the Kansas City Monarchs."

"To be sure, Jackie, to be sure," the colonel said. "How could I forget that Colonel Rickey brought you to our house?" Then in a loud stage whisper, Chandler hissed to the audience: "Rickey—that no good carpetbagger! What could he be thinking?"

More laughter rippled through the Waldorf ballroom. At the end of the evening, the master of ceremonies, columnist Dan Daniel of the *New York World Telegram*, proclaimed the burlesque "the best one yet." Arthur Daley of *The New York Times* devoted his next column to describing the show, complete with long passages of the mock dialogue between "Colonel Chandler" and "Robbie" the butler. "It was one of the best and most merciless ribbings the boys ever dealt out to anyone," Daley wrote. "The burlesque was so broad that the scribes were able to risk bringing into the cast of characters as delicate a subject as Jackie Robinson, the Negro shortstop whom Branch Rickey signed to a Montreal contract. But it all was such lampoonery that no one's feelings really were hurt."

To the contrary, one sportswriter was enraged. After reading the account of the burlesque in *The New York Times*, Wendell Smith denounced the white baseball writers in his next *Courier* column. While most of them paid lip service to giving Robinson a shot at the majors, he wrote, their "Nazi Opera" showed what they really thought. "They weren't courageous or brave enough to express their feelings in their respective newspapers, (that might affect circulation), so they put on this dastardly act behind closed doors," Smith fumed. After a decade of crusading for integration, Smith had finally seen a major league organization sign a black player. But the Waldorf dinner showed him that the struggle to get the men who ran and covered baseball, and the fans who filled the stands, to take Branch Rickey's "experiment" seriously had only begun.

Unbeknownst to his *Courier* readers, Smith now had a personal role in that experiment's next phase. Ever since the Royals press conference the previous fall, he had been in regular contact with both Robinson and Rickey. When Wendell wrote a column defending Jackie against skepticism from some white ballplayers and reporters, Jackie sent him a grateful letter. "I want to thank you and the paper for all you have done and are doing on my behalf," he wrote. "As you know I am not worried about what the white press or people think as long as I continue to get the best wishes of my people." In November, Jackie wrote again from Venezuela, where he was playing exhibition games with Negro League veterans. Wendell wrote back to say that he had informed Rickey of the example of "good conduct" Jackie was setting for South American fans.

Meanwhile, Smith was corresponding with Rickey about plans for Robinson's first spring training. Searching for a warm-weather location that would be hospitable to blacks, Rickey had decided to bring both the Dodgers and the Royals to Daytona Beach, on the northeast coast of Florida. Daytona had a small working-class black community and a practice ball field in the Negro section of town. It was also home to a black college, Bethune-Cookman, founded by Mary McLeod Bethune, the friend and adviser to Franklin and Eleanor Roosevelt. Anticipating problems with Daytona hotels, Rickey summoned Smith to Brooklyn and asked him to search for lodging for Robinson and another player he planned to offer a tryout, Grays pitcher Johnny Wright. Later Rickey wrote to ask Wendell to do the same in Sanford, Florida, a nearby town where he wanted to locate an "early camp" for first-time prospects.

Rickey proposed that Smith serve as Robinson's chaperone as well, to keep him company and keep him out of trouble. "This whole program was more or less your suggestion, as you will recall," Rickey wrote, "and I think I had a point that much harm could come if either of these boys were to do or say something out of turn." Smith wrote back to accept the offer, and to suggest that he take on chauffeur duties as well, since Robinson and Wright would often not be able to travel by bus with their teammates. At some point, Smith arranged to include Billy Rowe and his red Pontiac in the arrangement, and Rickey agreed to pay each man $50 a week—matching their *Courier* salaries. But Wendell's letters made it clear that he saw himself as having far loftier motivations than money. "I am most happy to feel that you are relying on my newspaper and me, personally," he wrote Rickey, "in cooperation in trying to accomplish this great move for practical Democracy in the most amiable and diplomatic manner possible."

As luck would have it, Wendell had a college classmate who lived in Sanford, Florida. Viola Brock was a schoolteacher whose husband, David Brock, ran the local bolita, the numbers-in-a-bag lottery racket. They owned one of the finest houses in the Negro section of town, a two-story white manse with a wide screened-in porch shaded by a large tree in the front yard. When the Brocks agreed to act as hosts, Rickey showed his gratitude by visiting them several days before Robinson and Wright were due to arrive. Sitting in a wicker chair on the porch, Rickey praised the property, unaware of the gambling operation that funded it. "This is the type of place they should be quartered in," Rickey proclaimed. "If we can't put them in hotels, then they should stay some place that represents something. This is the type of home."

The day after Jackie and Rachel Robinson's arrival in Daytona Beach, Smith and Rowe drove them to Sanford's Memorial Athletic Field, where hopefuls trying to make the Royals squad had been working out for two days. If Rickey had hoped to minimize the hoopla surrounding Robinson by starting his tryout in Sanford, it didn't work. Along with hundreds of walk-on prospects—many of them returning World War II veterans— the park was full of reporters. For the rest of the day, they peppered Robinson with questions as he did jumping jacks, fielded grounders, and took batting practice with a newfangled pitching machine called the "Iron Mike."

At the end of the day, as the white players returned to their hotel for dinner, Smith and Rowe took Robinson and Wright to the Brock home. As the group relaxed over drinks on the front porch, they waved at neighbors who wandered by, hoping to catch a glimpse of the famous visitor. Jackie felt the first day had gone well. "Everyone was swell to us, and we were expecting a cool reception," he told his hosts. David Brock nodded as he sipped a rum and cola. "You'll find good people every place you go," he said optimistically. "Yes, sir, even here in Florida."

But when the men returned to the Brock house for lunch the following day, they received a very different reception. Robinson and Wright had gone inside and Smith was sitting on the porch when a white man approached.

"You're chaperoning Robinson?" the man asked.

"That's right," Wendell replied.

"We want you to get those niggers out of town," the man said. He claimed that he had just come from a meeting of local businessmen at the town hall and that they wanted the two black ballplayers out of Sanford by nightfall.

Alarmed, Smith phoned Rickey, who was in Daytona Beach at the Dodgers camp. Rickey told Wendell to get Robinson and Wright away from Sanford as quickly as possible—but not to tell them what had happened until they were safely out of town. Both men had come to see how temperamental Jackie could be and they didn't want him to blow up again. That evening, when the two players returned to the Brock home following afternoon practice, the usually jovial *Courier* reporters seemed "exceptionally quiet and sober," Robinson recalled. Over dinner, they exchanged grave glances. Then Rowe stood up and announced that he was going to gas up his Pontiac.

"You guys leaving us?" Jackie asked.

"No," Wendell replied. "We're all going to Daytona. . . . Pack your duds, fellows. We're blowing."

Smith called Rickey to tell him they were on their way to Daytona. Overhearing the conversation, Robinson worried that the Royals might be letting him go. As he packed his bags, he cursed his decision to accept Rickey's offer and contemplated taking Rachel back to California. The group piled into the Pontiac, Smith and Billy Rowe in the front seat and Jackie, Rachel, and Johnny Wright in the back. In the middle of town, they stopped at a red light. A group of white townspeople looked on from a street corner.

"How can people like that call themselves American?" Billy grumbled.

"They're as rotten as they come," Wendell muttered.

Jackie was confused. "They haven't done anything to us," he said. "They're nice people as far as I'm concerned."

Wendell turned around to face the backseat. "Sure, they liked you," he seethed. "They were in love with you. . . . That's why we're leaving."

"What do you mean?" Jackie asked.

"Look, we didn't want to tell you guys because we didn't want to upset you," Wendell said. "But we're leaving this town because we've been told to get out. They won't stand for Negro ballplayers on the same field with whites."

In Daytona Beach, Smith and Rowe took the Robinsons to the home of another black couple—Joe Harris, a pharmacist, and his wife, Duff— while Wright lodged with a black family nearby. At night, the five stayed in the Negro section of town while the white players trying out for the Montreal team headed for a hotel on the beach. At Kelly Field, the ballpark in the black neighborhood where Rickey had arranged for the Royals to train, scores of locals appeared to cheer on their new heroes. Eager to impress the black fans as much as his coaches, Robinson strained his arm firing from shortstop on his first day of practice. Forced to switch to second base and then to first base, able to take only a few swings of batting practice, he grew increasingly frustrated and anxious.

Wendell and Billy did their best to buoy Jackie's spirits. They played cards with him at night and took him to a USO club with a Ping-Pong table and to the black movie theater in town. But Jackie remained in a funk until the Royals finally played the Brooklyn Dodgers in an exhibition game for the first time. Four thousand people showed up, a quarter of them black. When Robinson came to the plate, he heard a smattering of boos, but far more cheers. "Come on black boy, you can make the grade!" a white fan shouted. Jackie fouled out to the catcher and didn't get a hit in the rest of the losing effort, but he left encouraged. That night, he recalled, he "went to sleep, the applause still ringing in my ears."

Still, Robinson's slump continued. Rachel began to worry that her husband wouldn't make it past spring training. Finally, in a game against the St. Paul Saints, Jackie laid down a bunt along the third base line and beat it out for a single. Rickey was in the stands, and he gave Smith a vote of confidence to pass along to *Courier* readers. "He'll hit, and he'll be quite a ball player," Rickey said. "I'm sure of that. The only question is his arm. I only hope it comes around." Relieved, Rachel took over the kitchen of the Harris home and prepared a celebratory dinner of chicken and vegetables.

From that point on, Robinson's hitting and fielding gradually improved, but his temper—and the patience of his Pittsburgh minders—continued to be tested. On a Sunday in late March, the Royals traveled to Jacksonville to play the Jersey City Giants, only to find the ballpark padlocked. The city's Bureau of Recreation had called off the game at the last minute, leaving hundreds of fans stranded outside. When Montreal went to Deland, Florida, to play Indianapolis, Jackie scored a run in the first inning on a single, a stolen base, and a sacrifice fly. As he slid into home, a policeman walked onto the field and grabbed him by the collar. In a heavy drawl, the officer threatened to throw Robinson in jail if he didn't leave the field immediately. "We told y'all to leave them Nigra players home," he growled when Royals manager Clay Hopper protested.

In mid-April, as the Royals prepared to head north for the regular season, Smith added up the toll that racism had taken on their spring training. In addition to the incidents in Jacksonville and Deland, nine other Royals games had been called off. City officials in Savannah, Richmond, and Sanford had declared that they would allow play only if Robinson and Wright stayed away, and in each case Rickey had canceled the games rather than submit to the demands. For the first time, Wendell let *Courier* readers in on what had happened to Robinson and Wright in the days after their arrival in Florida. "Contrary to stories that were published from Sanford at the time, Robinson and Wright were definitely not wanted," Smith wrote. He explained that he hadn't reported the threats against them at the time for fear that "the power of suggestion" might encourage whites in other Florida towns to attempt similar intimidation.

As the Royals headed north by train for the regular season, Smith accompanied them, and Robinson confided to him how much he had felt the strain of expectation from black fans in Florida. "I could hear them shouting in the stands, and I wanted to produce so much that I was tense and over-anxious," Jackie said. "I started swinging at bad balls and doing a lot of things I would not have done under ordinary circumstance. I wanted to get a hit for them because they were pulling for me so hard."

In his next *Courier* column, Smith pleaded with "the Negro fan to help by taking some of the pressure off . . ." No celebrating before anything had happened, he cautioned. No disorderly conduct that might prove a distraction or an embarrassment. "The guy who is so stimulated by the appearance of Robinson and Wright in Montreal uniforms that he stands up in the stands and rants and raves, yells and screams before they have even so much as picked up a ball," Wendell wrote, "is the guy who will be cheering them out of Organized Baseball, rather than in."

Then, on opening day of the Royals' season, before 25,000 fans and a bevy of chorus line girls that the Jersey City Giants had hired for the occasion, Robinson put on a performance that black fans couldn't help but cheer. After a tense and unspectacular spring training, he suddenly displayed all the gifts that had led Wendell Smith and Branch Rickey to put so much faith in him. After grounding out to shortstop in the first inning, Jackie came to bat in the third with two men on base. On the first pitch, he blasted a 335-foot home run over the left field fence. In the fifth, he dropped a bunt single down the third base line, stole second, advanced to third, and scored on a balk after unnerving the pitcher with a feint to home. In the seventh, he singled to center, stole second again, moved to third on a single, and scored on a triple. In the eighth, he beat out another bunt, made it all the way to third on the next hit, and then induced another balk. On defense, playing second base, he had five put-outs. He made only one error, a bad throw on a double play ball that cost the Royals the one run in a 14–1 rout.

In the stands, Wendell Smith and Joe Bostic, *The People's Voice* reporter, savored the moment. "Our hearts beat just a little faster, and the thrill ran through us like champagne bubbles," Wendell recalled. Meanwhile, the

Courier's editorial page writers delivered a self-help lecture reminiscent of Robert L. Vann. Robinson's opening day triumph, they wrote, showed the importance for blacks to be ready to capitalize on the chances they demanded. "There is too much of a tendency for people nowadays to give more time to clamoring for opportunity than to preparing themselves for the opportunity when it arrives," they wrote. "Agitation is very well, but execution is far more important."

A week later, Robinson was in Montreal for the Royals home opener and the beginning of a season-long love affair with the team's fans. (After several bad outings, Johnny Wright was demoted to the class-C minor league, and the next year he returned to the Homestead Grays.) Jackie won the International League batting crown with a .349 average, stole 40 bases, scored 113 runs, and had the best fielding statistics of any second baseman in the minors. He led the Royals to 100 victories, the most in their history, and helped them come from behind to beat Louisville in the "Little World Series."

After the Royals won their final game at home, thousands of fans rushed onto the field and demanded to see their hero. "We want Robinson!" they shouted, and in French, *"Il a gagné ses épaulettes!"* (He has earned his stripes!) When Jackie finally stepped out of the dugout, the crowd mobbed him, lifted him off the ground, and paraded him around the infield. As he showered in the locker room, fans jammed the hallway outside blocking his exit as he tried to leave. Handing his bags to a friend, Jackie crouched in his old UCLA running back stance and made a break for the street. Fans chased him for three blocks until he jumped into a waiting car.

Sam Maltin, a Canadian journalist who covered the game for the *Courier*, couldn't help but note the irony of a white mob chasing a black man for something other than a lynching. When the Royals had played in Louisville earlier in the series, the crowd booed Robinson. Now, Maltin hoped, the scene in Montreal would teach them something. "To the large group of Louisville fans who came here for the first time, it may be a lesson of goodwill among men," Maltin wrote. "They couldn't fail to tell others down South of the 'riots'—not because of hate but because of love."

Wendell Smith stayed home in Pittsburgh, however, and was uncharacteristically subdued about Robinson's minor league championship. His only contribution to the coverage was a short interview by phone in which Robinson thanked Montreal for "a great year" and his wife, Rachel, for getting him through periods when he had been "down in the dumps." About the following season, Jackie said only: "I think I'm going to get a chance with the Dodgers; however, I haven't heard from Mr. Rickey, so I can't say." Even when Robinson came to Pittsburgh the following week with an exhibition team, Smith steered clear of writing about him. After helping Jackie get so far, it was as though Wendell didn't want to jinx his chances of taking the next step—or betray any concern that the welcome that awaited Robinson in cities across America might be less rapturous than the one he had received in Montreal.

IN JANUARY 1947, JOSH Gibson moved back in with his mother on Strauss Street on Pittsburgh's North Side. In the decade since Gibson had rejoined the Homestead Grays, he had remained one of the biggest draws in black baseball and helped lead the Grays to eight Negro National League championships, seven of them in a row. But years of heavy drinking, drug abuse, and womanizing had taken a severe toll. Gibson's once chiseled frame swelled with a mountainous beer belly, then withered as liver, kidney, and bronchial ailments spread. Dark bags framed his once boyish eyes. His erratic hitting had earned him a demotion to the back side of the Grays order, and his once awe-inspiring annual home run totals had dwindled into the teens.

Staying in Pittsburgh, Gibson skipped his usual winter swing through the Mexican and Caribbean leagues. On some days, he spent hours at the home of his late wife's mother, where his son Josh Jr. lived, trying to reconnect with the sixteen-year-old. On other days, he lay in bed in the room where he had once slept as a strapping teenager starting out in the sandlot leagues. When he felt better, he headed across the river to the Crawford Grill, only to lapse into another bender and end up slumped over the bar or lying in a Wylie Avenue gutter. One night, his teammate Sammy Bankhead got a call alerting him that Gibson had crawled out on the ledge of a Hill District hotel and was threatening to jump. Leaning out the window, Bankhead talked his friend down by calling his bluff. "Go ahead and jump, then," Bankhead said. "See if I care."

On a Sunday afternoon, Gibson was drinking at the Crawford Grill when his head started to hurt. Wanting to get away from bright lights, he decided to spend the evening at the Garden Theater, a movie house on the North Side. When the feature was over, patrons found Gibson passed out in his seat. They searched his wallet and found his doctor's name. When the physician arrived, he took Gibson back to Strauss Street and administered a sedative as Josh's mother, Nancy, and younger siblings Jerry and Annie looked on. Whether Gibson later rose in bed and asked for all his trophies to be brought to him, as his Annie claimed, isn't sure. What is certain is that by 1:30 in the morning on January 20, the man known as "the black Babe Ruth" was dead at the age of thirty-five.

The brief Associated Press story that marked Gibson's passing in newspapers across the country cited the cause as a stroke. But in his obituary tribute in the *Courier*, Wendell Smith blamed a more insidious culprit. "Perhaps if Josh Gibson hadn't been a victim of the vicious color line in the majors; if he had been given the chance to make the big league he so justly deserved; if he could have swung his bat against the type of competition for which he was born, he might be alive today," Smith wrote. "For he was a big leaguer, and he knew it. He was a thoroughbred and he should have been with them. But they slammed the door in his face, his kindly black face, and left him standing on the outer fringes of the glistening world to which he belonged. That treatment, more than anything else, sent the 'king' to his grave. . . . It sent him to the 'land of drink' and into the pitfall of human errors. Finally his health went and he slipped away into eternal darkness. . . . I know the real reason Josh Gibson died. I don't need a doctor's report for confirmation, either. He was 'murdered' by Big League Baseball."

In this case, however, Smith may have protested too much. He would later insist that he had tried to win Gibson a shot at the big leagues—by recommending him to Pirates owner William Benswanger in 1942, and by trying to bring him to the Red Sox tryout in 1945, before Grays owner Cum Posey vetoed the idea. But Smith's writing at the time indicated otherwise. By the mid-1940s he had stopped singing Gibson's praises, while insisting that white owners were looking for younger players. Just as Ches Washington and Bill Nunn had done in championing Joe Louis, Wendell calculated that comportment was as vital as ability in challenging white prejudice. Even if Gibson had the gifts to play in the big leagues, Smith knew, he lacked the maturity to handle the pressure and to avoid embarrassing himself off the field. So Smith never discussed Gibson with Branch Rickey, or included him in speculation about what players might follow Robinson to the majors. And that bitter knowledge—that he had been upstaged by younger players and replaced as the darling of his hometown newspaper—may have contributed to Gibson's decline every bit as much as the injustice of white baseball.

Ushering in 1947, Smith declared that Robinson had helped make "'46 the Greatest Year for Negro Athletes." Yet as the new baseball season approached, Rickey still had not made his intentions clear, and Jackie was getting anxious. Once again, the Dodger president had chosen a spring training spot with Robinson in mind. Not wanting to repeat the previous year's experience in Florida, Rickey had announced that the Dodgers and Royals would spend the preseason in Cuba. Beyond that, he had said only that "Robinson will go to Havana as a member of the Montreal squad."

From Los Angeles, Robinson sent a worried letter to Pittsburgh, and in early February Smith wrote back to reassure him. "As I see it you are definitely going to get a chance," Wendell predicted. "All you have to do is keep a cool head, play the kind of ball you are capable of playing and don't worry about anything. As you know, Rickey is no dummy. He is a very methodical man and will see to it that you are treated right."

Finally, as the Dodgers and Royals left Cuba to play a series of head-to-head exhibition games in Panama, Rickey began to show his cards. Safely away from the throng of reporters in Cuba, he invited Smith and Robinson to a meal at the Tivoli Hotel in Panama City. When the two guests arrived, a maître d' informed them that they could enter the dining room but would not be allowed to eat—a Jim Crow practice imported by Americans who built the Panama Canal. Huffily, Jackie replied that he had already eaten. The two men waited in the lobby, passing the time writing postcards, until Rickey appeared and took them to meet in his hotel room.

The exhibition series against the Dodgers, Rickey told the two men, was Robinson's chance to prove once and for all that he belonged in a Brooklyn uniform. He encouraged Jackie to be a "whirling demon" on of-fense. "I want you to hit that ball," Rickey said. "I want you to get on base and run wild. Steal their pants off." Just as important, Robinson needed to show that he could play first base—a position to which he had only just been assigned, to fill the team's weakest infield link, but where by his own admission he felt "terrible."

Over the next week, the Royals played the Dodgers seven times, and Jackie more than rose to Rickey's challenge. He got twenty hits in thirty at bats, stole seven bases, and played error-free defense at first. When he returned to Cuba, the word he had so long awaited finally arrived, via Wendell Smith. Jackie was reading in his Havana hotel room one night when Wendell walked in, beaming. "I just left Mr. Rickey's hotel room," he said. "He told me he's going to put you on the Dodgers on April 10th."

In the March 29 edition of the *Courier*, Smith shared the historic scoop with his readers. "An unimpeachable source revealed to The Pittsburgh Courier this week," he wrote, "that Jackie Robinson . . . will be promoted to the Brooklyn Dodgers on the night of April 10 and will play for the big league club on opening day against the Boston Braves." Jackie's tor-rid showing in Panama had sealed the deal, Wendell reported. But then he added an ominous note: "The only obstacle in his way currently is the possibility of a wholesale rebellion on the part of the present members of the Brooklyn Club."

During his meeting with Smith at the Havana hotel, Rickey had shared worrisome details about an attempted revolt in the Dodger clubhouse. Two players had tried to circulate a petition objecting to signing Robinson, but had backed down after they were called on the carpet. "If you want to play in the majors, don't try to pick the personnel of my ball club," Rickey lectured them. Without citing Rickey as his source, Smith reported on the resistance to Robinson in the *Courier*. He singled out Ed Stanley, a Texan who stood to lose his job at first base, and "Dixie" Walker, the right fielder from Georgia, as the players most opposed to Robinson. He added that second baseman Eddie Stanky "appears to be prejudiced, but will play with him"—an impression Wendell may have formed after watching Stanky hurl a ball into the stands after Robinson embarrassed the Dodger infield with two perfect bunts in Panama.

When it came time for the Dodgers and Royals to break camp, Rickey continued to leave nothing to chance. After playing a final game in Cuba on Easter Sunday, both teams were scheduled to take a boat to Miami, then travel by train through the South so that the Dodgers could play another exhibition in South Carolina. But at the last minute, the Royals management informed Robinson that they were putting him on a plane straight from Miami to New York City. Once in Manhattan, Jackie checked into the McAlpin Hotel on Herald Square and waited for the rest of the Dodgers and Royals to arrive for a final head-to-head preseason game scheduled for the 10th of April, the date that Smith had specified in his story predicting Robinson's promotion.

That morning, a phone call awoke Jackie from a sound sleep. "Good morning, this is Mr. Rickey's secretary," said a woman's voice. "He wants you to get over here right away and sign your contract." Dressing hurriedly, Robinson rushed to Brooklyn to find Rickey and his top lieutenants assembled on the fourth floor of 215 Montague Street. "Jackie, you're a big leaguer now," Rickey declared after he and Robinson signed the documents that made it official. "You're going to play with the Dodgers and we're announcing it to the world today."

Several hours later, Robinson donned his Montreal uniform for the last time. In the sixth inning, the Royals were threatening to tie the 4–2 game when Jackie hit into a double play. As fans in the stands moaned in disappointment, a Rickey aide named Arthur Mann walked into the press area of the bleachers and started handing out copies of a one-page press release. Suddenly dozens of sportswriters raced to find telephones to report the news that Wendell Smith had broken in the *Courier* two weeks earlier. "The Brooklyn Dodgers today purchased the contract of Jackie Roosevelt Robinson from the Montreal Royals," the press release announced. "He will report immediately."

When Robinson arrived at Ebbets Field at noon the following day, a locker still hadn't been assigned to him, but a uniform had, stitched with the number 42. Jackie's teammates greeted him with dutiful nods rather than welcoming handshakes. Quietly, he joined a pregame strategy session. Two days earlier, Commissioner Happy Chandler had abruptly suspended Leo Durocher for accusing Yankees owner Lee McPhail of consorting with gamblers. So it was coach Clyde Sukeforth, substituting as manager, who advised the players on what to expect when they met the Yankees in the first of a three-game exhibition series. In the middle of the chalk talk, Sukeforth turned to his newest rookie. "Robinson, how are you feeling today?" he asked. Fine, Jackie replied. "Okay, then you're playing first today," Sukeforth said matter-of-factly, as Robinson gulped hard.

In Pittsburgh, *Courier* editors pulled out all the stops in covering Robinson's first weekend as a Dodger. The next issue devoted six full pages to stories and photographs of the three games against the Yankees. More than 24,000 spectators showed up for the first game on Friday, followed by 30,000 on Sunday—the largest crowds ever for the annual subway series. Thousands of black fans jammed into the bleachers, cheering Robinson each time he took the field and booing Dixie Walker, the rumored leader of the player revolt. Scores of photographers jostled to take pictures, including one photo that would become an instant classic: of white youngsters from Ocean Parkway who suspended themselves over the dugout to beg for Jackie's autograph.

Robinson managed only two hits in three games and the Yanks took the series 2–1. Still, when the first game was over police had to block the dugout tunnel to keep fans from mobbing him. As Jackie emerged from the dressing room, more screaming fans chased him as he ran to Billy Rowe's Pontiac. In his diary for the *Courier* (ghostwritten as usual by Smith), Robinson thanked his fellow Dodgers for their support, and singled out one in particular for the advice he had given about how to play individual Yankees at first base. "Ed Stanky, a great player, helped me the first day," Jackie reported, making amends for the earlier doubts that Smith raised about Stanky.

In a special Managing Editor's note, Bill Nunn touted the paper's role in the historic breakthrough. "The Pittsburgh Courier, who first mentioned Jackie as a major league prospect and who followed his every move from the moment he first entered the ranks of organized baseball . . . has done its part, thus far," Nunn wrote. But then Nunn pleaded with black fans to do their part. "AND NOW . . . the real challenge faces Negro America," he wrote. "The challenge . . . to leave whiskey bottles at home or on the shelves of the liquor stores . . . to leave out loud talking, obscene language and indecent dress on the outside of the ballpark . . . to learn something about the game [so we] won't humiliate Jackie by our lack of knowledge . . . to stop our booing over some untoward incident which might happen on the ballpark. Remember that Jackie might be 'roughed up' some, because that's the way they play in the majors—for keeps."

Smith had more good news to report the following week after the Dodgers began their regular season at home. In two games against the Boston Braves and two more against the New York Giants, Robinson came alive for six hits in fourteen trips to the plate, including a homer and a double. He performed ably at first base, where he was gradually becoming more comfortable. Heartened by the public response, Branch Rickey joked that Jackie would soon need police protection—from his fans. At the McAlpin

Hotel, more than five hundred letters piled up, from as many white people as black, writing from as far away as the Deep South and the Far West. "Hi, Black Boy!" read one letter from Portland, Oregon. "Glad to read that you have arrived. Had good idea that you had the stuff and would make the grade. You are a credit to your race—the human race, son. Very glad to see you in the big leagues. Good luck. Sincerely, WHITE BOY."

The honeymoon didn't last long, however. After a brief trip to Boston, the Dodgers returned to Brooklyn to face the Philadelphia Phillies. As Robinson made his way to the on-deck circle in the first inning, he heard a chorus of catcalls from the Phillies dugout. "Hey, you black nigger!" one player shouted out. "Why don't you go back where you came from!" another jeered. "Yeah, pretty soon you'll want to eat and sleep with white players!" a third shouted. Robinson was startled at first, having grown used to racist taunts in the South but not expecting them so far north. Next he became enraged, and imagined himself rushing the Phillies dugout to respond with his fists. But then he reminded himself of Rickey's lectures on self-restraint, and instead he proceeded calmly to the plate and answered with his bat, by hitting a single.

The abuse didn't end there. For the rest of the game and the two more that followed, the Phillies baited Robinson with increasingly bigoted slurs: "Hey nigger, why don't you go back to the cotton field where you belong?"; "They're waiting for you in the jungles, black boy!"; "Hey, snowflake, which of those white boys' wives are you dating tonight?!" The insults were so relentless that they infuriated the rest of the Dodgers team as well, and caused Jackie's white teammates to come to his defense and to rally together to sweep the series, 3–0. The cantankerous Stanky was particularly offended. "Listen, you yellow-bellied cowards," he shouted in the Phillies' direction. "Why don't you yell at someone who can answer back?"

In the following days, the *Courier* exposed the source of the attacks. In an interview with the paper's Philadelphia reporter, the Alabama-born Phillies manager, Ben Chapman, bragged that he had encouraged his players to "ride Robinson unmercifully." Chapman said he was only observing the time-honored tradition of hazing rookies. But his boastful admission caught the attention of columnist Walter Winchell, who made them a national story by chastising Chapman and the Phillies in his Sunday radio program. With that, the incident became too big for Happy Chandler to ignore. Chandler phoned Phillies general manager Herb Pennock and informed him that no more insults on the basis of race would be tolerated. The *Courier* hailed Chandler's intervention as "the first time in the history of organized baseball that the commissioner has taken action in matters of a racial nature."

Yet Wendell Smith had a different response to the Phillies' display. Instead of expressing outrage, he encouraged Robinson to use it as a public relations opportunity, to show how philosophical and unperturbed he could appear. In the *Courier*, their "Jackie Robinson Says" diary dismissed the tormentors with a weary shrug and a wry quip. "Some of the Phillies bench jockeys tried to get me upset last week, but it didn't really bother me," the diary read. "The things the Phillies shouted at me from their bench have been shouted at me from other benches and I am not worried about it. . . . In fact, the fellows who are sitting on the bench when I come to bat probably don't have much work to do. If they did, they'd be out there playing, wouldn't they?"

In addition to reassuring black fans, the *Courier* diary offered cover to league officials. As Brooklyn prepared to meet the St. Louis Cardinals on their first long road trip, the *New York Herald Tribune* broke a sensational story: the Cardinals were planning to strike rather than play against Robinson. When the rumor reached Ford Frick, he issued a stern warning to the Cardinals. "The National League will go down the line with Robinson whatever the consequences," he declared. Applauding Frick's hard line, Smith argued that it had been made easier by the earnest image of Robinson that he had helped project in the *Courier*. "By maintaining his composure at all times and acting the part of a gentleman," Wendell wrote, "Robinson has given the offices of baseball plenty of ammunition to use against his would-be oppressors."

When the Dodgers reached St. Louis, there was no strike, but there was more razzing. When Robinson came to the plate for the first time, Joe Garagiola, the Cardinals' portly second-year catcher, yelled out to his teammates in the infield.

"Watch this guy!" Garagiola cried. "He gets all his hits bunting. That's the only way he can get them."

"I can't hit, eh?" Robinson snorted as he dug into the batter's box. "Well, Garagiola, what's your batting average?"

"Oh, about two points below yours," Joe responded, "but if I could run as fast as you, I'd have a real good average."

"No matter how fast you can run, Joe," Jackie shot back, "you couldn't hit as much as you weigh."

Historians would later cite the exchange as one more example of the bigotry Robinson had to endure during his rookie season. Yet Smith dismissed it as a harmless case of joking and "riding," and suggested that Garagiola was trying to rattle Robinson into *not* laying down a bunt.

Writing his weekly column on the train back to New York, Smith chose instead to describe what it was like now for Robinson on the road, where Wendell was his roommate. Far from the run-down buses and dusty roadhouses of the Negro Leagues, they were riding in Pullman cars and being put up at plush hotels such as the Stevens in Chicago and the Schenley in Pittsburgh. Only in St. Louis did they receive word that the Chase Hotel, where the Dodgers were booked, was "not anxious" to put up Robinson. Instead, Jackie and Wendell stayed at the black-run Deluxe Hotel, where the owner provided a suite of rooms and round-the-clock use of his Cadillac. Before the Dodgers left town, the Chase Hotel reversed itself and informed the team that Robinson would be welcome during their next visit, but Smith told *Courier* readers that it was "doubtful" Jackie would accept. He would "return to the Deluxe Hotel and stay with those who befriended him on his first visit there," Wendell reported.

On the next Dodger road trip, Smith and Robinson continued to use their *Courier* columns to show gratitude to welcoming teams and players. Arriving in Pittsburgh, they made a point of praising Hank Greenberg, the former Detroit slugger who had signed with the Pirates after serving a stint in the Army. In the first game of the series, Robinson was beating out a bunt when Greenberg reached for a wild throw from the pitcher and knocked Jackie to the ground. The next time Jackie got on base, Hank asked him if he was all right. Then he shared some wisdom earned as one of the first Jews to become a big league star. "Listen, I know it's plenty tough," Greenberg said, "but you're a good ball player, however, and you'll do all right. Just stay in there and fight back, and always remember to keep your head up." In his diary, Robinson wrote that Greenberg and Frank Gustine, the Pirates third baseman, "made me feel that they were glad to see me in the majors and that I was a real good player."

While in Pittsburgh, Smith was able to sit in the Dodgers dugout and observe the growing solidarity between Robinson and his teammates. Proof came when Pirates pitcher Fritz Ostermueller threw an inside pitch that clipped Jackie's arm and knocked him to the deck. For several minutes he lay on the ground grimacing with pain, and the other Dodgers all rose from the bench to see if he was all right. From the dugout steps, they shouted at Ostermueller and vowed to get even—with Eddie Stanky leading the chorus. "As profane as they were," Smith wrote, "the things the Brooks shouted were simply expressions of their regard for Robinson and they sounded good to anyone who once feared that Jackie couldn't win the support of his teammates." Yet when it came to describing the incident in Robinson's diary, Wendell once again rose above the fray. "Ostermueller is a very good pitcher," Jackie declared in the diary. "I am sure he didn't intend to hit me. It was just one of those things."

His teammates' growing acceptance of Robinson was becoming evident outside the ballpark as well. On the road, the other Dodgers welcomed him into their nonstop games of hearts, rummy, bridge, and pinochle. When the team stopped in Danville, Illinois, to play an exhibition game, Robinson and Smith snuck off to play a round of golf. A foursome including Pee Wee Reese was playing ahead of them, and after four holes they invited Jackie and Wendell to join them.

By the time the Dodgers returned from their second long road trip in late June, Jackie had hit in nine straight games and was leading the

National League in stolen bases, including the first time in the majors that he had stolen home. Although no one expected him to be chosen as starting first baseman in the All-Star Game over Stan Musial or Johnny Mize of the New York Giants, he received a surprising number of votes for a newcomer to the position. Most important, he had helped the Dodgers pull into first place, a position the scrappy "Bums" would cling to for the rest of the season.

Robinson's success had also emboldened Bill Veeck, the innovative young owner of the Cleveland Indians, to bring a second black player up the major leagues: second baseman Larry Doby of the Newark Eagles. As it happened, two Pittsburghers figured in that less remembered milestone as well. Hearing that Veeck was open to the idea of signing a black player, Bill Nunn traveled to Cleveland to lobby for Doby. "Look the kid over real good," he urged. Taking Nunn's advice, Veeck sent his public relations director to contact Doby. The PR man was Louis Jones, Lena Horne's ex-husband, who had moved from Pittsburgh to Cleveland after their divorce and taken the job with the Indians. When he tracked down Doby, Jones made it clear that Veeck was prepared to move fast. "I wouldn't be surprised if you were in Cleveland in three weeks," he said.

By mid-September the Dodgers were on their way to a pennant. They had a six-game lead and only one hurdle left: a three-game series against the second-place Cardinals. In the second inning of the first game, Robinson's nemesis, Joe Garagiola, came to the plate with a man on and hit a ground ball to short. Jackie tagged Joe out, but not before Garagiola's cleats dug into his foot, tearing Jackie's shoe. Garagiola would claim that he was only rushing to avoid a double play, but this time Jackie didn't laugh it off. When he came to the plate the next inning, he started jawing with the catcher. Garagiola leapt up and started shouting in Robinson's face. The umpire had to separate the two men, and Clyde Sukeforth rushed out of the Dodgers dugout to prevent a fight.

The photo of the heated exchange would haunt Garagiola for the rest of his life, well into his career as a popular TV broadcaster. But Smith made no mention of the incident in the *Courier*, preferring not to tarnish the glow around Robinson as he headed toward the World Series. Instead, Wendell dwelled on a happier development that week: *The Sporting News* had named Jackie Robinson "Rookie of the Year."

As the World Series between the Brooklyn Dodgers and the New York Yankees commenced, Smith predicted a contest between grit and brawn, and it turned out to be just that. After falling behind two games to one, the Dodgers tied the series three-all on the improbable heroics of pinch hitters named Cookie Lavagetto and Al Gionfriddo. But in game seven, the Yankees came back to win 5–2, clinching the championship, as Robinson went hitless in four at bats.

Yet even then, Smith chose to accentuate the positive in his report for the *Courier*. Brooklyn would not have even won the pennant had it not been for Jackie Robinson, who ended with a batting average of .297, 29 stolen bases, and only 16 errors, Wendell concluded. And now that Robinson had done Brooklyn and black America proud, he stood to make a well-earned killing. During the off-season, Smith predicted, Jackie would rake in as much as seven times his $5,000 Dodgers salary in appearance fees, endorsements, and exhibition games.

After the 1947 season, Wendell Smith received new opportunities as well. The *Chicago Herald-American* offered him a job as its first black sportswriter, at a salary his bosses in Pittsburgh couldn't match. (Out of loyalty, Smith continued to write his "Sports Beat" column in the *Courier* for several more years.) With the backing of the Hearst empire, Smith was finally admitted into the Baseball Writers Association of America. For the first time, Wendell was able to work in the press boxes of ballparks where he had previously had to sit alone in the bleachers, his typewriter on his lap.

Smith also helped Robinson get a contract to write *My Own Story*, a short autobiography about his life in baseball up to that point. Yet ironically, his collaboration with Jackie and Rachel Robinson on the book would mark the beginning of a chill in their friendship. Jackie came to view the ghostwritten book as too rose-colored, and later hired other collaborators to help him write two edgier memoirs. Meanwhile, as

Robinson's fame continued to grow, Wendell began to chafe at Jackie's prickly complaints about the profession that had helped make his break-through possible.

The rift broke into the open a year and a half later, during spring training for the 1949 season. In an intramural game with a minor league club, Robinson singled off a prospect from rural Wisconsin named Chris Van Cuyk and taunted him from first base, yelling that he would remain "a Class D busher for twenty years." In his next at bat, Van Cuyk retaliated with several brush-back pitches, and Jackie threatened to punch him out if ever did it again. When the incident drew a rare personal rebuke from Commissioner Happy Chandler, Robinson blamed reporters, saying they had blown the story out of proportion.

The excuse infuriated Smith. "This, it seems, is time for some one to remind Robinson that the press has been especially fair to him throughout his career," Wendell wrote indignantly in the *Courier*. "If it had not been for the press, Mr. Robinson would have been just another athlete insofar as the public is concerned. If it had not been for the press, Mr. Robinson would not have been in the majors today. If it had not been for the press—the sympathetic press—Mr. Robinson would have probably still been taking around the country with Negro teams, living under what he called 'intolerable conditions.'. . . Mr. Robinson's memory, it seems, is getting shorter and shorter. That is especially true in the case of the many newspapermen who have befriended him during his career."

Over the next two decades in Chicago—with the *Herald-American* and later the *Sun-Times*, and as a popular radio and TV broadcaster—Smith never stopped crusading. As more black players entered the major leagues, he wrote a series on the persistence of segregation in Florida training camps that shamed clubs into granting equal treatment to their black players. Along with other black sportswriters, he demanded recognition for Negro League players in baseball's Hall of Fame. When that time came, Wendell was named to the panel that chose the first players to be recognized at Cooperstown: Satchel Paige and Josh Gibson, the Crawfords and Grays stars whom he had covered in his first years in Pittsburgh.

Even when Smith fell gravely ill with pancreatic cancer in his late fifties, he devoted one of his last columns to insisting that it was high past time for a black manager in the major leagues.

Four months after Smith wrote that column, Jackie Robinson threw out the first pitch at the 1972 World Series. Called on to address the sold out crowd and a nationwide TV audience, Robinson echoed his old friend's last appeal. "I won't be satisfied until I look over at the coaches box at third base and see a black manager there," Jackie declared.

Nine days later, on October 25, 1972, Robinson suffered a fatal heart attack at his home in Connecticut. From his sickbed, Smith wrote a remembrance for the *Sun-Times* that was reprinted in the *Courier*. While other obituaries conjured up the image of Robinson that Smith had worked so hard to cultivate—of a quiet, dignified pioneer—Wendell celebrated the Jackie he had come to know, one filled with "black aggressiveness" and fearlessness in the face of controversy. "He never backed down from a fight and never quit agitating for equality," Smith wrote. "He demanded respect, too. Those who tangled with him always admitted afterward that he was a man's man, a person who would not compromise his convictions."

When Smith himself died of cancer a month later, he was remembered quite differently: as a quiet advocate whose geniality stood in sharp contrast to the militant vogue of the day. "We are in a period when some blacks seem to feel that the race is being betrayed when a brother wears a smile," columnist Louis Martin wrote in the *Courier*. "Wendell was a natural born smiler, if there ever was one. The menacing frown is the popular mien for many blacks now who seem so anxious to tell all whites how much they hold them in contempt. Wendell knew that whites, like blacks, come in all shapes, sizes and characters. . . . His freedom from malice and prejudice made him doubly-strong in the struggle he led to abolish the racial barriers in the world of sports. Earnest, honest and selfless, Wendell developed the kind of personality that was hard for any man to hate. Yet no angry civil rights leader nor fiery freedom fighter ever did more to open the doors of opportunity to black youth."

It was a fitting tribute to Wendell Smith's gentle spirit and lasting influence, but also a telling commentary on how much twenty-five years of struggle had changed black America—including black Pittsburgh—between the hopeful autumn of Jackie Robinson's rookie season and the bitter fall of Richard Nixon's landslide reelection.

Evelyn Cunningham (*center*), gossip columnist "Toki" Schalk (*far left*), and some of the other women who by the late 1940s were playing an increasingly prominent role at the *Courier*.

9

THE WOMEN OF "UP SOUTH"

EDNA CHAPPELL HAD GROWN tired of covering teas, weddings, and debutante parties. Ever since joining the *Courier* as Julia Bumry Jones's secretary, she had given her all to the Women's Activities pages. When Jones suffered a stroke, she had gone to Julia's home with a typewriter every week to help the boss dictate her "Talk O' Town" pieces from her bed. After Jones passed away, Chappell edited the section while a stylish woman from Boston named Toki Schalk took over the gossip column and gave it a new name, "Toki Types." But now a war was on, and Edna had had her fill.

This wasn't the kind of journalism Chappell had dreamed of as a girl, when her father, an itinerant AME preacher, told her about Ida B. Wells and her anti-lynching crusades. It wasn't what she imagined when she first read Carter Woodson's "The Negro in Our History" after the family moved to West Virginia, or when she watched her older sister take over the small local paper in Uniontown, a onetime stop on the Underground Railroad sixty miles south of Pittsburgh. It wasn't the reason that after graduating from high school, Edna had skipped college and moved to California, to work for one of her heroines, Almena Lomax, the founder of the *Los Angeles Tribune*, and to meet another, Charlotta Bass, the pioneering publisher of the *California Eagle*.

So Chappell took matters into her own hands. She had expressed her frustration to Wendell Smith, who was filling in as city editor during the war years, and he had offered to give her work. One day, in a foul mood over having to cover yet another wedding party, Edna gathered up her typewriter and pens and notepad and carried them to the large round table at the other end of the newsroom.

Bill Nunn charged out of his office and confronted her. "What are you doing?" the managing editor asked.

"I'm moving my things over to the city desk," Chappell said, tears streaming down the dark cheeks behind her thick glasses. "I'm not going to work over here anymore. I'm sick of it."

"Who said you could move?" Nunn demanded.

"Well, Wendell said I could work for him, so I'm moving," Edna replied.

Nunn took Chappell into his office and "read me the riot act," she recalled. She couldn't simply appoint herself to a new job, he scolded. But after several minutes, his wide jaw spread into a broad smile. "Anyone with that kind of goddamn nerve will make a good reporter," Nunn chuckled. "Go on over there and work."

The guys on the city desk didn't make life easy for Edna. They nicknamed her "Chappie" and "Scoop," mocking the fact that she had yet to break a big story. Knowing that she was squeamish about dead bodies, they took her to identify murder victims at the morgue. They played practical jokes on her, such as sending her to buy a "left-handed wrench" for the press room. But Chappell took it all in stride, and eventually she earned their respect. "I did everything the same way the fellas did," she recalled.

Like all the reporters and editors at the *Courier*, Chappell took great pride in her part in the Double V Campaign. She covered Double V parties and beauty contests for the Women's pages and later helped the reporters on the city desk keep track of war bond pledges. But once the victory abroad was won, it became clear to everyone at the newspaper, and to its hundreds of thousands of readers across the country, that the second victory they had dreamed of, over racial injustice at home, was as distant as ever.

During the war, the number of lynchings in the South had dwindled to as few as one or two a year. Now lynchings were on the rise again, up to six in 1946. In Washington, D.C., Jim Crow practices remained so prevalent that a *Courier* campaign to expose them stretched out for a year. By the time the Washington crusade ended in 1947, the paper was able to take credit for only a few token changes: the National Theatre had started to admit Negroes for the first time, and P.L. Prattis had been credentialed as the first black journalist to be admitted to the Senate and House press galleries.

Closer to home, the *Courier* set out to document the persistence of Jim Crow practices in western Pennsylvania, where a state law banning any form of public discrimination had been on the books since the 1930s. Calling Chappell into his office, Prattis gave her the lead assignment. He wanted her to visit restaurants across Allegheny County and report on how she was treated. Prattis told Edna to present herself respectfully and dress as she always did at work—in conservative long wool dresses and skirts and her bookish horn-rimmed glasses.

Even after living in the region for most of her life, Chappell was shaken by what she found. When she ordered a cup of coffee at one restaurant, the waitress simply pretended not to have any. "Why, we don't serve coffee," the woman lied. When Edna pointed to the listing for coffee on the menu, the waitress snapped again: "We don't have coffee!" In Clairton, a steel town down the Monongahela River, the message was even more blunt. "If you lived around here, you would know better than to come in here because we don't serve Negroes," the owner informed her. Every day for several weeks, Chappell returned home with similar stories. She typed up her notes, and then found herself breaking down in exhaustion and rage. "I was just so hurt I would cry myself to sleep," she recalled.

It was no wonder that the latest wave of black migrants had a new

name for Pittsburgh: "Up South." Some twenty thousand more would arrive in the two decades after the war, bringing the city's black population
to just over 100,000 for the first time. But when they stepped off the train
at Union Station or drove through the tunnel approaches on the Pennsylvania Turnpike, they no longer felt the sense of freedom and promise that
Robert L. Vann and previous generations of migrants had experienced.
Instead, they found conditions that didn't seem that different from what
they were used to in the South. The only homes they could hope to buy
were ones listed as "Colored" in the city newspapers. Many ended up
living in Pittsburgh's new federal housing projects, which were rapidly
turning into black ghettos as white residents fled. Swimming pools and
other public facilities banned Negroes or limited them to restricted areas
and hours. The two biggest department stores downtown, Kaufmann's
and Gimbels, wouldn't let black customers use their dressing rooms. Nor
would they hire Negroes who answered their "Help Wanted" notices—
until a two-year picketing campaign brought national press attention and
forced the stores to change those policies.

In 1943, black Pittsburgh had welcomed the opening of a local office of
the Fair Employment Practices Committee—the job fairness agency that
FDR created in a deal to stave off A. Philip Randolph's planned March
on Washington. The FEPC had helped win blacks new opportunities in
the city's steel and other manufacturing plants, and to secure previously
off-limits jobs such as driving trolley cars. But once the war was over, Congress cut off funding for the FEPC and the Pittsburgh office closed down.
Left behind were documents showing that 50 percent of all Allegheny
County businesses still refused to hire blacks. Negroes who had found
work in the war factories fell victim to the "last hired, first fired" syn-
drome, as plants cut back and unions invoked seniority to protect white
members. Homer S. Brown, a Pittsburgh judge who had been elected to
the Pennsylvania legislature, introduced a bill to create a state version of
the FEPC, but it would take him almost ten years to get it passed.

For P.L. Prattis and the other *Courier* editors who had worked so hard
advocating on behalf of Negro soldiers, it was particularly distressing to

witness the struggles of black servicemen returning from World War II. Two weeks after the Japanese surrender, the *Pittsburgh Post-Gazette* was already heralding the new world of opportunities for returning white vets. "Fraternity Pins Replace Medals: GI Joe Going Back to College," proclaimed a feature story on the hundreds of veterans who were enrolling at the University of Pittsburgh, Carnegie Tech, and Duquesne University under the year-old GI Bill of Rights. The paper gushed about how much more mature the vets seemed compared with the average "Joe College," with his "casual slouch, the sloppy socks, the carelessly knotted ties." The vets dressed sharply, stood erect, and were never late to class. "They're all business, these boys we're getting in here from the army," marveled a Pitt staff member. "Some of them even forget themselves enough to salute."

For poor whites from immigrant backgrounds, a service record could serve as the ticket to a new life. Joseph L. Murphy was an Irish kid from Avalon, a small town upriver from Pittsburgh. Murphy had dropped out of high school and worked as a stock clerk before enrolling in the Civilian Conservation Corps. When America entered the war, he was assigned to the Sixth Armored Division, where he was promoted to lieutenant. Upon returning to Pittsburgh, he walked into a veterans center and took an aptitude test that got him into a "retail merchandising" course at Pitt alongside college grads studying for business degrees. Married with a two-year-old son, Murphy had his sights set on becoming a store executive. "I may find myself in pretty fast company," he told the *Post-Gazette*, "but I'll take a chance because if I can make good this course will give me a five-year jump on anyone just starting in at retail merchandising."

When white vets like Murphy needed money, it was there for them. On Grant Street, in the heart of downtown, nine of the city's largest banks opened the Pittsburgh Clearing House Association, to help cut through red tape involved in applying for the new government-subsidized loans and mortgages. "Under the GI Bill of Rights," the *Post-Gazette* explained to its readers, "a veteran may borrow to buy or build a new home or repair one he already owns; buy a farm or equip one; buy a business or start one."

Around Pittsburgh and across America, those loans would transform the social landscape. Veterans would use them to learn new skills and launch new careers, to buy new homes in the suburbs, and to open and invest in new businesses that fueled an economic boom that lasted for the next quarter century, the longest in U.S. history.

For black veterans, however, it was a different story. In the last year of the war, a War Department survey found that of the Negro soldiers still in the field, more than thirty thousand had plans to return to full-time study. Some 200,000 more hoped to go to school part-time. But when they returned home, they encountered hurdles in every corner of the country and at every tier of education. Many black GIs from the South had been illiterate or semiliterate when they enlisted, but had acquired valuable reading and math skills in the service and now wanted to finish high school. Yet Jim Crow restrictions on the number of black students who could study within a given geographical area—called "pupil stations"—meant that thousands had to wait years for a classroom spot, or never got one at all. (As the deadline for applying for GI Bill educational benefits neared in the early 1950s, the *Courier* estimated that more than 300,000 eligible black vets in seventeen Southern states would lose those opportunities due to "limited Jim Crow facilities.")

In the North, better-educated blacks encountered a more genteel form of Jim Crow. Most of the five thousand Negroes who served as officers in World War II hailed from the North, and many came home with visions of completing college or pursuing graduate or professional degrees. But many of the schools to which they aspired continued to place unspoken limits on the number of nonwhite Christian students they admitted, to their student bodies as a whole or to specific departments, programs, and internships. In 1947, almost two years after the war had ended, a study funded by the Jewish War Veterans and the American Jewish Congress found that quotas for blacks, Jews, Catholics, and "persons of Italian descent" remained rampant. Outraged by the findings, Arthur Klein, a Democratic congressman from New York, introduced an amendment to the GI Bill that would have compelled the Veterans Administration to hold hearings on any school charged with discrimination. It would also have empowered the VA to "stop all further payment" of government subsidies "if the school refuses to end the practice."

The Klein bill went nowhere, which came as little surprise to the *Courier* reporter who covered the world of black World War II veterans. John H. Young III was the son of a well-to-do black family from Pine Bluff, Arkansas. He had graduated from Morehouse College and played semi-pro football before spending the war as a flight instructor at the Tuskegee Institute. When he left the Army, Young contacted the *Courier* and persuaded the editors to let him travel across the South and assess the mood and postwar prospects for blacks in different states. The resulting series, which appeared every week for several months in early 1945, grew increasingly pessimistic as Young traveled from South Carolina and Tennessee into the Deep Southern states of Mississippi, Alabama, and Louisiana, where he found "the spirit of the Negroes at its lowest ebb."

Moving to the *Courier*'s Washington bureau, Young took over the veterans beat. When he visited the Veterans Administration for the first time, he was alarmed to discover that its long-serving head, Frank T. Hines, did not have a single Negro on his staff. Soon afterward, President Harry Truman replaced Hines with General Omar Bradley, and Young held out hope that the hero of the Normandy invasion might rectify the situation. But when Young interviewed the general and pressed on the issue, Bradley grew defensive. He argued that to appoint a black adviser would look like an admission of discrimination, and that to hire a Negro as his administrative assistant would mean passing over more experienced white employees. Did that mean that Bradley had no plans to hire someone who could advise him on the concerns of black vets? Young asked. "Yes, I am not considering any such appointment," Bradley replied curtly.

Charting the legislative path of the GI Bill on Capitol Hill, Young identified all the ways in which its original 1944 version penalized Negro veterans. To be eligible for educational benefits, returning soldiers had to be twenty-five or younger—a provision that shut out older black enlistees. The bill only covered courses of study that lasted at least thirty-five weeks, excluding the part-time and shorter trade school training sought by blacks with limited time and money. Housing loans were available only for properties priced at "reasonable normal value"—a tough standard to meet in Northern urban neighborhoods where the price of real estate had skyrocketed since the beginning of the war. By the end of 1945, Young was able to report that amendments to the bill had eased some of the most punitive conditions, but not enough to eliminate numerous disadvantages for Negro vets.

In the most racially insidious feature of the GI Bill, administration of its benefits was left to individual states. In the South, especially, that allowed for a proliferation of petty obstacles designed to frustrate and disqualify Negro applicants. To investigate, Young traveled across Mississippi, Louisiana, and Texas, identifying himself as a veteran Army pilot seeking a GI Bill business loan. At every turn, he encountered a maze of maddening conditions: Loans were available only for property and equipment, not for merchandise needed to stock shelves. Applicants were required to provide an existing business address, and to have lined up a security guarantee *before* the local VA office approved the loan. Most discouraging, applicants had to show evidence of previous experience in their proposed line of work, making it impossible for them to pursue a new profession or to branch out beyond the world of black businesses serving black customers. When Young told one banker that he hoped to open a furniture store, the man scoffed. "I can't imagine a Negro wanting to go into the furniture business," he said.

In another monthslong *Courier* crusade, Young highlighted the plight of Negro soldiers who had received so-called blue discharges. By the end of the war, as many as 200,000 veterans—a disproportionate number of them black—had been sent home early with blue-tinted certificates indicating no specific misconduct but flagging "habits or traits of character which served to render retention in the service undesirable." The early discharges became notorious as a means of casting out bed wetters, klutzes, and suspected homosexuals; but they also gave white officers a way to get rid of blacks who offended them for any reason. Many Negro servicemen returned with stories of being deliberately enticed or harassed to take the releases, without knowing what they were signing. (Underscoring how widely misused the blue discharges were, 30 percent of recipients who protested the status to a War Department review board won those appeals and were instead issued the white or beige certificates denoting honorable service.)

For most vets with blue discharges, the consequences only became apparent once they got home. The original language of the GI Bill stated: "a discharge or release from active service under conditions other than dishonorable shall be a prerequisite to entitlement to veterans benefits." That did not appear to exclude blue discharges, which technically were not dishonorable. But in a series of exposés, Young documented how the Veterans Administration gave its local and regional officers free rein to deny benefits to the blue certificate holders. When challenged, VA officials fell back on semantics, arguing that the mere reception of a blue discharge amounted to a "dishonorable condition." The stories raised enough disturbing questions that a sympathetic member of the Senate Veterans Committee had them read into the Congressional Record—but ultimately, Young's crusade had little impact in altering the fate of the blue dischargees.

While Young campaigned on behalf of black vets, his bosses in Pittsburgh and their colleagues in the Negro press tried to pin down the new president on his civil rights agenda. After more than a decade of watching FDR kowtow to Southern Democrats, the black editors hoped for better from Harry Truman. In late May 1945, less than two months after Roosevelt's death, Truman did something his predecessor never had: he received a delegation from the National Negro Press Association. Robert L. Vann's widow, Jesse, and *Courier* president Ira Lewis were among fifteen black publishers and editors who met with Truman and presented him with a list of demands. Although Truman did no more than "listen with interest and cordiality," as the *Courier* described it, the group left encouraged. When Truman met with the group a second time in March 1946, Jesse Vann read him a statement "on behalf of 15,000,000 colored Americans" commending him for the handful of blacks he had named to his administration.

The publishers were even more encouraged a year later when Truman appointed a Commission on Civil Rights. Southern Democrats immediately threatened to block any of its recommendations, but Truman talked tough about persisting with the commission as he prepared to run for election in 1948. Once the race was under way, he further endeared himself to the Pittsburgh editors by praising a *Courier* story that blasted Republican foot-dragging on a housing bill. During a campaign stop in Los Angeles, an aide brought a copy of the *Courier* aboard the President's train. Later, the aide told a *Courier* reporter how happy Truman was to see the paper echo the "Do Nothing Congress" attacks he was making on the stump. "The boss got a kick out of the Courier telling off Congress on the Housing bill stall," the aide said.

As the race entered the home stretch in the fall of 1948, however, Truman turned evasive on the subject of civil rights. Southern Democrats had stormed out of the Democratic convention in Philadelphia after the adoption of a civil rights plank pushed by Hubert Humphrey and other Northern liberals. Forming the Dixiecrat Party, they had nominated South Carolina senator Strom Thurmond for president, a challenge that threatened to cost Truman crucial states in the Electoral College. In the meantime, the Republican nominee, Thomas Dewey, gave a series of forceful speeches denouncing bigotry and calling for a strong "legislative approach" to uprooting racial inequality. Impressed by the Republican candidate's rhetoric and frustrated by what it saw as continued "Southern control" over the Democrat Party, the *Courier* endorsed Dewey and joined every other newspaper and polling organization in America in predicting that he would defeat Truman handily.

Yet as Truman biographer David McCullough would note, one reporter remained conspicuously bullish on his prospects: John L. Clark of the *Courier*. Clark, the former "Wylie Avenue" columnist and publicist for Gus Greenlee's Pittsburgh Crawfords, had spent months aboard "the Truman special" as the train crossed the country and "had taken seriously the size of the crowds," as McCullough put it. In Clark's last dispatch before the election, he predicted that Truman would win Texas, Oklahoma, and Arkansas, despite Strom Thurmond's candidacy, as well as Ohio, for all of the power of Senator Robert Taft's Republican machine. In all, Clark put twenty-three states with a total of 252 electoral votes in Truman's column. While predicting a narrow Republican victory, Clark speculated that an upset in "one of the big states now conceded to Dewey" would be enough to put Truman over the top.

When Truman shocked the nation and won, Clark chalked it up to the black vote. In the end, Truman carried five more states than Clark predicted for a total of 303 Electoral College votes. In the largest of those, California, his edge among black voters was more than double his margin of victory. Truman's advantage among blacks also exceeded his overall victory margin in the pivotal Midwest states of Ohio and Illinois. The *Courier* gave Negro voters additional credit for Truman's wins in Virginia, Tennessee, Georgia, and Arkansas, which limited Strom Thurmond's inroads to four states. It was a convincing enough victory, the paper argued hopefully, to provide Truman "a mandate, the meaning of which cannot be forgotten" to make good on "his progressive position on civil rights for minorities."

Once the election was over, Truman finally did begin to make good on some of his grand promises on civil rights. Two weeks after the election, he put out word that there would be no racial segregation at his Inaugural Balls. In his next State of the Union Address, he laid out a plan for what would be one of his most heralded achievements: the official end to segregation in the U.S. armed forces.

In Pittsburgh, the *Courier's* editors took satisfaction in their role in bringing about that long overdue milestone, but it was tempered by sadness that two men hadn't lived to witness it. One was Robert L. Vann, who had led the fight on behalf of black serviceman for so long. The other was Ira Lewis, the loyal deputy who took up the cause after Vann's death. In the summer of 1948, Lewis had been named to a committee of sixteen Negro leaders appointed to advise the Truman administration on how military desegregation should be implemented. But just two months before the election, on a trip to New York, Lewis suffered a fatal stroke. In a sign of the esteem in which both he and the *Courier* were held, Truman wired his "heartfelt sympathy" to Pittsburgh. Thomas Dewey hailed Lewis as "a fine American . . . and an influential leader."

But now the Little Chief was gone, too, only eight years after the Big Chief. It would be left to Jesse Vann, Robert L. Vann's quiet, self-effacing widow, to try to preserve their legacy, less than a decade into her apprenticeship as the paper's treasurer and at a time when the *Courier*'s old rival, *The Chicago Defender*, was on the rise again.

At four o'clock on a Wednesday afternoon in March 1949, Jesse Vann was in her office at the *Courier* when she received a visit from a pressman named Felix Robinson. Could she come to the newsroom? Robinson asked. As soon as her tiny, gray-haired figure appeared in the doorway, a cry of "Surprise!" rang out. The paper's entire staff had assembled to wish their new publisher a happy sixty-fourth birthday. There were members of the old male guard that had built the paper with her husband: Bill Nunn; P.L. Prattis; Frank Bolden, now city editor; and Chester Washington, the sportswriter turned business manager who was about to depart for Los Angeles, to oversee the *Courier* operation there and later to run his own newspapers. There was Daisy Lampkin, the society matron and NAACP leader who was now the vice president of the *Courier* and the paper's largest shareholder after Mrs. Vann.

There was also a group of younger female reporters who would prosper under Jesse Vann's wing. They included Edna Chappell and Hazel Garland, a onetime maid who had joined the women's section staff and would one day rise to editor-in-chief. Of them all, the most striking was a statuesque redhead—nearly six feet tall in heels, sporting a pearl necklace and dressed in the latest New York fashion—who presented Mrs. Vann with her gift: a gold charm bracelet engraved with the name of every *Courier* department. They called Evelyn Cunningham "Big East," and she had just returned to Pittsburgh after reporting the first big story in the next front of the civil rights struggle, Down South.

ON A WARM GEORGIA evening in September 1948, six-year-old Dorothy Yvonne Nixon was gathering vegetables for dinner in the backyard of her family's farm when she heard the sound of a car pulling up out front. Her father, Isaiah, was inside, resting after a long day of picking tobacco and cotton and tending to livestock on his hardscrabble, sixty-eight-acre property in the town of Alston, some 180 miles south of Atlanta. Her mother, Sallie, was in bed, recuperating from giving birth a week earlier to the latest of the couple's six children, little Isaiah Jr. Her grandmother Daisy was sitting on the back porch, watching the sun go down, and together she and Yvonne, as she was known within the family, went to investigate the loud voices calling for Isaiah Sr. to come out of the house.

Two white men stood in the front yard, carrying guns. Yvonne recognized them as brothers who lived down the road: Johnnie and Jim A. Johnson. As she quietly curled up next to one of her sisters on the front steps, her father emerged in the doorway.

"Who did you vote for today?" Jim A. demanded to know.

"I guess I voted for Mr. Thompson," Isaiah replied.

"Mr. Thompson" was Melvin Thompson, the state's interim governor. Two years earlier, he had taken the place of Eugene Talmadge, the segregationist who had been reelected governor for the fourth time only to pass away shortly afterward. Now Thompson was running for a new term, but he faced opposition from Talmadge's son, Herman, who had the strong backing of the Ku Klux Klan. For only the second time since Reconstruction, Southern Democrats also faced a new reality: the Supreme Court had ruled that they could no longer exclude blacks from voting in their primaries. Since then, another Negro farmer named Dover Carter had been bravely defying the Klan and registering blacks in Georgia's Montgomery County to vote. Two of his newest recruits were Isaiah and Sallie Nixon, and that morning they had gone into Alston to cast their first primary ballots.

As Yvonne looked on, the brothers demanded that her father get into their car. When he didn't budge, Johnnie Johnson pointed his shotgun at the house. Then Jim A. lifted his pistol and fired at Isaiah, striking him three times. Behind her, Yvonne heard her mother's voice. "Fall, Isaiah, fall!" Sallie Nixon shouted as she ran out of the house.

It was a blur after that. The men got in their car and drove away.

Yvonne's mother dragged her bloodied husband into the house and called for a gypsy cab to take him to the hospital. Then there was a long two-day wait before her mother told Yvonne and her siblings the terrible news: Daddy was dead. The certificate listed the cause as a gunshot wound that had entered Isaiah Nixon's abdomen and destroyed parts of his stomach, liver, kidneys, and small intestine. But Grandmother Daisy told Yvonne that the real cause was that her father had dared to "step over the line" and exercise his right to vote—and that there was no way that in Georgia two white men would ever be convicted of the murder.

The ensuing days and weeks proved Daisy right. Announcing Nixon's death, the Montgomery County sheriff said that he had been killed for insisting on voting even after town folk had advised him not to do so. When the Johnson brothers were detained, they told a different story: that they had gone to the Nixon farm to offer Isaiah work and had shot him in self-defense after an argument broke out. The case was sped to trial by early November, and an all-white jury took less than three hours to find Jim A. Johnson not guilty. The judge also ruled that "there was no need to present a case against Johnnie Johnson" as an accessory. In the white press, coverage of the trial consisted of three perfunctory wire service reports that were picked up by a handful of newspapers around the country and ended as soon as the Johnsons were acquitted.

For the *Courier*, however, the rushed verdict was only the beginning of the story. The editors in Pittsburgh became fixated on another angle: what had become of the young wife and small children who had watched Isaiah Nixon shot dead before their eyes? To find out, they dispatched a stringer based in North Carolina, A. M. Rivera Jr., to Georgia. When Rivera got to Alston, friends of Sallie Nixon told him that she had fled, in fear of another visit from the Johnsons or the Klan once the brothers were free. Quietly, she had buried her husband's body in a faraway corner of a local cemetery, under a tiny gravestone marked "Father." Then she had left town with her six children and mother-in-law, bringing only as many belongings as they could carry.

Eventually Rivera received a tip that Sallie Nixon was in Florida, staying with an uncle in Jacksonville. He wrote a letter to her address, and in early December he received an answer. Sallie reported that her children and mother-in-law were alive and safe, but that their circumstances were precarious. All eight were sleeping in one room of her uncle's house, and the young ones had all come down with colds due to the change in climate. They were struggling with the adjustment to new schools and a town where they knew no one. Yet they were all terrified to return to Georgia. "Mama, I don't want to go back because them people killed daddy and we don't have anybody to stay with us," four-year-old Margaret had told her mother. "I am afraid to go back up there."

Like Edna Chappell before her, Evelyn Cunningham was working for the Women's Activities department at the *Courier* at the time of Isaiah Nixon's murder and trial. She had come to Pittsburgh from the Harlem office, where she had been hired on the recommendation of an aunt who was dating Edgar Rouzeau, the dashing bureau chief turned war correspondent. Evelyn's first job was to read through *The New York Times* every morning to identify stories of interest to black readers, then to rewrite them with a *Courier* spin. Her sharp eye and deft writing touch impressed the editors in Pittsburgh, who offered her a raise to work at headquarters. At first she hated it, finding Smoketown as sleepy as it was smelly and dark. But with her elegant looks and gift for gab, Evelyn quickly turned heads and made friends. Before long she was organizing office parties and playing in the weekly office poker game, the only woman invited to the table.

Pittsburgh wasn't so bad, Evelyn decided, but she, too, yearned to do more than cover weddings and teas. At thirty-one, she couldn't remember a time when the news of the day hadn't been part of her life. Born Evelyn Long in the small town of Elizabeth City, North Carolina, she would leaf through the local paper as a toddler to find the name of her Grandmother Ellen, who wrote for the paper's "colored section." When she was five, the Long family moved to Harlem, where her father, Clyde, drove a cab and her mother, Mary, sewed dresses. At the dinner table, they discussed the headlines in *The Pittsburgh Courier* and the *Amsterdam News* and encouraged Evelyn and her brother Clyde Jr. to ask questions. Evelyn's interest in writing blossomed as she attended two of the best public schools available to colored students in New York City: Hunter High School for Girls in Manhattan, and Long Island University in Brooklyn. When she landed a part-time job with the *Courier* while still a student at LIU, her father was so proud that he bought her a secondhand typewriter and taught her how to use it.

By 1948, Evelyn Long had been married and divorced once and had just wed her second husband, a man named Gerald Cunningham. But she had no interest in having children, or in settling down to the life of a housewife. Instead, she began to pester Bill Nunn for more challenging reporting assignments.

"Do I have to cover these card parties for the rest of my life?" Cunningham nagged. "I want to do more serious stories."

"Like what?" Nunn asked.

To test him, she cited the most horrific story in the paper at the time, the postwar spike in mob killings of Negroes. "Like the lynchings down south," she said.

When Nunn nodded "Okay" and said that he would keep her in mind, Cunningham suspected he might simply be humoring her. Perhaps he thought that once she had time to mull it over, she would decide that she was happy to stay in Pittsburgh and cover fashion shows. So when she read Sallie Nixon's letter, she had a bold idea. She went to Nunn and proposed that the *Courier* start a fund to aid the Nixons, and that Evelyn herself go south to meet the widow and dramatize her plight for the paper.

The week of Christmas 1948, *Courier* readers picked up the latest edition to find a picture of Evelyn Cunningham on the front page, handing Sallie Nixon a check for $117.48 to help her family celebrate the holiday. Dressed in a tailored short-sleeve dress, her hair professionally straightened and curled, Cunningham towered over the petite widow, who wore a plain white blouse and no makeup. Behind them stood a tiny tree that the children had decorated, and a picture of Sallie's late husband on the wall, his baby face framed by a farmer's fedora. "Christmas for the Nixons Will

Be Real," promised the headline on Cunningham's story, which conjured up the cramped two-room house in which the family was living. In one room, Sallie, her mother-in-law, and five children slept on two beds that had been pushed together, with baby Isaiah in a crib on the floor. In the other room were her unemployed uncle and his wife and child.

The next edition, published on New Year's Day, announced: "The Courier's Resolution for '49: A NEW HOME FOR THE NIXONS!" The paper reported that it had already collected $1,275 and called upon "clubs, churches, civil and social organizations, individuals and groups of all kind" to contribute. In a poignant profile, Cunningham described the state of mind of the five-foot-tall Georgia farm girl who found herself a widowed mother of six at the age of twenty-five. "Sallie Nixon isn't bitter about the death of her husband," Evelyn wrote. "The kind of sorrow she bears is in some sense worse than bitterness. She has a pitiful fear of white people, and way deep down I believe she feels that the brutal killing of her husband, at the hands of two white men, was inevitable . . . one of those things that happens to a colored man in the South." Yet Sallie carried on for the sake of her children. She was still able to marvel at seeing ocean water for the first time, and to laugh when told about the marriage proposals that had come into the *Courier* since it began printing her picture. "I wouldn't wish these children on any man," Sallie said.

The following week, Cunningham profiled the Nixon children, in a story accompanied by adorable photographs of the six in their finest hand-me-downs. She described ten-year-old Mary Ann as a shy but protective eldest child. When Evelyn took her and two-year-old Connie Louise into town and offered to buy them popsicles, Mary Ann told her that she and her sister would share. Seven-year-old Hubert was a budding "lady killer" with his father's good looks, a natural ease with hugging and kissing but also a habit of picking on his three younger sisters. Six-year-old Yvonne was quiet and kept to herself. Of them all, the most shaken by their father's death was Margaret, the pig-tailed four-year-old who "clung to her mother like a shawl." Meanwhile, the youngest, Isaiah Jr., had just turned four months old and would grow up with no memories of his father or of the brutal way in which he died. "He'll never remember any of it," Cunningham wrote.

Moved by the family's plight and Cunningham's touching stories, hundreds of *Courier* readers sent donations to the "Nixon Fund." Wendell Smith led the collection drive in the world of sports, eliciting contributions from several Negro League baseball teams and a $50 check from Abe Saperstein, the owner of the Harlem Globetrotters. Billy Rowe worked his entertainment contacts in New York City. But most of the money came from ordinary citizens and community groups, often in amounts of as little as a dollar or two. With Cunningham acting as chaperone, Sallie Nixon traveled north, appearing in black churches in Detroit and Pittsburgh and receiving a welcome from Pittsburgh mayor David Lawrence. By the time the trip was over, the fund had swelled to $3,336.76—enough to purchase a modest 55-by-25-foot lot in the black neighborhood of Jacksonville, within walking distance of a school.

From California, the most famous black architect in America extended his help. Paul Williams was a Los Angeles–born orphan who had grown up to become the first Negro west of the Mississippi River to earn an architect's license. By the late 1940s, he had developed a reputation as "Hollywood's architect" after designing the homes of numerous movie stars and marquee properties such as the MCA Building and the Palm Beach Tennis Club. Williams offered to design a home for the Nixons as his contribution to the fund, and within weeks the *Courier* published his drawing of a modest, five-room bungalow framed by palm trees and a picket fence.

The week before Christmas of 1949, a year after Evelyn Cunningham had proposed the crusade, Jesse Vann traveled to Jacksonville to present Sallie Nixon with the keys and deed to her new home. In the end, it had cost $7,300 to build, under the watchful eye of a Florida contractor named Leroy Argrett who also charged no fee or markups on materials. More than seven hundred individuals, churches, and other organizations had contributed just over $5,000 to the Nixon Fund. Mrs. Vann herself had made up the difference: $2,290.00. A separate fund announced by Cunningham raised several hundred dollars for furnishings, and half a dozen stores in Pittsburgh and Jacksonville donated appliances, tables, chairs, and bunk beds. "I'm too happy to say a word," Sallie sobbed as she entered the house, before composing herself to thank Mrs. Vann and assembling her children for a picture under a Christmas tree that had been purchased and surrounded with presents by Paul Williams's wife, Della.

Calling the Nixon Fund "one of the noblest campaigns in its history," the *Courier* reminded readers of its larger purpose. "It not only was the matter of Mrs. Nixon's family needing a home," the paper declared. "It was a direct slap in the face of those who sought to undermine democracy by denying a citizen the constitutional right to vote."

With time, Evelyn Cunningham's crusade on behalf of Isaiah Nixon's widow and children would be largely forgotten in the annals of the civil rights struggle. But it foreshadowed strategies and tactics to come: the broadening of the movement to the cause of voting rights; and the search for sympathetic, press-friendly victims who could inspire blacks and stir the conscience of whites. For Evelyn Cunningham, it was also the beginning of a new life on the road, one that would make her one of the first journalists, black or white, to arrive at the next great battlegrounds of the movement and to introduce the country to two of its towering figures.

OVER THE NEXT DECADE, Evelyn Cunningham would become the only civil rights reporter in America who dispensed romantic advice in her spare time. Capitalizing on her star power after the Nixon Fund campaign, Cunningham persuaded her editors in Pittsburgh to let her move back to the Harlem bureau and to give her a weekly column. She called it "The Women," and addressed it to a new generation of female readers. Instead of tea parties, she covered such topics as going on blind dates, conversing with awkward white men, and feigning interest in sports for women who didn't know "home plate from a hot plate." The *Courier* touted "The Women" as "spicy reading," and in her most provocative pieces Cunningham explored the art of picking up men in bars, the etiquette of accompanying them to striptease clubs, and the absence of data about black women in Alfred Kinsey's 1953 bestseller *Sexual Behavior in the Human Female*. ("Since, however, Negro women are women before they are Negro," Cunningham concluded, "I am inclined to believe—without benefit of a staff of researchers—that there would not have been any drastic differences in the Kinsey findings had he included Negro women.")

In a column entitled "Race Leaders with Sex Appeal," Cunningham playfully suggested that vision and eloquence weren't the only qualities that drew women to leading civil rights figures. For A. Philip Randolph, it was his seductive voice—"one of those deep, resonant, cultured larynxes that goes with the come-wiz-me-to-see-Casbah line." For diplomat Ralph Bunche, it was his worldly air: "When his cigarette dangles from his lips, when his eyes sparkle and he looks like he's going to wink but doesn't, a gal reporter has a tough time concentrating on weighty United Nations problems." For Congressmen Adam Clayton Powell, it was his wavy mane and rascal charm: "There's not much he has to say when he is appearing before a hysterical group of women, and a lock of hair falls down to the middle of his brow."

But it was no accident that Cunningham reserved her most affectionate assessment for Thurgood Marshall, the head of the NAACP's Legal Defense Fund. "With some very important court victories under his belt and a wealth of prestige and influence around the world," Evelyn wrote, "Marshall can still walk into a room and stumble over a chair and be assured that it will be put down to his 'boyishness.'"

Cunningham had first met Marshall while covering what became known as the "Groveland Four" case. In 1948, around the time that Isaiah Nixon was shot in Georgia, Norma Padgett, a seventeen-year-old woman from Groveland, Florida, accused four black men of raping her. Three of them—Samuel Shepherd, Charles Greenlee, and Walter Lee Irvin—were promptly arrested. The fourth, Ernest Thomson, fled Groveland's Lake County but was tracked down by a posse and killed on the spot. An all-white jury found the others guilty after Shepherd and Greenlee confessed. But an NAACP legal team, led by Marshall, appealed the death sentence for Shepherd and Irvin (Greenlee was given life as a minor), on the grounds that blacks had been excluded from the jury and that the confessions were coerced with savage beatings while the suspects were shackled to jailhouse ceiling pipes and forced to stand on broken glass. After three years, the case went to the Supreme Court, which overturned the verdict and ordered a new trial.

On a November night in 1951, Sheriff Willis McCall arrived at Raiford State Prison to transport the three black men back to the Lake County jail. On the way, according to McCall's account, a tire on his car went flat. When he pulled onto a dirt road to inspect the damage, Samuel Shepherd asked to get out of the car to relieve himself. Shepherd was handcuffed to Irvin, and as soon as they were on their feet they turned on McCall and attacked him. In self defense, McCall said, he shot both men, killing Shepherd and wounding Irvin, who survived by pretending to be dead.

Walter Irvin was rushed to a hospital in Eustis, Florida, and Cunningham was one of a handful of reporters to be allowed into his room. There, she found Thurgood Marshall and other members of his legal team huddled around the hospital bed as Irvin, gasping for air, gave his version of the shooting. It was after dark, he said, and Sheriff McCall was trailing another car driven by his deputy, James Yates. Yates pulled off onto a clay road, and McCall followed him. They stopped and got out of their cars to confer, then Yates peeled away. As McCall drove farther down the road, he started to complain about a flat tire. Stopping again, he ordered the prisoners to help him fix it. As the shackled pair shimmied off the front bench seat and tried to stand up, McCall pumped a bullet into each of them. Then he threw the men to the ground and fired two more times.

Wounded but still conscious, Irvin saw Deputy Yates reappear. "These SOB's tried to jump me and I did a good job on them," he heard McCall say. Yates shone a flashlight in Irvin's eyes. "This SOB's not dead," he said. "Let's kill him." Yates fired at Irvin for a third time, at close enough range that he assumed the shot was fatal.

Alex Akerman, one of the defense attorneys, leaned in toward Irvin's hospital bed. "I know you must be tired, but there are just one or two questions," he said. "Had you tried to jump him? The sheriff?"

"No, sir," Irvin replied.

Then Thurgood Marshall spoke. "Did you ever try to escape that night?"

"No, sir, never," Irvin said.

From the hospital, Cunningham went to Irvin's home, where she was the first person to describe the nature of his wounds to his parents. Delia Irvin insisted that her "Walt Lee," a World War II Army veteran, could not have committed the rape because he would never lie to his mother. "'I'm your mamma,'" she said. "'Tell the truth. Did you do that?' And Walt Lee said he didn't." Cleveland Irvin just wanted to visit his son in the hospital and bring him cigarettes. They talked of taking Irvin and his three younger brothers someplace else where it would be "good for us," but that hope was in vain. An all-white coroner's jury cleared Sheriff McCall of any wrongdoing. Despite Marshall's best efforts, Irvin was convicted in a second trial, after rejecting a plea deal that would have spared him the death penalty. He spent the next three years on death row until a new governor commuted his sentence to life imprisonment, and another thirteen behind bars before he was paroled. On a visit to Lake County two years later, Irvin was found dead in mysterious circumstances, his body slumped over the wheel of his car.

By the time Walter Irvin's second trial was over, Evelyn Cunningham and Thurgood Marshall had become fast friends. He encouraged her to keep asking for hard news assignments, and teased her when he saw a man's byline on a big story. "Why didn't you write that article?" he asked. Over time, Cunningham became one of the few reporters with whom Marshall let down his guard. To his biographer Juan Williams, Cunningham recalled one night when Marshall accompanied her to an illegal after-hours club in New York. Around three in the morning, police broke in and threw everyone in the crowded, smoke-filled place into a panic. Spotting a familiar policeman, Cunningham pleaded with him to let Marshall escape. "You can't arrest this man," she said. "He is very, very important. You have to let him go." The cop ushered the two out a side door, but as they were walking away Marshall tipsily threatened to go back. "I would like to defend these guys—these cops got no right doing this," he declared, before Cunningham yanked his coat sleeve and suggested that it was time for him to go home.

In the fall of 1953, as Marshall was organizing the NAACP lawyers to argue the case for desegregating America's schools before the Supreme Court, he allowed Cunningham into their inner sanctum: the cluttered offices of the Legal Defense Fund on 107 West 43rd Street in Manhattan. She described the chaotic informality with which Marshall oversaw a small army of fifty-two lawyers as they raced to meet the deadline that the justices had set for rehearing cases in thirty-seven states. She introduced *Courier* readers to Marshall's still largely unknown team of lieutenants: his bow-tied deputy, Robert Carter; Constance Baker Motley, the only woman on the team; and Jack Greenberg, the top white lawyer. (Later, Cunningham would write a strong defense of Greenberg when Marshall was named to the U.S. Court of Appeals and many blacks criticized the Legal Defense Fund for appointing a white man to succeed him.)

When the justices heard the arguments in December 1953, Cunningham was one of four reporters the *Courier* sent to Washington. Outside the Court, she interviewed blacks who had camped out overnight, warming themselves with Thermoses of coffee, to get one of the fifty seats inside that had been set aside for spectators. Inside, Bill Nunn and two other *Courier* reporters took notes as Marshall and his lieutenants argued before the justices. Also seated in the gallery, in a section reserved for Marshall's special guests, was Pittsburgh's Daisy Lampkin, who had led a joint *Courier*-NAACP fundraising drive that raised more than $13,000 to pay the Legal Defense Fund's expenses.

Six months later, in the consolidated decision that became known as *Brown v. Board of Education of Topeka, Kansas*, the Supreme Court unanimously struck down the doctrine of "separate but equal" education across the land. In Pittsburgh, the editors splashed the news that "SCHOOLS WILL BE MIXED!" across the front page. Yet along with praise for "Buster" Marshall, as the paper called him, the *Courier* also identified omens of trouble to come. Another front-page story quoted Southern officials, from Georgia to Louisiana, defiantly vowing to maintain segregated schools in their states. An editorial foresaw more political gerrymandering to make school districts increasingly white or black. In a story entitled "School Decision Fails to Excite Southern Mothers!" both white and black parents expressed fears that the ruling might be implemented too quickly and worried about what it would mean for their children.

In the year after the *Brown v. Board of Education* decision, Cunningham continued to dispense personal advice while keeping an eye out for big reporting opportunities. In her weekly column, she pondered the vogue for informal dinner parties and the dilemma of modern women expected to act feminine *and* help pay the bills. Meanwhile, she profiled the new director of the NAACP, Roy Wilkins, and soprano Marian Anderson, on the eve of her debut as the first black singer to perform with the Metropolitan Opera. As news of Emmett Till's murder spread, Cunningham rushed to a Harlem church were ten thousand people shared their anguish over the fourteen-year-old Chicago boy who had gone to visit relatives in Mississippi only to be kidnapped, mutilated, shot, and drowned for chatting with a white woman who ran the local grocery store.

In January 1956, another protest had begun to capture the attention of the country, and Cunningham urged her bosses in Pittsburgh to send her to cover it. In Montgomery, the capital of Alabama, virtually the entire community of forty thousand Negroes was refusing to ride the city's segregated buses. The protest had started on the first day of December 1955, when Rosa Parks, a seamstress who was also a secretary of the local NAACP, was arrested for refusing to give up her seat to a white passenger. Following a trial one-day strike, church leaders banded together with the local NAACP director, E. D. Nixon, to organize a sustained boycott. Instead of taking the bus, blacks car-pooled, hitchhiked, rode with Negro cab drivers, or simply walked. As word of the boycott spread over the Christmas holiday, black pastors across America praised it from the pulpit and took up collections of money and secondhand shoes to send to Alabama.

When Cunningham arrived in Montgomery, she checked into "a sad little hotel" in the heart of town, as she described it. On Tuesday, January 31, she was in her hotel room when she heard the sound of a loud explosion nearby. She followed the noise and smoke to Highland Street, to find that a firebomb had ripped into a tiny white bungalow house. It was the parsonage of Reverend Martin Luther King Jr., the young pastor of the Dexter Avenue Baptist Church who had been elected to chair the boycott committee, which called itself the Montgomery Improvement Association (MIA). King was speaking at another church, First Baptist, several blocks away at the time of the bombing, but his wife, Coretta, and their ten-week-old daughter, Yolanda, were inside the house. By the time King got there, it was surrounded by white policemen and scores of angry black town neighbors, some of them brandishing construction pipes and broken Coca-Cola bottles.

After checking to make sure his loved ones were all right, King emerged on what was left of the small, columned porch to urge calm. As Cunningham listened to his resounding voice and eloquent cadences, she could see why despite King's age—he had just turned twenty-seven—he had emerged as the leader of the Montgomery protest. "If you have weapons, take them home," King pleaded to the angry crowd. "If you do not have them, please do not seek to get them. We cannot solve this problem through retaliatory violence. We must meet violence with nonviolence. Remember the words of Jesus: 'He who lives by the sword will perish by the sword.' We must love our white brothers, no matter what they do to us. We must make them know that we love them. Jesus still cries out in the words that echo across the centuries: 'Love your enemies; bless them that curse you; pray for them that despitefully use you.'"

Within days of the firebombing, a grand jury with only one black member indicted King and other boycott organizers for conspiring to violate an obscure ordinance against interfering with local business. Rather than wait to be arrested, more than ninety of the city's most distinguished black citizens, dressed in their Sunday best, turned themselves in. Cunningham watched as they submitted to mug shots and fingerprints and posted $300 bail each, then posed for a group portrait on the courthouse steps. Later in the week, she attended the first MIA meetings opened to reporters. At one, the organization rejected by a vote of 3,998 to 2 a deal from the bus company, promising better treatment but retaining segregated seating. At another, the crowd resolved to carry on the protest by refusing to use any vehicles at all. "Now they're really going to see some walking!" an elderly lady called out after the motion passed.

As the streets of Montgomery filled with Negroes, defiantly but peacefully going about their business entirely on foot, Cunningham wrote a status report to her editors in Pittsburgh. "This situation here is something like I've never in life seen," she wrote. "It's difficult to believe what these people are doing and the almost Christ-like manner in which they're doing it. It is my considered—though womanly—opinion that this deal will be seen as bigger than the Supreme Court decision [on school desegregation] and that you ought to have somebody real close here for the next few months. I've never seen Negroes 'cool it' like these people. They KNOW they're right and they aren't going to quit for nothing or nobody. They aren't being excitable and emotional as we've always been. And they're slowly realizing that they've got a key to the whole race thing right in their pockets. In short, they don't give a damn what the entire white people do. They're ready, spiritually and psychologically, to be martyrs if need be. Honest to God, I've never been prouder of being a Negro. Love and kisses and forgive the sentimentality, but I'm moved.—EVELYN"

Cunningham became even more moved as she listened to the testimony during King's four-day conspiracy trial. As fellow ministers tried to play down King's role in organizing the boycott, his lawyers worked to establish the "just cause" of the protest by calling more than thirty black citizens, most of them women, to describe their experiences riding Montgomery's buses. The rule that Rosa Parks had violated—Negroes in the back half of the bus had to stand once the front half was full and whites needed more seats—was only the start of the indignities described. Blacks were forced to enter the front door to pay a dime for their ride, then to exit the bus and reenter through the back door. Often drivers pulled away before they could get back on. Buses routinely drove by stops in black neighborhoods, or peeled away before colored passengers found their footing. Virtually every black witness described vile names by which bus drivers had called them: "nigger," "boy," "shine," "black cow," "big black ape."

Yet instead of sounding angry or humiliated, the witnesses appeared eager to share their stories for the benefit of dozens of reporters, from as far away as France and India, who had descended on Montgomery to cover the trial. When Judge Eugene Carter tried to dismiss one woman from the stand, she didn't want to leave. "Y'all can ask me some more questions if you want to!" the woman said.

Carter pressed another woman about why she had stopped riding the bus on the specific date of December 5, 1955.

"Because we decided," the woman answered.

"Who decided?" the judge asked.

"We decided," the woman said.

"Who's we?" the judge asked.

"Fifty thousand Negroes of Montgomery!" the woman cried out— eliciting such a loud cheer from the black spectators in the courtroom that Carter threatened to jail them all if the commotion continued.

Faced with writing "The Women" column in the midst of the trial, Cunningham skipped her usual lifestyle tips. Instead, she opened up to her female readers about how the Montgomery assignment had changed her. "I've always felt that being a Negro was one of life's most interesting experiences," she wrote. "There have been countless times when certain individual Negroes have made me very proud to be part of them. And there've been times when I have been utterly ashamed. But for the most part, I've been resigned and indifferent. But here in Montgomery, I got a good shaking up. I learned so much that it was like I'd never known anything. And most of all I experienced sheer happiness that I am a Negro. I felt that I was part of the finest, noblest, most courageous people in the world. Even more amazing to me was to realize that this thing that sprinkled off on me was something that had been soaking into the people here a mighty long time. And I was ashamed for the times I had been ashamed."

As soon as the lawyers completed their summations, Judge Carter found King guilty of conspiracy and ordered him to pay a $500 fine or face jail time. King chose to go to prison for two weeks, transforming him for the first time into not just a leader but a martyr for his cause. Suddenly the interest of news organizations turned from the boycott to Reverend King himself. *Jet* magazine put his face on the cover. *The New York Times* commissioned a "Man in the News" profile. Yet for all the veteran reporters from around the world who were now assigned to the Montgomery story, none had gained more access to the young preacher than the tall, stylish woman from *The Pittsburgh Courier*.

When they first met, Cunningham hadn't tried to interview King but instead had engaged him in a casual conversation. "I just wanted to get to know him," she recalled, "and I wanted him to get to know me, because I was going to be around." Soon they were having long talks about King's philosophy of nonviolence, and he was teasing her about not being a true pacifist. "I'm listening to you!" he said. "I'm listening to your anger. I'm listening to how you want to shoot up and kill the bad guys!" Because he liked Cunningham—and because he understood the power and reach of her newspaper across black America—King began to introduce her to fellow protest leaders and other valuable sources. "This is Sister Cunningham, and she's from the Pittsburgh Courier," he would say. "But she's a New Yorker and she is not nonviolent."

In April 1956, five months into the boycott, that access allowed Cunningham to write the first truly personal profile of King to appear in the national press. *The New York Times* and other publications had reported the factual highlights: King's upbringing as the son of one of Atlanta's top Baptist preachers; his education at Morehouse College and Boston University's divinity school; his interest in the teachings of Gandhi, Kant, and Hegel. But in "The Life Story of Martin Luther King," published in three installments in the *Courier*, Cunningham provided details that no white or male reporter would likely have gleaned.

The moment that King had fallen in love with public speaking, Cunningham reported, wasn't when listening to his father or his maternal grandfather preach at Ebenezer Baptist Church. It was when he impressed all the other boys and girls at the local Elks Club by winning an oratory contest at the age of fourteen. At Morehouse, King was known more for his love of talking and socializing than for his schoolwork. Until his senior year, he had resisted the idea of becoming a minister. "I had the feeling that you had to make social sacrifices and I wasn't willing to make these particular sacrifices," King confessed to Cunningham. "I also had some intellectual doubts about religion. But I finally came to see that religion could be intellectually respectable as well as emotionally satisfying."

Cunningham coaxed King's wife of three years, the former Coretta Scott, into recounting their courtship. Inviting Evelyn to the parsonage, Coretta described how a mutual friend had tried to set her up with Martin when he was at Boston University and she was studying at the New England Conservatory of Music. At first she was wary. "I had an aversion to ministers because of a stereotyped impression of them," Coretta said. But Martin got her phone number from the friend, and "gave me a line I had never heard before" to convince her to have lunch. "He said he would be driving a green Chevy," Coretta said, "and that he usually made it from the University to the Conservatory in seven minutes, but that tomorrow he would make it in five." By the end of that lunch, Martin was talking about marriage, and he continued to do so during daily phone calls and dates for months until Coretta finally accepted his proposal.

At that point in the interview, King walked into the room where Coretta and Evelyn were talking. "Why don't you simply tell her that I swept you off your feet?" he joked. "And don't forget to mention that when you saw all those girls talking to me at that party in Waterbury, you started looking at me in a new light!" Coretta laughed. It was true, she admitted to Cunningham.

In the last story in her series, Cunningham described how King had emerged as the leader of the Montgomery movement. When the city's black leaders met on the night of Rosa Parks's arrest, he arrived late. Before then, there was talk of what to do next but no sense of who would be in charge. "It was an Alphonse-Gaston affair," as Cunningham put it. Then King walked in, one participant told her, and "it was like someone had sent him. He was it." Cunningham also captured the extraordinary gift for public speaking that had galvanized the protesters and that was beginning to awe blacks around the country as King traveled to raise funds for the boycott. "No one can leave one of his sermons without being profoundly moved," she wrote. "He speaks without notes and gives the impression of spontaneity. But his talks are well-prepared and studied. He never under-rates his listeners or talks down to them. . . . When he is delving deeply into a weighty subject matter he knows how to make it understandable without the least bit of condescension. He might well be termed one of the great orators of this century."

Cunningham's evocative stories on the Montgomery boycott caught the eye of editors at *The New York Times*, who hired her as a part-time stringer. For the next decade, she helped inform the *Times*'s slowly expanding cov-erage of civil rights while returning to the front lines of the struggle for the *Courier*. Covering the unrest in Birmingham, Alabama, she pushed her way through a crowd to try to interview Bull Connor, the city's defiantly pro-segregationist police chief. When she identified herself as working for *The Pittsburgh Courier*, Connors snorted: "Oh, that's that nigger paper up North, huh?"

Eventually, Cunningham landed another part-time job hosting a lunch-time talk show on WLIB-AM, a jazz radio station in New York City. Her first guest was Malcolm X, the fiery Nation of Islam leader who was just starting to gain national attention. Her last guest was New York governor Nelson Rockefeller, who offered her a job as an adviser and opened the door to a new career as a political consultant and civic activist.

Ever stylish, Evelyn became a muse of Bill Cunningham, *The New York Times* fashion photographer who shared her last name and delighted in including her in his weekly collages of city trendsetters. Upon her death at the age of ninety-four, he would pen a fond remembrance praising Ev-elyn's penchant for "long dangling earrings," "playful use of scarves," and figure-stretching combinations of short jackets and long Pucci and St. Laurent dresses and pants suits. "Her hands gave her the expressiveness of a Giacometti sculpture," the photographer wrote, "not unlike the style of Diana Vreeland."

Evelyn Cunningham's stay in Montgomery ended in June 1956, after a federal district court in Alabama found in favor of the boycotters in a civil case filed by the NAACP. It was the first step toward a Supreme Court ruling later that year which mandated an end to segregated seating on buses across the country. After six months of living in a hotel, Cunningham decided it was time to go back north, back to writing advice for modern women and to her next assignment for the *Courier*. But before leaving Alabama, she wrote a farewell column entitled "What I Like About Dixie."

Whenever she went south, Cunningham confided, she arrived full of rage over the injustices she was sent to cover. Then she enumerated the reasons that "I always wind up enjoying myself and hating to leave, lynch mobs notwithstanding." Southern blacks knew how to take life slowly, unlike rushing, shoving, subway-riding New Yorkers. They still enjoyed formal meals at dining tables, rather than eating on the run in cramped kitchens like apartment-dwelling Northerners. Most of all, they all seemed to know and look after one another. "If you go out and leave a pot boiling on the stove," Evelyn wrote, "you can always call a neighbor to go over and turn out the gas."

Cunningham ended with an observation that sounded gentle at the time, but that in the years ahead would be starkly confirmed in her second home of Pittsburgh, and captured in the work of the most illustrious of all its black native sons. "Being in Dixie always takes some of the smugness out of me about being a big city gal," she wrote. "They got a way of making me feel that I've got as many problems as they have."

August Wilson revisits his childhood home on the Hill, a cold-water flat (*rear*)
in the back of what was once Bella Siger's market on Bedford Avenue.

10

THE BARD OF A BROKEN WORLD

LIKE ROBERT L. VANN, Gus Greenlee, Billy Strayhorn, and Evelyn Cunningham, Daisy Wilson had North Carolina roots. She grew up in Spear, a tiny, remote town high in the Appalachian Mountains near the northern Virginia border. Raising Daisy and a younger brother by herself, her mother, Zonia, did her best to scratch out a living on their subsistence farm, but illiteracy limited her horizons. It kept Zonia from advertising her produce, from deciphering bills and contracts, and from otherwise protecting herself against cheats. Daisy was forced to leave school in Spear after the sixth grade to work on the farm, but not before she mastered the skill that she would pass along to her own children, along with the message that reading was the one thing that Negroes needed to survive in a hard world and to make the most of the gifts that God gave them.

Family lore had it that to start a new life for her family, Zonia Wilson walked all the way from North Carolina to Pittsburgh. That story was surely apocryphal, but by the late 1930s, she and her children had settled alongside the other black migrants and white immigrants in the Hill District. In her late teens, Daisy had a round, freckled face, slightly buck teeth, and an already womanly figure. While she was shopping at a grocery store one day, a trim white man with a high forehead and a German accent began chatting with her. Daisy shyly turned away, but a few days later, when she saw him again, she smiled and answered back. His name was Frederick August Kittel, and he went by "Fritz." Born in Bohemia, Austria, he had moved to Pittsburgh after World War I. Now, in his early forties, he was a baker by trade. Soon they became lovers and moved together into a cold-water flat above a store on Bedford Avenue and started a family. First came a girl they named Freda and then another, Linda Jean. But Fritz Kittel sorely wanted a male child, and when a third girl, Donna, arrived next, he didn't hide his disappointment. "Another split-ass," he sneered.

Finally, on April 27, 1945, Daisy gave birth to a boy. Fritz insisted on giving him his name—Frederick August Kittel Jr.—and the family nicknamed him "Freddy." He had his mother's broad face, freckles, and light mocha skin, and she doted on him. By the time Freddy was four, Daisy had taught him to read. By the time he was five, she had taken him to the Carnegie Library on Wylie Avenue to get his first library card. The first book he read by himself was *Curious George*. Before long, he had devoured all of the Hardy Boys books and his sisters' Nancy Drews. At ten, he started to read the Bible, resolving to finish the entire Old and New Testaments by the time he was grown.

Although Daisy wasn't Catholic, she wanted Freddy to be educated by nuns. She enrolled him in the Holy Trinity School at the corner of Crawford Street and Centre Avenue for third grade. In sixth grade, Sister Catherine encouraged Freddy to try his hand at poetry. Before the year was out, he was writing romantic odes to the girls in his class. He also delighted in infuriating the nuns with his precocious curiosity. "When they said no one could figure out the Holy Trinity, I was like, 'Why not?'" he later recalled. "I instantly wanted to prove that it could be done."

Freddy's experience of his father was far less happy. By the time his first son was born, Fritz Kittel's chronic drinking had curdled his relationship with Daisy Wilson. He had moved into a hotel and visited the family only for days or nights at a time. When he showed up, it was usually with flour-covered sacks stuffed with fragrant rolls and doughnuts to appease his wife and entice his children. But then Fritz would retreat with a newspaper and a gallon jug of Muscatel, demanding silence and drinking himself into a stupor. In the temper tantrums that sometimes ensued, baked goods were hurled across the apartment, and bricks thrown at the second-floor windows. Asked later to cite a warm memory of his father, his namesake recalled the day they went downtown together to shop for a pair of Gene Autry cowboy boots that Freddy coveted. But then as they entered the shopping district, his father handed him some coins to put in his pocket. "Jingle it!" Fritz said—to let the white folks know he had money.

Left to raise six children on her own—two more boys, Richard and Edwin, came after Freddy—Daisy did her best to steer them away from trouble while keeping their minds and bellies full. She ceased working as a cleaning lady and made do with welfare payments so that she wouldn't have to leave home. Every Monday evening at seven, she gathered the family around the radio for the weekly reading of the Rosary. Daisy encouraged her children to listen to Art Linkletter's *People Are Funny* show and the Top Forty music countdown, promising a nickel to the child who guessed which song would be Number One. At the time, their block of Bedford Avenue, on the border between the Lower and Middle Hill, was still mixed, and the Kittel children made friends with white neighbors as well as black. The girls sometimes helped out Bella Siger, the Jewish lady who ran Bella's Market, the store in front of their building. The boys played with the sons of the Italian shoe repairman next door, Mr. Butera, in a tiny backyard as Daisy kept watch from the kitchen window.

Daisy's closest friends were a black couple who lived across the street, Charley and Julie Burley. With his muscular build, thick eyebrows, and smartly parted hair, Charley was a well-known figure on the Hill, a former boxer who had almost gone all the way to the top. As a teen, he had worked his way up the city ranks to a national Golden Gloves title. As a professional, he had defeated the Cocoa Kid to win the World Colored

Welterweight Championship. But Burley had never earned a shot at a non-Negro title. Some said it was because contenders from Billy Conn to Sugar Ray Robinson ducked him; others whispered that it was because he was too proud to play the game and throw fights. A gifted baseball player, Charley had also tried out for the Homestead Grays but never made the team. By the late 1940s, he was working as a garbage collector for the city of Pittsburgh. But he still dressed the part of a champion, with his Stetson hats and Florsheim shoes, and exuded the toughness that had kept him from ever being knocked out in almost a hundred pro bouts. Disappointed by his white father, Freddy Kittel came to idolize Charley Burley and see him as a model of the kind of man he wanted to be.

Around this time, Freddy received another lesson in standing tall from his mother. One night, the family was listening to the radio when a contest was announced. A Speed Queen washing machine would go to the first person to call the station and correctly identify a popular advertising jingle. As a single mother who did laundry for six children by hand, scrubbing their clothes on a washboard and hanging them out to dry, Daisy could have used the help. And when the announcer read the slogan—"When it rains, it pours"—she recognized it immediately. There was no phone in the house, so she handed a dime to one of her daughters and told her to go to a pay phone outside and call in the answer: Morton's Salt.

Daisy won the contest, but she never got the Speed Queen. When Morton's discovered that she was black, the company sent her a certificate to buy a used washing machine at the Salvation Army instead.

Julie Burley urged her friend to use it. "Daisy, you got all them kids, what difference does it make?" Julie said. "Take the washing machine."

But Daisy refused, and she gave her son a prideful explanation he would never forget. "Something is not always better than nothing," she told him.

By the time Freddy was finishing grade school, Daisy had met and married a new man. David Bedford was a laborer for the Pittsburgh sewer department. He was black, and a book reader like Freddy, and at first the boy welcomed the new relationship. Like Charley Burley, Bedford was a man who carried the heavy weight of disappointment. A football star in high school, he hoped to get an athletic scholarship to college and study to become a doctor. But colleges didn't recruit black players at the time, and Bedford was too poor to afford tuition. So he foolishly tried to rob a store and shot a man in the attempt. He was found guilty of murder and spent the next twenty-three years in prison before emerging to salvage what he could from the rest of his life. But Bedford never spoke of his past, and Freddy only learned of it after his stepfather had passed away.

In the mid-1950s, as Freddy was nearing his teens, an alarming rumor swept through the Holy Trinity school: the Hill District was going to be torn to the ground, and everyone who lived there would have to move. Sam Howze, an older black student who had befriended Freddy, recalled the impact the news had on them and their classmates. "To kids, this was frightening," he said. "Will I have a new school? Will I have to find new friends? Why are they tearing our neighborhood down?" One day, Howze's parents announced that they were moving their eleven children from Fullerton Street to Bedford Dwellings, the housing project that had been built on the site of the old Greenlee Field, where the Pittsburgh Crawfords once played. Soon afterward, Freddy learned that his family was relocating even further away, to a neighborhood called Hazelwood along the Monongahela River to the south.

For Freddy, accustomed to the friendly mixing on the Hill, the move would bring his first experience of being singled out for the color of his skin. Hazelwood was home to a Jones & Laughlin steel mill and the European immigrants who worked there, and they were not happy about the sudden influx of black families from the Hill. One day, a brick was hurled through the window of Freddy's new home. When it came time for high school, his mother sent him to Central Catholic High, the huge parochial school run by the Christian Brothers three miles away in the Oakland neighborhood. As a freshman, Freddy was placed in a homeroom class in which he was the only black student. On many mornings, he would arrive at school to find the words "Go home, nigger!" and other hostile messages scrawled on his desk.

Beginning to grow into the broad-chested physique he would have as a man, Freddy tried out for the football team. But he soon quit, infuriating his stepfather and chilling their relationship. Instead, Freddy began to study the art of boxing, to survive his daily brawls on the way to and from school. The Christian Brothers sometimes had to send him home in a taxi-cab, but that did him no good in the mornings, when bullies awaited him along the route from Hazelwood. One day, his homeroom class was recit-ing the Pledge of Allegiance when Freddy heard the student in front call him "nigger." As soon as the words "with liberty and justice for all" were out of his mouth, he recalled, Freddy decked the boy. The two students were taken to the principal's office, and when Brother Martin told Freddy he was being sent home, Freddy responded that wouldn't be coming back.

He transferred to Connelly Trade School, a vocational academy for students from across the city. Even though the school was near his old home, on Bedford Avenue on the edge of the Hill, Freddy was even more miserable than he had been at Central Catholic. The reading assignments were at a fifth-grade level. Making tin cups out of sheet metal bored him to death. He treated his instructors with contempt, and they returned it. The breaking point came one day in shop class, when Freddy used a T-square to hammer a thumbtack. Furious at the indifference to his tools, the teacher punched Freddy and knocked him to the ground. Rising to his feet, Freddy shoved the instructor against the blackboard. "Give me a pink slip," he said. "I'm leaving this school."

Next Freddy enrolled in Gladstone High, the local school across the street from his home in Hazelwood. He was placed in the tenth grade but forced to repeat ninth-grade subjects he had never finished. More bored than ever, he sat in the back of his classes, doodling and day-dreaming. The one subject that held his attention was history, which happened to be taught by a black man called "Mr. B." by his students. Freddy became particularly engaged when Mr. B assigned the class to write a paper about a foreign leader. Freddy had always had a fascination with Napoleon, identifying with the story of the self-made soldier who rose to become an emperor. He threw himself into researching the sub-ject, checking out dozens of books from the library and paying his sister to type up a twenty-page paper with quarters he had earned cutting the lawn of a neighbor.

The day after Freddy turned in the assignment, Mr. B asked him to stay after class. On the title page of the Napoleon paper, the teacher had written two letters: an "A+" and an "E" (which at the time was sometimes used to indicate a failing grade, because it came after "D.") "I'm going to give you one of these grades," Mr. B said. Then the teacher asked Freddy to prove that one of his older sisters hadn't written the paper for him. Insulted, Freddy pointed out that the paper had a bibliography, and that Mr. B. never asked white students to prove their authorship. "Unless you call everybody in here . . . even the ones that went and copied out of the encyclopedia word for word, I don't feel I should have to prove anything," Freddy said. Mr. B circled the "E" and handed the paper back to Freddy, who promptly ripped it apart, threw the tattered pages into a trash can, and stormed out of the school, vowing never to return.

That night, however, Freddy had second thoughts. He dreaded breaking the news that he had dropped out of yet another school to his stepfather, who was still furious with him for quitting the football team at Central Catholic, and to his mother, who dreamed of his becoming a lawyer. So the next day, Freddy went back to the school with a basketball and spent the morning dribbling outside the principal's office. Perhaps, he imagined, the principal would have heard about the injustice that had been done and would rectify it by inviting him back to school. But the principal never appeared, and Freddy eventually picked up the basketball and left Gladstone High for good.

Freddy had run out of places to go—except one. A year earlier, on another walk home from playing basketball, he had wandered into the Hazelwood branch of the Carnegie Library. In a corner he had found a shelf marked "Negro," stacked with some thirty books. He picked out one entitled the *The Collected Poems of Paul Laurence Dunbar* and became so fascinated with the poet's unusual use of black dialect that he took the copy home and forgot to return it. He browsed a sociology text and came upon a phrase that captivated him: "the Negro's power of hard work." Freddy had never thought of sheer industriousness as being a special power, but the idea captivated him, and the next time he went to mow his neighbor's lawn he did so with a proud fury.

At Gladstone High, Freddy had made the acquaintance of an elderly drunkard who hung around outside the school. Usually they just traded playful insults, but one day the man pulled a novel out of his coat and recommended it to Freddy. On his next trip to the Hazelwood library, Freddy found a copy of the book—*Invisible Man*—and became instantly engrossed in Ralph Ellison's haunting tale of a promising black valedictorian led astray by bigoted white authority figures and selfish black militants.

Without telling his mother that he had quit school, Freddy began going to the library instead. He took the long walk each morning to the main branch of the Carnegie Library in Oakland, the massive marble building that was one of the very first of the more than ten thousand libraries that Andrew Carnegie funded with the fortune derived from Pittsburgh's steel mills. Day after day, until the hour at which he would have come home from school, Freddy wandered the stacks picking up volumes that caught his eye. He read the poems of Langston Hughes and the novels of Richard Wright. He read the autobiography of the playwright Moss Hart. He read accounts of the Civil War. He read the Constitution of the United States and the Emancipation Proclamation. He read academic textbooks on theology and anthropology; instruction manuals for automobiles, airplanes, trains, and boats; guides for pottery-making and table manners—more than three hundred books in all.

Eventually Daisy discovered that Freddy was no longer in school, and she was furious. She saw it as a betrayal of all the sacrifices she had made for her talented son, and she turned against him with a vengeance. She banished Freddy to the basement of the house in Hazelwood and told him that he would never amount to anything. She announced that he was no longer welcome at the dinner table, and locked groceries in her room so that he would have to forage for himself. Eventually the atmosphere grew so tense that Freddy decided to escape by enlisting in the Army. Setting his sights on becoming an officer, he took the test for Officer Candidate

School and got the second highest score in his battalion. But when he was informed that he would have to wait two years to start the program—officers had to be at least nineteen, and Freddy was still only seventeen—he lost interest in the military. Although the circumstances aren't clear, he managed to get himself discharged after only one year.

Freddy traveled across the country to California and worked in a pharmacy until, in early 1964, he learned that his father was gravely ill. By then, Daisy Wilson had divorced David Bedford and returned to Fritz Kittel, finally marrying him and taking his name. But when Freddy returned to Pittsburgh to help his mother and sisters look after his father, he discovered that Fritz's mind was gone. He could tell vivid stories of fighting in the Argonne forest during World War I but no longer recognized his own son. Fritz's death would come within a year, and it was then that his namesake rented a room in a boardinghouse on Crawford Street on the Hill and decided that it was time to get serious about the calling that he had chosen for himself.

Freda, the oldest of his sisters, was in college now, at Fordham University in New York, and she sometimes paid Freddy to write English papers for her. She had just sent him $20 for a paper he had entitled "Two Violent Poets: Robert Frost and Carl Sandburg." On the first of April, three weeks before his birthday, Freddy took the money to McFerran's, a typewriter store in downtown Pittsburgh. He picked out a Royal Standard typewriter advertised in the window for $20 and persuaded the salesman to sell it to him without adding tax. With no change for a cab or the trolley, he walked the heavy piece of metal all the way to Crawford Street. As soon as he was back in his room, he put the typewriter on a small table, fed a sheet of paper into the platen roller, and poked out his name: "Frederick A. Kittel."

It didn't sound much like a writer's name, he thought, so he started to play with other variations. He shortened his name to "Fred. A. Kittel." He substituted his mother's maiden name: "Frederick A. Wilson." Finally he dropped the first name and inserted the middle name he had inherited from his father: "August Wilson."

He liked how that sounded and the way it looked on the page. So it was settled. For everyone but his family and his oldest friends, to whom he would remain "Freddy," Frederick August Kittel Jr. would now be known as August Wilson. And with that name, he set out to make his way as a writer on the Hill, the once proud neighborhood whose bottom half had just been torn down and whose middle heart would soon be burned out.

RICHARD KING MELLON LIKED to say that it was his wife, Connie, who gave him the resolve to remake Pittsburgh. World War II had just ended, and the heir to the Mellon banking fortune had brought his bride of eight years, a banker's daughter and equestrienne from New York, back to his birthplace after spending several years working for the War Department in Washington. On their first night in town, they checked into the penthouse suite at the William Penn Hotel downtown. As Connie looked out the window, the sky was so dark with smoke and ash from the steel plants along the river that she could barely make out the lit silhouette of the Mellon National Bank just down the block.

"I had almost forgotten how bad it is," Connie said. "Now I understand why a lot of people leave and why a lot of people will never come back."

Mellon sensed what Connie was implying: that *she* might not want to return to Pittsburgh. "We must come back here," he said.

"Well, you have a lot of ideas about it," Connie challenged him. "Will they ever get done?"

"They must get done," Mellon replied.

A reserved man whose most memorable feature was his mane of gray-streaked hair, Mellon had not always been so civic-minded. He had spent much of his youth foxhunting, golfing, and fishing at Rolling Rock, the ten-thousand-acre country estate south of Pittsburgh that his grandfather Thomas Mellon had built and left to his father, Richard Beatty Mellon. But "R.K.," as he was called, had been persuaded to join and then take charge of the Mellon empire after his father died and his cousin Paul, the son of banker Andrew Mellon, showed no interest in the family business.

While in Washington, R.K. had time to contemplate his hometown's future, and it did not look bright. Despite Pittsburgh's contributions to the war effort, its dirty streets and sulfurous smell had turned it into a national laughingstock. *Harper's* magazine had captured the widespread view with a cover entitled "Is Pittsburgh Civilized?" Gilded Age companies founded there were threatening to leave, taking away precious tax revenue, and no replacements were in sight. So when an aide named Wallace Richards approached Mellon with a bold proposal to raze and revitalize the entire downtown area, he listened attentively. "We've got to do something about that place or give it back to the Indians," R.K. joked ruefully after one meeting between the two men in Washington.

In the spring of 1943, with Mellon's blessing, Richards convened a meeting of forty of Pittsburgh's top financial, business, and political leaders at the William Penn Hotel. By the time it was over, they had agreed to form a nonprofit group called the "Allegheny Conference on Post-War Community Development." ("Post-War" was later dropped and it became known as the "ACCD," or simply "the Conference.") The members accepted Mellon's suggestion that they meet—often over lunch and cocktails at the Duquesne Club—not as heads of companies but as concerned private citizens. Soon the group began plotting a push in the state legislature for a series of bills called the "Pittsburgh Package" that paved the way for aggressive smoke and garbage controls; new bridge and highway construction; a traffic commission, parking authority, and parks department; and broad taxing authority to pay for it all.

In the fall of 1945, Mellon gained an unlikely partner in the overall redevelopment scheme that became known as the "Pittsburgh Renaissance." David Lawrence, the Democratic firebrand who had risen in Pennsylvania politics as a protégé-turned-foe of New Deal senator Joseph Guffey, ran for mayor of Pittsburgh and won by only fourteen thousand votes. Mellon had supported the Republican in the race, but he took the advice of an associate and reached out to Lawrence. The publicity-hungry populist and the shy capitalist quickly formed a highly effective team. A onetime amateur boxer from a working-class Irish neighborhood in Pittsburgh, Lawrence relished the public fights and splashy ribbon cuttings that came

with the ambitious rebuilding plan. Mellon preferred to work behind the
scenes, picking up the phone to lobby and assuage heads of powerful
business interests—from Consolidated Coal and Alcoa to the Pennsylvania Railroad—that owed money to his family's banks, or counted Mellon
among their corporate directors.

So low-profile was Mellon that readers of *Time* magazine were likely
puzzled to see his face on the cover in October 1949. *Time* hailed the
choice as a tribute to the unprecedented experiment in "urban renewal"
that Pittsburgh was undertaking. By then, a new thirty-nine-story, $28
million home for Mellon National Bank and U.S. Steel was under construction. A thirty-story, $10 million headquarters for Alcoa was on the
drawing boards. Equitable Life Insurance had funded the clearing of the
"Point," an area at the intersection of Pittsburgh's three rivers that was littered with abandoned warehouses and an old rail station that had burned
down in a suspicious fire. In its place was planned a "Gateway Center" of
modern office buildings and a public park atop a parking garage.

Smoke controls requiring that homes burn less coal and wood and
cars reduce gasoline emissions had thinned the city's black horizon to a
smoggy haze, letting through a third more sunlight. New modern dams
were being built to protect against the devastating floods that periodically
engulfed Pittsburgh. A hole through Squirrel Hill had been dynamited
to make way for a tunnel to connect the business and university districts
with the Pennsylvania Turnpike and the expanding suburbs to the east. To
the west, a new airport was taking shape, spacious enough to serve as a
hub for a national carrier called All American Airways, later to be renamed
Allegheny Airlines.

That same year, two of Pittsburgh's most prominent Jewish leaders
added an exciting new cultural dimension to the "Renaissance." Abraham
Wolk was a city councilman whose family owned a successful furrier business. He was also an avid patron of the City Light Opera, and he had a
novel vision: a new home for the company with a mechanized roof that
could open for concerts under the stars during the summer and close to
protect against the cold and snow of Pittsburgh winters. Wolk shared the

idea with his friend and fellow opera buff Edgar Kaufmann, the owner of the city's largest department store. Taking the concept a step further, Kaufmann agreed to put up $1.5 million to make the structure a multipurpose civic arena that could host concerts and sporting events and attract corporate and political conventions to Pittsburgh.

The question was where to locate the "retractable roof" structure. Lawrence's first choice was Highland Park, a scenic area northeast of downtown along the southern banks of the Allegheny River. But Highland Park also happened to be the home of another member of the Mellon family, R.K.'s uncle Robert King. Neighborhood residents mobilized in opposition, gathering more than a thousand signatures. Then at a City Council hearing, King made a dramatic appearance. Hobbling in on a cane and dressed in a tuxedo and black tie, he offered to donate his sprawling estate for a new city park if Lawrence called off his plan. "I am in favor of light opera and musical comedy," King told the gathering, "but I am against the proposal by promoters who may think that this particular site, which is now a refuge for birds and wildlife, can be man-made by destruction into something better than God made it!" Enticed by King's park proposal and not wanting to antagonize his powerful nephew, Lawrence backed off. Instead he proposed another home for the Civic Arena: the lower end of the Hill District.

At first, black leaders welcomed the proposal. Homer S. Brown, the Pittsburgh judge who served in the state legislature, had been an early supporter of Mellon's grand scheme, helping to pass the "Pittsburgh Package" bills and to win approval for an Urban Redevelopment Authority. Now Brown supported the URA as it took charge of plans to clear the Lower Hill to make room for the civic arena. At the *Courier*, editors had been upset to see black areas omitted from the first phase of the "Renaissance." Once the Hill District was put into play in the spring of 1950, they assigned a reporter named Paul L. Jones to write a three-part series spelling out how its residents could benefit from urban renewal.

In "Is the Hill District Doomed?," Jones estimated that more than half of the area's homes—6,000 out of 11,500—were "substandard," with

major structural defects, no running water or outdoor toilets. Greedy land-
lords had made matters worse, carving up homes to create more rooms to
rent and refusing to make repairs. During a postwar real estate boom elsewhere in Pittsburgh, the assessed value of Hill properties had *fallen*—in
part because of their proximity to "numbers joints" and "painted ladies"
as well as TB and pneumonia rates three times the city average. Yet over-
crowding had only grown worse, as even blacks who could afford to leave
struggled to find "colored" rentals, to get approved for mortgages, or to
take advantage of GI Bill loans, which "haven't meant much to Negroes,"
as Jones put it, because of their stringent appraisal requirements.

Describing the Hill as "Hell with the lid taken off"—a term that had
first been applied to the soot-caked Pittsburgh of the 1860s—Jones cited
all the new housing options that urban renewal would create for its inhab-
itants. It would allow those who met the criteria, earning less than $2,500
a year, to move to Pittsburgh's first low-income housing projects: Bedford
Dwellings and Terrace Village. The federal Housing Act of 1949 had au-
thorized the construction of as many as fifteen thousand additional units
across the city. For homeowners who stood to lose property on the Hill,
"financial settlements will be negotiated," Jones predicted, or "the Urban
Redevelopment Authority will exercise its right of eminent domain and a
fair price will be set by a board of reviewers and approved by the courts."
All in all, the *Courier* writer concluded, "the dream of a good house for
everyone will be closer to realization, and that will be all to the good."

But Jones also raised concerns. "There are other considerations that are
important to Negroes aside from living in a sound pile of bricks and mor-
tar," he pointed out. "What is going to happen to the political power that
Negroes now have on the Hill? What about the churches whose membership may be scattered and whose sites may be taken? What about the informal neighborhood associations? Where will those not eligible for public
housing go? What about the probable hostility of some communities to
the influx of Negroes as renters, purchasers and builders? Will we wind
up with other ghettoes and heightened barriers or will a better democracy
come to our city?"

In the five years that followed, until the City Council formally approved the Hill clearance plan in May 1955, all of those prescient questions were put off. When the minister and members of the Bethel AME Church on Wylie Avenue—the oldest in black Pittsburgh—learned that the church was slated for destruction, they appealed repeatedly for a reprieve. But the URA rebuffed them, offering only to find another home for the church at "a reasonable price." Around the corner, the Loendi Club also sought to be spared, citing its long history as the premier gathering spot for the city's black elite. The URA turned a deaf ear to the well-heeled Loendi members, too, eventually giving them a final deadline to vacate just days before demolition began.

What the Hill petitioners didn't realize was how little leverage the URA actually had. The real powers behind the Pittsburgh Renaissance weren't the city agencies, or even David Lawrence's mayor's office, but R.K. Mellon and the other business leaders. Thanks to Mellon's Duquesne Club strategy, private firms and individuals had put up most of the $118 million for the city's renewal, compared to only $600,000 provided by the city itself. Those interests had little sense of the cultural significance of the Lower Hill for Pittsburgh's Negroes, or much concern for the human toll that their grand visions of a new Pittsburgh might take. In addition, the URA had the federal government to worry about. To finance the rest of the cost of the Hill project, it was seeking $88 million in "slum clearance" dollars provided by the 1949 Housing Act, providing an added incentive to portray the entire area as an unsalvageable ghetto.

In the meantime, the entire city became entranced by the futurist promise of the Civic Arena. Two local architects with degrees from the Carnegie Institute of Technology, James Mitchell and Dahlen Ritchey, designed a round, domed building that resembled a huge steel flying saucer. It spanned 170,000 square feet and called for more than three thousand tons of Pittsburgh's most famous product. The roof was divided into eight sections, with a patented engineering scheme to use gears and tracks to remove six of them in a matter of minutes. According to the elegant drawings and brochures produced by the ACCD, the arena was to be surrounded by high-rise garden apartments and a Symphony Hall that would help turn the area into a mecca for tourists and Pittsburghers of all stripes. So auspicious did the plan seem that at the end of 1954, Paul L. Jones himself left the *Courier* to take a job in the mayor's office as David Lawrence's secretary. (In her weekly gossip column, Toki Schalk greeted the news by reporting how much Jones would earn, $5,700 a year, and exclaiming "Swish!")

A year and a half later, at eleven o'clock on a May morning in 1956, Jones joined his boss at a ceremony to mark the beginning of the end of the Lower Hill. As a symbolic first target, the city chose a two-story house on Epiphany Street that dated as far back as the Civil War. The land on which it stood had even more history: it had once belonged to William Penn and was later owned by William Arthurs, the man for whom the surrounding area had once been known as "Arthursville." By the late 1940s, however, the house had fallen into disrepair and been seized by the city for nonpayment of taxes. Lifting an ax, David Lawrence chipped off a piece of the front doorway. Then he climbed atop a podium to announce to a crowd of Hill residents that the clearance of their neighborhood was officially under way. While the mayor and his associates repaired to lunch at the William Penn Hotel, trucks carrying cranes and wrecking balls lumbered onto Epiphany Street to begin tearing down the first of 1,300 structures that were earmarked for demolition over a span of ninety-five acres.

Yet almost immediately, it became apparent that the city agencies hadn't adequately prepared to resettle the more than eight thousand Hill dwellers. By the summer of 1956, some 230 families had moved to low-income housing units at Bedford Dwellings and Terrace Village. But at least one hundred earned too much to qualify and were struggling to find affordable housing elsewhere on the Hill or nearby. The URA had also failed to anticipate how many of the first wave of displaced residents would be single. By the following fall, 250 of them were living temporarily in the Improvement of the Poor shelter on Webster Avenue, a structure that itself was slated to be torn down in the next phase of demolition. A wrecking crew arrived at one house to find three single mothers with a total of twenty-one children still squatting there; city officials scrambled to find them a new home but had no capacity to provide additional child care help. At another home, workers had torn down everything but the basement when they came across a crippled alcoholic, so incapacitated that he couldn't move.

Delays and spotty communications left Lower Hill residents in the dark about when and where the "headache balls" would arrive. Less than three months before the second phase of demolition was scheduled to begin, clearing the twenty-acre expanse running from the bottom of Wylie Avenue to Bedford Avenue where the Civic Arena would sit, the city was still taking bids from private companies. Once the work began, it turned out that no one had planned for the mountains of decayed lumber that would pile up as more than 250 wooden structures were torn down. In an ironic twist, the city had to order a halt to the demolition under the new "smoke control" laws while it figured out how to cart away and burn the flammable debris in a way that didn't create a hazard.

Still, slowly but surely, youngsters who showed up to gawk at the demolition each day watched as many of the Hill's most storied gathering places disappeared. The wrecking balls laid waste to the Crawford Grill; to the Loendi Club; to the YMCA on Chatham Street; to the Bible Institute and the Improvement of the Poor shelter; to the Old Bath House that had served as a hiding place on the Underground Railroad; to the Washington Street Playground where Josh Gibson had first played sandlot baseball.

On a late July morning in 1956, Teenie Harris, the *Pittsburgh Courier* photographer, arrived at the corner of Wylie Avenue and Elm Street to document the last hours of the Bethel AME Church. It housed the oldest African Methodist Episcopal congregation west of the Allegheny Mountains, founded in a private home by three black freemen four decades before the Civil War. The church on Wylie Avenue dated back to 1906, and its enormous front facade was the most striking architectural sight on the Hill, with three tiled arched doorways and two enormous Romanesque towers. Harris had come to take pictures of the church four months earlier, before any demolition begun. He had returned several months later to shoot it once most of the surrounding blocks had been razed. Now Bethel stood alone, looming over a flat horizon of debris. As a wrecking ball went to work, dismantling the structure from back to front, Harris kept shooting, until, in a final image, there was nothing left but the entranceway and the bell towers and the outline of the new downtown skyscrapers in the smoggy distance.

Eight months later, in April 1958, Harris returned to the same spot to photograph the groundbreaking for the Civic Arena. With his usual showmanship, Mayor Lawrence presided over the event from the back of a dump truck, while a marching band serenaded the crowd and a huge Speedshovel backhoe stood at the ready. At the time, planners expected construction to take no more than two years. But the following year, a steel industry strike set the project back six months. Mounting material costs and unexpected design alterations kept adding to the budget, eventually increasing it to $22 million and necessitating a special bond offering. After more than three years, the project was far enough along to announce an opening day and a lavish $200,000 celebration. But at the last minute, that first dedication had to be called off when ticket sellers went on strike and construction workers refused to cross picket lines.

When a second Dedication Day was finally set for September 1961, it was greeted with more relief than excitement. David Lawrence, who had moved on to the governor's office, showed up briefly to join Pittsburgh's new mayor, Joseph Barr, for a low-key ribbon cutting. Customers who bought tickets for the arena's first event, an Ice Capades performance, were disappointed not to see the roof retract, since its movable parts had yet to be properly sealed. (When the roof was opened for the first time nine months later, at a Carol Burnett concert, the comedienne quipped: "Ladies and gentlemen, allow me to present . . . THE SKY!") The *Pittsburgh Post-Gazette* conceded that the arena had not lived up to the grandiose expectations that it would be the modern equivalent of "Rome's Coliseum and the arenas of Syracuse and Athens." Instead, the paper suggested, its greatest contribution to city life had been to provide a pretext for "some $75 million worth of blight clearance . . . in the Low Hill District, once notorious for its congestion of slums."

By then, black Pittsburgh had its own reasons to view the Hill clearance as a dismal failure. The additional fifteen thousand public housing units promised under the 1949 Housing Act had yet to materialize, forcing many more displaced families into the Bedford Dwellings and Terrace Village projects than had been originally anticipated. By some estimates, one third of them were technically ineligible to live there, since their household incomes were too high—making them vulnerable to eviction if the authorities decided to take action. Early hope for an increase in new housing construction to accommodate Negro buyers had evaporated. Instead, most Lower Hill residents who couldn't or didn't want to live in the projects had moved to nearby middle-class areas of the city where at least some black people lived, usually renting or moving in with friends and families because they couldn't afford house prices.

In the mid-1960s, word began to spread that city officials were seeking more federal money to tear down the Middle Hill. This time, a group of young civic leaders mobilized to stop them. One was Byrd Brown, the son of Homer S. Brown, the judge and former state legislator who had supported the early "Renaissance" efforts. After earning a college and law degree from Yale University, Byrd Brown had returned to Pittsburgh to take charge of the local NAACP. He galvanized the community with a slogan that would soon become a rallying cry for blacks across the cities of the North: "Urban Renewal Means Negro Removal." Another leader was James Jordan, the lone black on the Pittsburgh City Council, who took to publicly challenging Robert Pease, a Pollyannaish, Nebraska-born civil engineer who had been put in charge of the URA. Under the direction of two other leaders, Robert Lavelle and Frankie Pace, the activists formed a group called the Citizens Committee for Hill District Renewal and demanded that the city put money into improvement rather than destruction. As an emblem of their defiance, they erected a huge billboard at the northern edge of what was once the Lower Hill, at the corner of Centre Avenue and Crawford Street. "Attention: City Hall and URA," the billboard read. "No redevelopment beyond this point."

In early 1968, the *Courier* published a three-part series called "The

Black Mood in Pittsburgh" that reflected the militant spirit that was sweeping the country. Written by Carl Morris, a young city editor, the manifesto
noted that Pittsburgh had yet to experience the racial riots that had broken out in cities such as Los Angeles and Baltimore, but warned that
violence might be coming. Morris revealed that local militants planned a
"Burn Day" for sometime in May. They intended to march downtown to
serve notice that they would no longer be bound by the nonviolent strategy
of Martin Luther King Jr., who a year earlier had visited Pittsburgh and de-
fended that philosophy in a speech at the Pitt Student Union. But before
"Burn Day" could take place, news arrived on the night of April 4 that Dr.
King had fallen to an assassin's bullet in Memphis.

As darkness descended, residents of the Hill poured into the streets to
vent their grief and anger over King's murder. In the melee, a band of van-
dals broke into a meat market on Centre Avenue. Soon hundreds of looters
were roaming the streets, breaking into liquor stores to steal whiskey and
beer and setting fire to drugstores and supermarkets. Most of the targets
were owned by whites, but black businesses weren't immune: the city's
most prominent Negro realtor, Robert Lavelle, received a phone call warning that a building he had just constructed on the Hill might be firebombed.

Over the next two days, the rioting spread east to the neighborhoods
of Oakland and Homewood; south to Hazelwood; and across the river to
Manchester on the North Side. By the weekend, Mayor Joseph Barr had
issued a dusk-to-dawn curfew and the state's new Republican governor,
Raymond Shafer, had dispatched more than 4,000 National Guardsmen
and 350 state troopers to reinforce Pittsburgh's 1,400 city policemen.
Reverend LeRoy Patrick, a Presbyterian pastor in Homewood, walked out
of his church and saw bayonet-wielding troops in combat gear lining the
streets and military helicopters circling overhead. "I could hardly believe
this in Pittsburgh," he recalled.

In the end, the toll of the Holy Week Uprising, as the violence that
erupted in the aftermath of the King assassination came to be known, was
not as severe in Pittsburgh as it was in Washington, D.C., Baltimore, Chicago, or Kansas City. The hilly layout of the city and the work of clergymen

and civil rights leaders behind the scenes kept the looting from spreading to the downtown business district or affluent white neighborhoods such as Squirrel Hill and Shadyside. Still, over five days of unrest police made 1,300 arrests, firefighters combated more than 500 fires, and $620,000 worth of property was destroyed. When the smoke cleared, much of the Middle Hill was a burned-out shell, and all talk of rescuing it, either by renewal or by renovation, abruptly ended.

After the riots of 1968, still more blacks departed from the Hill to the nearby neighborhoods of Homewood, East Liberty, Manchester, and Beltzhoover. As they moved in, whites in those previously mixed enclaves steadily moved out, many seeking the peace and safety of the suburbs. Twenty years after August Wilson had grown up above Bella Siger's market on Bedford Avenue, Pittsburgh was no longer the jumble of ethnically mixed neighborhoods it had once been but an increasingly stark patchwork of white and black. And by 1971, even Robert Pease, the ever-upbeat head of the URA, had come to see that it had all started with the scheme to tear down the Lower Hill. "The Lower Hill project removed 1,000 units which were occupied by black people, and there was not in the city of Pittsburgh any additional new units earmarked for those people," Pease admitted to a *Post-Gazette* reporter. "So it caused a tightening of segregation in black neighborhoods and to that extent the renewal program contributed to segregation."

Then the engineer shrugged it off. "We have to learn by doing," he said.

WHEN FREDDY KITTEL MOVED to Crawford Street in 1965 and changed his name to August Wilson, he purchased an aged secondhand phonograph to keep in his boardinghouse room. Up Centre Avenue, there was a thrift shop run by the St. Vincent de Paul charity where he could buy used 78 rpm records for 5 cents apiece. He snapped up stacks at a time, whatever happened to be there, mostly old pop tunes like "(How Much Is) That Doggie in the Window?" by Patti Page. One day, he was sorting through his latest purchase and found a 78 whose faded title was covered with a yellowed, typed label that read: "Bessie Smith: Nobody in Town Can Bake a Sweet Jelly Roll Like Mine."

Wilson put on the record, and a piercing, plaintive voice filled the room:

> In a bakery shop today, I heard Miss Mandy Jenkins say
> She had the best cakes you see, and they were as fresh as fresh can be
> And as the people passed by, you would hear Miss Mandy cry . . .

Wilson listened to the end and immediately wanted to hear the song again. So he replayed it, and replayed it, and replayed it until he had played the record twenty-two times in a row. Each time, he heard something new in Miss Mandy's shop window call, so simple and yet so full of pride, perseverance, and sexual longing:

> Nobody in town can bake a sweet jellyroll like mine, like mine
> No other one in town can bake a sweet jellyroll so fine, so fine
> It's worth lots of dough, the boys tell me so
> It's fresh every day, you'll hear 'em all say
> Don't be a dunce, just try it once. You'll be right in line . . .

August Wilson had discovered the blues, and he was hooked. He started learning the names of the great blues singers and composers— Bessie Smith, Ma Rainey, W. C. Handy, Lead Belly—and looked for their records at the St. Vincent de Paul store. He had never studied music or played an instrument, so he knew nothing of the structure of the blues, of its major-to-minor chord progressions and three- and four-line stanzas. All he knew was that the music moved him in a spiritual way, and made him feel that he knew the characters in the songs, that he understood their history and felt their joy and pain.

Wilson knew little of the blues in part because it had never really been black Pittsburgh's music. In the 1920s and 1930s, that music had been the blend of ragtime and classical influences that inspired Earl Hines and Lois Deppe. Before World War II, it had been the swing music that

Billy Strayhorn absorbed in the dance halls of the Hill and raised to new heights of sophistication in his collaboration with Duke Ellington. After the war, it had been the bebop sound that Billy Eckstine brought to town with his sidemen Dizzy Gillespie and Charlie Parker; the elegant crooning of Eckstine and Nat King Cole, a frequent visitor; and the virtuoso piano stylings of Pittsburgh natives Mary Lou Williams, Ahmad Jamal, and Erroll Garner.

Now, in the mid-1960s, it was more likely to be the "soul-jazz" heard every night at the Hurricane Club on the Hill, the best known of the "chitlin' circuit" spots where Jimmy Scott, Shirley Scott, and Brother Jack McDuff made the Hammond B-3 organ swing. Run by Birdie Dunlap, a local legend whose great-grandfather was Lewis Woodson, the minister and Underground Railroad abolitionist, the Hurricane Club had also helped launch the career of the latest musical prodigy to come out of Pittsburgh, guitarist George Benson, who in his early twenties had already recorded several records with organist Jack McDuff.

Yet to August Wilson's ear, there was something about the blues that captured the world he saw around him on the Middle Hill. When he first moved into the rooming house on Crawford Street, he viewed his fellow boarders simply as down-on-their-luck artists, hustlers, and junkies. Once he heard Bessie Smith, however, he started to realize that each had a story, a cry that you could hear if you paid close enough attention.

For these people, the glory days of the Hill District were a distant memory. Downtown was no longer at the bottom of Wylie Avenue. It was a distant planet of skyscrapers on the other side of a parking lot moonscape, with a Civic Arena that looked like a spaceship in the middle of it. To the north, Sugartop, where the high yellow elite lived, seemed a universe away, now that the Loendi Club and the Crystal Barber Shop and the other venues where the black castes once mingled were gone. So, too, was the Penn Incline, the rickety funicular railway that had connected the Hill with the Strip District to the north. The city had ripped the funicular down in 1953 and never made good on promises to build a new one—because, rumor had it, there were plans to develop the Strip into a shopping district and downtown business interests didn't want Negroes there.

By the mid-1960s, even black sports heroes seemed distant to the folks who lived on the Hill. Once Joe Louis trained at the YMCA on Centre Avenue and dined at the Crawford Grill. Satchel Paige and Josh Gibson played for the Pittsburgh Crawfords at Greenlee Field on Bedford Avenue. Two decades after Wendell Smith and *The Pittsburgh Courier* helped Jackie Robinson break pro baseball's color barrier, some of the best players on the Pirates were black: outfielders Roberto Clemente and Willie Stargell, first baseman Donn Clendenon, and pitchers Bob Veale and Al McBean. But they belonged to white Pittsburgh now. They played at Forbes Field in Oakland, where ticket and concession prices made going to a ballgame more of a rare treat than a weekly ritual. Hill residents had little interest in the city's latest sports rage: the arrival of a new National Hockey League franchise called the Penguins, who were to make their home at the Civic Center. Nor did they have much use for the Steelers, a virtually all-white pro football team that hadn't won a championship in more than thirty years and was about to move to an expensive new stadium, named after Pittsburgh's three rivers, on the North Side.

The Pittsburgh Courier had gone into steep decline, and was no longer the source of unifying pride, debate, and gossip that it had long been. Ever since the bus boycott in Montgomery, white newspapers had started to cover the civil rights movement and to hire away many of the best reporters and editors from the Negro press. The *Courier*'s national readership had plummeted, and Jesse Vann had struggled to manage its finances after Ira Lewis's death. Searching for a new business partner, she sold a controlling interest to S. B. Fuller, a conservative black businessman from Chicago who had built the largest Negro cosmetics company in the country. Fuller swooped into town just as an upstart local newspaper, the *Urban Times-Record*, was making inroads covering the fight over urban renewal in Homewood. Fuller persuaded Mrs. Vann to adopt a new strategy that they unveiled at a press conference downtown and on the *Courier*'s front page. Instead of carrying on as a "Negro protest organ," the paper would focus on local issues, seeking to appeal to black and white readers alike by moving "its editorial policy in the mainstream of Pittsburgh's community life."

The new strategy was an utter failure. By 1966, the *Courier* had gone bankrupt. Hill residents watched as a "For Sale" sign was posted on the window of its Centre Avenue headquarters and desks, chairs, and type-writers were loaded onto a U-Haul truck to be sold to pay a small fortune in delinquent taxes. Robert L. Vann's pride and joy, his Hoe & Co printing press, was ordered to be put up for auction. In a turn of fate that would have appalled Vann and Ira Lewis, the paper was sold to John Sengstacke, the publisher of their longtime nemesis, *The Chicago Defender*. Sengstacke relaunched the paper as *"The New Pittsburgh Courier,"* with a modest footprint that ensured that it would never again match the *Defender* in readership or influence.

Soon the men who had led the *Courier* through the postwar years were all gone. P.L. Prattis retired, bitter over being called an Uncle Tom because he had come out against violence as a civil rights strategy in his last years as editor. Bill Nunn stepped down as managing editor and died just six years later, shortly after Maybelle, his high school sweetheart and wife of more than half a century. Their son, Bill Nunn Jr., who had risen to sports editor and managing editor, took a job as a scout for the Pittsburgh Steelers, encouraging the team to recruit from black colleges for the first time in its history and helping to build the dynasty that would win four Super Bowls from 1975 to 1980. Mrs. Vann retired to devote herself to charity work. On a late spring day in 1967, she suffered a stroke on her way to a club meeting. She died two days later, a loss that brought an out-pouring of tributes from across the country for the quiet orphan from Gettysburg who had made a journey worthy of *This Is Your Life*, the popular television show that had once featured Mrs. Vann as a guest.

No one August Wilson came into contact with on the Hill in the late 1960s would ever have qualified for that distinction. They were the folks that the city's declining manufacturing economy and the downtown "Renaissance" had left behind: the steel and coal workers who had lost their jobs; the cooks and waiters who worked for minimum wage and tips; the garbagemen and janitors who clung to lowly rungs on the city payroll; the hustlers and pushers who had turned to selling pyramid scheme products and street drugs to get by. But the blues made Wilson yearn to hear their stories, and he went about finding places where he could eavesdrop on them.

Wilson sat for hours in a booth at Eddie's Restaurant, nursing cups of coffee and scribbling down overheard conversations on napkins. He hung out at Pat's Place, a cigar store with a billiard table in the back where pensioners passed their days and where August came to be known as "Youngblood." Days after day, he ate lunch at a diner called Pan Fried Fish so that he could listen in on the conversation of gypsy car drivers who worked out of storefront "jitney station" next door—a collection of young hustlers and loquacious retirees who spent as much time telling tall tales and ribbing one another over games of checkers as they did answering the phone on the station wall that rang with calls for cheap rides around town.

To pay the rent, Wilson took odd jobs, usually as a cook in diners and hotel kitchens around town. The rest of the time, he pursued his dream of becoming a poet. He joined a community of struggling black artists who embraced the politics and aesthetics of the Black Power movement. Meeting in coffee shops and bars, they passed around copies of *The Autobiography of Malcolm X*. They quoted lines from LeRoi Jones, the radical black poet, playwright, and activist who would change his name to Amiri Baraka. They founded a journal of culture and politics called *Connections*, and Wilson served as poetry editor. While the others grew bushy Afros and dressed in dashikis, Wilson opted for a professorial look that he copied from his idol Dylan Thomas, whose poems he liked to recite in a Welsh accent. He scoured thrift shops for hand-me-down tweed jackets, knit ties, and porter's caps. After four years of rejection letters, he finally got a poem entitled "Muhammad Ali" published in *Negro Digest*. "Muhammad Ali is a lion," it began. "He is a lion that breaks the back of wind . . ."

Although Wilson had previously been interested in theater, he dipped his toe into that new art form. In 1968 he helped a friend named Rob

Penny form a troupe they called the "Black Horizon Theater." In schools and churches around town, they staged plays by Amiri Baraka, plays they found in issues of the *Tulane Drama Review*, and original plays that Penny wrote himself, dozens in all. Wilson tried his own hand at playwriting but struggled with creating dialogue, so he settled for directing instead.

By the early 1970s, Wilson had tired of the complications of street theater: the rehearsing after work; the worrying about whether unpaid actors would show up; the hawking of tickets at the last minute. He returned to writing poetry, some of it inspired by his troubled marriage. In 1970 he had wed a dark-skinned Pittsburgh woman named Brenda Burton and she had given birth to a girl they named Sakina Ansari, but they divorced after three years. Later Wilson would attribute the breakup to religious differences—Brenda had joined the Nation of Islam—but his sister Linda Jean offered another explanation. "In a nutshell, she thought his writing was a waste of time, that he wouldn't amount to anything," Linda Jean recalled of Burton.

Five years after his marriage dissolved, Wilson was still scraping by writing poetry in Pittsburgh when he was offered an unexpected change of scenery. A friend from the Hill named Claude Purdy had moved to St. Paul, Minnesota, and co-founded a small drama company. Purdy was looking for new works to stage, and he asked Wilson to fashion a satirical musical from some poems he had written about a fanciful Negro cowboy called "Black Bart." Wilson thought the idea was "ridiculous," he recalled, but he agreed to write a script he titled "Black Bart and the Sacred Hills." While the musical was in rehearsal, Purdy asked Wilson to help with revisions and sent him a plane ticket to St. Paul. Soon after Wilson arrived in Minnesota, Purdy's wife introduced him to her best friend, Judy Oliver, a white social worker with whom he fell in love and would later marry.

Even though the black community was much smaller in St. Paul than in Pittsburgh, Wilson liked the city's leafy calm and he decided to stay for a while. The decision became permanent when he found a job that allowed him to support himself as a writer. The Science Museum of Minnesota hired Wilson to write one-act plays for visiting schoolchildren that dramatized museum exhibits and explained the contributions of scientific pioneers such as Charles Darwin and anthropologist Margaret Mead.

Wilson began trying to write plays for himself again, and he made a stirring discovery. Back in Pittsburgh, he had seen a production of the South African play *Sizwe Banzi Is Dead*, which impressed him with its powerful yet utterly natural dialogue. In his attempts at playwriting until then, Wilson had tried to force words into the mouths of his actors. His friend Rob Penny had told him that was a mistake. "How do you make characters talk?" Wilson asked. "You don't," Penny responded. "You listen to them."

When Wilson started to listen in St. Paul, he began to hear the voices of the men and women he had overheard in the diners, rooming houses, and pool halls of Pittsburgh. Suddenly words began to pour out of him. Scribbling in notebooks and on napkins at Arthur Treacher's Fish & Chips, one of his new haunts, he took just ten days to write a one-act play called *Jitney* that consisted almost entirely of the banter he had heard from the gypsy cab drivers on the Hill. As soon as that play was finished, the voices of Southern migrants who had arrived in Pittsburgh in the 1940s began to speak to him, and he wrote a play about them called *Fullerton Street*. Encouraged by Penny, Wilson submitted both plays to the National Playwrights Conference, a prestigious summer theater workshop in Connecticut, but both times rejection letters came back in the mail.

How could he possibly improve on those plays? Wilson wondered. (After his first application was turned down, he had sent it again, thinking the rejection was a mistake.) But he was determined not to give up. He quit the science museum and took a job as a lunch cook at a Catholic charity, earning next to nothing but freeing up his afternoons to write. He went back to a story idea he had begun to toy with in Pittsburgh, about a studio session in the 1920s involving Ma Rainey, one of the first blues singers to have her voice committed to records. As Wilson wrote, the story grew into a tale about the conflicts between Ma's sidemen: Levee, a brash trumpeter who is trying to ingratiate himself with the record company; and Cutler and Toledo, a trombonist and piano player who are convinced that Negroes would always be kept down in the white-run music business.

This time, when Wilson submitted the play he called *Ma Rainey's Black Bottom* to the Playwrights Conference, he was accepted.

When Wilson arrived in Waterford, Connecticut, in July 1982, he was welcomed by one of the most revered black theater directors in America. Born in Canada and raised in Detroit, Lloyd Richards had abandoned law studies for a theater degree and gone on to direct the original Broadway production of *A Raisin in the Sun*. By the early 1980s, he was serving as dean of the Yale School of Drama and director of the summer Playwrights Conference. When Richards first read *Ma Rainey*, he was struck instantly by its original voice, by how accurately and beautifully it captured the kind of language he remembered from the Detroit barbershops of his youth. Richards was also impressed with how, using the blues as a metaphor, the play celebrated the difference between black culture and white culture. ("White folks don't understand the blues," Ma explains to the trumpeter Levee. "They hear it come out but they don't know how it got there. They don't understand that's life's way of talking. You don't sing to feel better. You sing because that's a way of understanding life.")

Richards believed that the play had the potential to go all the way to the New York stage, and he took the thirty-seven-year-old fledgling playwright and his fifty-three-page script firmly in hand. He picked actors for the workshop readings and directed them personally. He advised Wilson on how to tighten the play and build toward its bloody climax, when the trumpeter Levee stabs the trombonist Cutler and dooms himself to a prison sentence instead of a life of fame and fortune. For his part, Wilson was grateful to have found a mentor who could help him perfect his plays and serve as a kind of professional father figure. He took to calling Richards "Pop."

Relationships between fathers and sons were thus very much on Wilson's mind as he returned to St. Paul in the fall of 1982. So, too, was a workshop criticism of *Ma Rainey* that had stung him: that it was too much of an ensemble play, and that he needed to learn how to write bigger roles. Determined to show that he could do just that, Wilson began a new play that revolved around a central character who was an amalgam of two surrogate fathers from his own youth: his neighbor Charley Burley, the sanitation worker who had once been a boxing contender and Homestead Grays tryout; and his former stepfather and ex-con David Bedford.

The character, named Troy Maxson, is a former Negro League star who missed his shot at the pro leagues because he was serving time. Relegated to the life of a garbageman, Troy finds himself taking out his bitterness on his long-suffering wife, Rose, and on his son, Cory, who both fears and seeks to emulate his father. Wilson called the play *Fences*. He also situated it in the 1950s, as part of a new wildly ambitious goal he had set for himself: having already produced three works set in three different decades—*Jitney*, *Fullerton Street*, and *Ma Rainey*—he had resolved to write a collection of ten plays, one for every decade of the twentieth century.

In March 1983, around the time Wilson was putting his first draft of *Fences* in the mail to Connecticut, he lost his mother, Daisy, to lung cancer. They had long since reconciled, and he returned to Pittsburgh to give the maid who went on welfare to care for her children a proper burial alongside Gilded Era millionaires such as Henry J. Heinz in Greenwood Cemetery just outside Pittsburgh. Daisy Wilson would not live to witness the extraordinary success that her son was about to achieve, all made possible by the reverence she had taught him for the power of reading and writing.

That summer, Lloyd Richards invited Wilson back to the Playwrights Conference and staged a reading of *Fences*. The following year, he directed *Ma Rainey's Black Bottom* at the Yale Repertory Theatre in New Haven. From there *Ma* went to an off-Broadway theater in New York City, where it ran for 285 performances and won the coveted New York Drama Critics' Circle Award. The year after that, Richards brought *Fences* to Yale, fine-tuning it for a run on Broadway. In 1987 the play opened at the 47th Street Theatre, ran for more than two years, won the Tony Award for Best Play, and earned Wilson the Pulitzer Prize for Drama.

But Wilson had no time to celebrate. As one play after another went into production, he continued to work feverishly toward his goal of a "Century cycle." And as fate would have it, the inspiration for his next two plays came from another pioneering black artist who had spent his forma-tive years in Pittsburgh, the painter Romare Bearden.

Another North Carolina native, born in the Charlotte area, Bearden had moved to Pittsburgh as a youth and graduated from Peabody High School in the late 1920s. (Billy Eckstine was several years behind Bearden at Peabody, and later he recorded a song called "Seabreeze" written by the painter, who dabbled in jazz composition.) Bearden attended Lincoln University, outside Philadelphia, then moved to New York, where he fin-ished college at NYU and immersed himself in the downtown art scene. In the 1940s, after serving in World War II and living in Paris, he began to develop his signature technique and themes: using paint, paper, foil, fragments of photographs, and other materials, he constructed quirky but richly evocative collages conjuring up scenes of black life. In the late 1970s, after Wilson moved to St. Paul, his friend Claude Purdy intro-duced him to a book of Bearden's work called *The Prevalence of Ritual*. As he flipped through its pages, August recalled, he immediately recognized an "artistic mentor"—a visionary who had created a visual experience that he hoped to match in writing, capturing black culture in all its unique-ness, variety, celebration, and sorrow.

A Bearden collage entitled *Mill Hand's Lunch Bucket* particularly fas-cinated Wilson. It portrays a dejected-looking man in a crumpled hat, slumped at the table of a boardinghouse. Who was this man and what was his story? Wilson wondered. So he began writing a story imagining the answer. It became his 1910s play—and personal favorite—*Joe Turner's Come and Gone*, named after an old blues song about a Tennessee chain gang boss. The story revolves around Herald Loomis, a Southern preacher abducted and forced into hard labor for seven years. By the time Loomis is freed, his wife, Martha, has left him, and he travels north to Pittsburgh to find her. At a boardinghouse on the Hill, he meets Bynum, an elderly "conjure man" who tells him to stop looking elsewhere for salvation and to find his own "song." When Loomis finally locates Martha, she has em-braced a new faith and tries to convert him. Instead, Loomis pulls a knife and lashes his chest in a bloody act of self-resurrection. "I don't need anyone to bleed for me! I can bleed for myself!" he cries, before leaving the stage alone, shouting, "Herald Loomis, you shining! You shining like new money!"

The second Bearden collage that caught Wilson's attention, called *The Piano Lesson*, depicts a black girl playing an upright piano while a woman, perhaps her mother, looks on. It became the spark for Wilson's next play, set in the 1930s, about a family dispute over what to do with an heirloom piano. Boy Willie, a Southern sharecropper, comes to Pittsburgh to sell the piano so that he can buy land back home. But his sister Berniece refuses to part with the piano because it embodies so much family history: a slave owner named Sutter had sold their ancestors to pay for it, and their father had been shot stealing the piano back. "Mama Ola polished this piano with her tears for seventeen years," Berniece reminds her brother. "For seventeen years she rubbed on it until her hands bled. Then she rubbed the blood in, mixed it up with the rest of the blood on it. . . . You always talking about your daddy but you ain't never stopped to look at what his foolishness cost your mamma." Finally, just as Willy Boy is about to take the piano away, Berniece sits down at the keyboard and plays it for the first time in years, shouting out the names of her ancestors to cast out the ghost of Sutter from her house and convincing her brother to leave empty-handed.

As first *Joe Turner's Come and Gone* and then *The Piano Lesson* followed *Fences* to Broadway, critics began to dwell not just on the merits of the individual plays but on the overall scope of Wilson's achievement. *Joe Turner* won him a third Drama Critics' Award. *The Piano Lesson* won a Tony Award and a Pulitzer Prize, the second for Wilson in four years. A television production of the play aired on CBS's *Hallmark Hall of Fame*, introducing millions of non-theater-goers to Wilson's work for the first time. By now, Wilson's body of work was being compared to that of America's greatest playwrights, to Eugene O'Neill, Tennessee Williams, and Arthur Miller. His portrait of the Hill District was on its way to being likened to the most memorable depictions of a specific place and culture in all of English literature—to William Faulkner's Mississippi backwater of Yoknapatawpha County and to Thomas Hardy's Wessex countryside in southern England. With the arrival of two more plays—*Two Trains Running*, set in the 1960s, and *Seven Guitars*, set in the 1940s—Wilson's Pittsburgh was being etched in the national imagination as the definitive depiction of black American life in the twentieth century.

Yet how close to reality was it? For those familiar with Pittsburgh, there were numerous references to real places: Wylie Avenue, Logan Street, Lutz's Meat Market, Greenwood Cemetery. There were also clearly identifiable eras in the background of Wilson's plays. *Fences* harked back to the glory days of Negro League baseball, when the Pittsburgh Crawfords and the Homestead Grays reigned. *The Piano Lesson* recalled the day when pianos enjoyed a place of pride in the homes of Pittsburgh strivers. *Joe Turner's Come and Gone* captured the atmosphere of the pre–World War I boardinghouses where Southern migrants roomed. *Seven Guitars* conveyed the disillusionment of black men after World War II. *Two Trains Running* evoked the era of urban renewal and Black Power, with its story of an older restaurant owner worrying that his business will be torn down, a young militant planning to attend a street protest, and a long-suffering waitress enduring the casual sexism of both generations.

Much of black Pittsburgh's legacy, however, was missing from Wilson's work. There was little acknowledgment of the migrants who came to the city with high degrees of literacy and cultural sophistication, or the entrepreneurs who built barbershop chains, funeral parlors, and a thriving national newspaper that employed hundreds of Negroes. (One of the few businessmen with a major part in a Wilson play, the undertaker West in *Two Trains Running*, is a one-dimensional villain.) Apart from a fleeting reference to a raffle at the Loendi Club in *Seven Guitars*, there were few nods to the life of the Hill's black social elite, or the high-rolling racketeers like Gus Greenlee and Woogie Harris who were part of it. Other than the blues musicians who appeared in many of Wilson's plays, there was no sense of the fertile creative culture, fed by strong arts programs in the city's high schools, that produced Earl Hines, Billy Strayhorn, Erroll Garner, and Wilson's own hero, Romare Bearden. There was hardly a glimpse of Wilson's own cohort, struggling black poets and painters living a black American version of *La Bohème*.

To hear Wilson discuss his work, those omissions were quite deliberate. In dozens of interviews he gave once he became famous, he spoke eloquently of his desire to highlight the beauty and profundity of everyday black speech and to celebrate the heroism of the invisible black working class. But Wilson was just as outspoken in his belief, forged at the height of black nationalism, that blacks could rise into the middle class or beyond only by shedding their true racial and cultural identity. "America offers blacks a contract that says, 'If you leave all that African stuff over there and adopt the values of the dominant culture, you can participate,'" he told literary scholar Bonnie Lyons. "The ones who accept go on to become part of the growing black middle class and in some areas even acquire some power and participation in society, but when they finally arrive where they arrive, they are no longer the same people. They are clothed in different manners and ways of life, different thoughts and ideas. They've acculturated and adopted white values."

In Wilson's worldview, to be financially successful or socially elite was almost by definition to no longer be authentically black, since the essence of blackness was struggle. In a word, it was the blues. So what didn't fit his definition of blackness he ignored, even as he sought to encompass a century's worth of black experience in ten plays. In that sense, Wilson's own contribution to black Pittsburgh's heritage was to make it at once larger and smaller than it had been before him, to shrink the legacy even as he was enshrining it.

Yet while Wilson may have depicted only one dimension of black Pittsburgh's history, he managed to capture its larger spirit in two essential ways. One was his sheer ambition—the audacity to dream that he could capture a century's worth of experience in plays about life on the Hill. It was the sort of drive that, each in their own way, Cap Posey, Robert L. Vann, Gus Greenlee, Cum Posey, Billy Strayhorn, Lena Horne, Bill Nunn, P.L. Prattis, Frank Bolden, Billy Eckstine, Erroll Garner, Wendell Smith, Edna Chappell, and Evelyn Cunningham all possessed, and would have saluted in Wilson. So, too, would have Andrew Carnegie, Pittsburgh's ultimate example of white ambition; and as far as August Wilson was concerned, the respect was mutual. In 1999, Wilson made a special trip to Pittsburgh to speak at a hundredth-anniversary ceremony for the Carnegie Library in Oakland, the one that had put the world at his fingertips as a youth. "Labor historians do not speak well of Andrew Carnegie," Wilson told the crowd. "Among other things, they call him a scoundrel. But I can say nothing bad about a man who made it possible to sit in his library and read the labor historians' reports. Andrew Carnegie will forever be for me that man who made it possible for me to stand here today."

The second insight that Wilson absorbed in Pittsburgh and celebrated throughout his work was the power of community. Whether in the ordinary life of rooming houses and jitney stations, or in the grandest accomplishments of the Hill District in its heyday, the glory of Pittsburgh was always as much communal as individual, explained as much by the dynamics of fellowship and competition as by lonely suffering or genius. It was a power, Wilson believed, that black people understood far better than white people. "The basic difference in worldview between blacks and whites," he once said, "can be expressed as follows: Western culture sees man as being *apart from* the world, and African culture sees him as *a part of* the world." It was also why Wilson preferred his stories of ensembles to his most famous work, *Fences*, with its spotlight on the tragic protagonist Troy Maxson. ("I want to say here for the record, of the plays that I have written it is my *least* favorite play," Wilson said, with a laugh that conveyed that he knew that saying so might upset some of his fans. "It's *not* my signature play.")

To quibble with Wilson's contradictions—the shy biracial artist who romanticized the earthiness of the black working classes; the preacher of "Africanness" who had never traveled to Africa and lived in Minnesota; the advocate for all-black theaters who was the toast of Yale and Broadway—was also to miss the essence of his achievement. It was no accident that the first work that Wilson checked out of the Carnegie Library as a teenager was *The Collected Poems of Paul Laurence Dunbar*, and that it took him almost thirty years to return the book, long after he had left Pittsburgh and become an acclaimed playwright. For August Wilson was never a historian, or even a realistic dramatist, so much as a poet of the black experience.

Wilson understood that about himself. He freely admitted that he never did historical research and knew relatively little of other playwrights. But he spoke frequently of his debt to Aristotle's *Poetics* and what he saw as its message that plays didn't need "plot points" if they had strong enough characters. His gift was not for compelling story lines but for memorable characters defined by their indelible language. He took the way ordinary black people spoke, the kind of banter that he scribbled on napkins in the haunts on the Hill, and rendered it sublime. What his plays lacked in accuracy or action they made up for in powerful metaphors for the black experience: the music that his characters sang and played to endure suffering; the physical scars they bore, or inflicted upon themselves; and the prison terms they served, robbing them of time and opportunity just as the age of slavery had robbed an entire race.

Throughout the 1990s, Wilson continued to work day and night, as though he, too, was making up for lost time. He divorced Judy Oliver and moved to Seattle, Washington, with a third wife, Constanza Romero, a costume designer he had met at Yale and with whom he would have another daughter, named Azula. With a new century dawning, he was determined to finish his ten-play project. For his 1970s play, he expanded his early one-act play *Jitney* to two acts. For the 1980s, he wrote *King Hedley II*, the story of an ex-con whose scheme to open a video store is undone in part by the forces of Reaganomics. Finally, Wilson placed bookends on the cycle. He went back to the turn of the century in *Gem of the Ocean*, a play that revolves around the character of Aunt Ester, a boardinghouse oracle, said to be almost three hundred years old, who represents a spiritual link to Africa and the slave ships of the Middle Passage. Then in *Radio Golf*, set in the 1990s, Wilson brings Aunt Ester's story full circle, as Hill politicians and militants fight over the fate of the house that Ester left behind, now targeted to become the latest casualty of urban renewal.

While Wilson was working on *Radio Golf* in the early months of 2005, he began to experience nagging stomach pains. His wife, Constanza, took him to a doctor, who informed August that he had liver cancer. It was so advanced, the doctor said, that he only had a matter of months to live. Keeping the diagnosis secret from all but a few intimates, Wilson moved into a hotel with Constanza so that no one would know where to find him. He worked around-the-clock with his personal assistant, Todd Kreidler, to finish the play. Only in late August, after *Radio Golf* had premiered at Yale and then moved to a theater in Los Angeles, did Wilson start phoning old friends to tell them the bad news. One of the first was Dwight Andrews, a musician and United Church of Christ pastor who had taught at Yale and served as the musical director for Wilson's early plays. As they discussed plans for August's funeral, Constanza had suggested that Andrews preside over the service, and her husband had pronounced the idea "perfect."

"Man, I'm sick," Wilson told Andrews. "I only have a few months to live. I want you to put me down."

Wilson's instructions were clear: he wanted to be buried in Pittsburgh. When the end came in October, hundreds of America's most accomplished black actors, directors, and writers traveled there to join his family for the ceremony. It took place in Oakland, just east of the Hill, at the Soldiers and Sailors Memorial Hall, the largest military museum in the country, built during the Gilded Age to honor veterans of the Civil War. Charles Dutton, the actor who had risen to fame playing Levee in *Ma Rainey* and Willy Boy in *The Piano Lesson*, read a passage from *Fences*. "Death ain't nothing but a fastball on the inside corner," Dutton proclaimed, in the voice of Troy Maxson. "That's all death is to me." Phylicia Rashad transformed herself into Aunt Ester, the role from *Gem of the Ocean* for which she had earned a Tony Award nomination. Wilson's boyhood friend Sam Howze, who as an adult had changed his name to Sala Udin and become an activist and city councilman in Pittsburgh, shared memories of their early years and young adulthood hanging out in diners on the Hill, talking for hours over endless cups of coffee. "Those days were the genesis of *Jitney* and *Jitney* was the genesis of the Pittsburgh Cycle," Udin explained to the crowd.

As the ceremony drew to a close, Udin heard the sound of a trumpet offstage. He recognized the tune of "Danny Boy," the poignant Irish ballad of farewell. As the slow, plaintive melody filled the cavernous memorial hall, Udin looked around to see people sobbing and pulling out handkerchiefs to mop their tears. Then Wynton Marsalis appeared onstage, blowing his rust-colored horn, and walked into the seats. Marsalis played the haunting last notes of "Danny Boy," then without skipping a beat tore into the first, joyous bars of "When the Saints Go Marching In."

Suddenly the four hundred mourners were on their feet. They sang along. They stomped the floor. They waved handkerchiefs in the air. With Marsalis leading the way, they formed a New Orleans–style procession and marched out onto the street. As pallbearers loaded Wilson's casket into a silver hearse, the mourners climbed into their cars. In a long, snaking phalanx, they followed the hearse to Greenwood Cemetery, ten miles to the east, where Wilson would be laid to rest not far from the gravesite of his beloved mother, Daisy. But rather than take the direct route, the hearse and the cars made one last trip through the streets of August Wilson's youth and his imagined theatrical universe: from Bedford Avenue, where he was born, to Crawford Street, where he first listened to Bessie Smith sing the blues.

A hard rain was falling, but as Udin and the other mourners looked out from their car windows they could see hundreds of Hill residents lining the streets, holding aloft homemade signs. "May All Your Fences Have Gates," read one, quoting the inscription with which Wilson liked to sign his plays. "August, You Have Blessed Our Lives with Stories and Images Like No Other," read another placard. Rain be damned, the famous actors and directors and musicians rolled down the windows to wave and shout greetings, and the residents waved and shouted back, and for one wet day in autumn the Hill District once again felt like the Crossroads of the World.

ACKNOWLEDGMENTS

ALTHOUGH MOST OF the people I write about in this book are no longer living, I am grateful for the help I received from surviving family members and colleagues. Lynell Nunn welcomed me into her home in the Hill District and talked to me about her grandfather, *Pittsburgh Courier* managing editor Bill Nunn Sr., in the basement den where her father, Bill Nunn Jr., also a *Courier* editor and later a scout for the Pittsburgh Steelers, kept three generations' worth of memorabilia. Patricia Prattis Jennings, the retired principal keyboardist for the Pittsburgh Symphony Orchestra, sat by the piano where she still practices and reminisced about her father, *Courier* executive editor P.L. Prattis. Rod Doss, the current publisher of *The New Pittsburgh Courier*, shared personal and institutional memories of former *Courier* publishers Robert L. Vann, Jesse Vann, and Ira Lewis. Charlene Foggie-Barnett, the director of research for the Teenie Harris Archive, told me vivid stories of being photographed by Harris as a child, as well as family tales of her father, Bishop Charles Foggie, for decades the leader of the city's AME Zion flock, and her mother, Madeline Sharpe, a friend and confidante to Lena Horne during Lena's turbulent late teens and early twenties in Pittsburgh.

I am indebted to Pittsburgh scholars and journalists who have been studying its history for far longer than I have. Professor Laurence Glasco of the University of Pittsburgh helped me to understand how the culture of black Pittsburgh was shaped by the origins of its Southern migrants. He also warned about the limitations of what he calls "the Narrative": the tendency of black history written since the civil rights movement to focus primarily on black struggle and white oppression, often at the expense of appreciating the scope of black achievement. Larry was also kind enough to read an early version of the manuscript for historical accuracy and nuance.

David Shribman, the Pulitzer Prize–winning journalist who since 2003 has served as executive editor of the *Pittsburgh-Post Gazette*, shared insights into his adopted city and caught numerous errors and typos in the unedited manuscript. Frank Proctor—perhaps the leading oral historian of black Pittsburgh since Frank Bolden's death—regaled me with stories of growing up on the Hill and attending Schenley High School. Eliza Smith Brown, editor of books on the city's development and architecture, made me appreciate the importance of Pittsburgh's topography and neighborhood culture. Maxwell King, another part-time historian who runs the Pittsburgh Foundation, put the story in the context of two "Pittsburgh Renaissances": the post–World War II experiment in urban renewal that destroyed much of the Hill District and had tragic ripple effects for the black community; and the city's current revival, which has lifted Pittsburgh out of its Rust Belt doldrums but has sadly yet to reach most of its black residents.

During my trips to Pittsburgh, I benefited from the guidance and hospitality of Darryl Ford Williams, executive producer of the PBS American Masters documentary on August Wilson; her husband, Joe Williams III, judge on the Allegheny Court of Common Pleas; Eric and Cecile Springer, stalwarts of the black business and civil rights establishment;

Linda Lane, former superintendent of the Pittsburgh school system; Julie Swiderski, director of Westinghouse Academy; Rick Wertheimer, former charter school principal and education reformer; David Grinnell, archivist at the University of Pittsburgh Library, who helped me sort through the papers of P.L. Prattis, Frank Bolden, and Erroll Garner; and Robert "Rock" Robinson, president of the Pittsburgh Duffers golf league and his fellow weekend warriors. I must also give a special shout-out to my cousin Leslie Ann Smedley, who let me stay at her lovely home, shared many delicious meals, and helped me to assemble missing pieces of family lore.

For their willingness to read early versions of the book and offer feedback, I thank Gail Lumet Buckley, Henry Louis Gates Jr., David Hajdu, and Nicholas Lemann. For the special interest they showed in this project, I am grateful to Pittsburgh natives Howard Fineman, Allan Dodds Frank, and Elliot Wolk, to the great civil rights reporter Hank Klibanoff, and to longtime comrades Henry and Celia McGee, Jonathan Alter, Renee Edelman, and Jason Wright. As always, Lynn Nesbit gave me candid and wise advice before, during, and after this undertaking. Alice Mayhew edited the book with her usual mix of intellectual empathy, organizational genius, and tough love on deadline. Jonathan Karp was generous in his support, and Richard Rhorer, Stuart Roberts, Lisa Healy, Fred Chase, and Jackie Seow provided invaluable assistance and good cheer in getting the book to the finish line. Rachel and Matthew Whitaker kindly took time from their busy lives to read galleys and offer perceptive thoughts. As always, their mother, Alexis Gelber, was my first reader, my most honest critic, and my most enthusiastic cheerleader.

My parents divorced when I was six years old and my father was absent from my life for a long time afterward. I would not have the memories that inspired this book had my mother, Jeanne Theis Whitaker, not continued to drive her two mixed race sons all the way from eastern Massachusetts to Pittsburgh every year so that we would not lose touch with our grandparents, aunts, uncles, and cousins. I am so glad that at ninety-one, she is still here to read this book—and to receive my thanks for making it possible.

NOTES

PREFACE

xiv   *they came north:* Laurence Glasco, "Double Burden: The Black Experience in Pittsburgh," in Samuel P. Hays, ed., *City at the Point: Essays on the Social History of Pittsburgh* (Pittsburgh: University of Pittsburgh Press, 1989), pp. 71–72; Ervin Dyer, "Revisiting the Great Migration," *Pittsburgh Post-Gazette*, Feb. 25, 2001, p. G1.

xiv   *Pittsburgh's black population:* "Historical Census Statistics on Population Totals by Race, 1790 to 1990, and by Hispanic Origin, 1970 to 1990, for Large Cities and Other Urban Places in the United States," U.S. Census Bureau, Feb. 2005.

1. THE BROWN BOMBER'S CORNERMEN

1   *Seventy thousand spectators:* Lewis A. Erenberg, *The Greatest Fight of Our Generation: Louis vs. Schmeling* (New York: Oxford University Press, 2006), pp. 134–42.

2   *Bill Nunn was the first of the three:* P.L. Prattis, unpublished "Autobiography," University of Pittsburgh Archives, Collection no. AIS.2007.01, p. "add 91."

3   *No one had a better nose:* Interview with Bill Nunn's granddaughter, Lynell Nunn; World War I draft registration card for William Goldwin Nunn and death

certificate for father Junius N. Nunn, ancestry.com; Ulish Carter, "Guiding Force Behind Courier Editorial Greatness," *New Pittsburgh Courier*, "100 Years of Influence" supplement, Nov. 17–23, 2010, p. 3.

4 *Vann also knew one of the men:* Andrew Buni, *Robert L. Vann of the Pittsburgh Courier* (Pittsburgh: University of Pittsburgh Press, 1974), p. 252.

4 *"Ches," as everyone called him:* Reports on Chester Washington and family in the 1920, 1930, and 1940 U.S. Federal Census, ancestry.com; "Leaves for School," *Pittsburgh Courier*, Sep. 20, 1924, p. 4.

4 *When Washington started looking into Louis's record:* Chester L. Washington and William G. Nunn, "The Life Story of Joe Louis," *Pittsburgh Courier*, March 9, 1935, p. 4, March 23, 1935, p. 14.

6 *Chappie Blackburn had done a lot of fighting in Pittsburgh:* Joe Louis, *My Life Story* (New York: Duell, Sloan & Pearce, 1947), pp. 46–47; "Joe Broke Two of 'Em Here," *Pittsburgh Courier*, Jan. 26, 1935, p. 4.

6 *During this time in Pittsburgh:* Louis, *My Life Story*, p. 47; "Predict Sellout for Joe Louis Fight at Duquesne Gardens," *Pittsburgh Courier*, Jan. 12, 1935, p. 1; "Wylie Avenue," *Pittsburgh Courier*, Jan. 12, 1935, p. 6.

7 *compare their man to Jack Johnson:* Erenberg, *Greatest Fight*, pp. 42–47.

7 *an exhaustive profile:* Chester L. Washington and William G. Nunn, "The Life Story of Joe Louis," *Pittsburgh Courier*, Feb. 9, 16, March 9, 23, 30, April 6, 20, 27, May 4, 18, 25, June 1, 22, 1935.

8 *his toughest opponent yet:* Louis, *My Life Story*, pp. 48–51; Nunn and Washington, "Life Story," *Pittsburgh Courier*, April 6, May 25, 1935.

8 *the Courier held its presses:* Buni, *Robert L. Vann*, p. 253.

8 *"JOE LOUIS BATTERS NATIE BROWN":* *Pittsburgh Courier*, April 6, 1935, p. 6.

9 *Ches Washington was already inside:* Nunn and Washington, "Life Story," *Pittsburgh Courier*, April 6, 1936, p. 14.

9 *officials demanded to know:* Buni, *Robert L. Vann*, p. 252.

9 *"Joe Louis Flattens 245-Pound Chicago Giant":* *Pittsburgh Courier*, June 8, 1935, p. 16.

10 *Ches agreed to answer Joe's mail:* "Ches Sez," *Pittsburgh Courier*, Oct. 30, 1937, p. 16.

10 *"JOE LOUIS WINS!":* *Pittsburgh Courier*, June 29, 1935, p. 1.

10 *"Bill Nunn Writes His Story 10,000 Feet in the Air":* *Pittsburgh Courier*, June 29, 1935, p. 1.

11 *a vindication of the Great Migration:* "Ches Sez," *Pittsburgh Courier*, Feb. 15, 1936, p. 15.

12 *Washington immediately got Joe on the phone:* "Ches Sez," *Pittsburgh Courier*, April 4, 1936, p. 15.

12 *McClelland received a worrisome telegram:* "Ches Sez," *Pittsburgh Courier*, April 18, 1936, p. 15.

13   *"JOE IN TIP TOP CONDITION—CHES"*: "Ches Sez," *Pittsburgh Courier*,
      June 13, 1936, p. 17.

13   *why it would be "Louis Before the Fifth"*: Ibid.

13   *Washington liked to compare Joe to a panther*: "Ches Sez," *Pittsburgh Courier*,
      June 20, 1936, p. 15.

14   *poet Langston Hughes recalled*: Joseph McLaren, ed., *The Collected Works of
      Langston Hughes*, vol. 14 (Columbia: University of Missouri Press, 2003), pp.
      307, 308.

14   *his blood-streaked head in his hands*: "Ches Sez," *Pittsburgh Courier*, Oct. 30,
      1937, p. 16.

14   *Washington faulted Louis*: "Ches Sez," *Pittsburgh Courier*, June 27, 1936, p.
      16.

14   *Bill Nunn was even tougher*: "Courier City Editor Writes a Letter to Joe," *Pitts-
      burgh Courier*, June 27, 1936, p. 15.

15   *Washington attributed the turn of events*: "Ches Sez," *Pittsburgh Courier*, Feb. 13,
      1937, p. 19.

15   *Braddock knew that he could expect a much fatter gate*: Jeremy Schaap, *Cinder-
      ella Man: James J. Braddock, Max Baer, and the Greatest Upset in Boxing History*
      (New York: Houghton Mifflin Harcourt, 2005), p. 271.

16   *Ches Washington tagged along*: "Ches Sez," *Pittsburgh Courier*, May 19, 1937, p.
      17.

16   *"The King is dead"*: *Pittsburgh Courier*, June 23, 1937, p. 1.

16   *a celebratory ode entitled "Our Champ"*: Ibid., p. 13.

17   *an exclusive account of the title bout*: "Ches Sez," *Pittsburgh Courier*, July 3,
      1937, p. 17.

18   *Louis invited Washington to Detroit*: "Joe Louis Resolves to Beat Schmeling,"
      Pittsburgh Courier, Jan. 8, 1938, p. 17.

18   *"There's nothing to it!"*: *Pittsburgh Courier*, Jan. 8, 1938, p. 1.

19   *the political symbolism surrounding it*: Erenberg, *Greatest Fight*, pp. 137–38.

19   *Louis had his own reasons*: Louis, *My Life Story*, pp. 97–98.

19   *Louis was as antsy as a caged cat*: Ibid., pp. 100–101.

20   *It was pandemonium*: "Rouzeau Gives Glowing Account of Joe's Victory," *Pitts-
      burgh Courier*, June 25, 1938, p. 17.

20   *the referee summoned the fighters*: Louis, *My Life Story*, pp. 101–2; *Pittsburgh
      Courier*, June 25, 1938, p. 1.

21   *his share of the earnings*: Buni, *Robert L. Vann*, p. 256.

21   *"Joe was murderous"*: Ibid., pp. 256–57.

21   *"JOE KO'S MAX"*: *Pittsburgh Courier*, June 25, 1938, p. 1.

21   *the vicarious glee*: Buni, *Robert L. Vann*, p. 256.

22   *more than doubled the Courier's circulation*: Ibid., p. 257.

22   *Vann proudly cited the paper's contribution*: Ibid., pp. 257–58.

23　*"the Crossroads of the World"*: The Harlem Renaissance poet Claude McKay has been widely cited as coining this description of the Hill District—see Laurence Glasco, "Double Burden: The Black Experience in Pittsburgh," in Samuel P. Hays, ed., *City at the Point: Essays on the Social History of Pittsburgh* (Pittsburgh: University of Pittsburgh Press, 1989), p. 76—but it is unclear whether McKay ever used the phrase. Others attribute it to Mary Dee, a Pittsburgh disc jockey: see Hazel Garland, "Mary Dee Rests: First Female Disc Jockey Is Buried in Pittsburgh," *Pittsburgh Courier*, March 28, 1964, p. 1.

2. THE NEGRO CARNEGIES

25　*The boy's name was Cumberland Willis Posey*: Rachel Jones Williams, "Cumberland Willis Posey Sr.," *Pennsylvania Heritage Magazine*, Spring 2010.

25　*his father was ordained*: *Cyclopaedia of Biblical, Theological, and Ecclesiastical Literature*, vol. 8 (New York: Harper & Brothers, 1879), p. 436.

26　*As Cumberland Posey was entering his teenage years*: Thomas S. Ewell, "The Smoky City," *The Colored American Magazine* 4, no. 2 (December 1901), p. 136.

27　*Posey set his sights*: Ibid., pp. 136–37.

27　*The object of his affection*: Carole Wylie Hancock, "Honorable Soldiers, Too: An Historical Case Study of Post-Reconstruction African American Female Teachers of the Upper Ohio River Valley," PhD diss., Ohio University, March 2008, pp. 311–26; Carole Wylie Hancock, "Eminently Qualified," in Karen A. Johnson, Abul Pitre, and Kenneth L. Johnson, eds., *African-American Women Educators* (Lanham, Md.: Rowman & Littlefield, 2014).

28　*"Progress in the march of events"*: Carole Wylie Hancock, "Eminently Qualified," in Karen A. Johnson, Abul Pitre, and Kenneth L. Johnson, eds., *African American Women Educators* (Lanham, Md.: Rowman & Littlefield, 2014), p. 9.

29　*an event occurred in Athens*: "Lynching in Athens: Christopher C. Davis," Leona L. Gustafson, ed., *Ohio American Local History Network*, geneologybug.net.

30　*"I have used the freedom of giving your name"*: Len Barcousky, "Eyewitness 1758: Pittsburgh Gets Its Name," *Pittsburgh Post-Gazette*, Dec. 2, 2007, p. A2.

30　*three major "packet lines"*: Laurence A. Glasco, ed., *The WPA History of the Negro in Pittsburgh* (Pittsburgh: University of Pittsburgh Press, 2004), pp. 387–88.

31　*profitable mass production of steel*: David Nasaw, *Andrew Carnegie* (New York: Penguin, 2006), p. 179.

31　*The buyer was Andrew Carnegie*: Ibid., p. 247.

32　*As a child, Andrew Carnegie*: Ibid., pp. 1–53.

32　*But he would build his first fortune*: Ibid., pp. 54–88.

33　*In his early thirties*: Ibid., pp. 137–63.

33　*one of history's most generous philanthropists*: David Nasaw, "Giving Back, Big Time," *Los Angeles Times*, Nov. 2, 2006, accessed on latimes.com.

33 *George Westinghouse, a young inventor:* "George Westinghouse Jr.," *They Made America,* PBS.org.

33 *head-to-head with Thomas Edison:* Gilbert King, *Edison vs. Westinghouse: A Shocking Rivalry,* Smithsonian.com, Oct. 11, 2011.

33 *In 1869, Henry J. Heinz:* John N. Ingham, *Biographical Dictionary of American Business Leaders,* vol. 2 (Westport, Conn.: Greenwood Press, 1983), pp. 566–67.

34 *Andrew Mellon was still in his teens:* Ibid., pp. 918–22.

34 *Henry Clay Frick was a sickly child:* John N. Ingham, *Biographical Dictionary of American Business Leaders,* vol. 1 (Westport, Conn.: Greenwood Press, 1983), 417–19.

35 *Carnegie saw that he needed Frick:* Nasaw, *Andrew Carnegie,* pp. 209–10, 289–90.

35 *curbing the growing power of labor unions:* William Serrin, *Homestead: The Glory and Tragedy of an American Steel Town* (New York: Times Books,1992), pp. 66–95.

37 *denounced as a hypocrite:* Ibid., pp. 92–95; Nasaw, *Andrew Carnegie,* 456–72.

37 *Posey made his first investment:* Ewell, "Smoky City," pp. 137–38.

38 *Carnegie had befriended Booker T. Washington:* Nasaw, *Andrew Carnegie,* pp. 714–15.

38 *346 Negroes working in three Carnegie steel mills:* Helen A. Tucker, "The Negroes of Pittsburgh," *Charity and the Commons,* vol. 21, Oct. 1908–April 1909, p. 603.

38 *"for the industrial Negro to succeed":* Ibid., pp. 599–603.

39 *Four years after the Declaration of Independence:* "Pennsylvania's Gradual Abolition of Slavery," in Robert Hill and Laurence Glasco, eds., *Free at Last? Slavery in Pittsburgh in the 18th and 19th Century,* www.library.pitt.edu.

39 *the most prominent was Charles Avery:* "Notable Abolitionists of Pittsburgh," in Hill and Glasco, eds., *Free at Last?*

40 *Lewis Woodson, a minister and businessman:* Ibid.; Frank Bolden, "The Woodson-Proctor Family," *Pittsburgh Courier,* May 13, 1950, p. 17.

40 *a nineteen-year-old boy named Martin Delany:* "Notable Abolitionists of Pittsburgh," in Hill and Glasco, eds., *Free at Last?*; Glasco, *WPA History of Pittsburgh,* pp. 82–88.

41 *Along with Woodson and Delany:* "Notable Abolitionists of Pittsburgh," in Hill and Glasco, eds., *Free at Last?*

41 *an area known as Arthursville:* Ervin Dyer, "The Abolitionists of Arthursville," *Pittsburgh Post-Gazette,* Feb. 22, 1999, p. D1.

42 *a warm, windy afternoon:* Peter Charles Hoffer, *Seven Fires: The Urban Infernos That Reshaped America* (New York: PublicAffairs Books, 2006), pp. 63–103.

42 *After Congress passed the Fugitive Slave Law:* "Fugitive Slave Laws and Great Escapes," in Hall and Glasco, eds., *Free at Last?*

43 *Wealthy whites who had lost their homes:* Quentin R. Skrabec Jr., *The World's*

Richest Neighborhood: How Pittsburgh's East Enders Forged American Industry (New York: Algora Publishing, 2010).

43   *Frick's card table:* Ibid., p. 106.

43   *more millionaires than any neighborhood:* Ibid., pp. 3–22.

44   *Thomas Mellon met that demand:* "The Hill District: History," *Bridging the Urban Landscape,* Carnegie Library of Pittsburgh, andrew.cmu.edu.

44   *A number of well-to-do families:* Laurence Glasco, "Taking Care of Business: The Black Entrepreneurial Elite in Turn-of-the-Century Pittsburgh," *Pittsburgh History,* Winter 1996/96, pp. 177–82.

45   *"Our caterer is not a man of 'soft snap'":* Ewell, "Smoky City," p. 134.

45   *Caroline Wiley and her husband:* Frank Bolden, "The Wiley Family," *Pittsburgh Courier,* Feb. 4, 1950, p. 18.

45   *Samuel Rosamond:* Ewell, "Smoky City," pp. 147–48.

45   *He moved his family into a home in Homestead:* Ibid., pp. 136–38.

46   *Lewis Woodson's daughter Virginia:* Bolden, "The Woodson-Proctor Family."

46   *For the men of the black elite:* Ewell, "Smoky City," p. 138.

46   *the Loendi club:* Ron Ieriaci, "Loendi Club," Old Mon Music blog, oldmonmusic .blogspot.com.

46   *Wives and daughters had their own societies:* Ewell, "Smoky City," pp. 140–48.

47   *the education of their children:* Ibid., pp. 140–43.

47   *"a charming little belle":* Thomas S. Ewell, "The Smoky City," *The Colored American Magazine* 4, no. 2 (December 1901), p. 140.

47   *Cum Posey preferred sports to books:* John N. Ingham and Lynne B. Feldman, *African-American Business Leaders: A Biographical Dictionary* (Westport, Conn.: Greenwood Press, 1994), pp. 293–96.

48   *"adventurous and turbulent spirit":* W. Rollo Wilson, "Sports Shots," *Pittsburgh Courier,* Jan. 20, 1934, p 14.

49   *The first black-edited journal:* Glasco, *WPA History of Pittsburgh,* p. 247.

49   *a collection of verse:* Edward Nathanial Harleston, *The Toiler's Life: Poems* (Charleston, S.C.: BiblioLife LLC).

50   *rented in the home of the Tanner family:* Frank Bolden, "The Collins-Tanner Family," *Pittsburgh Courier,* May 27, 1950, p. 17.

50   *Harleston quickly ran out of savings:* Andrew Buni, *Robert L. Vann of the Pittsburgh Courier* (Pittsburgh: University of Pittsburgh Press, 1974), pp. 42–44.

3. THE CALCULATING CRUSADER

53   *Robert Lee Van hated kitchen odors:* Andrew Buni, *Robert L. Vann of the Pittsburgh Courier* (Pittsburgh: University of Pittsburgh Press,1974), pp. 3–7.

54   *the profession he had chosen:* Ibid., p. 7.

54   *"I learned to split rails":* Ibid., pp. 7–8.

55   *He managed to get a summer job:* Ibid., p. 9.

55   *It was the Waters Training School:* Ibid., pp 10–11.

56   *announced that he was going to Boston:* Ibid., pp. 11–12.

56   *he hailed Abe Lincoln as his hero:* Ibid., p. 12.

56   *Vann enrolled at Virginia Union University:* Ibid., pp. 13–14.

57   *opportunity for Negroes in the South was shrinking fast:* Ibid., pp. 16–19.

57   *"I'm going North":* Ibid., pp. 19–20.

58   *Charles Dickens himself:* Rick Seback, "What the Dickens?," *Pittsburgh Magazine,* November 21, 2012.

58   *Pittsburgh was very different:* Buni, *Robert L. Vann,* pp. 21–22.

59   *"The poorer Negroes live":* Helen A. Tucker, "The Negroes of Pittsburgh," *Charity and the Commons,* vol 21, Oct. 1908–April 1909, pp. 600–601.

59   *no one would have guessed that now:* Buni, *Robert L. Vann,* pp. 31–32.

60   *At Western University:* Ibid., p. 36.

60   *the sorrow of losing his mother:* Ibid., pp. 32–33.

60   *Vann found someone to fill the void:* Ibid., pp. 38–40.

61   *Vann began submitting items to* The Pittsburgh Courier: Ibid., pp. 42–47.

62   *"CORPSE AND PISTOL FOUND":* Pittsburgh Press, March 13, 1910, p. 4.

62   *one story more than any other:* Paula Uruburu, *American Eve: Evelyn Nesbit, Stanford White, the Birth of the "It" Girl and the Crime of the Century* (New York: Riverhead Books, 2008).

64   *The paper was produced:* Ibid., *Robert L. Vann,* p. 49.

64   *In August 1911, in another steel town:* Raymond M. Hyser and Dennis B. Downey, "'A Crooked Death': Coatesville, Pennsylvania and the Lynching of Zacharia Walker," *Pennsylvania History* 54, no. 2 (April 1987).

65   *Vann wrote a mournful editorial:* "Pennsylvania Falls," *Pittsburgh Courier,* May 11, 1912, p. 4.

65   *New York attorney John Frank Wheaton was celebrated:* "Success of a Foremost and Able Attorney," *Pittsburgh Courier,* May 25, 1912, p. 1.

65   *Scipio Africanus Jones, Esq. of Arkansas, was hailed:* Colored Lawyer Frees Client of Serious Charge," *Pittsburgh Courier,* March 2, 1912, p. 1.

65   *advertise his own legal services:* "Attorney Vann Triumps and T. Cash Is Free," *Pittsburgh Courier,* March 16, 1912.

66   *the paper was still in dire financial straits:* Buni, *Robert L. Vann,* pp. 50–51.

66   *He brought on Ira Lewis:* Ibid., pp. 53–54.

67   *The* Courier *needed to crusade on their behalf:* Ibid., pp. 55–86.

67   *Vann experienced firsthand:* Ibid., pp. 81–86.

68   *Of all the battles Vann waged:* Ibid., pp. 81–86.

69   *something bold needed to be done:* Ibid., pp. 119–21.

69   *Robert Abbott:* John N. Ingham and Lynne B. Feldman, *African-American Business Leaders: A Biographical Dictionary* (Westport, Conn.: Greenwood Press, 1994), pp. 1–12.

69 *Ira Lewis made a special trip to Chicago*: Buni, *Robert L. Vann*, p. 119.

70 *"more sensational and morbid stories"*: Ibid., p. 132.

70 *growing roster of memorable writers*: Ibid., pp. 136–45.

70 *Julia Bumry was destined*: "Julia Bumry Jones 1895–1945," Homewood Cemetery Historical Fund, facebook.com/The-Homewood-Cemetery-Historical-Fund/.

71 *Vann and the* Courier *lost Cap Posey*: "C. W. Posey Is Victim of Illness," *Pittsburgh Courier,* June 13, 1925, p. 1.

72 *he decided to splurge on a Cadillac*: Buni, *Robert L. Vann*, p. 117.

72 *"NAACP 'SLUSH FUND' AIRED"*: *Pittsburgh Courier*, Oct. 9, 1926, p. 1.

73 *Johnson gave a hot-tempered address*: Buni, *Robert L. Vann*, p. 152.

73 *"SLUSHES OVER SLUSH FUND"*: *Pittsburgh Courier*, Oct. 23, 1926, p. 1.

73 *Du Bois joined the attack*: The Crisis, no. 127, Jan. 27, 1927.

73 *"The old boy is dead on his feet"*: "The Black Man's Balance, 1926," *Pittsburgh Courier*, Jan. 1, 1927, p. 20.

73 *virtually every black newspaper*: Buni, *Robert L. Vann*, pp. 159–60.

74 *"'BURY THE HATCHET'"*: *Pittsburgh Courier*, Sep. 14, 1929, p. 1.

74 *"I am glad it happened"*: Buni, *Robert L. Vann*, p. 161.

74 *The second battle*: Ibid., pp. 161–71.

74 *When Randolph came to Pittsburgh*: "Randolph Receives Ovation at Loendi," *Pittsburgh Courier*, Feb. 19, 1927, p. 1.

74 *Vann made no bones*: Buni, *Robert L. Vann*, p. 163.

75 *Vann called for Randolph's resignation*: "Open Letter to Pullman Porters and Maids," *Pittsburgh Courier*, April 14, 1928, p. 1.

75 *Randolph was irate*: Buni, *Robert L. Vann*, pp. 168–71.

75 *Vann's top priority*: Ibid., pp. 171–73.

76 *the job of writing about the new press*: "Grad Student at Pitt Hails Courier's Plan as Great Achievement," *Pittsburgh Courier*, Dec. 14, 1928, p. 8.

77 *H. L. Mencken praising the Courier*: "'Courier Best' Says Mencken," *Pittsburgh Courier*, Dec. 20, 1930, p. 1.

77 *"the Great White Father"*: Buni, *Robert L. Vann*, p. 172.

77 *Mike Benedum had always had a nose*: "Michael Benedum's Enduring Lessons," *Claude Worthington Benedum Foundation 2008 Annual Report*.

78 *Benedum asked his black valet*: "Races: Elks and Equality," *Time*, Aug. 12, 1935, pp. 9–10.

78 *"What has the Negro ever gotten"*: "Races: Elks and Equality," *Time*, Aug. 12, 1935, pp. 9–10.

78 *It was a bitter conclusion*: Buni, *Robert L. Vann*, pp. 1975–190.

79 *the* Courier *endorsed Calvin Coolidge*: "For President, in 1924, Calvin Coolidge," *Pittsburgh Courier*, Aug. 25, 1923, p. 16.

79 *the blame for the patronage slights*: "Voices of the City," *Pittsburgh Courier*, Feb. 8, 1930, p. 13.

79   *"Neediest Family Drive":* "Courier Gang Does Its Bit for Needy," *Pittsburgh Courier*, Dec. 6, 1930, p. 1.

80   *to go through Guffey's closest adviser:* Buni, *Robert L. Vann*, p. 191.

80   *a Hill resident named Eva Deboe Jones:* "Eva DeBoe Jones, 90, Political Legend, Buried," *New Pittsburgh Courier*, Feb. 25, 1967, p. 2.

80   *"Mr. Vann'd like to see your brother":* Joseph Alsop and Robert Kitner, "Behind the Headlines," *The Spokesman Review*, Nov. 1, 1938, p. 2.

80   *at first Guffey wasn't interested:* Buni, *Robert L. Vann*, p. 192.

80   *Guffey was persuaded:* Ibid., pp. 192–93.

81   *he was presented with just such an opportunity:* Ibid., p. 193.

81   *"The Patriot and the Partisan":* Full text in *Pittsburgh Courier*, Sep. 17, 1932, p. 12.

83   *Vann paid to have pamphlets:* Buni, *Robert L. Vann*, p. 194; "You Can Get One," *Pittsburgh Courier*, Nov. 5, 1932, p. 1.

83   *one of FDR's most memorable speeches:* "Campaign Address on the Federal Budget at Pittsburgh," Franklin D. Roosevelt, Oct. 19, 1932, *The American Presidency Project,* presidency.ucsb.edu.

84   *Julia Bumry Jones, who gushed:* "Talk O' Town," *Pittsburgh Courier*, Oct. 22, 1932, p. 9.

84   *scores of the black residents:* "5th Ward Republicans 'Go Democratic' . . . ," *Pittsburgh Courier*, Nov. 5, 1932, p. 3.

84   *a majority of blacks on the Lower Hill:* Buni, *Robert L. Vann*, p. 197.

85   *Negroes had tipped the race:* "Close to 2,000,000 Negroes Voted," *Pittsburgh Courier*, Nov. 19, 1932, p. 2.

85   *the hard evidence:* Nancy J. Weiss, *Farewell to the Party of Lincoln: Black Politics in the Age of FDR* (Princeton, N.J.: Princeton University Press, 1983), pp. 30–31.

85   *no less an authority:* Alsop and Kitner, "Behind the Headlines."

86   *FDR didn't need much persuading:* Buni, *Robert L. Vann*, pp. 198–99.

86   *big enough news:* "The Presidency," *Time*, July 31, 1933, p 9.

86   *some of the most powerful men:* Buni, *Robert L. Vann*, pp. 199–202.

86   *a banquet that Ira Lewis threw:* "Talk O' Town," *Pittsburgh Courier*, Aug. 5, 1933, p. 9.

86   *After the testimonials:* Buni, *Robert L. Vann*, p. 202.

4. THE RISE AND FALL OF "BIG RED"

89   *In the early afternoon of April 29, 1932:* Chester A. Washington, "Sportively Speaking," *Pittsburgh Courier*, May 7, 1932, p. 15.

90   *a classic pitching duel:* "Hubbard Pitches Three-Hit Game to Beat Paige, 1 to 0," *Pittsburgh Courier*, May 7, 1932, p. 15.

91   *William Augustus Greenlee was born:* John N. Ingham and Lynne B. Feldman,

African-American Business Leaders: A Biographical Dictionary (Westport, Conn.: Greenwood Press, 1994), pp. 298–99.

91 *He was assigned to the 367th Infantry:* Emmett J. Scott, *The American Negro in the World War*, 1919, Chap. 11.

92 *a shrapnel wound:* Rob Ruck, *Sandlot Seasons: Sport in Black Pittsburgh* (Urbana, Ill.: University of Illinois Press, 1993), p. 138.

92 *Greenlee's taxicab was waiting for him:* Ingham and Feldman, *African-American Business Leaders*, pp. 298–99.

93 *Police promptly raided it:* "Gambling and Clubs Are Also Under Ban," *Pittsburgh Daily Post*, March 25, 1925, p. 3.

93 *more credible accounts:* Ruck, *Sandlot Seasons*, pp. 140–41.

94 *"Teenie Little Lover":* Laurence Glasco, "An American Life, an American Story: Charles 'Teenie' Harris and Images of Black Pittsburgh," in Cheryl Finley, Laurence Glasco, and Joe W. Trotter, *Teenie Harris Photographer: Image, Memory History* (Pittsburgh: University of Pittsburgh Press, 2011), p. 2.

94 *Working as "cut buddies":* Ruck, *Sandlot Seasons*, p. 146.

94 *Greenlee and Harris usually derived their numbers:* Ibid., p. 140.

94 *their runners filled the streets:* "Numbers Racket Menaces 'Hill' Real Estate Values," *Pittsburgh Post-Gazette*, Sep. 26, 1930, p. 1.

95 *a brutal August heat wave:* "Fields Afire as Dry Spell, Heat Continue," *Pittsburgh Post-Gazette*, Aug. 4, 1930, p. 2.

95 *gamblers wrote the simplest number:* Ruck, *Sandlot Seasons*, pp. 144–45.

95 *a nightclub he called the Crawford Grill:* "Gus Greenlee" entry on Pittsburgh Music History Web blog, sites.google.com/site/pittsburghmusichistory.

96 *a vice squad barged into the Crawford Grill:* "Jewish Syndicate Claims Concession on 'Numbers' Through Aid of Vice Squad," *Pittsburgh Courier*, March 10, 1934, p. 1.

96 *police used axes and crowbars:* "Six Are Taken in Numbers Raid," *Pittsburgh Post-Gazette*, Aug. 10, 1934, p. 3.

96 *Greenlee courted the Republican politicians:* "Gus Greenlee (Big Mogul of Pittsburgh)," *Pittsburgh Courier*, Nov. 19, 1932, p. 8.

97 *Greenlee hired a part-time publicist:* Mark Ribowsky, *The Power and the Darkness: The Life of Josh Gibson in the Shadows of the Game* (New York: Simon & Schuster, 1996), p. 76.

98 *One of his closest white friends:* Rob Ruck, Maggie Jones Patterson, and Michael P. Weber, *Rooney: A Sporting Life* (Lincoln, Neb.: University of Nebraska Press, 2010), p. 80.

99 *the Crawfords had assembled a raw but imposing roster:* Jim Bankes, *The Pittsburgh Crawfords* (Jefferson, N.C.: McFarland, 2001), pp. 16–17.

99 *The players decided to approach Greenlee instead:* Ruck, *Sandlot Seasons*, pp. 152–53.

100 *Cum Posey introduced night baseball:* "Grays-Monarchs Set for Night Games Here," *Pittsburgh Courier*, July 19, 1930, p. 14.

100 *Cum Posey may have been a late bloomer:* Ruck, *Sandlot Seasons*, pp. 130–36.

100 *"Posey played the saint":* Bankes, *Pittsburgh Crawfords*, p. 16.

101 *the Grays projected an image:* Ribowsky, *The Power and the Darkness*, pp. 73–74.

101 *The morning of the game:* "Grays-Monarchs Set for Night Games Here," *Pittsburgh Courier*, p. 14.

102 *a problem became apparent:* Judy Johnson account in Bankes, *Pittsburgh Crawfords*, pp. 38–39.

102 *According to another version:* Ribowsky, *The Power and the Darkness*, pp. 42–43.

103 *his economical hitting technique:* Ibid., pp. 33–34.

103 *the longest drive they had ever seen at Forbes Field:* "Grays Set for Lincoln Series," *Pittsburgh Courier*, Sep. 20, 1930, p. 15.

103 *the stuff of baseball legend:* Rob Neyer, "Did Gibson Hit One Out of Yankee Stadium?," ESPN.com, May 19, 2008.

103 *praised the 1930 Grays:* "Ches Sez," *Pittsburgh Courier*, Dec. 11, 1930, p. 15.

104 *Posey proclaimed it as good as a world championship:* "Grays Undisputed Champs," Cum Posey, *Pittsburgh Courier*, Oct. 10, 1931, p. 15.

104 *There hadn't been one single unified black league:* Bankes, *Pittsburgh Crawfords*, pp. 3–11.

104 *Posey called for the formation of a new "East-West League":* "'Cum' Posey's Pointed Paragraphs," *Pittsburgh Courier*, Jan. 30, 1932, p. 15, Feb. 13, 1932, p. 15.

104 *Gus Greenlee was turning the upstart Crawfords:* Bankes, *Pittsburgh Crawfords*, pp. 3–11.

105 *an impressive no-hit shutout:* "Streeter Pitches No Hit Game Here," *Pittsburgh Courier*, June 13, 1931, p. 14.

105 *Greenlee seized an opportunity:* Larry Tye, *Satchel: The Life and Times of an American Legend* (New York: Random House, 2009), pp. 51–58.

105 *living up to his nickname:* Leroy (Satchel) Paige, *Maybe I'll Pitch Forever* (Lincoln, Neb.: University of Nebraska Press, 1993), pp. 17–18.

105 *When the day came:* Tye, *Satchel*, p. 68.

106 *a private celebration:* Paige, *Maybe I'll Pitch Forever*, pp. 63–65.

107 *a list of high-handed conditions:* "Crawfords' Owner Makes First Statement About the Team, New Park and Plans," *Pittsburgh Courier*, Feb. 27, 1932, p. 14.

107 *a professional-quality stadium:* John L. Clark, "The Rise and Fall of Greenlee Field," *Pittsburgh Courier*, Dec. 10, 1938, p. 17.

107 *Greenlee went to war:* Bankes, *Pittsburgh Crawfords*, p. 22.

108 *Gibson had signed a new contract:* Ribowsky, *The Power and the Darkness*, p. 84.

108 *Greenlee had the more binding contract:* "Crawfords, Grays Claim Gibson for '32 Season," *Pittsburgh Courier*, Feb. 6, 1932, p. 14.

108 *a tour of the sunny South:* Bankes, *Pittsburgh Crawfords*, p. 22.

108 *he arranged for wealthy black families:* "I Believe You Should Know," *Pittsburgh Courier,* April 16, 1932, p. 15.

108 *"CRAWFORD'S BASKING IN SPA'S SUNLIGHT":* *Pittsburgh Courier,* April 2, 1932, p. 15.

108 *he invited Robert L. Vann to throw out the first pitch:* "Courier 'Chief' in Action," *Pittsburgh Courier,* May 7, 1932.

108 *Cum Posey threw in the towel:* "Sports Shots, by W. Rollo Wilson," *Pittsburgh Courier,* June 4, 1932, p. 14.

108 *The Grays agreed to merge:* "Grays, Detroit to Merge; League Shifts Loom," *Pittsburgh Courier,* June 11, 1932, p. 15.

109 *Several players became so worried:* "Sportively Speaking," *Pittsburgh Courier,* July 2, 1932, p. 15.

109 *Cum Posey was still finding ways to snub him:* "Posey Picks Foster, Lundy, Wilson on All-Star Team," *Pittsburgh Courier,* Nov. 19, 1932, p. 15.

109 *Greenlee targeted Cool Papa Bell:* Bankes, *Pittsburgh Crawfords,* pp. 48–49.

110 *Satchel Paige swore he once saw:* William "Brother" Rogers, "Cool Papa Bell," Mississippi Historical Society Website, mississippihistory.org.

110 *In an open letter:* "Posey Reveals Why Grays Left Nat'l Ass'n," *Pittsburgh Courier,* July 8, 1933, p. 14.

110 *Clark fired back:* "Clark Continues Exposure on Grays' League Status," *Pittsburgh Courier,* July 29, 1933, p. 15.

111 *the idea of a black all-star game:* "Posey's Points," *Pittsburgh Courier,* Aug. 15, 1942.

111 *Played on a raw, rainy September day:* Bankes, *Pittsburgh Crawfords,* pp. 94–95.

112 *Gus Greenlee had made good on his vow:* Ibid., pp. 48, 70–81.

112 *Paige recalled going 31–4:* Paige, *Maybe I'll Pitch Forever,* p. 75.

113 *Greenlee claimed that Josh Gibson:* Ribowsky, *The Power and the Darkness,* p. 121.

113 *In a defiant piece in the* Courier: "Negro National League Clubs to Be Called to Powwow Soon," *Pittsburgh Courier,* Dec. 16, 1933, p. 14.

113 *Greenlee was making plenty of money:* Paige, *Maybe I'll Pitch Forever,* pp. 65–73.

114 *the best season of his career:* Tye, *Satchel,* pp. 65–66.

114 *More than ten thousand fans:* "Paige Hurls No-Hit Classic," *Pittsburgh Courier,* July 7, 1934, p. 1.

115 *Bewildered by the way Paige's fastball:* Tye, *Satchel,* p. 67.

115 *Gus Greenlee gloated while Cum Posey fumed:* *Pittsburgh Courier,* July 7, 1934, p. 15.

115 *the second East-West Classic:* "As 'Speedball' Satchel Paige Ambled into the East-West Game and Simply Stole the Show," *Pittsburgh Courier,* Sep. 1, 1934, p. 14.

115 *"It's Paige":* Paige, *Maybe I'll Pitch Forever,* p. 82.

116 *In the* Chicago Daily Times: "Writer Calls East-West Tilt Most Colorful in Sports History," *Pittsburgh Courier,* Sep. 8, 1934, p. 15.

116 *Big Red showed his gratitude:* Paige, *Maybe I'll Pitch Forever*, pp. 86–88.

116 *"'Satch' Says 'I Will' Twice":* *Pittsburgh Courier*, Nov. 3, 1934, p. 4.

116 *"a powerful lightness":* Paige, *Maybe I'll Pitch Forever*, p. 86.

117 *"Heroes come and go":* "Ches Sez," *Pittsburgh Courier*, April 20, 1935, p. 14.

117 *the Crawfords were so good by 1935:* Bankes, *Pittsburgh Crawfords*, pp. 72–73.

117 *Paige had found his year in Bismarck stressful:* Paige, *Maybe I'll Pitch Forever*, pp. 88–90.

117 *As the 1936 season began:* "Flash—Satchell Paige Returns to Crawfords—Flash," *Pittsburgh Courier*, April 25, 1936, p. 14.

118 *When the Crawfords reached New Orleans:* Paige, *Maybe I'll Pitch Forever*, pp. 115–20.

118 *It appeared that Rafael Trujillo:* Bankes, *Pittsburgh Crawfords*, pp. 105–7.

118 *he was in no position to fight back:* Ingham and Feldman, *African-American Business Leaders*, p. 303.

119 *Greenlee Field had become a perennial money-loser:* Clark, "The Rise and Fall of Greenlee Field."

119 *Paige soon pulled out:* Paige, *Maybe I'll Pitch Forever*, pp. 119–20.

119 *But when Paige approached Greenlee:* Tye, *Satchel*, pp. 117–18.

119 *His name was Rufus "Sonnyman" Jackson:* "Ches Sez," *Pittsburgh Courier*, Jan. 2, 1937, p. 14.

120 *"GRAYS GET GIBSON":* *Pittsburgh Courier*, March 27, 1937, p 16.

120 *That turned out to be an understatement:* Ruck, *Sandlot Seasons*, pp. 170–74.

120 *Cum Posey began to take a public stand:* "Pirates Owner Would Favor Sepia Players in Organized Baseball; Lauds Gibson, Satchel," *Pittsburgh Courier*, Feb. 12, 1938.

121 *John L. Clark didn't hide his bitterness:* Clark, "The Rise and Fall of Greenlee Field."

5. BILLY AND LENA

123 *In the fall of 1935:* David Hajdu, *Lush Life: A Biography of Billy Strayhorn* (New York: Farrar, Straus & Giroux, 1996), pp. 22–29.

123 *A wiry go-getter:* Ralph E. Koger Westinghouse High School yearbook entry, 1932, ancestry.com.

123 *he filed stories to the Courier:* "Junior Branch NAACP," *Pittsburgh Courier*, Dec. 12, 1931, p. 9.

123 *According to the posters:* "Flyer from the Strayhorn inspired 1935 high school musical *Fantastic Rhythm*," *Media Gallery*, billystrayhorn.com.

124 *"Musical Divorces":* "Junior Jottings," *Pittsburgh Courier*, May 26, 1934.

124 *Strayhorn outdid himself:* "Westinghouse Grads Honored by Keystone Civic League, Inc.," *Pittsburgh Courier*, June 22, 1935, p. 3.

124 *On the second day of November:* "'Fantastic Rhythm' Is Big Success," *Pittsburgh Courier*, Nov. 9, 1935, p. 9.

125   *Despite a torrential rainstorm:* "'Fantastic Rhythm' Shows Real Talent," *Pitts-*
      burgh Courier, Nov. 16, 1935, p. 3.

125   *In his youth:* Hajdu, *Lush Life,* pp. 3–12.

127   *"a black teacher associated with Volkwein's":* Ibid., p. 12.

127   *the distinctive way she wore her hair:* Charlotte Catlin photos, Teenie Harris Ar-
      chive, Carnegie Museum of Art, teenie.cmoa.org.

127   *Catlin was also descended:* Frank Bolden, "The Enty Family, 1783–," *Pittsburgh*
      Courier, March 4, 1950, p. 18.

127   *Charlotte's mother's family story:* Ibid.

128   *The man Charlotte married:* Details of the Enty/Catlin family of 7425 Monticello
      Street, Pittsburgh, in the 1940 U.S. Federal Census, ancestry.com.

128   *In her early twenties:* "Chapter History," Alpha Kappa Alpha Sorority, akapitts
      burghaao.net.

129   *connected to a musical tradition:* Laurence A. Glasco, ed., *The WPA History of*
      the Negro in Pittsburgh (Pittsburgh: University of Pittsburgh Press, 2004), pp.
      307–25.

129   *a man arrived on a steamboat:* Ibid., pp. 325–33.

129   *In Duquesne:* Stanley Dance, *The World of Earl Hines* (New York: Da Capo,
      1983), pp. 7–32.

130   *Opened in 1916:* "Schenley High School to Open with Fall Term, *Pittsburgh*
      Daily Post, Sep. 17, 1916, p. 14.

130   *But he also continued to seek knowledge:* "Earl Hines Explains His Influences and
      Technique," youtube.com.

131   *"a kind of genius":* Dance, *World of Earl Hines,* p. 20.

131   *"If I catch you here again":* Ibid., pp. 31–32.

131   *Earl Hines did come back:* "Earl Hines Returns Friday for Week's Engagement at
      Stanley," *Pittsburgh Courier,* June 4, 1932, p. 17.

131   *among the best jazz performances:* Jeffrey Taylor, "Louis Armstrong, Earl Hines,
      and 'Weather Bird,'" *The Musical Quarterly* 82, no. 1 (Spring 1998): 1–40.

132   *At the age of six:* Linda Dahl, *Morning Glory: A Biography of Mary Lou Williams*
      (Berkeley: University of California Press,1999), pp. 3–36.

132   *another Pittsburgh high school:* "Westinghouse High School Dedicated; Portrait
      of Its Patron Is Presented," *Pittsburgh Daily Post,* May 27, 1925, p. 5.

132   *After issuing a $3 million bond offering:* "Westinghouse High School to Be Com-
      pleted," *Pittsburgh Post-Gazette,* Dec. 22, 1920, p. 5.

133   *"Tough on Black Asses":* Dahl, *Morning Glory,* p. 38.

133   *Erroll Garner was the baby:* Whitney Balliett, "Being a Genius," *The New Yorker,*
      Feb. 22, 1982, pp. 59–72.

133   *Billy Strayhorn stood out:* Hajdu, *Lush Life,* pp. 13–15.

134   *When he was nineteen:* "Convention Highlights," *Pittsburgh Courier,* Sep. 1,
      1934, p. 7.

134   *Continuing to work at Pennfield Drug Store:* Hajdu, *Lush Life,* pp. 30–45.

135   *Billy began to work on a solo piano piece:* Ibid., pp. 34–36.

135   *One of those places was a small club:* Ibid., p. 43; John M. Brewer Jr., *African Americans in Pittsburgh* (Charleston, S.C.: Arcadia Publishing, 2006), p. 53.

136   *Teddy Horne was an unlikely racketeer:* Gail Lumet Buckley, *The Hornes: An American Family* (New York: Alfred A. Knopf, 1986, Applause paperback), pp. 3–106.

138   *By the time Lena was sixteen:* Lena Horne and Richard Schickel, *Lena* (New York: Doubleday, 1965), pp. 45–76.

139   *Teddy Horne surfaced again:* Ibid., pp 77–103.

139   *the* Courier *ran a story:* "'Love at First Sight' Romance Ends at Altar," *Pittsburgh Courier,* Jan. 23, 1937.

140   *Within another month Lena was pregnant:* Horne and Schickel, *Lena,* pp. 87–88.

141   *the biggest news of the year:* "Lena Horne Accepts Hollywood Film Offer," *Pittsburgh Courier,* Feb. 5, 1938, p. 20.

141   *Woogie's little brother:* Laurence Glasco, "An American Life, An American Story: Charles 'Teenie' Harris and Images of Black Pittsburgh," in Cheryl Finley, Laurence Glasco, and Joe W. Trotter, *Teenie Harris Photographer: Image, Memory History* (Pittsburgh: University of Pittsburgh Press, 2011), p. 11.

141   *But it was a very different scene:* "Refuses to Appear at Premiere of Own Film," *Pittsburgh Courier,* June 18, 1938, p. 20.

142   *But the gossips didn't know the full story:* Horne and Schickel, *Lena,* p. 91.

142   *So when Lena received another show business offer:* Ibid., pp. 91–97.

142   *When Lena told her father:* Ibid., pp. 97–98.

143   *the experience of singing with Charlotte Catlin:* Ibid., pp. 99–100.

144   *it wasn't enough to save Lena's marriage:* Ibid., pp. 100–3.

144   *Billy left for New York on an odyssey that began:* Hajdu, *Lush Life,* pp. 47–63.

147   *Then a showdown in the music industry:* Ibid., pp. 81–88.

148   *While Duke was there:* Ibid., pp. 90–92.

148   *Fleeing Pittsburgh for New York:* Horne and Schickel, *Lena,* pp. 105–21; Buckley, *The Hornes,* pp. 137–47.

149   *They began a secret affair:* Buckley, *The Hornes,* pp. 145–47.

149   *Duke helped convince her:* Horne and Schickel, *Lena,* pp. 122–26.

150   *One of the first things Billy and Lena talked about:* Hajdu, *Lush Life,* p. 94.

150   *Billy and Lena became inseparable:* Horne and Schickel, *Lena,* pp. 124–26; Hajdu, *Lush Life,* pp. 95–97.

151   *the awful news about Pearl Harbor:* Horne and Schickel, *Lena,* p. 125.

6. THE DOUBLE V WARRIORS

153   *When Percival Leroy Prattis left Chicago:* Charles A. Rosenberg, "Percival L. Prattis: The Pittsburgh Courier's Man in Chicago," *Western Pennsylvania History,* Fall 2014, pp. 48–60.

155   *Lillian fled to New York again"* "Talk O' Town," *Pittsburgh Courier,* March 13, 1937, p. 9.

155   *When Prattis proposed marriage:* Rosenberg, "Percival L. Prattis," p. 58.

155   *he was seen as an outsider:* P.L. Prattis, unpublished "Autobiography," University of Pittsburgh Archives, Collection no. AIS.2007.01.

155   *Prattis was also not charmed:* Rosenberg, "Percival L. Prattis," p. 58.

156   *Drafted at the age of twenty-two:* Percival Leroy Prattis WI Registration Card and U.S. Department of Veterans Affairs benefits application, ancestry.com.

156   *After World War I:* Andrew Buni, *Robert L. Vann of the Pittsburgh Courier* (Pittsburgh: University of Pittsburgh Press, 1974), pp. 299–300.

156   *For Vann, it had been a sobering time:* Ibid., pp. 203–21.

157   *a near-fatal skull fracture:* "Local Attorney Critically Hurt," *Pittsburgh Post-Gazette,* Sep. 16, 1933, p. 1.

157   *While the Vanns were in Los Angeles:* Robert L. Vann, "Saw Shirley Temple . . . and Bill Robinson," *Pittsburgh Courier,* Nov. 23, 1935, p. 17.

157   *In a mordant letter":* Buni, *Robert L. Vann,* p. 221.

157   *P.L. Prattis sent Vann a letter:* Prattis, unpublished "Autobiography."

158   *The war correspondent idea:* Buni, *Robert L. Vann,* pp. 244–48.

158   *Vann gave himself the assignment:* Robert L. Vann, "Hitler Salutes Jesse Owens," *Pittsburgh Courier,* Aug. 8, 1936, p. 1.

159   *But in Vann's letters home:* Buni, *Robert L. Vann,* p. 259.

159   *Jesse Vann hosted a welcome home picnic:* "The Courier 'Gang' Welcomes The Chief Home!," *Pittsburgh Courier,* Sep. 5, 1936, p. 9.

159   *Vann threw the* Courier's *clout:* Buni, *Robert L. Vann,* pp. 264–72.

160   *The rift would break wide open:* Ibid., pp. 277–81, 291–93.

160   *Three issues in particular rankled him:* Ibid., pp. 283–84.

160   *Vann's high-minded opposition:* "Editorial of the Day: Changing the Supreme Court," *Chicago Daily Tribune,* March 7, 1937, p. 15.

160   *Vann himself was touted:* Buni, *Robert L. Vann,* pp. 285–86; "Head of the National Bar Association Endorses Vann for Supreme Court," *Pittsburgh Courier,* Jan. 22, 1938, p. 2.

161   *As Mencken put it:* "The Unchanging Mencken," *St. Louis Post-Dispatch,* March 5, 1938, p. 4.

161   *"We will never get anything":* Buni, *Robert L. Vann,* p 286.

161   *Vann's third and most passionate cause:* Ibid., pp. 299–313.

161   *In the letter: Pittsburgh Courier,* April 2, 9, 16, 23, 30, May 7, 21, 1938, all p. 14.

162 *an unlikely source:* Buni, *Robert L. Vann*, pp. 306–10.

162 *a second audience with Roosevelt:* "Courier Editor Discusses Farm Bill, Negro Division with President Roosevelt," *Pittsburgh Courier*, Nov. 5, 1938, p. 1.

162 *Vann refused to give up:* Buni, *Robert L. Vann*, pp. 310–12.

163 *the* Courier *congratulated itself:* "We Thank All Who Helped Us," *Pittsburgh Courier*, Sep. 28, 1940, p. 1.

163 *he wrote his friend Claude Barnett:* Rosenberg, "Percival L. Prattis," p. 58.

163 *he had been diagnosed with abdominal cancer:* Buni, *Robert L. Vann*, pp. 316–18.

164 *"You cannot afford":* Ibid., p 317.

164 *But on an October morning in 1940:* "Talk O' Town," *Pittsburgh Courier*, Nov. 2, 1940, p. 9.

164 *within days he slipped into a coma:* "Courier Editor Succumbs Fighting," *Pittsburgh Courier*, Nov. 2, 1940, p. 1.

165 *"NATION EULOGIZES VANN":* *Pittsburgh Courier*, Nov. 2, 1940, pp. 1, 3.

165 *FDR didn't need the Courier's backing in 1940:* Buni, *Robert L. Vann*, pp. 322–23.

165 *Hundreds of mourners attended:* "Notables from All Sections of Country Attend Last Rites for Robert L. Vann," *Pittsburgh Courier*, Nov. 2, 1940, p. 28.

166 *Floral tributes were sent:* "Floral Tributes to Robert L. Vann," *Pittsburgh Courier*, Nov. 2, 1940, p. 4.

166 *Vann's casket to Homewood Cemetery:* Buni, *Robert L. Vann*, p. 323.

166 *P.L. Prattis and dozens of other mourners stayed behind:* Teenie Harris Archive, photo no. 2001.35.18388.

166 *P.L. Prattis embarked on a mission:* "Gladden the Heart," *Pittsburgh Courier*, April 26, 1941, p. 15.

166 *In a series of articles:* "Sent Illiterates to Skilled Units," *Pittsburgh Courier*, June 14, p. 2; "Race Soldiers May Get Officers Training in Army Schools If—," *Pittsburgh Courier*, May 31, 1941, p. 1.

167 *Then on an August night at Fort Bragg:* "Ft. Bragg's 'Night of Terror,'" *Pittsburgh Courier*, Aug. 16, 1941, p. 1.

167 *the NAACP called for an investigation:* "Developments!," *Pittsburgh Courier*, Aug. 16, 1941, p. 1.

167 *an unprecedented response:* "Was in Command at Fort Bragg on 'Night of Terror,'" *Pittsburgh Courier*, Oct. 18, 1941, p. 1; "Successful Courier Campaign Places Negro M.P.'s at Fort Bragg," *Pittsburgh Courier*, Nov. 22, 1941, p. 13.

168 *"We Remember 1919":* *Pittsburgh Courier*, Feb. 7, 1942, p. 13.

168 *In another column:* "Rogers Says," *Pittsburgh Courier*, Jan. 24, 1942, p. 7.

168 *Prattis set out to discover the sailor's name:* Transcript of Frank Bolden interview for *The Black Press: Soldiers Without Swords*, a film by Stanley Nelson, pbs.org/blackpress.

168 *"MESSMAN HERO IDENTIFIED!":* *Pittsburgh Courier*, March 14, 1942, p. 1.

169   *A bill was introduced in Congress:* "Congressional Medal Sought for Dorie Miller," *Pittsburgh Courier,* March 21, 1942, p. 1.

169   *Instead, Knox hastily arranged:* "Navy Cross for Dorie Miller," *Pittsburgh Courier,* May 16, 1942, p. 1.

169   *James Gratz Thompson was a cafeteria worker:* George S. Schuyler, "'Make Democracy Real,' Says Double V Originator," *Pittsburgh Courier,* April 18, 1942, p. 5.

170   *he wrote a letter to the* Courier: "Should I Sacrifice to Live 'Half-American'?," *Pittsburgh Courier,* Jan. 31, 1942, p. 3.

170   *Holloway's drawing appeared: Pittsburgh Courier,* Feb. 7, 1942, p. 1.

171   *The response from* Courier *readers:* "Race Unites for Drive to Secure Real Democracy," *Pittsburgh Courier,* March 7, 1942, p. 12.

171   *In the next edition, the editors officially announced: Pittsburgh Courier,* Feb. 14, p. 1.

171   *Beatrice Williams: Pittsburgh Courier,* Feb. 21, 1942, p. 1.

171   *Singer Marian Anderson: Pittsburgh Courier,* March 7, 1942, pp. 12–13.

171   *the National Baptist Convention:* "NBC Baptists Endorse Courier's 'Double V' Drive," *Pittsburgh Courier,* March 21, p. 15.

171   *on behalf of the NAACP:* "NAACP Joins Courier's 'Double Victory,'" *Pittsburgh Courier,* May 23, 1942, p. 4.

171   *The Pullman Porters and Maids Association:* "Future of Negro Depends on 'VV'— Porters," *Pittsburgh Courier,* Sep. 5, 1942, p. 15.

171   *the United Automobile Workers:* "UAW Endorses 'Double V,'" *Pittsburgh Courier,* Aug. 15, 1942, p. 6.

171   *Thomas Dewey:* "Denounces Limit Placed on Negro in War Efforts," *Pittsburgh Courier,* Feb. 28, 1942, p. 1.

172   *Pearl Buck:* "'Racial Predjudices Must Go,' Pearl Buck Warns in Speech," Ibid.

172   *From Hollywood:* Pat Washburn, "The Pittsburgh Courier's Double V Campaign in 1942," presented at Annual Meeting of the Association for Education in Journalism, August 1981, p. 5.

172   *Clare Boothe Luce:* "Clare Luce Asks for 'Double V' in America," *Pittsburgh Courier,* Nov. 28, 1942, p. 15.

172   *the campaign even had a theme song:* "Razaf, Johnson to Compose 'Double V' Song," *Pittsburgh Courier,* March 14, 1942, p. 21; "Louis Jordan Will Feature 'Double V' Song on Tour," *Pittsburgh Courier,* June 20, 1942, p. 21.

172   *Double V hairdo: Pittsburgh Courier,* May 30, 1942, p. 24.

172   *"Double V Girl of the Week": Pittsburgh Courier,* March 28, p. 1.

172   *Double V bathing suit contests: Pittsburgh Courier,* Sep. 5, 1942, p. 15.

173   *membership in "Double V Clubs":* Washburn, "Double V Campaign," pp. 1, 8–9.

173   *a very different response in Washington:* Patrick S. Washburn, *A Question of Sedition: The Federal Government's Investigation of the Black Press During World War II* (New York: Oxford University Press, 1986), pp. 41–65.

174 *"When are you going to indict the seditionists?":* Geoffrey R. Stone, *Perilous Times: Free Speech in Wartime from the Sedition Act of 1798 to the War on Terrorism* (New York: W. W. Norton, 2004), pp. 256–57.

174 *FBI agents began showing up:* "Cowing the Negro Press," *Pittsburgh Courier,* March 14, 1942, p. 6.

174 *"expressed dissatisfaction":* Patrick S. Washburn, *The African American Newspaper: Voice of Freedom* (Evanston, Ill.: Northwestern University Press, 2006), p. 167.

174 *"Hoover's flunkies":* Washburn, *A Question of Sedition,* p. 84.

175 *The report singled out a brief account:* "'Now Is the Hour to Strike for Race Justice'—Powell," *Pittsburgh Courier,* May 2, 1942, p. 4.

175 *he reached out directly to Roosevelt:* Washburn, *A Question of Sedition,* p. 87.

175 *Instead of Prattis, it was John Sengstacke:* Ibid., pp. 87–92.

175 *When Sengstacke arrived at the Justice Department:* Ethan Michaeli, *The Defender: How the Legendary Black Newspaper Changed America* (New York: Houghton Mifflin Harcourt, 2016), pp. 246–48.

176 *one of the three most influential crusades:* Washburn, *The African American Newspaper,* p. 144.

176 *virtually all of the nearly one thousand articles:* Washburn, "Double V Campaign," pp. 14–26.

176 *director Stanley Nelson suggested:* "Section 4: Treason?," in Study Guide Index for *The Black Press: Soldiers Without Swords,* a film by Stanley Nelson, pbs.org/ blackpress.

176 *its wartime financial windfall:* Washburn, *A Question of Sedition,* p. 133.

176 *a new sense of optimism:* "1942 in Retrospect Shows Gains Outweigh Losses," *Pittsburgh Courier,* Jan. 2, 1943, p. 5.

177 *In one photo, smiling riveters:* "Air Force Signs Women Mechanics," *Pittsburgh Courier,* Dec. 19, 1942, p. 11.

177 *When the* Courier *recapped the year:* *Pittsburgh Courier,* Jan. 2, 1943, p. 5.

177 *"We Gain by War":* *Pittsburgh Courier,* Oct. 10, 1942, p. 13.

178 *When* Courier *reporter Frank Bolden reflected back:* Washburn, *African American Newspaper,* p. 162.

178 *ten accredited war correspondents:* John D. Stevens, "From the Back of the Foxhole: Black Correspondents in World War II," *Journalism Monographs,* no. 27, Feb. 1973, p. 10. Of the ten *Courier* war correspondents, three—Frank Bolden, Fletcher Martin, and George Padmore—were also assigned to black newswires.

178 *lift its circulation to all-time high:* "Taxes Owed, U.S. Claims," *Pittsburgh Post-Gazette,* Nov. 21, 1967.

178 *Blazing trails was nothing new:* "Biography," Frank E. Bolden Papers, University of Pittsburgh Library System, Collection no. AIS.2008.05, May 2010.

179   *Vann offered him a full-time job*: Bolden interview in *Frank Bolden: The Man Behind the Words*, a film by Daniel Love, 2001.

179   *a gift for coining colorful phrases*: "Reporter, Raconteur Frank Bolden Dies at 90," *Pittsburgh Post-Gazette*, Aug. 29, 2003, p. 1.

179   *Under War Department rules*: Michael S. Sweeney, "Press Accreditation During WWII," nojobforawoman.com.

180   *As soon as Bolden arrived at Fort Huachuca*: "'Arizona Is No Place for Negro Soldiers,'" *Pittsburgh Courier*, Jan. 13, 1934, p. 7; Truman K. Gibson, *Knocking Down Barriers: My Fight for Black America* (Evanston, Ill.: Northwestern University Press, 2005), pp. 156–62.

180   *Bolden labored to turn the drudgery of tank maneuvers*: "Fort Huachuca Division Looks Good in Bayonet and Gas Mask Drills," *Pittsburgh Courier*, July 4, 1942, p. 20.

180   *To bypass the military censors*: Bolden interview in Love, *Frank Bolden: The Man Behind the Words*.

180   *After one story about a gunfight*: "Three Soldiers Wounded in Huachuca Gun Battle," *Pittsburgh Courier*, July 11, 1942, p. 12.

181   *a troubled marriage*: Frank E. Bolden Papers, Folders 46–48.

181   *But unhappily for Rouzeau*: "The Courier's Edgar T. Rouzeau Is at the War Front!," *Pittsburgh Courier*, July 18, 1942, p. 1.

181   *Seven months passed before Rouzeau*: "Negro Troops Land in Liberia on Sunday," *Pittsburgh Courier*, Dec. 12, 1942, p. 19.

181   *FDR inspected black troops in the field*: "Roosevelt Reviews Famed 41st," *Pittsburgh Courier*, Feb. 6, 1943, p. 1.

181   *the squadron was treated like an "orphan" unit*: "U.S. Gambled Millions; 99th Made Good—Rouzeau," *Pittsburgh Courier*, Dec. 11, 1943.

181   Time *magazine reported*: "Army & Navy—Experiment Proved?," *Time*, Sep. 20, 1943.

182   *Rouzeau's upbeat accounts*: "99th Pilots Tell of Death-Defying Moments," *Pittsburgh Courier*, Oct. 16, 1943, p. 2.

182   *a story entitled "A Behaviour Pattern"*: *Newsweek*, March 26, 1945, p. 37.

182   *In* The New York Times: "Americans Lose Ground in Italy," *New York Times*, Feb. 14, 1945, p. 5.

182   *P.L. Prattis had made two unlikely choices*: "Eight Courier Men Gave You Ringside Seats During European Campaigns," *Pittsburgh Courier*, May 12, 1945, p. 5; "Collins George Dead: He Was First Black Critic," *Detroit Free Press*, Feb. 16, 1980, p. 3.

183   *Almond also told the black troops*: Gibson, *Knocking Down Barriers*, p. 185.

183   *the Buffalos were widely mocked*: Mary Penick Motley, ed., *The Invisible Soldier: The Experience of the Black Soldier, World War II* (Detroit, Mich.: Wayne State University Press, 1987), pp. 258–59.

183 *But the Buffalos never forgot Collins George:* "Collins George Made Blacks Feel Like Heroes," *Detroit Free Press,* March 13, 1980, p. 8.

183 *a frustrating ordeal:* P.L. Prattis, "Days of Courier Past . . . ," in Henry G. La Brie III, ed., *Perspectives of the Black Press: 1974* (Kennebunkport, Maine: Mercer House Press, 1974), p. 71.

184 *arrived at the beaches of Normandy two weeks later:* "My Trip Across the Channel," *Pittsburgh Courier,* July 22, 1944, p. 9.

184 *Stanford arrived in France:* "New Courier Writer Abroad," *Pittsburgh Courier,* May 10, 1945, p. 1.

184 *In Steven Spielberg's* Saving Private Ryan: Linda Hervieux, *Forgotten: The Untold Story of D-Day's Black Heroes, at Home and at War* (New York: Harper, 2015), p. 263.

184 *a minor hero of Billy Rowe himself:* "93rd Warriors Trap Japanese" and "Billy Rowe Aids Wounded Soldiers," *Pittsburgh Courier,* May 6, 1944, p. 1.

185 *Bolden's excitement was palpable:* "Army, Navy 'One Big Family' on Transport to Middle East," *Pittsburgh Courier,* Aug. 5, 1944, p. 3.

185 *It was the desert monarchy of Iran:* "Our Troops in Gulf of Persia Master Language of Natives," *Pittsburgh Courier,* Oct. 7, 1944, p. 18.

185 *the most ambitious engineering project of the war:* Anand Sankar, "On the Road to China," *Business Standard,* May 24, 2008, business-standard.com.

186 *"They don't need engineers here":* "Engineers Keep Supplies Moving Through Deluge," *Pittsburgh Courier,* Aug. 4, 1945, p. 18.

186 *Bolden described the mission as "Green Hell":* "Tan Yank Engineering Feat Was 'Impossible,'" *Pittsburgh Courier,* April 14, 1945, p. 19.

186 *The nearest "Negro Rest Club":* "GIs Get New Rest Camp in India-Burma Theatre," *Pittsburgh Courier,* March 31, 1945, p. 19.

187 *When the Ledo Road finally reached China:* "Deny Move on to Keep Tan GIs Out of China," *Pittsburgh Courier,* Feb. 17, 1945, p. 15.

187 *When Bolden ran into two old friends:* "Pittsburgh Boys Enjoy Happy Reunion on Stilwell Road," *Pittsburgh Courier,* Jan. 30, 1945, p. 3.

187 *When word of V-E Day reached Burma:* "V-E News Brings No Rejoicing," *Pittsburgh Courier,* May 19, 1945, p. 1.

188 *"So you have come all the way":* "'Nehru Finds India's Problems Akin to U.S. Negroes'—Bolden," *Pittsburgh Courier,* Aug. 11, 1945, p. 1.

188 *Jinnah took a very different tone:* "Jinnah Explains Stand of India's Moslems to Frank Bolden," *Pittsburgh Courier,* Aug. 18, 1945, p. 18.

189 *When Gandhi invited Bolden:* "'British Must Go if India Is to Have Unity'— Gandhi," *Pittsburgh Courier,* Aug. 18, 1945, p. 23.

189 *When the Japanese finally surrendered:* "Tan Yanks Invade Japan," *Pittsburgh Courier,* Sep. 1, 1945, p. 1.

189 *"Peace Means These GIs Can Leave Jungle Hell":* *Pittsburgh Courier,* Sept. 1, p. 9.

190   *Winston Churchill's prediction:* "Burma's Stilwell Road: A Backbreaking World War II Project Is Revived," *Los Angeles Times,* Dec. 30, 2008, latimes.com.

190   *"600,000 Negroes Face Job Loss in Cutbacks":* Pittsburgh *Courier,* Sep. 1, 1945, p. 1.

7. THE COMPLEX MR. B

193   *Teenie Harris joined the* Courier: Laurence Glasco, "An American Life, an American Story: Charles 'Teenie' Harris and Images of Black Pittsburgh," in Cheryl Finley, Laurence Glasco, and Joe W. Trotter, *Teenie Harris Photographer: Image, Memory History* (Pittsburgh: University of Pittsburgh Press, 2011), p. 13.

193   *He photographed Johnny Woodruff:* Teenie Harris archive, Carnegie Museum of Art, teenie.cmoa.org. no. 2001.35.27670.

193   *Harris recorded the hero's welcome:* Ibid., no. 2001.35.38374.

193   *they trooped to Teenie's private studio:* Ibid., no. 2001.35.38624.

194   *"It's Eckstine Now!":* Pittsburgh *Courier,* Aug. 19, 1944, p. 13.

194   *a shot that would prove historic:* Harris archive, no. 2001.35.3088.

194   *it was a national sensation:* "Billy Eckstine's Ork Wows Swing World," *Pittsburgh Courier,* Oct. 14, 1944, p. 13.

194   *a blur in Teenie's photos:* Harris archive, no. 2001.35.11516.

194   *Billy Eckstine was as big an attraction:* Ibid., no. 2001.35.3033.

194   *When a cake was brought out:* Ibid., no. 2001.35.7176.

195   *Eckstine was placed at the head table:* Ibid.

195   *recorded a new song:* "Eckstine Waxes New Vocadiscs," *Pittsburgh Courier,* Dec. 9, 1944, p. 13.

195   *"press agented into a sepia Sinatra":* "Hill's Side," *Pittsburgh Courier,* Feb. 17, 1945, p. 13.

196   *His name, William Clarence Eckstein:* Cary Ginell, *Mr. B: The Music and Life of Billy Eckstine* (Milwaukee, Wisc.: Hal Leonard Books, 2013), pp. 1–5.

196   *his first taste of entertaining:* "'Hep-Cat' Billy Eckstine Credits Mother for Fabulous Career," *Pittsburgh Press,* Dec. 21, 1952, p. 55.

196   *Mary Ann Smith was an "Old Pittsburgher":* "Pioneer North Side Woman Succumbs," *Pittsburgh Courier,* June 27, 1931, p. 8.

197   *his first introduction to business:* "Scores of Hustling Lads Get Splendid Training in Thrift and Salesmanship," *Pittsburgh Courier,* March 15, 1930, p. 19.

197   *a radio column called "Wave Lengths":* Pittsburgh *Courier,* Jan. 2, 1932, p. 9.

197   *By his senior year:* Ginell, *Mr. B,* pp. 7–14.

198   *Eckstine moved to Chicago:* Ibid., pp. 15–19.

198   *Eckstine lent a needed dash of youth:* Ibid., pp. 21–27.

199   *On the train ride back north to Chicago:* Stanley Dance, *The World of Earl Hines* (New York: Da Capo,1983), pp. 238–39.

200   *Worried that he would never perform again:* Ginell, *Mr. B,* p. 27.

200   *The session took place:* Ibid., pp 29–35.

200   *the orgasmic finale left no doubt:* "1941 Hits Archive: Jelly, Jelly—Earl Hines (Billy Eckstine vocal)," uploaded by MusicProf18 to youtube.com.

200   *a "triumphant homecoming":* "Matthews Secures Earl Hines for Tri-State Tour During Christmas Holidays in Big Deal," *Pittsburgh Courier,* Nov. 16, 1940, p. 20.

201   *it was an instant craze:* Ginell, *Mr. B,* pp. 33–34.

201   *they went after two up-and-coming musicians:* Ibid., pp. 43–47.

201   *"Diz had his head on straight, man":* Eckstine interview in Dizzy Gillespie, *To Be or Not to Bop* (New York: Doubleday, 1979, Da Capo paperback edition), pp. 174–75.

202   *"These greasy muthafuckas cruised me":* Gillespie, *To Be or Not to Bop,* p. 174.

202   *Dizzy Gillespie was fifteen years old:* Ibid., pp. 32–33.

202   *Born on the North Side:* John Chilton, *Roy Eldridge: Little Jazz Giant* (New York: Continuum, 2002), pp. 1–23.

203   *he teamed up with his brother Joe:* "Brothers' Rhythm Kings Ready to Serve Public," *Pittsburgh Courier,* May 13, 1933.

203   *When Dizzy Gillespie moved to Philadelphia:* Gillespie, *To Be or Not to Bop,* p. 58.

203   *Teddy Hill was so taken:* Ibid., p. 65.

204   *Kenneth Spearman Clarke had grown up:* Phillip Daquila, "Keeping Time: *Klook* Remembers Jazz Drummer's Place in History," *Pittsburgh History,* Spring 1995, pp 46–48.

204   *"the beginnings of modern drumming":* Gunther Schuller, *The Swing Era: The Development of Jazz, 1930–1945* (New York: Oxford University Press, p. 421.

204   *he and Dizzy Gillespie clicked immediately:* Gillespie, *To Be or Not to Bop,* pp. 9–100.

205   *"It wasn't only":* To Be or Not to Bop, p 99.

205   *managing a small nightclub:* Rudi Blesh, "Flying Home," in Robert Gottlieb, ed., *Reading Jazz: A Gathering of Autobiography, Reportage and Criticism, from 1919 to Now* (New York: Vintage, 1999 paperback edition), pp. 529–34.

206   *Minton's became a nightly musical laboratory:* Gillespie, *To Be or Not to Bop,* pp. 134–51.

206   *another Pittsburgher became a nightly presence:* Ibid., pp. 148–51; Linda Dahl, *Morning Glory: A Biography of Mary Lou Williams* (Berkeley: University of California Press, 1999), pp. 182–83.

207   *When the band reached Hartford:* Gillespie, *To Be or Not to Bop,* pp. 128–33.

208   *playing in the Hines band gave them the chance:* Ibid., pp. 176–77.

209   *another raw but extraordinary young talent:* Ginell, *Mr. B,* pp. 49–53.

209   *the bandleader suggested another title:* Dance, *The World of Earl Hines,* p. 90.

210   *"the incubator of bop":* Richard Harrington, "Earl Hines: Piano Man," *Washington Post,* April 15, 1983, washingtonpost.com.

210   *In early August of 1943:* Ginell, *Mr. B,* pp. 52–53.

210   *So Billy began reassembling the old Hines bandstand:* Ibid., pp. 55–62.

210   *a skinny dark-hued teenager:* Ibid., pp. 60–61.

211   *"B didn't take no shit off nobody":* Ibid., p. xviii.

211   *For the other members in the orchestra:* Ibid., pp. 61–62.

211   *In his first year as a bandleader:* Ibid., pp. 63–71.

212   *Eckstine was ready for a change as well:* Ibid., pp. 85–90.

213   *he privately resented singing the blues:* Ibid., p. 34.

213   *"nothing approaching the blues about it":* Ibid., p. 82.

213   *In Boston, a drunken woman:* Ibid., p. 93.

214   *an admiring telegram from Frank Sinatra:* "After the Thin Man," *The Billboard,*
      Jan. 11, 1947, p. 15.

214   *he was striking out on his own:* Ginell, *Mr. B,* pp. 95–98.

214   *one of Eckstine's first trips:* "Frogs' 'Night of Stars' Set for Mosque, August 7,"
      Pittsburgh Courier, July 13, 1946, p. 21; "'Night of Stars' Greatest Show in Frogs'
      History," *Pittsburgh Courier,* Aug. 16, 1947, p. 16.

215   *the hottest American male vocalist of the late 1940s:* Ginell, *Mr. B,* pp. 99–102.

215   *almost as famous for his look and his lifestyle:* Ibid., pp. 103–6.

215   *Walter Winchell reported:* Cincinnati Enquirer, April 29, 1947, p. 7.

215   *Thousands of fans on Easter break:* Ginell, *Mr. B,* pp. 108–10.

216   *By the time Eckstine returned to the Paramount:* "He's Idol of the Bobby-Sox
      Brigade," *St. Louis Post-Dispatch,* May 17, 1950, p. 42.

216   *At the end of his act:* Ginell, *Mr. B,* p. 109.

216   Life *magazine commissioned a profile:* "Mr. B: Bobby Soxers Become Billy Soxers
      to Boost Baritone Billy Eckstine," *Life,* April 24, 1950, pp. 101–4.

216   *a new club called Bop City:* "Broadway, by Mark Barron," syndicated in *Fitch-
      burgh Sentinel,* May 12, 1949, p. 6.

217   *Holmes snapped a photo:* "Mr. B," *Life,* p. 101.

217   *Holmes later said the photograph was her favorite:* David Hajdu, *Heroes and Vil-
      lains: Essays on Music, Movies, Comics, and Culture* (New York: Da Capo, 2009),
      p. 13.

217   *Life readers leapt to their own:* Ginell, *Mr. B,* p. 115.

218   *"It changed everything":* Hajdu, *Heroes and Villains,* pp. 13–14.

218   *In fact, the fallout:* Ginell, *Mr. B,* pp. 119–26.

219   *the role of Joe in* Carmen Jones: Ibid., pp. 131–32.

219   *But Eckstine also couldn't win for trying:* Ibid., pp. 127–31.

219   *In 1954, the bottom started to fall out:* Ibid., pp. 133–37.

220   *"Is Billy Eckstine Through?":* Jet, Jan. 20, 1955.

220   *Billy returned to Pittsburgh:* Ginell, *Mr. B.,* pp. 139–43.

220   *He signed a new deal with Roulette Records:* Ibid., pp. 147–50.

221   *Levy pulled a pistol from his desk:* Ibid., p. 148.

221 *To celebrate the poll's fourth anniversary:* "Courier's Carnegie Music Hall Concert Smash Hit," *Pittsburgh Courier,* March 22, 1947, p. 16.

222 *Like so many other kids from black Pittsburgh:* Transcript of 1996 Ray Brown interview with WKCR disk jockey Ted Panken, posted on tedpanken.wordpress. com, Oct. 13, 2011.

222 *the remarkable versatility for which he would become known:* "Ray Brown, Master Jazz Bassist, Dies at 75," *New York Times,* July 4, 2002, p. B6.

222 *By the time he was an upperclassman at Schenley High School:* Brown interview, tedpanken.workpress.com.

223 *Ray and Ella fell in love:* "Ella Fitzgerald, the Voice of Jazz, Dies at 79," *New York Times,* June 16, 1996, p. 1.

223 *For Ray, one of those projects:* "Ray Brown, Master Jazz Bassist," *New York Times.*

223 *In 1949, a young Canadian pianist named Oscar Peterson:* "Ray Brown: Jazz Master," *Pittsburgh Music History,* sites.google.com/site/pittsburghmusichistory.com.

223 *Jones hailed him:* Matthew Rybicki, *Ray Brown: Legendary Jazz Bassist* (Hal Leonard Corp. e-book), 2013.

224 *Christian McBride, was even more specific:* Brown interview, tedpanken.word press.com.

224 *He remembered one peer in particular:* Ibid.

224 *There was one place Erroll Garner couldn't play:* "Erroll Garner: Jazz Piano Giant," *Pittsburgh Music History,* sites.google.com/pittsburghmusichistory.

224 *he set out for New York City:* "Erroll Garner: Jazz Piano Giant," *Pittsburgh Music History.*

224 *Martha Glaser also hailed from the Pittsburgh area:* "Martha Glaser 1921–2014," *Jazz Promo Services,* Dec. 3, 2014, jazznewsyoucanuse.com.

225 *Martha lit up in Erroll's presence:* "Erroll & Martha" Exhibit, University of Pittsburgh Library, online at pitt.libguides.com.

225 *It was an appeal summed up:* Billy Rowe's Notebook," *Pittsburgh Courier,* Sep. 16, 1950, p. 14.

225 *Arriving minutes after his sidemen:* "The Day Mr. Piano Amazed Broadway," *Pittsburgh Courier,* May 29, 1954, p. 23.

226 *Erroll was flying from San Francisco to Chicago:* Whitney Balliett, "Being a Genius," *The New Yorker,* Feb. 22, 1982, pp. 69–70.

226 *To earn a little extra cash:* Thomas Cunniffe, "Erroll Garner: The Complete 'Concert by the Sea,'" JazzHistoryOnline, 2007.

227 *One buyer was a gentleman:* Ruth Garner Moore interview in *Erroll Garner: No One Can Hear You Read,* a film by Atticus Brady, First Run Features, 2012.

228 *During one* Tonight Show *appearance:* Tonight Show clip in ibid.

228 *he collapsed onstage:* "Erroll Garner, Jazz Pianist; Composed 'Misty,' 'That's My Kick,'" *New York Times,* Jan. 3, 1977, p. 24.

228   *Jamal had an answer for the critics:* Ahmad Jamal interview in *No One Can Hear You Read.*

8. "JACKIE'S BOSWELL"

231   *On a hot Florida afternoon:* Chris Lamb, *Blackout: The Untold Story of Jackie Robinson's First Spring Training* (Lincoln, Neb.: University of Nebraska Press, 2004), pp. 5–19; Wendell Smith, "Robinson Arrives in Fla. Camp," *Pittsburgh Courier,* March 9, 1946, p. 17.

233   *referred to himself as "Jackie's Boswell":* Citation for "1993 J. G. Taylor Spink Award Winner Wendell Smith," National Baseball Hall of Fame, baseballhall. org.

234   *Smith grew up around white people:* Wendell Smith interview in Jerome Holtzman, *No Cheering in the Press Box* (New York: Henry Holt, 1973, paperback edition), pp. 323–24.

234   *a soapbox on the subject of race:* "Smitty's Sport Spurts," *Pittsburgh Courier,* May 14, 1938, p. 17, Jan. 14, 1939, p. 14.

235   *Wendell proposed a new one:* Holtzman, *No Cheering,* p. 314.

235   *Smith's investigation was a big hit: Pittsburgh Courier* sports pages, July 15, 22, 29, Aug. 5, 19, 1939.

235   *"I've seen a million": Pittsburgh Courier,* Aug. 5, 1939, p. 16.

235   *an open letter to Kenesaw Mountain Landis:* "Ches Sez," *Pittsburgh Courier,* May 30, 1942, p. 17.

236   *White sportswriters picked up on the theme:* "'If Negro's Good Enough for Navy, He's Good Enough for Majors'—Parker," *Pittsburgh Courier,* July 25, 1942, p. 17.

236   *shamed Landis into taking a position:* "Commissioner Landis' Emancipation Proclamation," *Pittsburgh Courier,* July 25, 1942, p. 17.

236   *the commissioner finally consented:* Wendell Smith, "Publishers Place Case of Negro Players Before Big League Owners," *Pittsburgh Courier,* Dec. 11, 1943, p. 1.

236   *the morning's most memorable remarks:* "Ira F. Lewis' Factual Speech to Judge Landis and Major League Owners," *Pittsburgh Courier,* Dec. 11, 1943, p. 14.

237   *When Smith chased him down for comment:* Wendell Smith, "Frick Says Owners Were Impressed by Publishers," *Pittsburgh Courier,* Dec. 11, 1943, p. 14.

237   *"a subtle 'fence game' on this question":* "'Smitty's' Sports Spurts," *Pittsburgh Courier,* Dec. 2, 1944, p. 12.

238   *Benswanger had backed out of a promise:* Jules Tygiel, *Baseball's Great Experiment: Jackie Robinson and His Legacy* (New York: Oxford University Press, 1983, 2008 paperback edition), p. 39.

238   *four black men walked into the Dodger spring training camp:* "McDuffie, Thomas

First Negroes in Big League Uniforms," *Pittsburgh Courier*, April 14, 1945, p. 12.

238 *McDuffie and Thomas were too old:* "'Smitty's' Sports Spurts," *Pittsburgh Courier*, April 14, 1945, p. 12.

239 *The* Courier *had first written about him in 1940:* "Jackie Robertson [sic] Stars on Diamond," *Pittsburgh Courier*, March 16, 1940.

239 *Now Smith was working at lining up a pro tryout:* Holtzman, *No Cheering*, pp. 318–20.

239 *Jackie was accustomed to being around white people:* Arnold Rampersad, *Jackie Robinson: A Biography* (New York: Ballantine, 1997), pp. 62–112.

240 *witness his short temper for the first time:* Howard Bryant, *Shut Out: A Story of Race and Baseball in Boston* (New York: Routledge, 2002), p. 31.

240 *The previous year, Gus Greenlee:* "'Smitty's' Sports Spurts," *Pittsburgh Courier*, April 28, 1945, p. 12.

241 *Smith called Rickey to check out the story:* Holtzman, *No Cheering*, pp. 313–14, 320–21.

242 *Robinson was playing for the Monarchs:* Jackie Robinson and Wendell Smith, *Jackie Robinson: My Own Story* (New York: Greenburg Publishers, 1948), pp. 14–23.

242 *"it would have killed it":* Holtzman, *No Cheering*, p. 321.

242 *When that day arrived two months later:* Robinson and Smith, *My Own Story,* pp. 28–30.

243 *many didn't give Robinson much of a chance:* "What 'Name' Writers Wrote About Signing of Jackie Robinson," *Pittsburgh Courier*, Nov. 3, 1945, p. 12.

243 *One was a first-person account:* "'Glad of Opportunity and Will Try to Make Good'—Robinson," *Pittsburgh Courier*, Nov. 3, 1945, p. 1.

243 *The other was a two-hour interview:* "Branch Rickey Tells Courier Why He Signed Jackie Robinson to Play with Montreal Club," *Pittsburgh Courier*, Nov. 3, 1945, p. 1.

244 *"We're not here to give anything away":* "Posey Skeptical About Tryouts for Sepia Stars in Big Leagues," *Pittsburgh Courier*, Aug. 29, 1942, p. 16.

244 *For a brief time after the Royals announcement:* Tygiel, *Baseball's Great Experiment*, pp. 86–89.

244 *In the days after Cum Posey succumbed:* "Sports World Pays Final Tribute to Cum Posey," *Pittsburgh Courier*, April 6, 1946, p. 17.

245 *It was the most important social night of the year:* Arthur Daley, "At the Baseball Writers Show," *New York Times*, Feb. 4, 1946, p. 23.

246 *Wendell Smith denounced the white baseball writers:* "The Sports Beat," *Pittsburgh Courier*, June 1946, p. 12.

247 *Jackie sent him a grateful letter:* Robinson letter to Smith, dated Oct. 31, 1945, Wendell Smith archive, National Baseball Hall of Fame (NBHF), baseballhall.org.

247 *Jackie wrote again from Venezuela*: Robinson letter to Smith, undated, NBHF archive.

247 *the example of "good conduct"*: Smith letter to Robinson, dated Dec. 4, 1945, NBHF archive.

247 *plans for Robinson's first spring training*: Holtzman, *No Cheering*, pp. 321–22.

247 *Rickey proposed that Smith serve as Robinson's chaperone*: Rickey letter to Smith, dated Jan. 8, 1946, NBHF archive.

247 *far loftier motivations than money*: Smith letter to Rickey, dated Jan. 14, 1946, NBHF archive.

248 *They owned one of the finest houses*: Francis Coleman Oliver, "The Brock House," Goldsboromuseum.com.

248 *Rickey showed his gratitude*: "The Sports Beat," *Pittsburgh Courier*, March 9, 1946, p. 16.

248 *The day after Jackie and Rachel Robinson's arrival*: Robinson and Smith, *My Own Story*, pp. 66–70.

249 *they received a very different reception*: Holtzman, *No Cheering*, p. 322; Lamb, *Blackout*, p. 88, based on interview with Billy Rowe (see p 196, note 33).

249 *when the two players returned to the Brock home*: Robinson and Smith, *My Own Story*, pp. 70–73.

250 *In Daytona Beach*: Lamb, *Blackout*, pp. 92–93; Robinson and Smith, *My Own Story*, pp. 75–77.

250 *their best to buoy Jackie's spirits*: Robinson and Smith, *My Own Story*, pp. 74–75.

250 *but he left encouraged*: Ibid., pp. 78–79.

251 *he gave Smith a vote of confidence*: Rampersad, *Jackie Robinson*, pp. 146–47.

251 *When Montreal went to Deland*: Robinson and Smith, *My Own Story*, pp. 80, 97–98.

251 *Smith added up the toll that racism*: "Cancels 9 Games When Towns Bar Negro Players," *Pittsburgh Courier*, April 13, 1946, p. 14.

252 *he had felt the strain of expectation*: "The Sports Beat," *Pittsburgh Courier*, April 20, 1946, p. 16.

252 *savored the moment*: "The Sports Beat," *Pittsburgh Courier*, April 27, 1946, p. 16.

253 *a self-help lecture reminiscent of Robert L. Vann*: "Making Good in Baseball," *Pittsburgh Courier*, April 27, 1946, p. 6.

253 *a season-long love affair*: Robinson and Smith, *My Own Story*, pp. 104–7.

253 *After the Royals won their final game*: Ibid., pp. 107–10.

253 *the irony of a white mob*: "Fans 'Mob' Jackie in Great Tribute to Star," *Pittsburgh Courier*, Oct. 12, 1946, p. 1.

254 *His only contribution*: "The Sports Beat," *Pittsburgh Courier*, Oct. 19, 1946, p. 12.

254 *In January 1947, Josh Gibson*: Mark Ribowsky, *The Power and the Darkness: The Life of Josh Gibson in the Shadows of the Game* (New York: Simon & Schuster, 1996), pp. 291–95.

255 *cited the cause as a stroke:* "Josh Gibson Dead," Associated Press, Jan. 21, 1947.

255 *Wendell Smith blamed a more insidious culprit:* Ribowsky, *The Power and the Darkness,* pp. 297–98.

256 *"46 the Greatest Year for Negro Athletes":* "The Sports Beat," *Pittsburgh Courier,* Jan. 4, 1947, p. 12.

256 *Rickey still had not made his intentions clear:* "The Sports Beat," *Pittsburgh Courier,* Jan. 18, 1947, p. 16.

256 *Robinson sent a worried letter to Pittsburgh:* Robinson letter to Smith, dated Feb. 4, 1947, NBHF archive.

257 *he invited Smith and Robinson to a meal at the Tivoli Hotel:* "Robinson Segregated in Panama?," *Pittsburgh Courier,* March 29, 1947, p. 4.

257 *He encouraged Jackie to be a "whirling demon":* Robinson and Smith, *My Own Story,* p. 120.

257 *Jackie more than rose to Rickey's challenge:* "Jackie Bats .667 in Tilts," *Pittsburgh Courier,* March 29, 1947.

257 *the word he had so long awaited finally arrived:* Robinson and Smith, *My Own Story,* pp. 120–21.

257 *Smith shared the historic scoop:* "Jackie on First for Brooklyn," *Pittsburgh Courier,* March 29, 1947, p. 1.

258 *Smith reported on the resistance:* "The Sports Beat," *Pittsburgh Courier,* April 12, 1947, p. 14.

258 *That morning, a phone call awoke Jackie:* Robinson and Smith, *My Own Story,* pp. 123–24.

259 *Arthur Mann walked into the press area:* Rampersad, *Jackie Robinson,* pp. 166–67.

259 *When Robinson arrived at Ebbets Field:* Robinson and Smith, *My Own Story,* p. 126.

259 *Sukeforth turned to his newest rookie:* Rampersad, *Jackie Robinson,* p. 167.

259 Courier *editors pulled out all the stops:* "Jackie Robinson Packing 'Em In," *Pittsburgh Courier,* April 19, 1947, p. 1.

260 *As Jackie emerged from the dressing room:* "The Sports Beat," *Pittsburgh Courier,* April 19, 1947, p. 18.

260 *"Ed Stanky, a great player":* "Jackie Robinson Says," *Pittsburgh Courier,* April 19, 1947, p. 18.

260 *Bill Nunn touted the paper's role:* "Let's Take It in Stride," *Pittsburgh Courier,* April 19 1947, p. 18.

260 *Smith had more good news to report:* "Jackie Robinson Bats .429 in First Week in Majors," *Pittsburgh Courier,* April 26, 1947, p. 15.

260 *Branch Rickey joked:* "Fans Swamp Jackie; Public Affairs Out," *Pittsburgh Courier,* April 26, 1947, p. 1.

261 *more than five hundred letters piled up:* "The Sports Beat," *Pittsburgh Courier,* April 26, 1947, p. 14.

261 *The honeymoon didn't last long*: Robinson and Smith, *My Own Story*, pp. 128, 145.

261 *The abuse didn't end there*: Rampersad, *Jackie Robinson*, pp. 172–73.

261 the Courier *exposed the source of the attacks*: "Phillies Warned by Baseball Czar over Robinson Incident," *Pittsburgh Courier*, May 10, 1947, p. 1.

262 *dismissed the tormentors with a weary shrug*: "Jackie Robinson Says," *Pittsburgh Courier*, May 3, 1947, p. 15.

262 *When the rumor reached Ford Frick*: "Frick's Actions Avert Big Strike," *Pittsburgh Courier*, May 17, 1947, p. 14.

262 *there was more razzing*: "The Sports Beat," *Pittsburgh Courier*, May 31, 1947, p. 14.

263 *what it was like now for Robinson on the road*: Ibid.

263 *they made a point of praising Hank Greenberg*: "Jackie Robinsons Says," *Pittsburgh Courier*, May 24, 1947, p. 14.

264 *While in Pittsburgh, Smith was able*: "The Sports Beat," *Pittsburgh Courier*, May 24, 1947, p. 14.

264 *Robinson and Smith snuck off to play a round of golf*: "The Sports Beat," *Pittsburgh Courier*, June 28, 1947, p. 14.

264 *By the time the Dodgers returned*: "In Midst of Nine Game Hit Streak," *Pittsburgh Courier*, June 28, 1947, p. 14.

265 *Robinson's success had also emboldened Bill Veeck*: "The Sports Beat," *Pittsburgh Courier*, July 12, 1947, p. 14.

265 *Robinson's nemesis, Joe Garagiola*: Rampersad, *Jackie Robinson*, pp. 184–85.

266 *Smith predicted a contest between grit and brawn*: "Wendell Smith's Sports Beat," *Pittsburgh Courier*, Sep. 27, 1947, p. 13.

266 *Smith chose to accentuate the positive*: "Yanks Win; Jackie Big Factor in Dodgers Showing," *Pittsburgh Courier*, Oct. 11, 1947, p. 15.

266 *he stood to make a well-earned killing*: "Jackie's Off to Hollywood," *Pittsburgh Courier*, Oct. 18, 1947, p. 1.

266 *Wendell Smith received new opportunities*: "About Wendell Smith," NBHF archive.

266 *a chill in their friendship*: Rampersad, *Jackie Robinson*, pp. 206–7.

267 *The excuse infuriated Smith*: "Wendell Smith's Sports Beat," *Pittsburgh Courier*, March 19, 1949, p. 10.

267 *Smith never stopped crusading*: "Wendell Smith and Jim Crow" and "Wendell Smith and the Hall of Fame," NBHF archive.

268 *he devoted one of his last columns*: "Black Manager Seen on Scene," *Chicago Sun-Times*, reprinted in *The Billings Gazette*, June 4, 1947, p. 64.

268 *"I won't be satisfied"*: Wendell Smith, "The Jackie Robinson I Knew," *The New Pittsburgh Courier*, Nov. 4, 1972, p 9.

268 *From his sickbed, Smith wrote a remembrance*: "Wendell Smith: The Jackie Robinson I Knew," reprinted in the *Pittsburgh Courier*, Nov. 4, 1972, p. 9.

268 *When Smith himself died:* Louis Martin, "We Mourn a Notable Friend," *Pittsburgh Courier*, Dec. 9, 1972, p. 3.

9. THE WOMEN OF "UP SOUTH"

271 *Edna Chappell had grown tired:* Evelyn Cunningham interview transcript, *The Black Press: Soldiers Without Swords*, a film by Stanley Nelson, pbs.org/black press.

273 *In Washington D.C., Jim Crow practices:* "Courier Intensifies Crusade," *Pittsburgh Courier*, Jan. 18, 1947, p. 1.

273 *P.L. Prattis had been credentialed:* "Race Newsman (at Long Last) Admitted to Senate and House Press Galleries," *Pittsburgh Courier*, March 22, 1947, p. 1.

273 *Chappell was shaken by what she found:* Cunningham transcript, *Soldiers Without Swords*.

273 *the latest wave of black migrants:* Joe W. Trotter and Jared N. Day, *Race and Renaissance: African Americans in Pittsburgh Since World War II* (Pittsburgh: University of Pittsburgh Press, 2010), pp. 44–89.

274 *a two-year picketing campaign:* "Break Job Barriers in Pittsburgh Department Stories," *Pittsburgh Courier*, Feb. 8, 1947, p. 22.

274 *Homer S. Brown, a Pittsburgh judge:* Trotter and Day, *Race and Renaissance*, pp. 59–60.

275 *opportunities for returning white vets:* "GI Joe Going Back to College," *Pittsburgh Post-Gazette*, Sep. 13, 1945, p. 11.

275 *Joseph L. Murphy was an Irish kid:* "Tests Show Veteran Was Right About Job," *Pittsburgh Post-Gazette*, Feb. 11, 1956, p. 17.

275 *When white vets like Murphy needed money:* "Banks to Open Office to Help Vets on Loans," *Pittsburgh Post-Gazette*, May 9, 1945.

276 *plans to return to full-time study:* "30,000 Negro Soldiers Eye Post-War Education, *Pittsburgh Courier*, Jan. 13, 1945, p. 2.

276 *Yet Jim Crow restrictions:* "300,000 Vets Lose GI Rights," *Pittsburgh Courier*, June 24, 1950, p. 1.

276 *Outraged by the findings:* Arthur G. Klein, "Discrimination Against Veterans by Schools," *The Jewish Veteran*, April 1947, pp. 11–12.

277 *The resulting series:* John H. Young, "The White South Speaks," *Pittsburgh Courier*, Jan. 6, 13, 20, 17, Feb. 3, 10, 24, March 3, 10, 17, 24, 31, April 7, 14, 1945.

277 *But when Young interviewed the general:* "No Post for Negro in Vets' Administration," *Pittsburgh Courier*, Nov. 3, 1945, p. 1.

277 *Charting the legislative path:* "Congressional Wrangling May Leave GI Bill Hopeless Mess," *Pittsburgh Courier*, June 16, 1945, p. 3.

278 *Young was able to report:* "Easier for Veterans to Buy Homes Under Revised Bill," *Pittsburgh Courier*, Dec. 1, 1945, p. 1.

278 *To investigate, Young traveled:* "Rules May Make Vet Loans Difficult for Race GIs to Obtain," *Pittsburgh Courier*, March 17, 1945, p. 9.

278 *Young highlighted the plight of Negro soldiers:* "Courier Launches Probe of Army's Blue Discharges," *Pittsburgh Courier*, Oct. 20, 1945, p. 1.

279 *a sympathetic member of the Senate Veterans Committee:* "Courier Articles Put into Record," *Pittsburgh Courier*, Nov. 17, 1945, p. 1.

279 *he received a delegation:* "Extra! Newspaper Publishers Call on President Truman," *Pittsburgh Courier*, June 2, 1945, p. 1.

279 *When Truman met with the group a second time:* "Publishers Laud Pres. Truman's Fair Policy," *Pittsburgh Courier*, March 9, 1946, p. 13.

279 *The publishers were even more encouraged:* "Publishers OK Truman Charter," *Pittsburgh Courier*, March 6, 1948, p. 1.

280 *praising a Courier story:* "Truman Is Courier Fan," *Pittsburgh Courier*, June 26, 1948, p. 1.

280 *Truman turned evasive:* John L. Clark, "It's the South vs. Negro Vote," *Pittsburgh Courier*, July 17, 1948, p. 1.

280 *one reporter remained conspicuously bullish:* David McCullough, *Truman* (New York: Touchstone, 1992), p. 710.

280 *In Clark's last dispatch before the election:* "John L. Clark Says Truman May Win Vote in 23 States but Still Won't Have Enough," *Pittsburgh Courier*, Oct. 30, 1948, p. 2.

281 *Clark chalked it up to the black vote:* "Negro Vote in 3 Key States Big Factor in Dems' Victory," *Pittsburgh Courier*, Nov. 13, 1948, p. 1.

281 *no racial segregation at his Inaugural Balls:* "Truman Wasn't Kidding!," *Pittsburgh Courier*, Dec. 18, 1948, p. 1.

281 *Lewis suffered a fatal stroke:* "Nation Mourns Courier President," *Pittsburgh Courier*, Sep. 4, 1948, p. 1.

282 *Jesse Vann was in her office:* "Toki Types," *Pittsburgh Courier*, March 5, 1949, p. 8.

282 *On a warm Georgia evening:* Caela Abrams, "Bullets and Ballot Boxes: The Isaiah Nixon Story," *The Georgia Civil Rights Cold Cases Project*, Emory University, scholarblogs.emory.edu.

283 *Yvonne, as she was known within the family:* In *Courier* stories about the Nixon family cited in this chapter, the name of the third child was spelled "Evarn." In fact, the name on her birth certificate was "Dortha Evon." As explained to me by Dorothy Nixon Williams, the married name she goes by now, her parents didn't know how to spell her intended name. Only when she began school did she discover the correct spelling and become known outside the family as Dorothy. When she retired many years later, she had her given names legally changed to Dorothy Yvonne.

284 *Announcing Nixon's death:* "Georgia Negro Fatally Shot After Demanding His Vote," *Pittsburgh Press*, Sep. 12, 1948, p. 1.

284 *The judge also ruled:* Abrams, "Bullets and Ballot Boxes."

284 *When Rivera got to Alston:* "Nixon Family Missing," *Pittsburgh Courier,* Dec. 4, 1948, p. 1.

284 *Eventually Rivera received a tip:* "Courier Finds Nixons," *Pittsburgh Courier,* Dec. 11, 1948, p. 1.

285 *Evelyn Cunningham was working:* Yanick Rice Lamb, "Evelyn Cunningham: The Pittsburgh Courier's 'Lynching Editor,'" submitted to *Journal of Women's History,* June 2014, yanickricelamb.com.

285 *an aunt who was dating Edgar Rouzeau:* Evelyn Cunningham interview for *National Visionary Project,* visionaryproject.org.

285 *she, too, yearned to do more:* Lamb, "Evelyn Cunningham"; Cunningham interview, *National Visionary Project.*

286 *she had a bold idea:* "Toki Types," *Pittsburgh Courier,* Sep. 17, 1949, p. 8.

286 *Evelyn Cunningham on the front page:* "Christmas for Nixons Will Be Real!," *Pittsburgh Courier,* Dec. 25, 1948, p. 1.

287 *In a poignant profile:* "Fear of Whites Haunts Nixons, Writer Reveals," *Pittsburgh Courier,* Jan. 1, 1949, p. 1.

287 *Cunningham profiled the Nixon children:* "Nixon Kids Like All Others, Except—," *Pittsburgh Courier,* Jan, 8, 1949, p. 1.

288 *hundreds of* Courier *readers sent donations:* "Sports, Theatrical Worlds Join Nixon Fund Campaign," *Pittsburgh Courier,* Jan. 22, 1949, p. 1.

288 *Sallie Nixon traveled north:* "Sallie Nixon Finds Warm Hearts in Ice-Cold North," *Pittsburgh Courier,* Feb. 5, 1949, p. 1.

288 *the most famous black architect in America:* Karen E. Hudson, *Paul R. Williams, Architect* (New York: Rizzoli,1993).

288 *Jesse Vann traveled to Jacksonville:* "Nixon Family in New Home," *Pittsburgh Courier,* Dec. 24, 1949, p. 1.

289 *touted "The Women" as "spicy reading":* Pittsburgh Courier, Jan. 12, 1952, p. 5.

289 *the absence of data about black women:* "Race Women Not Included," *Pittsburgh Courier,* Aug. 29, 1953, p. 1.

290 *"Race Leaders with Sex Appeal":* Pittsburgh Courier, Feb. 9, 1952, p. 10.

290 *the "Groveland Four" case:* Gilbert King, *Devil in the Grove: Thurgood Marshall, the Groveland Boys, and the Dawn of a New America* (New York: HarperCollins, 2012).

291 *Cunningham was one of a handful of reporters:* "Move Wounded Prisoner from Hospital to Jail," *Pittsburgh Courier,* Nov. 17, 1951, p. 1.

292 *Cunningham went to Irvin's home:* "Irvin's Parents Bent with Grief by New Events," *Pittsburgh Courier,* Nov. 17, 1951, p. 4.

292 *teased her when he saw a man's byline:* Lamb, "Evelyn Cunningham."

293 *Cunningham recalled one night:* Juan Williams, *Thurgood Marshall: American Revolutionary* (New York: Times Books, 1998), pp. 191–92.

293 *he allowed Cunningham into their inner sanctum:* "Legal Aces Battling Segregation," *Pittsburgh Courier,* Sep. 12, 1953, p. 13.

293 *When the justices heard the arguments:* "Washington Pipeline," *Pittsburgh Courier,* Dec. 12, 1953, p. 13.

293 *a joint* Courier-NAACP *fundraising drive:* "'EE' Fund Hits $13,000 Mark," *Pittsburgh Courier,* Dec. 12, 1953, p. 1.

293 *"SCHOOLS WILL BE MIXED!":* Pittsburgh Courier, May 29, 1954, p. 1.

294 *"School Decision Fails to Excite Southern Mothers!":* Pittsburgh Courier, May 29, 1954, p. 3.

294 *Roy Wilkins:* "Roy Wilkins . . . NAACP's Man of the Hour," *Pittsburgh Courier,* June 25, 1955, p. 24.

294 *Marian Anderson:* "Marian to Courier: 'Never Gave Up Hope,'" *Pittsburgh Courier,* Oct. 16, 1954, p. 1.

294 *Emmett Till's murder:* "Harlem Protests Lynching," *Pittsburgh Courier,* Oct. 1, 1955, p. 1.

294 *In January 1956:* Taylor Branch, *Parting the Waters: America in the King Years, 1954–63* (New York: Simon & Schuster, 1988), pp. 143–68.

294 *When Cunningham arrived in Montgomery:* Lamb, "Evelyn Cunningham."

295 *Rather than wait to be arrested:* "Montgomery's Folks Prove Negroes Can Get Together," *Pittsburgh Courier,* March 3, 1956, p. 4.

295 *she attended the first MIA meetings:* "'More Determined than Ever,'" *Pittsburgh Courier,* March 3, 1956, p. 3.

296 *Cunningham wrote a status report:* "Confidential Report from the Courier's Evelyn Cunningham," *Pittsburgh Courier,* March 3, 1956, p. 3.

296 *calling more than thirty black citizens:* "Tired of Being Called 'Apes,'" *Pittsburgh Courier,* March 31, 1968, p. 2.

297 *she opened up to her female readers:* "The Women," *Pittsburgh Courier,* March 10, 1956, p. 33.

298 *a "Man in the News" profile:* "Battle Against Tradition," *New York Times,* March 21, 1956, p. 28.

298 *When they first met:* Lamb, "Evelyn Cunningham."

298 *the first truly personal profile of King:* "The Life Story of Martin Luther King, Jr.," *Pittsburgh Courier,* April 7, 1956.

299 *Cunningham coaxed King's wife:* "Choosing the Ministry Was Not an Easy Decision but He Had No Trouble Selecting the Right Girl!," *Pittsburgh Courier,* April 14, 1956, p. 6.

299 *In the last story in her series:* "Why and How This Young Pastor Became Leader of Bus Boycott," *Pittsburgh Courier,* April 21, 1956, p. 6.

300 *Covering the unrest in Birmingham, Alabama:* Lamb, "Evelyn Cunningham."

300 *Eventually Cunningham landed another part-time job:* Ibid.

300 *Upon her death at the age of ninety-four:* "On the Street; Luminous," *New York Times*, May 16, 2010, accessed nytimes.com.

301 *"What I Like About Dixie":* Pittsburgh Courier, July 7, 1956, p. 14.

10. THE BARD OF A BROKEN WORLD

303 *Daisy Wilson had North Carolina roots:* August Wilson, "Living on a Mother's Prayer," *New York Times*, May 12, 1996, p. E13.

303 *reading was the one thing that Negroes needed:* August Wilson, "Feed Your Mind, the Rest Will Follow," *Pittsburgh Post-Gazette*, March 28, 1999, p. B1.

304 *While she was shopping at a grocery store one day:* John Lahr, "Been Here and Gone," *The New Yorker*, April 16, 2001, p. 55.

304 *"The first book he read by himself:* Bill Moyers, "August Wilson: Playwright," in Jackson R. Bryer and Mary C. Hartig, eds., *Conversations with August Wilson* (Jackson, Miss.: University Press of Mississippi, 2006), p. 66.

304 *he had devoured all of the Hardy Boys books:* Wilson, "Feed Your Mind."

304 *She enrolled him in the Holy Trinity School:* Laurence Glasco and Christopher Rawson, *August Wilson: Pittsburgh Places in His Life and Plays* (Pittsburgh: Pittsburgh History and Landmarks Foundation, 2011), p. 64.

304 *delighted in infuriating the nuns:* Lahr, "Been Here," p. 55.

304 *Freddy's experience of his father:* Ibid.

305 *Daisy did her best:* Ibid., pp. 54–55.

305 *the Kittel children made friends:* Laurence Glasco, "August Wilson and the Hill District," *Pittsburgh Post-Gazette*, Feb. 25, 2007, p. H6.

305 *Daisy's closest friends:* Recollections of Burley in *August Wilson: The Ground on Which I Stand*, Sam Pollard, director, *American Masters*, PBS, 2014; Allen Rosenfeld, *Charley Burley: The Life and Hard Times of an Uncrowned Champion* (Bloomington, Ind.: AuthorHouse, 2007).

306 *another lesson in standing tall:* Dinah Livingston, "Cool August: Mr. Wilson's Red-Hot Blues," in Bryer and Hartig, eds., *Conversations*, p. 47.

306 *Julie Burley urged her friend:* Lahr, "Been Here," p. 55.

306 *David Bedford was a laborer:* Ibid., p. 56; Mary Ellen Snodgrass, *August Wilson: A Literary Companion* (Jefferson, N.C.: McFarland, 2004), p. 7.

307 *an alarming rumor:* Sala Udin, "Growing Up with August," in Laurence Glasco and Christopher Rawson, *August Wilson: Pittsburgh Places in His Life and Plays* (Pittsburgh History and Landmarks Foundation, 2011), p. xvii.

307 *his first experience of being singled out:* Lahr, "Been Here," p. 56.

308 *The one subject that held his attention:* Livingston, "Cool August," pp. 43–44.

309 *"Unless you call everybody in here":* Lahr, "Been Here," pp. 56–57.

309 *Freddy had run out of places to go—except one:* Wilson, "Feed Your Mind."

310 *she was furious:* Lahr, "Been Here," p. 57.

311   *he learned that his father was gravely ill:* Ibid., p. 57.

311   *finally marrying him and taking his name:* Research by University of Pittsburgh historian Laurence Glasco for a forthcoming book on August Wilson

311   *Freda, the oldest of his sisters:* Lahr, "Been Here," p. 57.

312   *Richard King Mellon liked to say:* "Pennsylvania: Mr. Mellon's Patch," *Time*, Oct. 3, 1949, accessed on time.com/vault.

313   *"Is Pittsburgh Civilized?":* Harper's, Oct. 1930.

313   *approached Mellon with a bold proposal:* Dan Fitzpatrick, "A Story of Renewal," *Pittsburgh Post-Gazette*, May 21, 2000, p. C2.

313   *Richards convened a meeting:* Roy Lubove, *Twentieth Century Pittsburgh: Government, Business and Environmental Change* (Pittsburgh: University of Pittsburgh Press, 1995), p. 109.

313   *Mellon gained an unlikely partner:* Fitzpatrick, "A Story of Renewal," p. 30.

314   *his face on the cover:* "Pittsburgh's Richard Mellon: For the Golden Triangle, a New Sidewalk Superintendent," *Time*, Oct. 3, 1949.

314   *he had a novel vision:* "CLO Names 50 to Hall of Fame," *Pittsburgh Post-Gazette*, May 4, 1996, p. 46.

315   *Kaufmann agreed to put up $1.5 million:* "Assuring the Arena," *Pittsburgh Post-Gazette*, Dec. 5, 1953, p. 6.

315   *King made a dramatic appearance:* Fitzpatrick, "A Story of Renewal," p. C3.

315   *black leaders welcomed the proposal:* Cheryl A. Dudley, "Homer S. Brown Biography," biography.jrank.org.

315   *At the* Courier, *editors had been upset:* "Housing Authority Omits Hill from Postwar Plans," *Pittsburgh Courier*, April 14, 1945.

315   *"Is the Hill District Doomed?":* Pittsburgh Courier, April 22, p. 32, April 29, p. 14, May 6, p. 31, May 13, 1950, p. 35.

316   *"Hell with the lid taken off":* Matthew Newton, "Hell with the Lid Taken Off," *Oxford American*, Spring 2017, oxfordamerican.org.

316   *"that will be all to the good":* "Hill Housing Future, What Will It Mean?," *Pittsburgh Courier*, May 6, 1950, p. 31.

317   *they appealed repeatedly for a reprieve:* "Bethel Acts to Stay in Same Area," *Pittsburgh Courier*, May 26, 1951, p. 1.

317   *the Loendi Club also sought to be spared:* "Loendi Members Must Plan for New Location," *Pittsburgh Courier*, Nov. 16, 1957, p. A3.

317   *The real powers behind the Pittsburgh Renaissance:* Fitzpatrick, "A Story of Renewal," p. C1.

317   *Two local architects:* "Biography/History" in description of Mitchell & Ritchey Collection, Carnegie Mellon University, andrew.cmu.edu.

317   *a patented engineering scheme:* "Case Studies: Moveable Civic Arena Roof Rolls on Wheels Designed by Heyl & Patterson," heylpatterson.com.

318   *"Swish!":* "Toki Types," Pittsburgh Courier, Dec. 11, 1954, p 8.

318 *the beginning of the end of the Lower Hill:* "Razing of Old Homestead Starts 'New Hill' Project," *Pittsburgh Post-Gazette*, May 20, 1956, p. 32.

318 *the city agencies hadn't adequately prepared:* "Lower Hill Resettlement Progresses on Schedule," *Pittsburgh Post-Gazette*, Aug. 15, 1956, p. 15.

318 *A wrecking crew arrived:* Robert Voelker, "How Goes the Renaissance: Was It Business Before People," *Pittsburgh Post-Gazette*, Oct. 16, 1971, p. 6.

319 *the city was still taking bids:* "Bulldozers to Begin Clearing 20 Acres in Lower Hill March 1," *Pittsburgh Post-Gazette*, Jan. 9, 1957, p. 17.

319 *In an ironic twist:* "Smoke Control Snags Project," *Pittsburgh Post-Gazette*, Aug. 23, 1957, p. 17.

319 *the Hill's most storied gathering places disappeared:* "Progress Demands These Lower Hill Landmarks," *Pittsburgh Courier*, Aug. 27, 1955, p. 3.

319 *the last hours of the Bethel AME Church:* Teenie Harris photograph no. 2001.35.4127 in Cheryl Finley, Laurence Glasco, and Joe W. Trotter, *Teenie Harris Photographer: Image, Memory History* (Pittsburgh: University of Pittsburgh Press, 2011), p. 27.

320 *the groundbreaking for the Civic Arena:* Teenie Harris photograph no. 2001.35.9140 in Ibid., p. 144.

320 *But the following year:* "City's Auditorium Opens Its Doors Today," *Pittsburgh Post-Gazette*, Sep. 17, 1961, p. 1.

320 *When the roof was opened:* Sharon Eberson, "The Stars Came Out," *Pittsburgh Post-Gazette*, July 25, 2010, p. E1.

320 *the arena had not lived up to the grandiose expectations:* "City's Public Auditorium Now Is a Dream Fulfilled," *Pittsburgh Post-Gazette*, Sep. 17, 1961, p. 38.

321 *black Pittsburgh had its own reasons:* Laurence Glasco, "That Arena on the Hill: The Complex Legacy for Black Pittsburghers," *Pittsburgh Post-Gazette*, July 4, 2010, p. B7.

321 *As an emblem of their defiance:* Teenie Harris photograph no. 2001.35.9463 in Finley et al., *Teenie Harris*, p. 166.

321 *a three-part series: New Pittsburgh Courier*, March 2, 9, 16, 1968.

322 *As darkness descended:* "Guard, State Troopers Sent in to Quell Hill District Disorder," *Pittsburgh Post-Gazette*, April 8, 1968, pp. 1, 8.

322 *Reverend LeRoy Patrick:* Joe W. Trotter and Jared N. Day, *Race and Renaissance: African Americans in Pittsburgh Since World War II* (Pittsburgh: University of Pittsburgh Press, 2010), pp. 105–6.

323 *Then the engineer shrugged it off:* Voelker, "How Goes the Renaissance," p. 6.

323 *When Freddy Kittel moved to Crawford Street:* Moyers, "August Wilson," in Bryer and Hartig, eds., *Conversations*, pp. 63–64.

325 *every night at the Hurricane Club:* "Hurricane Club: Birdie Dunlop's Organ Soul Jazz Mecca Where the 'In-Crowd' Mingled," *Pittsburgh Music History*, sites. google.com/site/pittsburghmusichistory.

325 *So, too, was, the Penn Incline:* Bob Hoover, "The 17th Street (Penn) Incline," in "Lost Pittsburgh," *Pittsburgh Post-Gazette Magazine,* July 11, 1993, pp. 4–5.

326 *Searching for a new business partner:* "S.B. Fuller Changes Editorial Format," *New Pittsburgh Courier,* Nov. 17–23, 2010, p. 11.

327 *Hill residents watched as a "For Sale" sign:* Teenie Harris Archive, Carnegie Museum of Art, teenie.cmoa.org., accession no. 2001.35.3232.

327 *In a turn of fate:* "Taxes Owed, U.S. Claims," *Pittsburgh Post-Gazette,* Nov. 21, 1967, p. 4.

327 *P.L. Prattis retired:* P. L. Prattis, "Days of The Courier Past . . . ," Henry G. La Brie III, ed., *Perspectives of the Black Press: 1974* (Kennebunkport, Maine: Mercer House, 1974), p. 69.

327 *Bill Nunn stepped down:* "William G. Nunn, Ex-Courier Editor, Buried in Pittsburgh," *New Pittsburgh Courier,* Nov. 22, 1969, p. 1.

327 *shortly after Maybelle:* "Toki Types," *Pittsburgh Courier,* Sep. 20, 1969, p. 11.

327 *Their son, Bill Nunn Jr.:* "Bill Nunn Jr., Football Pioneer Who Scouted Steelers Legends, Dies at 89," *Pittsburgh Post-Gazette,* May 7, 2014.

327 *she suffered a stroke:* "Mrs. Vann of Pittsburgh Courier Fame Dies at 82," *Jet,* June 22, 1967, p. 25.

328 *Wilson sat for hours in a booth:* Glasco and Rawson, *Pittsburgh Places,* p. 89; *August Wilson: The Ground on Which I Stand,* PBS.

328 *He hung out at Pat's Place:* Vera Sheppard, "August Wilson: An Interview," in Bryer and Hartig, eds., *Conversations,* pp. 101–2.

328 *August came to be known as "Youngblood":* Lahr, "Been Here," p. 59.

328 *he ate lunch at a diner called Pan Fried Fish:* " 'Jitney' Captures Drama Behind Hill Substitute Taxi-Cab Service," *New Pittsburgh Courier,* Nov. 20, 1982, p. 7.

328 *a community of struggling black artists:* Recollections of Wilson and friends in *August Wilson: The Ground on Which I Stand,* PBS.

328 *They founded a journal:* Lahr, "Been Here," p. 59.

328 *his idol Dylan Thomas:* Research by University of Pittsburgh historian Laurence Glasco for a forthcoming book on August Wilson.

328 *"Muhammad Ali is a lion":* Sandra G. Shannon, "August Wilson Explains His Dramatic Vision: An Interview," in Bryer and Hartig, eds., *Conversations,* pp. 118–19.

329 *Wilson tried his own hand at playwriting:* David Savran, "August Wilson," in Bryer and Hartig, eds., *Conversations,* p. 21.

329 *his troubled marriage:* Lahr, "Been Here," p. 59.

329 *unexpected change of scenery:* Ibid.; Research by University of Pittsburgh historian Laurence Glasco for a forthcoming book on August Wilson.

330 *he made a stirring discovery:* Savran, "August Wilson," p. 23; Lahr, "Been Here," p. 62.

331 *When Wilson arrived in Waterford:* Lahr, "Been Here," pp. 62–63; J. Wynn Rousuck, "August Wilson's Plays Shepherded by His Collaborator Lloyd Richards," *Baltimore Sun*, May 10, 1992, baltimoresun.com.

331 *using the blues as a metaphor:* Samuel G. Freedman, "A Playwright Talks About the Blues," *New York Times*, April 13, 1984, p. 3.

331 *He took to calling Richards "Pop":* Shannon, "Dramatic Vision," in Bryer and Hartig, eds., *Conversations*, p. 134.

331 *a workshop criticism of Ma Rainey that had stung him:* Wilson interview in *August Wilson: The Ground on Which I Stand*, PBS.

332 *a proper burial:* Photo of gravesite for "Daisy Kittel: March 12, 1920–March 15, 1983," Greenwood Cemetery, Sharpsburg, Pennsylvania, FindaGrave.com.

332 *That summer, Lloyd Richards invited Wilson back:* Chronology of Wilson plays, productions, and awards, in Bryer and Hartig, eds., *Conversations*, pp. xix–xxii.

333 *he recorded a song called "Seabreeze":* Ruth E. Fine, *The Art of Romare Bearden* (New York: Harry N. Abrams, 2003), pp. 24, 214.

333 *Purdy introduced him to a book:* Ladrica Menson-Furr, *August Wilson's Fences* (London: Bloomsbury, 2009), p. 7.

333 *A Bearden collage:* Sheppard, "Interview," in Bryer and Hartig, eds., *Conversations*, pp. 111–12.

334 *compared to that of America's greatest playwrights:* Richard Hornby, "New Life on Broadway," *The Hudson Review*, Autumn 1988, p. 518.

334 *the most memorable depictions:* Christopher Rawson, "Charting 20th-Century Black America," *Pittsburgh Post-Gazette*, Sep. 5, 1999, p. 14 of Sunday supplement.

336 *"America offers blacks a contract":* Bonnie Lyons, "An Interview with August Wilson," in Bryer and Hartig, eds., *Conversations*, p. 206.

337 *Wilson made a special trip to Pittsburgh:* Wilson, "Feed Your Mind," p. B1.

337 *"The basic difference in worldview":* Sheppard, "Interview," in Bryer and Hartig, eds., *Conversations*, p. 106.

337 *It was also why Wilson preferred:* Sandra G. Shannon and Dana A. Williams, "A Conversation with August Wilson," in Bryer and Hartig, eds., *Conversations*, p. 251.

338 *almost thirty years to return the book:* Wilson, "Feed Your Mind."

338 *Wilson understood that about himself:* Savran, "August Wilson," in Bryer and Hartig, eds., *Conversations*, p. 23; Lyons, "Interview," in Bryer and Hartig, eds., *Conversations*, p. 213.

338 *Throughout the 1990s:* Chronology in Bryer and Hartig, eds., *Conversations*, pp. xxi–xxii.

339 *While Wilson was working on* Radio Golf: Interviews with Constanza Romero, Todd Kreidler, and Dwight Andrews in *August Wilson: The Ground on Which I Stand*, PBS.

339 *he wanted to be buried in Pittsburgh:* "August Wilson's Final Act," *Pittsburgh Post-Gazette,* Oct. 9, 2005, p. 1.

340 *As the ceremony drew to a close:* Udin interview in *August Wilson: The Ground on Which I Stand,* PBS.

340 *A hard rain was falling:* Footage in *August Wilson: The Ground on Which I Stand,* PBS.

IINDEX

Page numbers in *italics* refer to map and illustrations.

Abbott, Robert, 69–70, 153, 159, 165, 176
abolitionists, 39–43, 46, 49, 57, 325
"Act for the Gradual Abolition of Slavery" (Pennsylvania; 1780), 39
Adams, Johnny, 187
Addis Ababa, 158
African American Newspaper, 176
African Methodist Episcopal (AME) Church, 25–26
Aged Women's House, 47
"Air Mail Special" (song), 222
Akerman, Alex, 291
Alabama (Los Angeles nightclub), 150
Alexander, Jane Pattoddn, 134
All-American football team (*Courier*), 70
Allegheny Airlines, 314
Allegheny City, Pa., 32, 39, 58, 59
"Allegheny Conference on Post-War Community Development" (ACCD), 313, 317–18
Allegheny County, Pa., 84, 273
Allegheny River, xiii, 12, 30

All-Star Games (major leagues):
   of 1937, 111
   of 1965
"All the Way" (song), 220
Almond, Edward "Ned," 182, 183
Alpha Kappa Alpha, 128
Alpha Phi Alpha, 179
Alsop, Joseph, 85
Alston, Ga., 282–84
Amalgamated Association of Iron and Steel Workers, 35–36
American Federation of Labor, 177
American Federation of Musicians, 205, 210
American Jewish Congress, 276
American League, 111
American Society of Composers, Authors and Publishers (ASCAP), 147
Ammons, Gene, 212
Amos 'n' Andy (radio show), 7
Amsterdam News, 285
Anderson, Ivie, 138, 146
Anderson, Marian, 171, 294
Andrews, Douglas, 339
"Ann, Wonderful One" (song), 199, 200, 201

Apollo Theater (Harlem), 140, 194, 195, 197, 201, 206, 209, 212
Appalachian Mountains, xiii
Aragon Ballroom (Pittsburgh), 194, 210
Argrett, Leroy, 288
Aristotle, 338
Armstrong, Louis, 129, 131, 203, 216
Armstrong High School (Washington, D.C.), 197
Army, U.S., all-black units in, 176
Arthurs, William, 42, 44, 318
Arthursville (neighborhood), 41–42, 46, 59, 318
Askew, C. E., 166
Askew, John, 53
Associated Negro Press (ANP), 153, 154, 166
Associated Press, 255
Athens Messenger, 28
Athens, Ohio, 27
"A-Tisket, A-Tasket" (song), 221
Aurora Reading Club, 46
Austria, Nazi occupation of, 19
Autobiography of Malcolm X, The (Malcolm X and Haley), 328
Avakian, George, 225–26, 227
Avery, Charles, 39–40, 57
Avery Trade School for Colored Youth, 39–40
Aybar, José Enrique, 118

Baer, Max, 8, 11, 155
Baird, Tom, 244
Baker, Chet, 220
Baker, Vernon, 183
Baltimore Afro-American, 9, 73
Baltimore Black Sox, 103
Bankhead, Sammy, 255
Baraka, Amiri (LeRoi Jones), 328
Barnet, Charlie, 149
Barnett, Claude, 153, 154, 155, 163, 166
Barr, Joseph, 320, 322
Barrow, Lillie, 7, 18, 21
Barrow, Munroe, 7
baseball, integration of, xv, 22, 120–21
    Landis and, 235–37
    Negro Leagues and, 243–44, 245
    Wendell Smith's crusade for, 233–35, 243–44, 246
    see also Rickey, Branch; Robinson, Jackie
Baseball Writers Association of America, 235, 266
    Robinson as target of roast by, 245–46
Basie, Count, 219, 220, 221, 222
Bass, Charlotta, 174, 272

"Battle of Monticello Street," 68
Bearden, Romare, 149, 333–34, 335
bebop, xvi, 202, 206–12, 221, 225, 228, 325
Beckwith, John, 101
Bedford, David, 306–7, 311, 332
Bedford Avenue, 89, 121, 302, 304, 305, 308, 319, 323, 326, 340
Bedford Dwellings, 316, 318, 321
Bedford Land Company, 107
Belafonte, Harry, 215, 217, 219
Bell, "Cool Papa," xv, 109–10, 111, 112, 113, 115, 117
    with Crawfords, 112–13
Bella Siger's Market, 302, 305, 323
Belmont Hotel (Pittsburgh), 96, 137, 139
Belpre, Ohio, 26
Beltzhoover (neighborhood), xxiii, 45
Benedum, Michael Late, 86
    Courier printing plant financed by, 76, 78
    as FDR supporter, 78
    as oil wildcatter, 77–78
Bennett, Tony, 218
Benson, George, 325
Benswanger, William, 120, 238, 256
Bergman, Ingrid, 172
Berkman, Alexander, 37
Berlin, Irving, 130
Berlin Olympics (1936), 19, 158–59, 193
Bessemer, Henry, 31
Bethel AME Church, 128, 317
    demolition of, 319–20
Bethune, Mary McLeod, 164, 175, 247
Bethune-Cookman College, 247
Bibb, Joseph D., 168, 177
Biddle, Francis, 174
    in meeting with Sengstacke, 175–76
Billboard, 213, 215
Billy Eckstine Orchestra, 194, 195, 210
Billy Eckstine's Imagination (album), 220
"Birdland All-Stars" concert, 220
Birkie, Hans, 5–6
Birmingham, Ala., 300
Birmingham, England, 58
Black, Hugo, 160, 161
Black, Julian, 4, 5, 6–7, 8, 10, 12, 21, 166
Blackbirds of 1938 (musical revue), 142
Blackburn, Jack "Chappie," 4, 5–6, 9–10, 13, 14, 17, 18, 19, 20
Black Harlem Theater, 328–29
black nationalism, 41
Black Power, 328, 335
Black Press, The: Soldiers Without Swords (film), 176

Black Sox scandal, 136, 236
black veterans:
    blue discharges of, 278–79
    Courier's crusade for, 277–78
    Jim Crow laws and, 276–79, 316
Blake, Eubie, 131
Blakely, Art, 194
    in Billy Eckstine Orchestra, 210–11
Blanton, Jimmy, 150, 222
Bluebird Records, 200, 201
blues, 200, 202, 206, 213
    Wilson and, 323–24, 325, 328, 330–31,
        335, 336, 340
"Blue Suede Shoes" (song), 220
Bogart, Humphrey, 172
Bolden, Frank, 174, 178, 191, 282
    background of, 178–79
    in Burma, 185–86, 189–90
    at Fort Huachuca, 180
    India independence movement covered by,
        188–89
    in 1943 return to Pittsburgh, 181
    Vann's hiring of, 179
    as war correspondent, 178, 179–80, 184–85,
        189–90
Book Shoe (baseball team), 105
Boothe, A. C., 55
Bop City (Pittsburgh nightclub), 216–17
Bossa Nova, 220
Bostic, Joe, 238, 252
Boston, Mass., 56, 239
Boston Braves, 239, 260
Boston Red Sox, 239, 240
Boston University, 298, 299
Bougainville, 184
Bowman, Madge, 133
Boyd, Charles N., 135
Boyd, Herbert, 187–88
Bracken, Milton, 182
Braddock, Edward, 29–30
Braddock, Jim, 15–18, 155
Braddock, Pa., 31
Bradley, Omar, 277
Brock, David, 248
Brock, Viola, 248
Brooklyn, N.Y., 136
Brooklyn Brown Dodgers, 240–41, 242
Brooklyn Dodgers, xv, 230, 237, 240–41,
    256–58
    growing solidarity between Robinson and
        teammates on, 264
    Robinson with, 257–66
Brotherhood of Sleeping Car Porters, 74–75

Brothers (Los Angeles nightclub), 150
Brown, Byrd, 321
Brown, Calvin, 55, 56
Brown, Homer S., 274, 315
Brown, Natie, 8
Brown, Ray, 120, 121
    background of, 222
    Fitzgerald's marriage to, 223
    Gillespie and, 222, 223
    Peterson and, 223
Brown Bomber Chicken Shack (Detroit), 18
Brown Chapel AME Church, 59
Brown v. Board of Education of Topeka, Kansas,
    293–94
Buck, Pearl, 172
Bulge, Battle of the, 184
Bunche, Ralph, 290
Burke, Johnny, 226
Burley, Charley, 305–6, 332
Burley, Fletcher, 132, 133
Burley, Julie, 305–6
Burma Road, 185, 186
Burnett, Carol, 320
Burton, Brenda, 329

Café Society (New York nightclub), 149, 207
California, University of, at Los Angeles
    (UCLA), 239
California Eagle, 174, 272
Calloway, Cab, 201, 207–8
Calvin, Floyd J., 71
Capitol Records, 219, 220
Capone, Al, 131, 198
Capone, Ralph, 131, 198
Carmel-by-the-Sea, Calif., 226
Carmichael, Hoagy, 197
Carnegie, Andrew, 31, 32–33, 38, 43, 58, 337
    Cap Posey and, 38–39
    Frick's partnership with, 35
    Homestead Strike and, 37, 38
    philanthropy of, 33, 35, 37, 38, 47
Carnegie, Margaret, 32
Carnegie, Tom, 35
Carnegie, William, 32
Carnegie Hall (New York), 220
Carnegie Institute of Technology, 128, 275,
    317
Carnegie libraries, 47, 304, 309–10, 337
Carnegie Music Hall (Pittsburgh), 221
Carnera, Primo, 9–11, 20
Carney, Harry, 146
Carson, Johnny, 228
Carter, Dover, 283

Carter, Eugene, 297
Carter, Robert, 293
Cash, Thomas, 65–66
Catlin, Charles, 128
Catlin, Charlotte Enty, 133, 134, 150, 195
    Lena Horne and, 143, 144
    musical talent of, 127, 128
    Strayhorn's lessons with, 128–29
Central Catholic High School (Pittsburgh), 307
Centre Avenue YMCA (Pittsburgh), 114, 128
Century Cycle (Wilson), xvi, 332–33, 334–35, 338–39
Chandler, Albert Benjamin "Happy," 245, 259, 262, 267
Chapman, Ben, 261–62
Chappell, Edna, 172, 282
    in move to Courier city desk, 271–72
Charities and the Commons, 38
Charleston, Oscar, 101, 107, 109, 111, 112, 113, 117
Chase Hotel (St. Louis), 263
"Chelsea Bridge" (song), 148
"Cherokee" (Noble), 149
Chiang Kai-shek, 185
Chicago, Ill., 3, 7–8, 16, 153–54
Chicago American Giants, 111
Chicago Bee, 73
Chicago Daily Times, 116
Chicago Daily Tribune, 160
Chicago Defender, 3, 9, 14, 22, 64, 69, 153, 159, 165, 166, 175, 282, 327
Chicago Herald-American, 266
Chicago Sun-Times, in continued crusade for equality in baseball, 267–68
Chicago Whip, 73
China, 185
Christian, Charlie, 206
Christian Brothers, 307, 308
Christian Recorder, 41
Churchill, Winston, 170, 190
Cinquale Canal fiasco, 182, 183
Citizens Committee for Hill District Renewal, 321
City Council, Pittsburgh, 317
City Light Opera (Pittsburgh), 314
Civic Arena (Pittsburgh), 314–21, 325, 326
civil rights, 68, 163, 300
    Truman and, 279–80, 281
civil rights movement, xv, 22, 225, 282, 289, 290, 326, 342
    Montgomery boycott in, 294–300, 301
Civil War, U.S., 23, 33

Clairton, Pa., 273
Clark, John L., 70, 97–98, 108, 110, 113, 121, 280–81
Clark Memorial Baptist Church, 244
Clarke, Kenny, 203–6, 223
    Gillespie and, 204–5
Clarke, Ramon, 76–77
Clemente, Roberto, 326
Clendenon, Donn, 326
Cleveland, Ohio, 81–82
Cleveland Gazette, 73
Cleveland Indians, 265
Club DeLisa (Chicago nightclub), 198
Club Plantation (Los Angeles nightclub), 195
Club Riviera (St. Louis nightclub), 210–11
Coast Guard, U.S., blacks in, 176
Coatesville, Pa., 64–65
Cole, "King," 111
Cole, Nat King, 219, 325
Coleman Industrial Home for Negro Boys, 204
Collected Poems of Paul Lawrence Dunbar, The, 309, 337
colleges, racial quotas and, 276
Collins, Harry, 131
Colored American Magazine, 45, 47
Columbia Records, 225, 227
Columbia University, 60
Comiskey Park, 16, 111, 242
Commission on Civil Rights, 280
Committee for Participation of Negroes in the National Defense, 162
Como, Perry, 214
concentration camps, 19
Concert by the Sea (album), 227
"Concerto for Piano and Percussion" (Strayhorn), 134
Congress of Industrial Organizations, 177
Congress, U.S., military draft implemented by, 162–63
Congress Party, Indian, 188
Connections, 328
Connelly Trade School, 308
Connie Mack's All Stars, 103
Connor, Bull, 300
Contrasts (album), 226
Coolidge, Calvin, 79
Cooper, Gary, 1, 172
Cooper, Ralph, 140–41
Copley Square Hotel (Boston), 56
Cornelius, Ira, 140
"Cottage for Sale, A" (song), 213
Cotton Club (Harlem), 138

Courier Hour, The (radio show), 71
Coyne, Jimmy, 97, 98, 99
Crawford Grill, 13, 88, 95–96, 97, 105, 106, 111, 114, 116, 145, 255, 319, 326
police raids on, 96
Crawford Street, 311, 323, 325, 340
Crisis, 9, 72, 73
Cronin, Joe, 240
Crutchfield, Jimmie, 112
Crystal Barber Shop, 93–94, 325
Cuba, Dodgers/Royals spring training in, 256–58
Cummings, Homer, 157
Cunningham, Bill, 300
Cunningham, Evelyn, 270, 282
background of, 285–86
Brown case covered by, 293
Greenland Four case and, 291
King and, 298–99
Marshall's friendship with, 292–93
Montgomery boycott covered by, 294–95, 301
as *New York Times* stringer, 300
in Nixon Family Fund campaign, 286–89
radio talk show of, 300
"The Women" column of, 289–90, 294, 297, 301
Cunningham, Gerald, 286
Curtiss-Wright, 177

Daley, Arthur, 246
Daniel, Dan, 246
Danville, Ill., 264
Darcel, Denise, 218
Darrow, Clarence, 72
Davis, Benjamin O., 165
Davis, Benjamin O., Jr., 181, 182
Davis, Christopher C., 29
Davis, Miles, 210–11
Dawson, Mary Cardwell, 129, 133, 135
Dayton, Ohio, 125
Daytona Beach, Fla., 231–32, 247, 249
D-Day invasion, 193
Dean, Dizzy, 112, 235
Declaration of Independence, 39
Deland, Fla., 251
Delany, Martin, 40–41, 43, 48, 49
Delta Coal Company, 37
Delta Sigma Theta, 71
Deluxe Hotel (St. Louis), 263
Democratic Party, xv, 78
black migration to, 85, 165
Dempsey, Jack, 5

Deppe, Lois, 130–31, 214, 324
Detroit, Mich., 7, 8–9
Detroit Owl, 73
Dewey, Thomas, 171–72, 280, 281
Dickens, Charles, 58
Dihigo, Martin, 101
discrimination, 22, 57, 69, 81, 136, 162, 164, 174, 177
against black veterans, 276–78, 316
Courier crusades against, 68, 273–74
see also military, U.S., blacks in; segregation
Dixiecrat Party, 280
Dixon, Randy, 183–84
Doby, Larry, 265
Dominican Republic, 118
Dorham, Kenny, 212
Double Victory Campaign, xv, 151, *152,* 170–74, 176, 178, 191, 235, 272
Douglass, Frederick, 41
Downbeat, 216, 220
Downtown (neighborhood), *xxiii*
draft, 162–63
Dragones de Cuidad Trujillo, Los (Dominican baseball team), 118
Drama Critics' Award, 334
Du Bois, W. E. B., 68, 168
Courier's feud with, 72–74
Duke Is Tops, The (film), 141–42
Dunlap, Birdie, 325
Duquesne, Pa., 129
Duquesne Club (Pittsburgh), 46, 313, 317
Duquesne Gardens (Pittsburgh), 201
Duquesne University, 275
Durocher, Leo, 235, 236, 238, 259
Dutton, Charles, 339

Early, Stephen, 175
East End (neighborhood), *see* Point Breeze
East Liberty (neighborhood), *xxiii,* 132
East-West Classic, 2, 111–12, 115–16, 121
East-West League, 104, 106–9
Ebbets Field, 121, 240
Eckstein, Aileen, 196
Eckstein, Charlotte "Lottie," 196
Eckstein, Clarence, 196, 220
Eckstein, Maxine, 196
Eckstine, Billy, xv–xvi, *192,* 194–95, 209, 228, 325, 333
background of, 196
with Earl Hines Orchestra, 198–99, 208–9, 213
education of, 196–98
IRS problems of, 219

Eckstine, Billy (*cont.*)
   June's divorce from, 218, 219
   June's marriage to, 210, 215
   Life photo controversy and, 217–18, 221
   MGM contract of, 214, 215, 218
   solo career of, 213–14
   voice and piano lessons of, 196–97
Eckstine, June Harris, 210, 215, 218
Eddie's Restaurant, 328
Edison, Thomas, 33
education, xiv, 39, 40, 47–48, 91, 180, 197
   black veterans and, 276, 277
   segregation and, 47, 73, 293
813th Pioneer Infantry Brigade, 156
Eldridge, Blanche, 202
Eldridge, Joe, 202–3
Eldridge, Roy, 202–3, 206
elections, U.S.:
   of 1932, 78–85, 97
   of 1936, 159–60
   of 1940, 163–64, 165
   of 1948, 280–81
Elks (Negro Elks Clubs), 2, 171, 224, 299
Ellington, Duke, xv, 145, 197, 222, 325
   Lena Horne's affair with, 149
   Strayhorn's first meeting with, 145–46
Ellington, Mercer, 147–48
Ellison, Ralph, 310
Enty, Clever "Frank," 127
Enty, Mary Jane Litte, 127, 128
Enty, Peter, 127
Enty, Tobias, I, 127
Enty, Tobias, II, 127
Esquire, 212
Ethiopia, Italian invasion of, 157–58
Ewell, Thomas, 45, 47
Ewing, Buck, 102

Fair Employment Practices Committee, Congress's
   defunding of, 274
Fantastic Rhythm (musical revue), 123–25,
   134, 146, 148
Farley, Jim, 79, 80, 85, 86
Fascism, 19, 157
Faulkner, William, 334–35
Fedd, Eddie William, 188
Federal Bureau of Investigation (FBI), black
   editors investigated by, 173, 174
Feldman, Harry, 84
Fences (Wilson), xvi, 332, 334, 335, 337, 339
Fifteenth Amendment, 57
Fifth Army, U.S., 183
Finch, Robert, 238

Fish, Hamilton, 156, 161–62
Fitzgerald, Ella, 138, 197, 221
   Ray Brown's marriage to, 223
Flash, 141
"Flower Is a Lovesome Thing, A" (song), 148
"Flying Home" (song), 222
Foggie, Charles, 166
Forbes, John, 30
Forbes Field (Pittsburgh), 83, 119, *230,* 326
   Homestead Grays games at, 100, 101–2,
      103, 105–6
Ford, Henry, 234
Fort Bragg, 176
   "Night of Terror" at, 167, 173
Fort Duquesne, Battle of, 16, 29–30
Fort Huachuca, 176, 180
Fort Pitt, 30
41st Engineers Regiment, 181
Foster, Rube, 104, 109, 110
Fowler, "Boggy," 124, 125
Fox, Ed, 198–99
Frick, Ford, 237, 262
Frick, Henry Clay, 34–35
   attempted assassination of, 37
   Cap Posey's partnership with, 38–39
   Carnegie's partnership with, 35
   Homestead Strike and, 35–36, 37, 38
   Point Breeze mansion of, 43
"FROGS Week," *192,* 214–15
From Here to Eternity (film), 218
Fugitive Slave Law (1850), 42
Fuller, S. B., 326
Fullerton Street, 23
Fullerton Street (Wilson), 330, 332

Gable, Clark, 1
Gandhi, Mahatma, 188–89
Garagiola, Joe, 263, 265
Garner, Erroll, xv, *192,* 214, 225, 325, 335
   death of, 228
   Glaser as manager of, 225–26
   influence of Pittsburgh musical culture on,
      228–29
   as musical prodigy, 133, 224
Garner, Ruth, 227
Garvey, Marcus, 41
Gem of the Ocean (Wilson), 338, 339
George, Collins, 182–83
Germany, Nazi, 19
Gershwin, George, 125
Gettysburg, Pa., 60, 61
GI Bill of Rights, 188, 275–76, 279
   black veterans penalized by, 277–79, 316

Gibson, Josh, xv, 90, 109, 112, 113, 120, 121, 267, 319, 326
  with Crawfords, 99, 107–8, 111, 112–13, 117
  death of, 255
  drinking and drug abuse by, 254–55
  with Grays, 102–4, 120–21
Gibson, Josh, Jr., 254
Gibson, Nancy, 254, 255
Gillespie, Dizzy, xvi, 194, 206, 221, 325
  in Billy Eckstine Orchestra, 210–11
  Calloway and, 207–8
  Clarke and, 204–5
  departure from Eckstine Orchestra of, 212
  with Earl Hines orchestra, 201–2, 208–9
  Parker and, 208–9
  Ray Brown and, 222, 223
  with Teddy Hill Orchestra, 203–4
Gimbels department store, 274
Ginell, Cary, 213
Gionfriddo, Al, 266
Gladstone High School (Pittsburgh), 308–9, 310
Glaser, Martha, 224–25
  as Gerner's manager, 225–26
Gold Star Mothers, 82
"Good Jelly Blues" (song), 194
Goodman, Benny, 149
Gordon, Dexter, 194, 212
Gothic Line, 183
Gould, Joe, 15–16
Gould, Joseph Howard, 78
Grand Terrace Café (Chicago), 131, 198–99, 213
Granz, Norman, 223, 225
Great Depression, 79, 89, 94, 97, 105, 108–9
Great Migration, xiv, 11, 57, 58–59, 67, 69, 77, 78, 129, 169
Great Pittsburgh Fire of 1845, 42, 43, 44, 49
Greenberg, Hank, 263–64
Greenberg, Jack, 293
Greenlee, Charles, 290–91
Greenlee, George, 96
Greenlee, George, Jr., 145–46
Greenlee, Gus "Big Red," xv, 13, 79, 84, 88, 130, 136, 145, 150, 166, 240, 244, 335
  background of, 91
  as bootlegger, 92–93
  Crawford Grill of, see Crawford Grill
  as Crawfords' owner, see Pittsburgh Crawfords
  Cum Posey's rivalry with, 111, 115, 119, 121
  East-West Classic and, 111–12
  Greenlee field built by, 89–91
  loans and poverty relief by, 97–98
  money difficulties of, 118–19
  as numbers racketeer, 93–95, 112
  Paige's relationship with, 106, 113–14, 117
  as Republican loyalist, 96
  in World War I, 91
Green, Madeline, 209
Greenlee Field (Pittsburgh), 89–91, 107, 108, 109, 114, 326
  demolition of, 121
  financial problems of, 119–20
Greenwood Cemetery, 332, 340
Grieg, Edvard, 134
Griffiths, Clark, 244
Grove, Lefty, 103
Groveland, Fla., 290
Groveland Four, 290–91
Guffey, Emma, 86
Guffey, Joseph, 80, 86, 160, 166, 313
Guinyard, Freddie, xxiv
Gustine, Frank, 264

Hajdu, David, 127, 218
Hallmark Hall of Fame (TV show), 334
Hall of Fame, black players in, 267
Hammond, Jack, 149
Hammond and Gerlach music store, 204
"Hamp's Boogie-Woogie" (song), 222
Hampton, Lionel, 172, 221–22
Hampton Institute, 38
Hance, William, 50
Handy, W. C., 324
Harding, Warren, 78–79, 81
Hardy, Thomas, 335
Hargrove, Hondon, 183
Harlem, 10, 13, 18, 20, 21, 22, 74, 136, 137, 138, 141, 144, 146, 147, 155, 195, 198, 201, 204, 205, 206, 207, 210
  Courier bureau in, 22, 71, 181, 231, 238, 285–86, 289
Harlem Globetrotters, 111, 288
Harlem Renaissance, 71
Harleston, Edward Nathaniel, 49–50, 61–62
Harper's, 313
Harrellsville, N.C., 55
Harrington, Ollie, 182
Harris, Charles "Teenie," 94, 95, 100, 141
  athletic talent of, 98–99
  as Courier photographer, 193–94, 319
Harris, Joe and Duff, 250
Harris, Vic, 120
Harris, William "Woogie," 93–95, 136, 137, 141, 193, 335

Hart, Moss, 310
Harvard Medical School, 41
Hawkins, Coleman, 203, 206
Hayes, Edgar, 204
Hayes, Stewart, 27
Hazelwood (neighborhood), *xxiii*, 307, 310, 322
Hearst, William Randolph, 49
"Heartbreak Hotel" (song), 220
Heinz, Henry J., 33–34
　　Point Breeze mansion of, 43
Henderson, Fletcher, 125, 203
Herron Avenue, *iv*
Highland Park (neighborhood), *xxiii*
Hill, Herman, 195
Hill, Teddy, 203, 205–6
Hill City Auditorium, 194
Hill District (neighborhood), *ii*, xvi, *xxiii*, 6, 23, 44, 46, 88, 93, 96, 116, 128, 204, 304, 338
　　Civic Arena project in, 314–21, 325, 326
　　failure to provide for displaced residents of, 318–19, 321
　　squalid living conditions in, 59, 67
Hillsborough, N.C., 125, 126
Hines, Earl "Fatha," xv, 129, *192*, 198–202, 208, 213, 214, 216, 224, 324, 335
　　jazz lessons of, 130–31
　　as musical prodigy, 129–30
　　at Schenley High School, 130, 131
Hines, Frank T., 277
Hines, James, 129, 130
Hitler, Adolf, 1, 2, 15, 19, 23, 159
Hocking River, 27
Hodges, Johnny, 146
Holiday, Billie, 138
Holloway, Wilbert, 170–71
Holmes, Martha, 216
Holy Ghost College (Duquesne University), 48–49
Homestead, Pa., *24*, 29, 45, 119
　　steel mill at, 31, 35–36
Homestead Grays, xv, 48, 100–104, 110, 114–15, 244, 306, 335
　　Cum Posey as manager of, 49
　　Gibson with, 102–4, 120–21
　　Jackson as co-owner of, 119–20
　　night games played by, 100, 101–2
Homestead High School, 48
Homestead Strike, 35–37, 38
Homewood (neighborhood), *xxiii*, 3, 44, 126, 128, 322
Homewood AME Zion Church, 128

Homewood Cemetery, 166
Hoover, Herbert, 79, 81–82, 83
Hoover, J. Edgar, 1
　　in campaign against black press, 173, 174
Hopper, Clay, 251
Horne, Burke, 136
Horne, Corn Calhoun, 136
Horne, Edna Scrotton, 136–37, 138, 139
Horne, Edwin, 136
Horne, Edwin "Little Teddy," 143, 149
Horne, Edwin "Teddy", Jr., 136–37, 144, 150
　　Lena's relationship with, 138, 139, 142, 144, 149
　　in move to Pittsburgh, 137
　　as racketeer, 96, 137–38
Horne, Erroll, 136
Horne, Frank, 136, 137
Horne, Irene, 137, 139
Horne, Lena, *122*, 194
　　in *Blackbirds of 1938*, 142
　　Catlin and, 143, 144
　　with Charlie Barnet band, 148–49
　　childhood of, 137
　　children of, 140, 143, 149
　　Cotton Club job of, 138
　　Ellington's affair with, 149
　　Joe Louis's affair with, 149
　　Louis Jones's marriage to, 139–44
　　in move to Los Angeles, 150
　　in Noble Sissle band, 138–39
　　pregnancies of, 140
　　Strayhorn's arrangements for, 150–51
　　Strayhorn's friendship with, 150–51
　　Teddy's relationship with, 138, 139, 142, 144, 149
　　in *The Duke is Tops*, 141–42
"Hot Box" (song), 222
Hot Five band, 131
House of David (baseball team), 117
House of Representatives, U.S., Military Affairs Committee of, 156, 162
housing, segregation, 67–68, 323
Housing Act (1949), 316, 321
Howard Theatre (Washington, D.C.), 197, 198, 199, 210
Howard University, 48, 70, 182, 195, 198
Howe, Louis, 80
Howze, Sam, *see* Udin, Sala
Hubbard, Jesse, 90
Hubbell, Carl, 235
Hughes, Langston, 14, 310
Human Rights Commission, 225
Humphrey, Hubert, 280

Hunter, Nate, 112
Hunter High School for Girls (New York), 286
Hurok, Sol, 227–28
Hurricane Club (Pittsburgh nightclub), 325

"I Apologize" (song), 218, 219
Ickes, Harold, 86
"I'll See You in C-U-B-A" (song), 130
"I'm in the Mood for Love" (song), 213
India, independence movement in, 188–89
Ink Spots, 221
Institute of Alabama, black pilots trained at, 176
Internal Revenue Service, 78
International League, 242, 253
Invisible Man (Ellison), 310
Iran, 185
Irvin, Walter Lee, 290–91
Italy, Ethiopia invaded by, 157–58
"I've Got It Bad and That Ain't Good" (song),
    148
"I Want to Talk About You" (song), 195

Jackson, Milt, 223
Jackson, Robert, 44
Jackson, Rufus "Sonnyman," 119
Jacksonville, Fla., 251, 288–89
Jacobs, Mike, 8, 9, 11, 15–16, 21
Jamal, Ahmad, 228–29, 325
Jay McShann band, 206
Jazz at the Philharmonic, 223, 225
"Jelly, Jelly" (song), 200, 201, 210, 213
Jersey City Saints, 251
Jet, 220, 298
Jethroe, Sam, 239
Jewish War Veterans, 276
Jews, Louis and, 19
Jim Crow, see discrimination
Jinnah, Muhammad Ali, 188
Jitney (Wilson), 330, 332, 338, 339
jobs, blacks' postwar losses of, 190–91
Joe Turner's Come and Gone (Wilson), 333–34,
    335
John Mann Street Chapel (Winchester), 26
Johnson, Budd, 198, 200, 201
Johnson, Jack, 7
Johnson, James C., 172
Johnson, James Weldon, Courier's feud with,
    72–74
Johnson, Jim A., 283–84
Johnson, Johnnie, 283–84
Johnson, Judy, 101, 102, 109, 111, 112, 117
Jones, Anna, 201
Jones, Eva DeBoe, 80

Jones, Gail, 140, 142, 144
Jones, Julia Bumry, 6, 12, 70–71, 83–84, 86,
    97, 128, 154, 164, 271
    Prattis's relationship with, 155
    stroke of, 172
Jones, LeRoi (Amiri Baraka), 328
Jones, Louis, 143, 265
    Lena Horne's marriage to, 139–44
Jones, "Papa Jo," 204
Jones, Paul L., 315–16, 318
Jones, Quincy, 220, 223
Jones, Rachel Lovett, 46
Jones, Scipio Africanus, 65
Jordan, James, 321
Jordan, Louis, 172
Jordan, Ralph Burdette, 168
Jump for Joy (musical), 148, 150
"Just Squeeze Me" (song), 148

Kansas City Monarchs, 100, 101–2, 104, 119,
    243, 244
    Robinson with, 233, 239, 241–42
Kaufmann, Edgar, 315
Kaufmann's department store, 274
KDKA (radio station), 128, 131
King, Coretta Scott, 295, 299
King, Martin Luther, Jr.:
    assassination of, 322
    Cunningham and, 298–99
    jailing of, 297–98
    in Montgomery boycott, 295–96, 299–300
King, Robert, 315
King, Yolanda, 295
King Hedley II (Wilson), 338
Kinsey, Alfred, 290
Kirk, Andy, 206–7
Kittel, Frederick August "Fritz," 304–5, 311
Kittel, Frederick August, Jr., see Wilson, August
Klein, Arthur, 276
Kline, Charles, 96–97
Knights of Pythias, 46, 86
Knights Templar, 46
Knox, Frank, 169, 235
Knox, Philander, 43
Koger, Ralph "Projoe," 123–24, 147
Kraken, Jack, 4, 8
Krall, Diana, 223
Kreidler, Todd, 339
Ku Klux Klan, 160, 283
Kuller, Sid, 148

labor unions, 35–36
Lampkin, Daisy, 66, 68, 128, 282, 293

Landis, Kenesaw Mountain, 235
Landon, Alf, 160
Latrobe, Pa., 93
Laughlin, Thomas, 62
Lavagetto, Cookie, 266
Lavelle, Robert, 321
Lawrence, David, 80, 86, 160, 244, 288, 313–14, 318, 320
Lead Belly, 324
Leader House (Pittsburgh), 130
Ledo Road (Stilwell Road), 185–88, 189–90
Leonard, Buck, xv, 114, 115, 120, 121
Levy, Morris, 220, 221
Lewis, Ira, 71, 86, 164, 327
    as *Courier* managing editor, 6
    as *Courier* publisher, 168, 236–37, 279
    as *Courier*'s business manager, 66, 69–70, 154–55, 159
    Cum Posey's eulogy delivered by, 244
    death of, 281, 326
Lewis, John, 223
Lewis, John Henry, 114, 119, 121
Lewis, Lew, 142
Liberia, 181
Life, 216–18, 220–21
"Life Story of Joe Louis, The" (*Courier* series), 7
"Life Story of Martin Luther King, The" (Cunningham), 298–99
Lincoln, Abraham, 56, 78, 82
Lincoln University, 70
Lionel Hampton Orchestra, 221–22
Little, George, 128
Little, James Edward, 127–28
"Little Haiti" (neighborhood), 44
Little Troc (Los Angeles nightclub), 151
Loendi Big Five, 48
Loendi Club, 46, 50, 59, 61, 71, 74, 111, 128, 129, 141, 194, 317, 319, 325, 335
Lomax, Almena, 272
Long, Clyde, 285
Long Island University, 286
Look, 218
Los Angeles Tribune, 272
"Lotus Land" (Scott), 134
Louis, Joe, *xxiv*, 117, 121, 138, 154, 166, 215, 237, 326
    Blackburn as trainer of, 4, 5–6, 9–10, 13, 14, 17, 18, 19, 20
    in Braddock title fight, 15–18
    in Carnera fight, 9–11, 20
    Courier's championing of, xv, 2, 4, 7–8, 9, 10, 14, 16–17, 18, 22, 154–55, 256

early matches of, 4–6, 7–8
    first Pittsburgh visit of, 6–7
    in first Schmeling fight, 13–15
    Jacobs as promoter of, 9, 11
    Lena Horne's affair with, 149
    marriage of Marva and, 155
    and 1936 Pittsburgh flood benefit, 12
    Nunn and, xv, 2–4, 5, 10, 14–15, 16, 22, 154, 256
    personality of, 6, 9
    in Schmeling rematch, 1–2, 19–21
    Washington's close relationship with, 13, 14, 17
Louis, Marva Trotter, 13, 18, 21, 155
Louisville, Ky., 253
Lower Hill (neighborhood), 84, 173, 204, 315, 317–19, 321, 323
Luce, Clare Boothe, 172
Luce, Henry, 217
Luckey, Lucinda, 29
Lunceford, Jimmie, 172
"Lush Life" (song), 135
lynchings, 29, 64–65, 73, 78–79, 160, 176, 177, 271, 273, 286
Lyons, Bonnie, 336

McAlpin Hotel (New York), 258, 260–61
MacArthur, Douglas, 189
McBean, Al, 326
McBride, Christian, 224
McCall, Willis, 291
McCarthy, Marvin, 116
McClelland, D. W., 12
McCullough, David, 280
McDuff, Jack, 325
McDuffie, Terry, 238
McGhee, Howard, 212
McKees Rocks, Pa., 94
McKelvey High School (Pittsburgh), 99
McKinley, William, 44, 56
McPhail, Lee, 259
McShann, Jay, 201–2
McVicker, Carl, 133–34
Mad Hatters, 135
Madison Square Garden, 9, 15, 16, 63
Malcolm X, 300
Maltin, Sam, 253–54
Manchester (neighborhood), *xxiii*
Manley, Abe and Effie, 113, 119
Marable, Fate, 129, 150
Ma Rainey's Black Bottom (Wilson), 330–31, 332, 339
Marine Coal Company, 37

Marines, U.S., blacks in, 176
Marsalis, Wynton, 340
Marshall, Thurgood:
  Brown case and, 293
  Cunningham's friendship with, 292–93
  Groveland Four case and, 290
Martin, Louis, 268
Martin, Pepper, 235
Massera, Charlie, 5
Mathewson, Christy, 116
Mathis, Johnny, 226
Matlock, Leroy, 112, 117
Medal of Honor, 169
Mellon, Andrew, 34, 79, 83, 312
Mellon, Connie, 312
Mellon, Richard Beatty, 312
Mellon, Richard King "R.K.," 312–13
  and Pittsburgh Renaissance, 313–14, 317
Mellon, Thomas, 34, 44, 312
Mellon National Bank, 312, 314
Memorial Athletic Field (Sanford), 248
Memphis Red Sox, 104–5
Mencken, H. L., 77, 157, 160–61
Messenger, The (journal), 74, 75
Methodist Episcopal Church, 26
Metronome, 216
MGM records, 214, 215, 216, 218
Middle Hill (neighborhood), ii, 305, 321, 323, 325
Milholland, Harry, 196
military, U.S., blacks in:
  combat training of, 176
  Courier stories on, 166–67, 173
  Vann's crusade for, 156, 161–62, 165
  see also specific units
military, U.S., desegregation of, 281
Miller, Arthur, 334
Miller, Doris "Dorie," 168–69, 176, 235
Miller, Emma Guffey, 80
Mills Brothers, 221
"Minertown" (neighborhood), 44
Minton, Henry, 205–6
Minton's Playhouse (New York nightclub), 205–6
Mississippi River, 30
Mister Kelly's (Chicago nightclub), 228
"Misty" (song), 226
Mitchell, Arthur, 177
Mitchell, James, 317
Modern Jazz Quartet, 223
Monk, Thelonius Sphere, 206, 207, 225
Monongahela House (Pittsburgh), 42, 78
Monongahela River, xiii, 12, 30

Montgomery, Ala., bus boycott in, 294–300, 301, 326
Montgomery Improvement Association (MIA), 295–96
Monticello-Delany Rifles, 48
Montreal Royals, 233, 242–43, 247–54, 256–58
Moonlight Harbor Orchestra, 123, 124, 125
Moore family, 59
Morehouse College, 298, 299
Moreland, Mantan, 141
Morgan, J. P., 58
Morris, Carl, 322
Motley, Constance Baker, 293
Mount Washington (neighborhood), xxiii, 45
Muchnick, Isadore, 239
Murphy, Joseph L., 275
Muslims, 188
Mussolini, Benito, 157
"My Little Brown Book" (song), 148
My Own Story (Robinson), 266
Mystery Mansion (Pittsburgh after-hours club), 135
Mystery, The (journal), 41, 49

Napoleon I, Emperor of France, 308–9
Nashville Elite Giants, 105
National Association for the Advancement of Colored People (NAACP), 9, 72, 162, 171, 294, 301, 321
  Courier's feud with, 72–74
  Legal Defense Fund of, 290, 293
National Association of Colored Women, 46–47
National Association of Negro Musicians, 134
National Association of Negro Women, 164
National Baptist Convention, 171
National Bar Association, 161
National League, 111, 244, 265
National Negro Opera Company, 135
National Negro Press Association, 236, 279
National Playwrights Conference, 330–31
Navarro, Fats, 212
Navy, U.S., expanded role of blacks in, 176
Navy Cross, 169
Negro Digest, 328
Negro Elks Clubs, 2, 171, 224, 299
"Negro in America, The" (Carnegie), 38
"Negroes of Pittsburgh, The" (Tucker), 38
Negro Leagues, xv, 238, 239, 263, 288, 335
  all-star game of, 3
  East-West League of, 104, 106–9
  and integration of major leagues, 243–44, 245
  see also specific teams

Negro National League, 110, 117, 254
  Crawfords' dominance of, 112–13
  East-West Classic of, 2, 111–12, 115–16, 121
  Grays' dominance of, 120
  Greenlee's resignation from, 121
  near-collapse of, 113
  see also specific teams
Negro National Publishers Association (NNPA), 175, 176
Negro World Series, 109
Nehru, Jawaharlal, 188
Nelson, Stanley, 176
Nesbit, Evelyn, 63–64
Newark Eagles, 113, 119, 238, 265
New Deal, 121, 151, 164
New England Conservatory of Music, 299
New Pittsburgh Courier, 327
Newsweek, 182
New York Black Yankees, 89, 90, 101, 120
New York Cubans, 113, 117, 238
New York Daily Mirror, 236
New York Daily News, 243
New York Drama Critics' Circle Award, 332
New York Giants, 260
New York Herald Tribune, 262
New York Lincoln Giants, 103
New York Times, 182, 246, 298, 300
New York World Telegram, 246
New York Yankees, 259–60, 266
"Night in Tunisia, A" (song), 209, 212
92nd Infantry Division (Buffalo Soldiers), 91–92, 182, 183
93rd Infantry Division, 180, 184
99th Pursuit Squadron (Tuskegee Airmen), 181–82, 193
Nixon, Connie Louise, 287
Nixon, Dorothy Yvonne, 282–84, 287
Nixon, E. D., 294
Nixon, Hubert, 287
Nixon, Isaiah, murder of, 283–84, 290
Nixon, Isaiah, Jr., 283, 287–88
Nixon, Margaret, 285, 287
Nixon, Mary Ann, 287
Nixon, Richard, 269
Nixon, Sallie, 283–84, 286, 289
Nixon Family Fund campaign, 286–89
Noble Sissle Society Orchestra, 139
Noel, Hattie, 141
nonviolent strategy, 189, 295, 298, 322
North Side (neighborhood), 45, 59, 322
North Star (journal), 41
numbers racket, 93–95

Nunn, Bill, 6, 7, 8, 70, 88, 265, 282, 293
  and Chappell's move to city desk, 272
  as city editor, 3
  as Courier managing editor, 166, 168, 221, 260, 273, 286
  death of, 327
  East-West Classic and, 111
  Louis championed by, xv, 2–4, 5, 10, 14–15, 16, 22, 154, 256
  Prattis's relationship with, 155, 167
Nunn, Bill, Jr., 327

Oakland (neighborhood), xxiii, 44, 130, 322
Oakmont, Pa., 52, 159, 165–66
Odd Fellows, 46
O'Dowd, Jack, 5
Office of Facts and Figures (OFF), 173
Ohio, 40
Ohio River, xiii, 30
"Oh Lady Be Good" (song), 221
Olympia Stadium (Detroit), 8
O'Neill, Eugene, 334
Ostermueller, Fritz, 264
Ott, Mel, 235
"Our Champ" (Courier poem), 16–17
Owens, Jesse, 19, 158

P-40 Warhawk fighters, 177, 181
P-51 Mustang fighters, 182
Pace, Frankie, 321
Padgett, Norma, 290
Padmore, George, 183
Page, Ted, 90, 101, 112
Page, William Nelson, 50, 59
Paige, Janet Howard:
  extravagant lifestyle of, 116
  Satchel's courtship of, 106
  wedding of Satchel and, 116
Paige, Leroy "Satchel," xv, 88, 90, 110, 120, 121, 267, 326
  with Crawfords, 105–6, 111, 112–16
  in defection from Crawfords, 116–17
  Dominican Republic's poaching of, 118–19
  extravagant spending by, 114, 116
  Greenlee's relationship with, 106, 113–14, 117
  marriage of, see Paige, Janet Howard
  1934 season of, 114
  post-Crawfords career of, 119
  in return to Crawfords, 117–18
Panama, 257
Pan Fried Fish, 328
Paramount Inn, 93, 94

Paramount Theatre (New York), 215–16
Parker, Charlie, xvi, 194, 206, 223, 224, 325
  in Billy Eckstine Orchestra, 210–11
  departure from Eckstine Orchestra of, 212
  drug habit of, 208, 212
  with Earl Hines orchestra, 201–2, 208–9
  Gillespie and, 208–9
Parker, Dan, 236
Parker, John J., 82
Parks, Rosa, 294, 296
"Passion Flower" (song), 148
Patrick, LeRoy, 322
"Patriot and the Partisan, The" (Vann), 81–83
Pat's Place, 328
Patterson, Joe, 190
Payton, Mr., 26, 27
Peabody High School (Pittsburgh), 195, 196, 333
Pearl Harbor, Japanese attack on, 151, 167–69
Pearlman, David, 145
Pease, Robert, 321, 323
Peck, John, 41
Pennfield Drug Store, 126, 144–45
Penn, William, 318
Penn Hills (neighborhood), 94
Penn Incline, 325
Pennock, Herb, 262
Pennsylvania, discrimination in, 273
Pennsylvania River, 32
Pennsylvania State University, 48
Penny, Rob, 328–29, 330
Peoples, Lucy, 54, 60
People's Voice, 238, 252
Pershing, John, 92
Peterson, Oscar, 223
Philadelphia Phillies, 261
Philadelphia Tribune, 73
Piano Concerto in A Minor (Grieg), 134
Piano Lesson, The (Bearden), 334
Piano Lesson, The (Wilson), xvi, 334, 335, 339
pianos, in black cultural life, 129, 207, 222, 335–36
Pickens, Willis, 190
Pinchot, Gifford, 79
Pinkerton guards, 35–36
Pittsburgh, Pa., xxiii
  black population of, xiv, xxiii, 58, 67, 77, 274
  flood of 1936 in, 12
  founding of, 29–30
  Great Fire of 1845 in, 42, 43, 44, 49
  King assassination riots in, 322–23
  postwar discrimination in, 274
Pittsburgh, Pa., black culture of, xiv–xvi

mixing of racketeers and elite in, 97, 137–38, 335
musical traditions of, 129, 324–25, 335
pianos and, 207, 222, 335–36
social clubs in, 46–47
Pittsburgh, University of, 76, 179, 275
  see also Western University of Pennsylvania
Pittsburgh African Education Society, 40
Pittsburgh Anti-Slavery Society, 41, 42
Pittsburgh Bessemer Steel Company, 31
Pittsburgh City League, 105
Pittsburgh Clearing House Association, 275
Pittsburgh Courier, xvi, 3, 65, 174, 182, 190, 253, 268, 270, 285, 319, 326
  All-American Ball Club list of, 3, 109
  All-American football team of, 70
  anti-discrimination crusades of, 68, 273–74
  baseball integration pushed by, 120–21
  Berlin Olympics covered by, 158–59
  as bestselling black newspaper in U.S., 52
  "Black Mood in Pittsburgh" series of, 321–22
  in black veterans' rights crusade, 277–79
  Chappell's move to city desk of, 271–72
  Chicago edition of, 153–54
  circulation of, xiv, 22, 70, 71, 75, 77, 157, 159, 173, 178
  Civic Arena project and, 315–16
  crusading attitude of, xiv–xv, 7, 67–69
  decline of, 326–27
  Double Victory Campaign of, 151, 152, 170–74, 176, 178, 191, 235, 272
  Ethiopian war covered by, 158
  financial difficulties of, 66, 69
  Fort Bragg report of, 167, 173
  founding of, 50–51, 61–62
  Greenlee-Posey feud and, 110
  Hoe printing press of, 8, 76, 77, 327
  J. E. Hoover's campaign against, 173
  as largest black newspaper, 22
  leadership shuffle at, 166
  Lewis hired as business manager of, 66
  Louis championed by, xv, 2, 4, 7–8, 9, 10, 14, 16–17, 18, 22, 154–55, 256
  on Louis's victory over Schmeling, 21–22
  "Neediest Family Drive" of, 79
  Nixon Family Fund campaign of, 286–89
  Nixon murder and, 284
  Nunn named managing editor of, 166
  Pittsburgh Crawfords coverage in, 108
  Prattis hired by, 154–55
  in price-hike scheme with Chicago Defender, 69–70

Pittsburgh Courier (*cont.*)
  Robinson coverage by, 259
  Robinson-Dodgers scoop of, 257–58
  Robinson's "diary" in, 243, 260, 262, 263, 264
  Smith as sports editor of, 231–32, 234
  sports coverage of, 2–3
  Thompson's letter to, 170
  Vann as majority owner of, 72
  Vann's focus on crime stories in, 64–65
  war correspondents of, 178, 180–88
  Willkie endorsed by, 163–64, 165
  "The Women" column in, 289–90, 294, 297, 301
  women reporters at, 282; *see also specific writers*
  writers at, 70–71; *see also specific writers and editors*
  see also Vann, Robert Lee
Pittsburgh Courier Band Poll, 221–22
Pittsburgh Courier Newsies Club, 197
Pittsburgh Crawfords, xv, 88, 89, 90, 98–99, 326, 335
  Bell signed by, 109–10
  dominance of, 112–13
  exhibition games played by, 112, 113
  Gibson and Johnson traded by, 120
  Gibson with, 99, 107–8, 111, 117
  Grays players poached by, 107–8
  Greenlee Field built for, 107
  Greenlee-Posey rivalry and, 106–9, 110, 111, 115, 119, 121
  Greenlee's purchase of, 99–100
  Greenlee's sale of, 121
  Greenlee's signing of players for, 104–5
  Paige's defection from, 116–17
  Paige's return to, 117–18
  Paige with, 105–6, 111, 112–16
Pittsburgh Gazette, 62
Pittsburgh High School, 47
Pittsburgh Music Institute, 135
Pittsburgh Penguins, 326
Pittsburgh Pirates, 100, 120, 230, 235, 237–38, 256, 263–64, 326
Pittsburgh Post-Gazette, 275, 320, 323
Pittsburgh Press, 62, 64, 196
Pittsburgh Renaissance, 22–23, 313–14, 317, 327–28
Pittsburgh Star-Telegraph, 111
Pittsburgh Steelers, 98, 326
Pitt, William (the Elder), 30
Poetics (Aristotle), 338
Point Breeze (neighborhood), *xxiii,* 32, 43–44

Pollock, Jackson, 216
Pompez, Alex, 99–100, 113
Poole, W. T., 84
Port Tobacco, Md., 25–26
Port Tobacco River, 25
Posey, Alexander, 25–26
Posey, Angeline Stevens "Anna," 24, 27–28, 31–32, 45–46, 71
  marriage of Cap and, 29
  as schoolteacher, 28–29
Posey, Beatrix, 47
Posey, Cumberland "Cap," Sr., 24, 31–32, 49, 58
  Carnegie and, 38–39
  childhood and adolescence of, 25–26
  coal businesses of, 37–38
  death of, 71
  Frick's partnership with, 38–39
  Homestead mansion of, 45–46
  marriage of Anna and, 29
  as steamboat engineer, 27
  Vann and, 59–60
Posey, Cumberland "Cum," Jr., xv, 47–48, 111, 256
  athletic talent of, 48–49
  death of, 244–45
  East-West League formed by, 104, 106–9
  as Grays owner-manager, 100–102, 104, 114
  Greenlee's rivalry with, 106–9, 115, 119, 121
  hired as Grays manager, 49
  integration of baseball pushed by, 120
  poaching of ballplayers by, 101, 102
  womanizing by, 101
Posey, Elizabeth Willis, 25
Posey, Stewart Hayes "See," 47, 48, 102, 107
Posey Coal Dealers and Steam Boat Builders, 37
Posey family, 47
Post Office, U.S., *Courier* investigation of, 174–75
Potomac River, 25
Povich, Shirley, 11
Powell, Adam Clayton, Jr., 175, 290
Powell, Bud, 223, 225
Powers, Jimmy, 243
Prattis, Helen Sands, 155, 163
Prattis, Lillian Sherman, 154–55
Prattis, Patricia, 163
Prattis, Percival Leroy "P.L.," 2–3, 157–58, 161, 168, 191, 282, 327
  anti-discrimination crusade of, 273, 274
  in Chicago, 153–54

Courier war correspondents overseen by, 178, 179, 182, 183–84
Double Victory Campaign and, 170
FBI investigation of, 173, 175
and FDR administration's censorship campaign, 174
Helen Sands's marriage to, 155, 163
Joe Louis marriage scoop of, 155
Julia Bumry Jones's relationship with, 155
Lillian Sherman's marriage to, 154–55
named *Courier* executive editor, 166
Nunn's relationship with, 155, 167
segregated Army base stories of, 166–67, 173
in World War I, 156
Presley, Elvis, 220
Prevalence of Ritual, The (Bearden), 333
"Prisoner of Love" (song), 214, 221
Proctor, Jacob, 46
Proctor, Virginia Woodson, 46
Pulitzer, Joseph, 49, 60
Pulitzer Prize for Drama, 332, 334
Pullman Company, 74–75
Pullman Porters and Maids Association, 171
Purdy, Claude, 329, 333
Pythian Temple on the Hill (Pittsburgh), 87, 125, 194, 198

Queen, Howard, 182, 183

race riots, 168, 210, 322–23
Racine, Hector, 242–43
racism:
August Wilson and, xvi, 307–8
Robinson and, 232–33, 245, 247, 249–50, 251, 253–54, 261–62
see also discrimination; segregation
racketeers, 93–95, 97, 112, 137–38, 335
Radcliffe, Ted, 107
Radio Golf (Wilson), 338–39
railways, 31, 33
"Rain Check" (song), 148
Rainey, Ma, 324, 330
Raisin in the Sun, A (Hansberry), 331
Ramage, Lee, 5
Randolph, A. Philip, 68, 74–75, 274, 290
Randolph, Lillie, 141
Rashad, Phylicia, 339
Razaf, Andy, 172
RCA, 220
Reconstruction, 57, 81
"Red Summer" race riots (1919), 168
Reed, David, 156

Reese, Pee Wee, 264
Reformers, 46
Republican Party, xv, 96
blacks' loyalty to, 78–79, 82
R. Hoe and Company, 8
Richards, Lloyd, 331, 332
Richards, Wallace, 313
Richmond, Va., 57
Richmond Planet, 57, 73
Rickey, Branch, xv, 237, 256
Robinson and, 233, 242, 256–57, 258–59
Wendell Smith and, 240–42, 243, 247–48, 258
Riddle, Nelson, 219
Ritchey, Dahlen, 317
Rivera, A. M., Jr., 284
Roach, Max, 223
Robeson, Paul, 149, 236
Robinson, Bill "Bojangles," 20, 111, 116, 141, 157
Robinson, Felix, 282
Robinson, Jackie, xv, *230*, 239, 245–46
Army service of, 239
college sports career of, 239
death of, 268
with Dodgers, 257–66
with Kansas City Monarchs, 233, 239, 241–42
with Montreal Royals, 242–43, 247–54, 256–58
in Panama exhibition games, 257
racism and, 232–33, 245, 247, 249–50, 251, 253–54, 261–62
Red Sox tryout of, 240
Rickey's relationship with, 256–57, 258–59
Rickey's signing of, 233, 242
rift between Wendell Smith and, 266–67
in Royals spring training, 250–51
short temper of, 232, 240, 241, 251, 267
as *Sporting News* Rookie of the Year, 266
teammates' growing solidarity with, 264
in trip to Daytona Beach, 231–33, 248
Wendell Smith's relationship with, 233, 246–48, 254, 263, 268, 326
Robinson, Rachel Isum, 232, 248, 249, 250, 254
Rockefeller, Nelson, 300
"Rocks in My Bed" (song), 148
Rogers, Joel Augustus, 158, 168
Romero, Constanza, 338, 339
Rooney, Art, 98
Roosevelt, Franklin Delano, 2, 78, 159–60, 173, 181, 188

Roosevelt, Franklin Delano (*cont.*)
  "Black Cabinet" of, 157, 175
  black newspapers viewed as seditionist by, 174
  death of, 240
  in 1932 election, 78–85, 97
  in 1936 election, 159–60
  in 1940 election, 163–64, 165
  Vann's criticisms of, 160
  Vann's meetings with, 80, 162
  wartime censorship and, 173–74
Rosamond, Samuel, 45, 46, 50
Roseland Ballroom (New York City), 199
Roulette Records, 220, 221
Rouzeau, Edgar, 181–82, 285
Rowe, Billy:
  as *Courier* entertainment columnist, 175, 288
  as *Courier* war correspondent, 184, 189
  as Robinson's chauffeur, 231–33, 247–50, 260
Roxborough, John, 4, 5, 6–7, 8, 9, 12, 17, 18, 21, 166
runaway slaves, 40, 42–43
Russell, "Pistol Johnny," 104
Russell, Ross, 225
Russell, Sylvester, 71
Ruth, Babe, 111

Sadie (Hines's aunt), 130, 131
St. Clair, Stephanie, 93
St. James AME Church (Cleveland), 82
St. James AME Church (Pittsburg), 133
St. James Literary Forum, 81
St. Louis Cardinals, 112, 262–63, 265
St. Louis Stars, 104, 109
Saint-Mihiel, Battle of, 92
St. Paul, Minn., 329
St. Paul Saints, 251
"Salt Peanuts!" (song), 209
Sanford, Fla., 247, 248
San Juan Hill, 82
Saperstein, Abe, 111, 288
Saving Private Ryan (film), 184
Savoy Ballroom (Pittsburgh), 125, 198, 202
Schalk, Toki, 270, 271, 318
Schenley High School (Pittsburgh), 130, 131, 222
Schenley Hotel (Pittsburgh), 235
Schmeling, Max, 15, 18
  in Louis rematch, 1–2, 19–21
  Louis's first fight with, 13–15
Schuller, Gunther, 204

Schultz, Dutch, 136
Schuyler, George, 71
Science Museum of Minnesota, 329–30
Scoop (Waugh), 158
Scott, Cyril, 134
Scott, Jimmy, 325
Scott, Shirley, 325
Scottsboro Boys, 7
"Seabreeze" (song), 333
"Second Balcony Jump" (song), 212
segregation:
  in education, 47, 73, 293
  of housing, 67–68, 323
  urban renewal and, 323
  see also desegregation; military, U.S., blacks in
Selassie, Haile, Emperor of Ethiopia, 157, 158
Selective Training and Service Act, 163
Sengstacke, John, 165, 166, 236
  Biddle's meeting with, 175–76
  Courier purchased by, 327
Serchio Valley, 182
784th Tank Battalion, 184
Seven Guitars (Wilson), 335
Seven Years War, 29
Sexual Behavior in the Human Female (Kinsey), 290
Shadyside (neighborhood), *xxiii*, 44, 126, 145
Shafer, Raymond, 322
Shallenberger, O. B., 45
Sharpsburg, Pa., 33
Shearing, George, 218, 219
Shepherd, Samuel, 290–91
Shuffle Along (musical revue), 123
Sifford, Charlie, 216
Siger, Bella, 305, 323
Sigma Pi Phi, 74
Simla, India, 188
Simms, William, 65
Simon, John, 54–55
Sims, Zoot, 220
Sinatra, Frank, 214, 215, 218, 219, 220
Sissle, Noble, 138–39
Sizwe Banzi Is Dead (Fugard), 330
Skirts Ahoy! (film), 219
"Skylark" (song), 213
Smith, Al, 79
Smith, Bessie, 324, 325
Smith, Jimmy, 238
Smith, Wendell, xv, 88, 120–21, 272, 288
  background of, 234
  baseball integration crusade of, 233–35, 243–44, 246

Baseball Writers roast denounced by, 246
as *Courier* sports editor, 231–32, 234
death of, 268–69
on Gibson's death, 255–56
major league dreams of, 234
in move to *Chicago Herald-American,* 266
pro tryout for Robinson sought by, 238–39
Rickey and, 243, 247–48, 258
rift between Robinson and, 266–67
Robinson and, 240–42
Robinson-Dodgers scoop of, 257–58
Robinson's *Courier* "diary" ghostwritten by,
    243, 260, 263, 264
Robinson's relationship with, 233, 240–42,
    246–48, 254, 263, 268, 326
"Solitude" (song), 146
"Something to Live For" (song), 146, 148
"Sophisticated Lady" (song), 145
Southern Democrats, 280
Spangler, Thelma, 146
Sparrow, Roy, 111
Spear, N.C., 303
Spearman, Charles, 204
Spearman, Martha Grace, 204
Spectacular, N.Y., 2
Spielberg, Steven, 184
Sporting News, 266
Squirrel Hill (neighborhood), *xxiii*
Stanford, Theodore, 184
Stanky, Eddie, 258, 261, 264
Stanley, Ed, 258
Stanley Theatre (Pittsburgh), 96, 131, 145,
    146, 194
"Stardust" (song), 197, 201
Stargell, Willie, 326
steel industry, 30–31, 33, 34–39, 58
Stein, A. C., 68
Stephens, Jake, 101, 107
Stevens, Aquilla, 28
Stevens, Eliza Brackston, 28
Stewart, Rex, 203
Stewart, Slam, 224
Stilwell, Joseph, 186
Stilwell Road (Ledo Road), 185–88, 189–90
Stitt, Sonny, 194
stock market crash of 1929, 76
"Stormy Monday Blues" (song), 201
Stotz, Edward, 130
Strayhorn, Billy, xv, *122,* 324–25, 335
    Catlin as piano teacher of, 128–29
    childhood and youth of, 125–27
    classical music as first love of, 134
    drug store job of, 126, 134–35, 144–45

as Ellington's collaborator, 147–48
Ellington's first meeting with, 145–46
as *Fantastic Rhythm* composer and lyricist,
    124–25, 134, 146, 148
first piano of, 127
homosexuality of, 135, 147
Lena Horne's friendship with, 150–51
in move to Harlem, 147
Westinghouse High School music studies
    of, 124, 133–34
Strayhorn, James, 125–26
Strayhorn, Jobe, 126
Strayhorn, Lillian Young (mother), 125, 126,
    147
Strayhorn, Lilly (grandmother), 126
Streeter, Sam "Lefty," 105, 106
Strip District (neighborhood), *xxiii,* 325–26
Sugartop (neighborhood), *ii, 4,* 44, 143, 155,
    179, 325
Sukeforth, Clyde, 241, 242, 259, 265
Sullivan, Maxine, *192,* 214
Supreme Court, U.S., 160, 177, 301
    Brown decision of, 293
Sweet, Ossian, 72
Syria Mosque, 12, 214

Taft, Robert, 280
Taft, William Howard, 62
"Take the 'A' Train" (song), 147, 148
"Talk O' Town" (*Courier* column), 71, 83–84,
    271
Talmadge, Herman, 283
Tannehill, Adamson, 44
Tanner, Benjamin Tucker, 41
Tanner, Henry Ossawa, 46
Tatum, Art, 222, 225
Taylor, Billy, 218
Teddy Hill Orchestra, 202, 203, 204, 207
Temple, Shirley, 157
10th Cavalry Regiment, 81–82, 180
Terrace Village, 316, 318, 321
Tesla, Nikola, 33
textile industry, 32
Thaw, Harry Kendall, 63–64
Theatre Owners Bookers Association (TOBA),
    132–33
Third Ward Voters League, 96
"This Is the Inside Story" (song), 215
This Is Your Life (TV show), 327
Thomas, Dave "Showboat," 238
Thomas, Dylan, 328
Thomas, Hawk, 90
Thompkins, James, 187

Thompson, James Gratz, 169–70, 172
    Double Victory Campaign suggested by, 170
Thompson, Melvin, 283
Thomson, Ernest, 290
Thornbury, Will, 226
366th Infantry Regiment, 182, 183
367th Infantry Regiment, 91–92
369th antiaircraft regiment, 193
370th Infantry Regiment, 183
Thurmond, Strom, 280, 281
Tiant, Louis, Sr., 117
Till, Emmett, 294
Time, 181, 314
Tinker, Hooks, 104, 105–6
Tito brothers, 93, 107, 119
Toiler's Life, The (Harleston), 50
Tonight Show, 228
Tony Awards, 332, 334
Trees, Joe, 77
Trocadero (Los Angeles nightclub), 149, 150
Trujillo, Rafael, 118, 119
Truman, Harry, 277
    black voters and, 281
    civil rights and, 279–80, 281
    and desegregation of military, 281
Tucker, Helen A., 38, 59
Tucson Times, 73
Tuesday Evening Study Club, 47
Tulane Drama Review, 329
Tuskegee Airmen (99th Pursuit Squadron),
    181–82, 193
Tuskegee Institute, 38
    black pilots trained at, 181
24th Infantry Regiment, 81–82
"Two Sleepy People" (song), 146
Two Trains Running (Wilson), 335

Udin, Sala (Sam Howze), 307, 339
Underground Railroad, 41, 42–43, 319, 325
United Automobile Workers, 171
United States League, 240
Unity, Pa., 65
Urban League, 160–61
Urban Redevelopment Authority (URA), 315,
    316, 317, 318, 321, 323
urban renewal, xvi, 314, 315, 316, 323, 326,
    335, 338
Urban Times-Record, 326
U.S. Steel Company, 58, 67, 79, 314

Van Cuyk, Chris, 267
Van Heusen, Jimmy, 220
Vann, Albert, 54

Vann, Jesse Matthews, 6, 21, 60, 86, 128, 157,
    159, 165, 279, 288–89, 326
    as *Courier* publisher, 282, 288, 326
    as *Courier* treasurer, 168
    death of, 327
    marriage of Robert Vann and, 61
    women reporters championed by, 282
Vann, Robert Lee, 2, 4, 6, 7, 10, 16, 21, 22, 52,
    66, 89, 108, 151, 154–55, 156, 173, 179,
    197, 281, 327
    anti-discrimination campaigns of, 68
    Berlin Olympics covered by, 158–59
    blacks in military as cause of, 156, 161–62,
        165
    cancer of, 163, 164
    Cap Posey and, 59–60
    childhood and adolescence of, 53–56, 81
    Cleveland speech of, 81–83
    college education of, 56–57, 60
    as *Courier*'s majority owner, 72
    as crusader, xiv–xv, 67–69, 156
    death of, 164–65
    FDR administration's sidelining of, 156–
        57
    FDR criticized by, 160
    in FDR's 1932 campaign, 81–85
    FDR's meetings with, 80, 162
    in feud with J. W. Johnson and Du Bois,
        72–74
    in founding of *Courier*, 50–51
    Justice Department appointment of, 86–88,
        157
    in law school, 60
    legal career of, 61, 65–66
    marriage of Jesse and, 61
    in move to Pittsburgh, 57–58
    named *Courier* editor, 62
    in remaking of *Courier*, 64
    as Republican loyalist, 78–79
    sensationalism disliked by, 70
    sleeping car porter job of, 60, 74–75
    social circle of, 59–60
    in switch to Democratic Party, 80–81
    writing staff assembled by, 70–71
Vashon, John, 41
Vaughan, Sarah, xvi, 194, 219, 220
    in Billy Eckstine Orchestra, 211, 212
    with Earl Hines orchestra, 209–10
Veale, Bob, 326
Veeck, Bill, 265
Veterans Administration, 276–77, 279
Vigilance Committee, 42
Virginia Union University, 56–57

Volkwein's Music Store, 127
V for victory sign, 170

Wagner, Honus, 235
Walker, Dixie, 258, 259
Walker, Frank, 174–75
Walker, Zachariah, 64–65
Wallace, Joe, 187
Waller, Fats, 222
War Department, U.S., 179, 184–85
    Fort Bragg shakeup of, 167
War Production Board, 177
Wartime Prohibition Act (1919), 92
Washburn, Patrick, 176
Washington, Booker T., 38, 41, 57
Washington, Chester "Ches," xv, xxiv, 2, 4, 6,
    7, 8, 9–10, 11, 12, 16, 22, 70, 99, 103,
    117, 120, 138, 139, 166, 282
    Louis and, 4–5, 13, 14, 17, 256
Washington, D.C.:
    discrimination in, 273
    Homestead Grays games in, 120
Washington, George, 30
Washington Post, 11
Washington Senators, 244
Waterford, Conn., 331
Waters Training School, 55–56, 60
Watts High School (Pittsburgh), 98–99
Waugh, Evelyn, 158
Wavell, Lord, 188
Webster, Ben, 206
Wells, Ida B., 176, 271
Western University of Pennsylvania, 40, 57,
    59, 60
    see also Pittsburgh, University of
Westinghouse, George, 33, 44, 128
    Point Breeze estate of, 43
Westinghouse High School (Pittsburgh), 3,
    123–24, 132, 133–34, 224
West Virginia, USS, 169
West Virginia State College, 234
Wheaton, John Frank, 65
Whitaker, C.S., Sr., v
Whitaker, Edith McColes, v
White, Stanford, 63–64
White, Walter, 71, 74, 162, 171
Wiley, Caroline, 45
Wiley, James, 193
Wiley, Thomas, 45
Wilkins, Roy, 9, 162, 294
Wilkinson, J. L., 100, 244
William Morris Agency, 200
William Penn Hotel (Pittsburgh), 86, 312, 313

Williams, Beatrice, 171
Williams, Bobby, 104
Williams, Chester, 104, 109
Williams, Della, 289
Williams, Joe, 206–7
Williams, Joe "Smokey Joe," 100–101, 102,
    105
Williams, John, 133
Williams, Juan, 292
Williams, Lou, 214
Williams, Marvin, 239
Williams, Mary Lou Scruggs, xv, 192, 206-7,
    325
    as musical prodigy, 132
Williams, Paul, 288, 289
Williams, Tennessee, 334
Willkie, Wendell, 163–64, 165
Wilson, August, xvi, 302
    army service of, 310–11
    blackness as viewed by, 336, 337
    blues and, 323–24, 325, 328, 330–31,
        335, 336, 340
    Century Cycle of, 332–33, 334–35, 338–39
    childhood and youth of, 304–11
    death of, 339–40
    Hill residents' stories absorbed by, 327–28,
        330, 338
    journeyman playwriting by, 329–30
    marriage of Brenda Burton and, 329
    marriage of Constanza Romero and, 338,
        339
    marriage of Judy Oliver and, 329, 338
    in move to St. Paul, 329
    poetry ambitions of, 328, 329
    racism and, 307–8
    Richards as mentor of, 331, 332
    as voracious reader, 304, 310
    writing career chosen by, 311–12
Wilson, Daisy, 303, 306, 310, 332, 340
Wilson, Freda, 311
Wilson, Jud "Boojum," 101
Wilson, Judy Oliver, 329, 338
Wilson, Shadow, 201, 202, 210
Wilson, Tom, 105
Wilson, W. Rollo, 70
Wilson, Zonia, 303–4
Winchell, Walter, 18, 215, 262
Winchester, Va., 26
Winton, N.C., 55
WLIB-AM, 300
Wolk, Abraham, 314–15
Woodruff, Johnny, 158–59, 193
Woodson, Caroline Robinson, 40

Woodson, Carter, 271
Woodson, Jemima, 40
Woodson, Lewis, 40, 42, 46, 325
Woodson, Thomas, 40
Working Girls Home, 47
Works Progress Administration, 85
World Series, of 1947, 266
World War I, 67, 82, 91–92
    black soldiers in, 156, 168
    Prattis in, 156
World War II:
    black correspondents in, 178, 179–88
    black troops in, xv, 23, 176, 178, 180–88, 193
    in Burma, 185–86
    Courier's "Double V Campaign" and, 151, *152*
    Italian campaign of, 182–83
    Japanese surrender in, 189
    U.S. entry into, 151, 168
World War II homefront, black workers in, 177–78
Wright, Johnny, 247, 248–50, 253

Wright, Richard, 310
Writt, John, 44–45, 46
Wylie Avenue, 23, 46, 47, 59, 64, 71, 93–94, 95, 96, 130, 135, 137, 193, 204, 304, 317, 319, 325
"Wylie Avenue" (*Courier* column), 97–98

Yale Repertory Theatre, 332
Yale School of Drama, 331
"Yankee Doodle Tan, A (the Double V Song)," 172
Yankee Stadium, 1, 10, 13–14, 103
Yates, James, 291
YMCA (Centre Street), 4, 6, 114, 128, 319, 326
"You Don't Know What Love Is" (song), 213
Young, Felix, 149, 151
Young, John H., III, in black veterans' rights crusade, 277–79
Young, Lester, 206, 220

Ziff Corporation, 70

ABOUT THE AUTHOR

MARK WHITAKER is the author of the critically acclaimed memoir *My Long Trip Home*. The former managing editor of CNN Worldwide, he was previously the Washington bureau chief for NBC News and a reporter and editor at *Newsweek*, where he rose to become the first African-American leader of a national newsweekly.